STUDIES
IN ISLAMIC HISTORY AND INSTITUTIONS

STUDIES IN ISLAMIC HISTORY AND INSTITUTIONS

BY

S. D. GOITEIN

Reimpression of the first edition

LEIDEN
E. J. BRILL
1968

First edition 1966

Reprinted 1968

PRINTED IN THE NETHERLANDS

CONTENTS

PART ONE

THE NATURE AND DEVELOPMENT OF ISLAM

PART TWO

ISLAMIC RELIGIOUS AND POLITICAL INSTITUTIONS

PART THREE

ISLAMIC SOCIAL HISTORY

PREFACE

For years colleagues have urged me to bring out a selection of studies of mine dealing with Islamic institutions and social history. As I had already been engaged in the writing of a comprehensive work on Mediterranean Society as portrayed in the documents of the Cairo Geniza, I was reluctant to respond to this expression of friendship and appreciation. Now, with *Mediterranean Society* nearing completion, it seemed useful to publish a collection of articles which will not be incorporated in that book nor in any other publication contemplated by me. Therefore, studies dealing specifically with the relationship of Islam and Judaism or with the ethnology and dialects of the Yemenites, let alone my publications of Geniza texts have not been included.

The articles presented here have been selected with an eye to their possible usefulness for university teaching. On one hand, they provide a general introduction to Islamic civilization by one who, so to speak, has lived all his life with Islam. On the other hand, most of them are the fruit of specialized research. Thus, while adding up, it is hoped, to a rounded view of important aspects of Islamic civilization, they provide the student with an opportunity to acquaint himself not only with the results of research, but also with the methods by which they were obtained.

With the exception of chapters I and III, the studies included in this volume have previously appeared in print in one form or another and in four different languages. None, however, was incorporated without revision and many were worked over in their entirety and greatly expanded. Such changes were necessary, for scientific papers are responses to momentary challenges, while chapters of a book form, or should form, parts of an enduring contribution. Only those articles which were written in recent years with a view to being integrated in a general book on Islam are rendered here more or less as they were originally published.

The image of Islamic history formed by the author in the course of forty years of research is summarized in the introductory essay (Chapter I). It contains a considerable number of viewpoints which appear here in print for the first time. In general, the studies assembled in this book approach Islam from three different directions. By thorough perusal and a new appraisal of the vast literary sources they try to get at the origin and true character of things. This applies to both religious and political institutions, as well as to social phenomena (Chapters I, III-VI, VIII-IX, XI). Through the study of documentary evidence (Ch. XIV) and fieldwork with genuine oriental communities (see Ch. XIX) they strive to understand "the man in the street" within Islamic civilization, his economic and social, as well as his spiritual life (XII-XIX). Finally, Islam is approached through comparison with Judaism. This has been done because Islam and Judaism, even from the mere typological point of view, betray an amazing degree of affinity. The question of how far the former is "indebted" to the latter is of secondary or no importance and partly outside the reaches of exact research. On the other hand, a study of parallel developments is highly conducive to a better understanding of both religions. Chapter X is a case in point, but similar considerations guided the argument also in other chapters—expressly or implicitly.

Islam is understood in this book as a human experience of divine things. How far this experience represents a real or imaginary encounter is left to the intellectual and spiritual perceptiveness of the individual reader. The author is aware of the fact that he is addressing a mixed audience. He has adopted the same attitude in his biblical studies. To those who, like himself, believe in the possibility of a real encounter, he owes an apology for letting his sources everywhere speak in their own language, the unmistakable language of human imperfection. By doing so, he hopes to serve not only the cause of truth, but that of religion as well.

At the risk of being labeled a pedant, the writer has attached summaries to studies with more involved argumentation. This was done for the benefit of both the busy scholar and the fledgling student. The latter is advised to read the summary before the chapter to which it is attached. With a few exceptions such as *j* instead of *dj* and *q* for *ḳ*, Arabic words are spelled as in the new edition of the Encyclopaedia of Islam.

I am indebted to distinguished colleagues and some of my students for ideas emerging while discussing with them problems treated in this volume. I am particularly grateful to Dr. Richard Ettinghausen, Head Curator of Near Eastern Art in the Freer Gallery of Washington, for continuous encouragement and many useful suggestions.

Sincere thanks are extended herewith to the editors and publishers of journals and books for the permission granted to use here material published first in their columns (see list below. p. XIII); to the librarians and the keepers of manuscripts of the libraries in which the author made his studies of Geniza documents (specified acknowledgments will be made in a volume devoted to Geniza studies in the process of writing); and to the American Philosophical Society for a grant enabling the author to prepare the manuscript of this book for publication. Professor N. Golb of the University of Chicago graciously and untiringly assisted me in the arduous task of proofreading.

REFERENCES TO PRIOR PUBLICATION OF STUDIES INCLUDED IN THIS VOLUME

II. The Intermediate Civilization. *Islamic Studies, Karachi,* 2 (1963), pp. 217-233.

IV. Ramadan etc. Partial use of *Der Islam* 18 (1929), pp. 184-194. In German.

V. The Origin and Nature of the Muslim Friday Worship. *The Muslim World* 49 (1959), pp. 183-195.

VI. The Birth-Hour of Muslim Law. *The Muslim World* 50 (1960), pp. 23-29.

VII. The Sanctity of Jerusalem etc. Based on *JAOS* 70 (1950) and *Bulletin of the Palestine Exploration Society* 12 (1945-6), pp. 120-6. The latter in Hebrew.

VIII. A Turning Point in the History of the Muslim State. *Islamic Culture,* Hyderabad, 23 (1949), pp. 120-135.

IX. The Origin of the Vizierate etc. *Islamic Culture* 16 (1942), pp. 255-262, 380-392. Appendix: *JAOS* 81 (1961), pp. 425-6.

X. Attitudes towards Government etc. Based on *Tarbiz* 19 (1948), pp. 153-159. In Hebrew.

XI. The Rise of Middle Eastern Bourgeoise etc., *Journal of World History* 3 (1957), pp. 583-604.

XII. The Mentality of the Middle Class etc., *Colloque sur la Sociologie Musulmane, Actes,* 11-14 Septembre 1961, *Centre pour l'Étude des Problèmes du Monde Musulman Contemporain,* Brussels, pp. 249-261.

XIII. The Working People of the Mediterranean Area, etc. *Annales Economies, Sociétés, Civilisations,* 1964, pp. 847-868. In French.

XIV. The Documents of the Cairo Geniza etc. Based on articles in *Studia Islamica,* Paris, 3 (1955), pp. 75-91, and *JOAS* 80 (1960), pp. 91-100.

XV. The Unity of the Mediterranean World etc. *Studia Islamica* 12 (1960), pp. 29-42.

XVI. Medieval Tunisia etc. *Études d'Orientalisme dédiées à la mémoire de Lévi-Provencal,* Paris 1962, pp. 559-579. In French.

XVII. Letters and Documents on the India Trade etc. *Islamic Culture* 27 (1963), pp. 188-205, with partial use of *Speculum, A Journal of Medieval Studies,* 29 (1954), pp. 181-197.

XVIII. The Beginnings of the Kārim Merchants etc. Based on *JESHO* 1 (1958), pp. 175-184.

XIX. The Present Day Arabic Proverb etc. Based on *Islamic Culture* 26 (1952), pp. 1-11.

ABBREVIATIONS

BSOAS	Bulletin of the School of Oriental and African Studies, London
EI^1 EI^2	The Encyclopaedia of Islam, first and new edition respectively
Der Islam	Der Islam, Zeitschrift für Geschichte und Kultur des islamischen Orients
JAOS	Journal of the American Oriental Society
JESHO	Journal of Economic and Social History of the Orient
JQR	Jewish Quarterly Review
JRAS	Journal of the Royal Asiatic Society
REJ	Revue des Études Juives
ZDMG	Zeitschrift der Deutschen Morgenländischen Gesellschaft

The Koran is quoted according to the official Egyptian edition (in the translation provided by the author). Where the edition by G. Flügel, Leipzig 1869, differs in the numbering of the verses, the numbers used by the latter are added, introduced by the sign /.

PART ONE

THE NATURE AND DEVELOPMENT OF ISLAM

CHAPTER ONE

THE FOUR FACES OF ISLAM

What is Islam? Is it the Ultimate Revelation, as claimed by Islam itself, "confirming", i.e. superseding the two older monotheistic religions and denying the right of any other form of belief except monotheism to exist? Was it merely a Christian heresy, as was assumed by some of its earlier Christian observers, or an Arabicized Judaism, as was believed by various medieval scholars? (Both attitudes have been echoed in modern historical research.) Or, seeing that Islam once formed a state and a formidable empire and that Pan-Islamism has been a political slogan even in our own century, are we bound to say that Islam is more than a religious faith, that its believers also form a body politic? Furthermore, it has become customary to use terms such as Islamic art, Islamic science, Islamic philosophy, which indicate that Islam denotes a whole civilization. If so, what is the specific character of this civilization, what are its roots and formative stages, and—is it still alive? Finally, we are puzzled when we find today, many young—and not so young, Muslims who do not have much use for religion in the strict sense of the word, and who possess only a faint knowledge of the tenets and history of Islam, but nevertheless are professed and even enthusiastic Muslims. What does Islam mean to such people?

In order to answer these questions it is necessary to define their various elements with more precision. We shall do this under four headings: Islam as the self-realization of the Arab nation; Islam as a great monotheistic religion; Islam as a body politic; Islam as a civilization. With regard to each of these four concepts we shall try to find out how they affect present day life and thought of the peoples concerned.

I

Islam was founded by the Prophet Muhammad, an Arab from the Arab town and desert emporium, Mecca. In 622 A.D. Muhammad moved with his followers northwards to Medina, an agricultural oasis, also predominantly Arab. The very considerable Jewish population of Medina, although thoroughly Arabicized, did not join Muhammad's community, which thus remained purely Arab during his lifetime. Even more important is the fact that Muhammad, while founding his new religion, originally claimed that he was merely providing his countrymen with an Arabic version of God's Book revealed before to other peoples. Again and again he emphasizes that he was sent to promulgate *qur'ānan ʿarabiyyan*, an Arabic scripture similar to that already in the hands of "the Possessors of the Book".[1]

To be sure, the driving force behind Muhammad's life work was religion. As has often been noted, it was the fear of the imminent Day of Judgment, the belief that the end of the physical world was at hand, which prompted Muhammad to assume the role of "Warner". There had been others in Arabia who had pondered about the world to come. However it was Muhammad, a born leader and a man concerned not only with his own salvation, but also with that of his countrymen who became the founder of a new faith.

Muhammad's emigration to Medina did not sever his allegiance to the Ka ʿba, the pagan sanctuary of his native city, as well as to the other holy places in the environs of Mecca, which had been national shrines of the Arabs before Islam. On the contrary. He incorporated their rites in the new religion and, by doing so, made it obligatory on his followers to fight until they would conquer the holy places, including his home town. Thus, undoubtedly sincere religious impulses blended with political expediency to result in ever stronger emphasis on the specifically Arab character of the new faith.

At the same time, the close daily contact with a large monotheistic community, the Jews of Medina, produced a similar effect. Here was an example of an all-permeating religion whose injunctions and practices regimented the entire life of its members. To the extent that Muhammad followed the example of the Jews, he did so not because he wanted to win them over. This view, although generally held by Western Islamists, is not vindicated by a critical examination of the sources.[2] He was inspired in Medina by Jewish rites and laws for the same reason which induced him in Mecca to incorporate in the Koran the stories of the Bible along with the religious tenets and ethical concepts of "the Possessors of the Book". He believed that all these aspects of religion were instituted by God and therefore worthy

[1] Koran 12:2, 39:28/29, 41:3/2, 42:7/5, 43:3/2, etc.
[2] See below, pp. 33-43 and 86.

of emulation. In any case, in Medina the prophet became a lawgiver. While acting as such, he took over basic ideas and a number of details from the older monotheistic religion, but as far as social institutions were concerned, such as the law of war and peace or family law, he naturally had to rely on local traditions. The result of this was that Muhammad, who had started out with the idea that all monotheistic religions were essentially one, that they represented different copies of one and the same heavenly book, and that he was called upon only to expound it "in clear Arabic", ended by founding a new church of a specific localized nature.

The essentially Arab character of Muhammad's religious creation was borne out by the events which followed his death. In the name of Islam the Arabs conquered most of Southwest Asia and North Africa and established an Arab kingdom in the countries occupied. The subject populations paid tributes or taxes, while the Arabs, who were the soldiers, governors, or otherwise privileged persons, enjoyed the use of the enormous riches that had become available by the liquidation of the previous rulers. Non-Arabs could become Muslims, but only in the same way as, prior to Islam, outsiders were admitted to an Arab tribe. A member of the subject population, when adopting Islam, had to attach himself to an Arab family, whose name he henceforth bore, and he also had to adopt an Arabic first name. In other words, in order to become a Muslim, one had to become an Arab first.

The Arabization of Southwest Asia and North Africa was a complicated and long process, the details of which are still subject to scientific controversy. However, the main reason for its rapid success was the fact that during the decisive first hundred years of its existence, the Muslim empire was an Arab state which granted immense privileges to persons of Arab race or affiliation.

There was another factor favoring the Arabization process, to which perhaps more attention should be given than has been done so far, a process which had begun long before Islam. It may be called the Arabization of the Arabs themselves.

This statement bears some elucidation. It has often been said that Muhammad created the Arab nation, that by his prophetical leadership he transformed a motley group of unruly and mutually hostile tribes into a cohesive and orderly community. In this respect, Muhammad and the Arabs have been compared to Moses and the ancient Israelites. "On this very day", says Moses, in the book of Deuteronomy, to the children of Israel "you have become a people to the Lord, your God". In other words, through the revelation separate tribes were converted into a spiritual and, in due course, a political unit.

In this respect, however, there was a great difference between ancient Israel and the Arabs in so far as the latter possessed *a secular national culture of their own* long before they were united politically under the banner of Islam. I am referring to the miracle of pre-Islamic poetry and literary language. Many decades before Muhammad started to issue his rather disconnected prophetical utterances there had been in existence a highly developed art of Arabic poetry, strict in its linguistic and literary forms and fantastically rich in vocabulary and observation of detail. This phenomenon of pre-Islamic Arabic poetry was a miracle in more than one respect. First, we see primitive people, camel breeding bedouins, developing an accomplished and refined means of expression, and, secondly, and even more astonishing, one and the same literary language, with small negligible dialectical differences, was used by mostly illiterate persons scattered over an area as large as one third of Europe. From Yemen in the south to Syria in the north, from the fringes of Iraq to the borders of Egypt, pre-Islamic Arabic poetry used one and the same idiom and the same literary techniques. How this was achieved we do not know and most probably shall never learn. The fact itself, however, is perhaps the most decisive in the whole history of the Arabs. The Arab nation was born through the development of a secular national culture confined in the main to rhetoric and poetical expression, and this was at a time when it had no political organization whatsoever.

The Arabs themselves, after having come into close contact with distant peoples and civilizations, were fully aware of their specific national genius. The Chinese, they say, excel in arts and crafts, the Indians in wisdom and story telling, the Persians in statecraft and moral maxims, the Children of Israel in prophecy, the Greeks in philosophy and science, and the Arabs in eloquence and poetry. It was this common literary achievement of illiterate tribesmen which molded them into a civilized nation.

The origin of Islam itself has to be viewed in the light of this miraculous linguistic and literary development. Monotheism was in the air; a nation like the Arabs, coming of age, could not remain outside its pale of influence. Christian and Jewish missionaries were active in the Arabian peninsula—not so much missionaries in the formal sense of the word, although these too were not wanting, but itinerant merchants, rabbis and monks travelling in the country. In various parts of Arabia the local populations had adopted one or another form of Christianity or Judaism. However the bulk of the Arab people did not consent to this. It had to have its Arabic scripture, a revelation not translated from a foreign language, but in its own 'clear Arabic'. Seen in this way, *Islam itself was a part of that miraculous linguistic process by which the Arab nation came into being.* Islam was a form of self-assertion and self-realization of the emerging Arab nation.

Consequently, the Arabic element is very conspicuous in Islamic religion.Although four-fifths of the Muslims do not have Arabic as their mother tongue, the prayers are invariably said in that language.[1] This insistence of Islam on the use of Arabic in prayer and the recitation of the Koran should not be compared with the role of Latin in the Catholic church. The Catholic service is performed by priests and other professionals while the congregation's participation is limited in scope. The Muslim prayer is an individual obligation, mostly absolved not in the mosque, but in the fields, in the workshop or the living room, while the study of the Koran is incumbent, at least in theory, on every Muslim man and woman. It has often been said that Arabic spread so widely because it is the language of the Koran. Historically speaking, we have to reverse this statement. Because the Arabs were so very much dedicated to their language, they forced its knowledge upon the peoples who wanted to read the Koran, or, rather they simply could not imagine that anyone could understand it properly except when studying it in Arabic. In contradistinction, the Jews translated the Hebrew Bible into Greek and Aramaic for the use of their own brethren. It is not the sanctity of a book which causes the diffusion of its language, but the strength of the language which forces the believers to study the original of a holy scripture.

[1] The nationalist and secular regime of Kemal Atatürk abolished the use of Arabic for the call to prayer from the minarets in Turkey. How significant, however, is the following passage from Bernard Lewis, "Islamic Revival in Turkey", *International Affairs* 28 (1952), p. 43: "In June 1950 the recitation of the call to prayer in Arabic was permitted. The call to prayer in Turkish, which had previously alone been tolerated, was not abolished, but the use of Arabic was made optional. As far as I could ascertain, the call is now read almost exclusively in Arabic."

In addition to the Koran, which, according to Muslim belief, is not the work of Muhammad, but the uncreated, eternal word of God, the whole religious and ethical literature of Islam, developed during its first five centuries, is written in Arabic, although the authors were largely non-Arabs. All the basic works on the oral traditions ascribed to the Prophet, on law and theology, on pietism and mysticism are composed in that language. Little wonder that Islam adopted the maxim that "the knowledge of Arabic is a part of one's religion".

The pilgrimage to the holy places in Arabia, the *ḥajj*, one of the five "pillars" or main duties of the Muslim, is another element preserving the intrinsically Arab character of Islam. During the early stages of expansion and colonization, when the Muslims discovered that, owing to the enormous distances, it was extremely difficult to fulfill this duty, some attempts were made to find substitutes.[1] However the upsurge of commerce and international trade which set in with the second century of Islam gave a mighty impetus to the holy pilgrimage. Commerce and *ḥajj* became so intimately associated that a pilgrim was normally blessed with the formula: "May God accept your *ḥajj*, condone your sins and let you find a good market for your wares". As is shown in another part of this book, the religious scholars of early Islam belonged largely to the merchant class and mostly were engaged in commerce themselves.[2] It is thus not surprising that we find in the biographies of nearly all of them that they made the pilgrimage to Mecca and most of them made it more than once. Many would remain in the holy city for a year or more, which "sojourn in the neighborhood of God" had the side effect of thoroughly Arabicizing the sojourner. In our own days, when people make the pilgrimage by plane, the effect is less profound. But what is lost in quality is made good by quantity, an enormous mass of pilgrims from all over the Muslim world being able to participate.

According to the theory of Muslim public law the caliph, or legal ruler of the Muslims, must be of the tribe of the Prophet, just as according to Jewish and Christian concepts the Messiah, or anointed king, must be of the house of David. This theory had the great practical consequence that it prolonged the rule of the Abbasid caliphs for a full four hundred years after they had lost all political power. It was terminated not by revolt from within, but by a pagan conqueror, the Mongol Hulagu who executed the last caliph of

[1] Cf. pp. 137-138.
[2] See Chapter XI.

Bagdad in 1258. Although the Near East became dominated by Turks and other warrior peoples from approximately 1000 A.D., the long rule of the Abbasid caliphs gave to the history of Islam the semblance of Arab supremacy.

Against this background we are able to understand the curious position of Islam in the more developed parts of the present day Arab world, such as the U.A.R. The wheel has come full circle: Islam itself now forms a part of the national, of the secular national culture. This has its corollary in that the very considerable Christian population takes part, or is forced to take part, in this cultural heritage. Islamic texts are included in the syllabus of the state schools, and the Christian schools find it extremely difficult to maintain themselves or to preserve their denominational character. While traditional Islam left a very high degree of legal autonomy to the religious minorities, i.e. Christians and Jews, and granted them the right to educate their children according to the ideals and substance of their faiths, the present day Arab states are less tolerant. By incorporating Islam in the national heritage, they impose it to a certain degree on non-Muslims. However, since Islam, as we have seen, was the highest form of self-realization of the Arab people, it seems perfectly legitimate that a Copt or a Syrian Christian, as soon as he identifies himself as a member of the Arab nation, should be required ta acquaint himself to some extent with Islam.

Within Islam itself, the Arab element has been utilized as an argument in favor of religion. Against the secularist tendencies unmistakably at work today, the fundamentalists make the following point: Before Islam the Arabs were of no consequence. After and through acceptance of Muhammad's message, they became the masters of the world. This proves that Islam is the source of Arab greatness. Consequently, only by strict adherence to their religion can the Arabs regain their former position.[1]

II

Yet Islam is not the religion of the Arabs alone, it is a universal, a world religion. As is well known, the Arabs constitute a minority among the Muslims. The largest single group of Muslims is formed by peoples speaking Indo-European languages: Iranians, Afghans,

[1] This point is made e.g. in the pamphlet *Al-Muslimoon* of the Islamic Centre in Geneva, Issue IV, February 1963, pp. 1-2.

and the Muslims of Pakistan and India, altogether about 180 million, over twice as many as the Arab peoples. The second largest group are the Indonesians and Malayans, who comprise the overwhelming majority of the inhabitants of Indonesia itself and a very considerable part of the population of Malaysia. Third in number, but certainly not less than second in historical importance, are the Turks. Turkish Muslims are found not only in the state called Turkey, but all over Central Asia. People of Turkish extraction have ruled the Middle East from the eleventh to the twentieth centuries and left their imprint on the history of this region. The fourth non-Arab group of Muslim peoples, much in the news in these days, is represented by black Africa, by Africans of various races, many of whom have adopted Islam only in recent times, when European colonial rule in various ways facilitated its spread. Strange as it may seem, it was Christian rule in Africa which was instrumental in the expansion of Islam. For the lower officials in the service of the European administrations, those with whom the population had actual contacts, had been largely Muslims from the Mediterranean countries, and the Muslim merchant, always the natural missionary of Islam, could more easily penetrate into remote districts when protected by a strong European government. Finally, it has been estimated that around the middle of this century about 50 million Muslims were found in China.

The very expansion of Islam was largely the work of non-Arab peoples. The Iranians islamized the Turks and the Mongols. All these three together conquered India for Islam. The conversion of most of the Malayan and Indonesian peoples was accomplished by Indian Muslims. The Chinese Muslims were either of Turkish and Mongol extraction themselves or were mainly attracted to Islam by persons of those races.

Thus we see that Islam, like Catholicism, was adopted by many peoples, separated from each other by great distances and differing in language, character, and historical background, even more than for example, the Catholic countries of South America, France and Poland.

The wide diffusion of Islam was due both to specific historical circumstances and to the innate character of the faith initiated by Muhammad.

The very success of the Arabs as a nation made their religion supernational. After their sweeping victories in the first century of Islam, which brought them to the shores of the Atlantic in the West and to the valleys of the Himalays in the East, they found themselves a small minority in their own empire. Mere expediency, if no other reasons, recommended both tolerance and missionary activity. Mass conversions of large sections of the subject population ensued, mostly caused by the social and economic advantages conferred by the adherence to the ruling religion, but partly as the result of the preaching of Islam. It is natural that the converts transferred to the new religion the yearnings, concepts and customs connected with their former persuasions and thus made Islam more diversified and appealing to a far greater variety of peoples and far richer than it would have been had it remained the monolithic faith of a single national group.

Let us imagine for a moment that the military expeditions of the Arabs which started immediately after the death of Muhammad had not been crowned with success; that the armies of Byzantium and the Sassanid kings had been strong enough to repel them and to confine them to the Arabian peninsula. In that case, Islam, if surviving at all, would have remained crude, primitive, starkly national and local in character and its appeal to other peoples would have been necessarily limited. Yet even in that case, it would not have lacked a strain of universality. This is proven by the evidence of the Koran, the basic document of Islam and the only one which was completed before the Arabs set out on their expeditions outside Arabia.

To begin with, by its very nature, monotheism is universalistic. The belief in one God has as a corollary the concept of one world with one human race. The Hebrew Bible does not open with a theomachy, or a fight between gods, and a first dynasty of kings of a city or a country, as we have in otherwise so highly developed ancient Babylonia. Instead we learn about the creation of the world through the mere word of the one God and about Adam and Eve, the father and mother respectively of all mankind. The Koran continuously and most emphatically refers to these two stories and connects them with the central themes of Muhammad's own message: "the second creation", i.e. the new world arising after the Last Judgment, and the personal responsibility of each individual, who faces punishment for his deeds like his first ancestor.[1]

This concept of individual responsibility is another great uni-

[1] Cf. Heinrich Speyer, *Die biblischen Erzählungen im Qoran*, Hildesheim, 1961, pp. 1-83.

versalistic idea which pervades the whole of the Koran. Muhammad, at the beginning of his prophetical vocation, certainly regarded himself as sent to "his next of kin", to "the city of Mecca and those around it".[1] However, he did not approach them as a tribe, he did not preach to them as a people. From the outset he addresses "man", the individual "soul", and never tires to emphasize that neither a brother, nor father and mother or wife and children are able to do a thing for a man when he stands before his eternal Judge.[2] This was a complete breach with the notions of pre-Islamic Arab society, where the family stood up for the misdeeds of its members and where the individual had no status except through his tribe. Muhammad was fully aware of this contrast between ethical monotheism and the traditional views of his countrymen. Therefore he stresses the responsibility of man as man incessantly in an exaggerated way reminiscent of Ezekiel.[3]

In view of this, there is not much point in the long-standing controversy as to whether Muhammad thought of himself as a prophet sent to the Arabs or to mankind in general. The various passages from the Koran adduced for the two opposing views allow of different interpretations.[4] However, from the very first word we hear from the Prophet's mouth, it is evident that he came to the Arabs not as Arabs, and in order to solve specifically Arab problems, but as human beings whom he felt himself obliged to guide in the same way as other human beings had been guided before.[5] Therefore it is correct to say that Muhammad's message was universal in character from its very inception.

This view is confirmed by Muhammad's prophetology, by the ideas which he nourished with regard to his own calling and that of his predecessors. Very much has been written about the subject. It seems, however, that its treatment was inspired too much by our

[1] Koran 26:214, 42:7/5, 6:92.
[2] *Ibid.* 90:4, 91:7, 80:34-37.
[3] Ezekiel 3:17-21. 14:12-20. 18:1-32. 33:12-20.
[4] The literature about the subject in F. Buhl, "Fasste Muhammed seine Verkündigung als eine universale, auch für Nichtaraber bestimmte Religion auf?" *Islamica* 2 (1926), pp. 135-149, and in F. Buhl, *Das Leben Muhammeds*, Leipzig 1930, pp. 295, 325 and 379.
[5] Koran 96:1-7. "Recite in the name of your Lord who has created, created *man* etc. ... He taught *man* what he did not know. Nay *man* ... ."
This sura is regarded by the Muslim scholars as Muhammed's first revelation. Naturally we have no means to check the truth of this assumption. But internal evidence proves that it is one of the oldest suras.

own knowledge about the theory of prophecy in fully developed religions such as the Jewish, Christian, Judeo-Christian and gnostic theologies, including the "traditions" and theories of the Muslim scholars themselves. Taking the inner evidence of the Koran as our guide and remaining aware of the necessary limitations of our knowledge, we arrive at the following approximate picture of Muhammad's early development.

Sometime around 600 A.D., a group of itinerant monotheistic preachers active in Arabia came to the conclusion (familiar from other missionary quarters) that the best way to spread the word of God among pagan peoples was letting it be propagated by members of those peoples themselves. This is alluded to in the earlier parts of the Koran where we read so frequently that to such and such a people *their brother* So and So was sent[1] and when they did not listen to him they were punished by destruction. This also explains why we find other prophets arising simultaneously with Muhammad in various parts of Arabia including one prophetess and one leader who was regarded by the Muslims as a dangerous rival of their own prophet.[2] Muhammad differed from his rivals in that he was a genius, he was the elect one and the others were not.

The testimony of the older sections of the Koran indicates that those itinerant preachers must have confined themselves to the most rudimentary essentials of their respective faiths. They called to repentance in the name of God, condemned certain practices such as sexual promiscuity and the burying alive of female babies, and recommended honesty in commercial transactions (most of them were probably engaged in commerce themselves). There was, however, one means by which they made a tremendous and almost magical impression on their illiterate audience. They held in their hand scrolls of parchment, purporting that these were sent down by God and contained the same terrible threats of punishments for unbelieving peoples which they had themselves just described. Adapting themselves to the local milieu (also a well known missionary device) they used the familiar stories about legendary or historical Arab peoples which had disappeared—and the ruins of whose alleged former habitations were still known—in order to drive home their lessons.

[1] In the last instance, the formulation may go back to Deuteronomy 18:18, "I shall raise up a prophet for them from *among their own brothers*."

[2] Cf. the instructive article "Musailima" in EI[1] (by F. Buhl).

Muhammad, as the son of a caravan city living on a farflung international trade, certainly was familiar with the existence of several religions, although he could not have but a faint idea about the differences between them. Thus his Meccan fellow citizens, as we shall presently see, knew that the Christians worshipped the "Messiah", but, failing to grasp the nature of trinity, simply regarded him as another God. It is also suggested by a number of Koranic passages that they were aware of the existence of various Christian denominations. The Meccan summer caravan traded with Palestine and Syria, and no visitor to those countries could but observe the antagonism between the local, Aramaic speaking population, which adhered to the monophysitic persuasion, and the orthodox Greeks, who oppressed them. The Meccan merchants visiting Alexandria, we read in one reliable source, were put up in the hospice of a church. Thus it is natural to assume that in Egypt too they had opportunity to notice the bitter contest between the Coptic Christians of that country and the Byzantine rulers who belonged to the orthodox church. The theological details of the conflict certainly escaped them entirely, but as it was accompanied by social discrimination and persecutions, it was blatant enough to attract the attention of even a casual visitor. The same applied, and to a higher degree, to the Jews living in those countries. Moreover, many Jewish settlements were situated on the caravan routes between Syria, Mecca and Yemen, and some strange Jewish customs, such as the Sabbath, the weekly day of rest (on which one was not permitted for example to travel in a caravan) were easily noted by the outsider, as is again shown by the many references to it in the Koran.

In the light of these propositions, we are now able to visualize the origins of Muhammad's so called "theory of revelation", i.e. his ideas about his own role within the general framework of the guidance of mankind by God's messengers. While listening to the foreign preachers, Muhammad, like some of his Arab contemporaries, was seized by the idea that he was called upon to carry the message of God's judgment to his next of kin, just as other messengers, according to the sermons heard, had been sent to other Arab peoples before him. Unlike the "Warners" contemporary with him, however, he began to ponder about those scrolls of parchment which contained God's message and on which the preachers based their claims. Those scrolls were written in a foreign language. But how could God, the gracious, withhold his word from the multitude of the Arabs and thus condemn them to ignorance and perdition? While meditating on this question, there ripened in him the conviction that God's message must be revealed some day in an Arabic version—and through none other than himself. There could be also no doubt as to the content of that book, for listening to preachers of different denominations he found that all said basically the same things. And how could it be otherwise? Were they not all sent by the same God? Consequently, as Muhammad reiterates again and again, the scripture promulgated through himself could also contain nothing else except what had been revealed before. This conviction was strengthened in time by the simple fact that during the whole of his formative period, most of the years of his activities in his native city, he knew of only one book preceding him: the book of Moses.[1] Thus it was perfectly natural that after the one book on which all relied there should be another one expounding its subject matter to those who for linguistic reasons had no access to the first.

The universalism of Muhammad's "theory of revelation", which dominates the early stages of his career, thus finds its full explanation in the circumstances which gave rise to his assumption of the role of God's messenger. The surmise that this "doctrine" came to him ready made from some Judeo-Christian gnostic circles is redundant and entirely out of place.[2] There could not be imagined a greater contrast than that existing between the esoteric and abstract theosophy of the gnostics and the pristine and broadly human belief of Muhammad in the one truth revealed to all mankind. Precisely because of its origin in a most personal experience, was this belief so strong and simple. It is, we may add at once, also a great asset to Islam in our own time, when we can hardly imagine a true faith other than one apt to encompass the whole human race; or at least one conceding that other religions contained the same basic truth.

Our understanding of the beginning of Islam disposes also of another old controversy, namely the question of Muhammad's sincerity. Here again we can rely on the self testimony of the Koran,

[1] Cf. below, pp. 97-99 and the Notes ibid. To the koranic passages adduced there, sura 6:91-2 may be added: "... Who sent down the book which brought Moses as a light and guidance to mankind? ... And this is a book which We sent down, a blessed one and confirming the *one* preceding it."

[2] This conjecture would not have been mentioned here, had it not been upheld by the eminent historian of religion Tor Andrae, *Mohammed, the Man and His Faith*, Chapter IV, Mohammed's Doctrine of Revelation (Harper Torchbook 1960, p. 94ff.).

so convincing in its innocent simplicity. In the early disputes between the Prophet and his compatriots who refused to believe in his message, reference is frequently made to a man or men from the "Children of Israel"[1] who, according to the Meccans, were the source of Muhammad's knowledge, or, vice versa, were adduced by him as corroborating the truth of his message. Thus we read in sura 25:5—6: "The disbelievers say: 'This is nothing but a fraud which he has devised'" —namely Muhammad's assertion of the heavenly origin of his message—"'and others have helped him with it'. They have said too: 'These are old-world tales, which he has written down for himself; they are recited to him every morning and evening (i.e. frequently)'". Likewise, in sura 16:103, Muhammad quotes his opponents as saying: "It is only a human being who teaches him". That means: not God. To this, Muhammad retorts: "The language of him at whom they point is foreign, but this is clear Arabic speech". This problem of the language of revelation is taken up again in sura 41:43—44: "Nothing is being said to you which has not been said to the messengers before you ... Had We made it a Koran (a scripture, or rather "a lection") in a foreign language, they would have said: would that its verses had been explained in both the foreign language and in Arabic". In other words: Why use a translation, if God's word can be had in the original? Sura 26:192—9 is particularly outspoken: "This is a revelation of the Lord of the World, brought down by the trustworthy Spirit to your heart so that you should be a Warner in clear Arabic speech. It is contained in the scriptures of the ancients. Is it not a sign"—i.e. a proof— "to them that the learned of the Children of Israel know it? Had We sent it down through one of the foreigners and had he recited it to them, they (the Arabs) would not have believed in it".

Muhammad's argument is most revealing: it was the miracle of language, the fact that he promulgated in clear Arabic what he had heard from his mentors in an outlandish diction which convinced him that it was God who spoke through his mouth, not those foreigners who could not make themselves properly understood. According to the Muslim theologians, the language of the Koran is a miracle of perfection which proves its heavenly origin. Whatever we may think about the merits of this assertion[2]—which, by the way, is typical

[1] Cf. the article "Banū Isrā'īl" in EI² (by S. D. Goitein).

[2] A long list of linguistic imperfections of the Koran is contained in the *Neue Beiträge zur semitischen Sprachwissenschaft*, pp. 1-30, by Theodor Nölde-

of a language-minded civilization—it certainly expresses well Muhammad's own concept of his mission.

The passages quoted above allude also to a further stage of Muhammad's prophetical career. Having become convinced that he was destined to deliver a holy scripture to his countrymen, he naturally had to find material for its composition. For this reason he joined the company of "the learned men of the Children of Israel" and accepted from them whatever fit into his scheme. Muhammad's familiarity with the Jewish and Christian heritage was very great. It is evident in the many Biblical narratives, in particular from the Old Testament and its aggadic embellishments, included in the Koran, and even more so by its language of prayer and hymn, preaching and polemics. A scrutiny of the religious phraseology of the Koran reveals an astonishing similarity to that used in Jewish and Christian literature. This can be explained only by prolonged and intimate personal contacts coming on top of the influence exercised on pre-Islamic Arabic through missionary activities.[1]

When we find that the references in the Koran to details contained in the older monotheistic scriptures are often strange, we should always remember that he had to rely on oral transmission and on casual informants whom he had to exchange frequently. Just as it is absurd for modern Muslim apologists to have recourse to the results of higher Biblical criticism in order to explain away the discrepancies between the biblical original and the Koran, so it would be unhistorical on our part to judge the Koran on the basis of our knowledge of the Bible. To give just one example. In a well known passage of the Koran Pharaoh, the Egyptian tyrant, asks Haman, the Persian vizier from the book of Esther, to build for him something which is definitely reminiscent of the Tower of Babylon (cf. Genesis 11:1—4): "O Haman, burn for me bricks and make me a tower that I may ascend to the god of Moses".[2] It would be entirely out of place to

ke. Considering, however, that Muhammed had to create almost out of nothing not only a religious vocabulary, but also styles of preaching, prayer and legislation, his performance, in this field too, is very remarkable.

[1] The language of Koranic prayer and hymn in its relationship with pre-Islamic religious phraseology was studied extensively (but certainly not exhaustively) in the present writer's Ph.D. thesis *Das Gebet im Qor'ān*, Frankfurt 1923, of which only a short summary was printed. I still hope to find time to return to this intriguing subject and to publish a revised version of the thesis. Cf. also below, Chapter III.

[2] Koran 28:38. A similar combination is found in other suras, cf. H. Speyer, *Die biblischen Erzählungen im Qoran*, p. 283.

comment here on Muhammad's ignorance. Muhammad did not study the Bible and was not supposed to do so. He had listened to preachers, and these, as we know both from numerous examples in rabbinical literature and from the sermons of the Syriac Fathers of the Church, would mention in one breath a number of haughty men, such as Pharaoh, Haman and the people of the Tower of Babylon, who revolted against God and demonstrated by their downfall the futility of rebellion. The Koran is not a history book. The stories included in it are but exempla destined to drive home a lesson.

In view of this it is also of no great import to find out which religious tradition it was from which Muhammad received the material for his exempla. Since specifically Christian stories are entirely absent from the fifty or so most ancient suras, while they contain aggadic, i.e. Jewish folkloristic elements, it is probable that the "learned men of the Children of Israel" or at least some of them, referred to in sura 26 (cf. p. 16) were Jews. It even seems that the very subject of Jesus was brought up first by Muhammad's pagan adversaries. For when he started to preach monotheism and attack their idols—a subject which became prominent only in his second Meccan period—he was refuted with the argument that even some of the people of the Book worshipped a god besides Allah, namely "Jesus, the son of Mary". "Are our gods better or he?"—they asked.[1] To which Muhammad retorted that Jesus was but a servant of God, a position which he retained throughout the Koran.

However, once a problem was raised, either by his adversaries or his own followers,[2] or, we may assume, his personal thinking, Muhammad tried vigorously to obtain new information. Step by step we are able to trace in the Koran Muhammad's ever widening knowledge of the older monotheistic religions. These endeavors bore rich fruit. They gave Muhammad's original universalism breadth and depth and completed the affinity of his creation, Islam, with its older sisters. The result of all this was far-reaching. The same basic religious and ethical notions, the same general framework of religious history which has educated in the past the peoples of the Middle East and Europe, of America and Australia and New Zealand, has also deeply affected large sections of the population of Asia and Africa beyond the Middle East.

According to the Koran, there is only one God and this God is the

[1] Koran 43:57-58.
[2] Many passages in the Koran open with the phrase: "They ask you".

creator of the world and its permanent and paramount lord. He guides mankind through successive acts of revelation, comparable to the covenants of the Old Testament which, beginning with Adam and Noah were renewed again and again. The main figures of Biblical history are as familiar to Muslims as they are to Christians or Jews, and Biblical names are as common among the former as they are among the latter.[1] Islamic religion is an ethical monotheism like its predecessors. God's uniqueness entails that man is constantly responsible for his deeds to one God, the God of justice and mercy. This world is only a preparatory stage for the world to come, which will be initiated by the Day of Judgment, an event which Muhammad expected to occur in his own lifetime or at least very soon thereafter. The main institutions of Islam, such as prayer, the Friday worship, fasting, almsgiving and many others have their origins and parallels in Christianity and Judaism. Islamic prayer uses the ideas and literary forms of the Christian and Jewish liturgy. The Fātiḥa, the opening chapter of the Koran, which is the main constituent of Muslim daily prayer, does not contain a single phrase which could not be traced to the liturgy of the older religions and which could not be said by every believing Christian or Jew.

The Koran is the holy scripture of Islam. Yet it forms only the basis on which the centuries following Muhammad's death (632 A.D.) erected a huge edifice of religious lore, law and thought. This system was completed in its rudiments about two hundred years after Muhammad and reached its pinnacle in the lifework of the "renewer of Islam" the theologian and mystic Ghazālī, who died in 1111. Islam develops as long as there exist believing Muslims and therefore new aspects of Islam are discernible in our own time as well. It is, however, correct to say that the Koran itself contains all or most of the essential traits of developed Islam.

In this respect, the role of the Koran in Islam is very much different from that of the Old Testament in Judaism. Even the most thorough study of the Old Testament is unable to provide an adequate idea of the beliefs and practices of Judaism (wherefore Christians and Muslims identifying Judaism with the Old Testament remain ignorant of the former). Contrariwise, the Koran, complemented by some information about Islamic practices, such as details concerning the five daily prayers, is a true mirror of Islam.

[1] Of course in Arabicized form. Thus the present head of the state of Pakistan is called *Ayyūb*, which is the Arabic equivalent of Hebrew *Iyyōv*, the Biblical Job.

The reason for this difference is twofold. The Hebrew Bible is not a book, it is a library. It constitutes the remnants of the literature of an ancient people, written in the course of over a thousand years and originally serving very diverse purposes. The Koran is the creation of one single man with one specific and immediate objective in mind, namely of supplying what the Koran actually is: a holy scripture for a new religion. With this, another and most important contrast is connected. Judaism is the outcome of a long development, discernible in the Old Testament itself, but continued after its conclusion for at least another half millenium, such central ideas as the beliefs in resurrection and the world to come, the celestial paradise and hell being next to absent from the Hebrew Bible. By the time of Muhammad, Judaism had become a complete and well rounded system of ideas, values and practices, on which any new creation could conveniently draw.

The situation was somewhat similar with regard to Christianity. The New Testament is far more homogeneous than the Hebrew Bible, but still far less uniform than the Koran. Christianity also needed hundreds of years until its creeds and practices crystallized. One needs only to remember how late such basic institutions as Christmas and Sunday were introduced (the latter is referred to in the Koran as a deviation from the Jewish Sabbath). First and foremost, however, Islam must be compared with Judaism, because the two religions are so very similar to each other, or, from the typological point of view, are identical in pattern. There is no need to emphasize the dissimilarity between Muhammad's message and religions such as Brahmanism, Buddhism or Taoism. But Christianity, too, is essentially distinct from Islam, although the latter is indebted so much to the former, as we shall presently see. The Christian faith is based on the belief in the redeeming power of the Savior and is realized in symbolic acts of sacraments.[1] Islam, like Judaism, is a religion of commandments, in which the minute observance of ritual and ethical injunctions is intended to sanctify every moment of the believer's life

[1] Wilfred Cantwell Smith, "Some Similarities and Differences between Christianity anf Islam," *The World of Islam*, ed. by J. Kritzek and R. Bayly Winder, London 1959, pp. 57-8, suggests that a Muslim, while memorizing the Koran, the pre-existent Word of God, might have a religious experience similar to that of a Christian in Communion. This suggestion, made by a deep searching student of Islam, who is a practicing Christian, is certainly noteworthy, but does not do away with the difference stated above.

Cf. also Marshall G. S. Hodgson, "A Comparison of Islam and Christianity as Framework for Religious Life," *Diogenes* 32 (1960), pp. 49-74.

and to make him continuously aware of his being but a servant of God.

These commandments are incorporated in God's law, which consists of two parts: the Scripture given directly through revelation, the written Torah (called *Kitāb*, corresponding to the Hebrew *tōrā shebi-Ketāv*, the written Torah), and an oral law (*Ḥadīth*, literally "something told", the equivalent of *tōrā shebeʿal pē*, the oral Torah). The latter is of course of lesser religious status, but in practice, its interpretation of the written law is of higher authority than the literal meaning of the scripture. The expounders of the Law, often lacking any official position and not forming an organized clergy, are the true representatives of both religions. In both, the study of the Law, or "the seeking of knowledge" as it is called in Islam, is an act of worship and a religious duty incumbent on everyone.

In addition to these conceptual and institutional similarities, Islam and Judaism have in common what could properly be called the spirit of religion. Theirs is a stern monotheism, an awesome reverence for an entirely transcendent God, mixed with a seemingly incongruous attitude of familiarity with the Highest Being, who will never fail to be considerate toward the adherents of the true faith. It has often been remarked that Muslims unlike Jews (and, of course, Christians) never say in their prayers "Our Father in Heaven". This discrepancy in religious parlance should not be overrated. The Muslims begin every work and superscribe every letter, book and legal deed with the words: "In the name of God, the Merciful, the Compassionate". As we have seen, the idea of the gracious God, who could not have left the Arabs without guidance, was at the very root of Islam, and the word *Raḥmān*, the Merciful, commonly occurs in the Koran as a designation for God (it was the proper name of God in Jewish usage during the centuries preceding Islam). A careful perusal of both learned and popular religious literature as well as actual observations prove that the believing and practicing Muslims and Jews feel themselves protected and secure. The almost permanent contact with God, established through the innumerable little injunctions which accompany the believer throughout life create in him the confidence that he is constantly watched and provided for. This feeling gives him strength to endure hardship and fills him with hope for reward in this world or, at least, in the world to come.

How is this amazing typological identity of Islam and Judaism to be explained? There is no need to recall that Medina, where koranic theology and religious language, lore and law received their final formulation, was the seat of a large Jewish community. Every page of the Medinese suras bears testimony to familiarity with Jewish things. We have also suggested that at least some or one of the "learned men of the Children of Israel" to whom Muhammad referred at a very early stage of his Meccan career must have been Jewish. However, such a great historical phenomenon as the type and essence of a religion should not be explained merely by influences. For the existence of an example does not imply at all that it would be followed. There must be a predisposition and readiness on the receiving end before any influence can become effective. Therefore, while it is useful and conducive to a fuller understanding of Islam and Judaism to study points of contact between them, we had better leave the greater question of their aboriginal affinity unanswered. It is, as a great Muslim historian would formulate it, "a secret of the secrets of God".

There are, however, three elements in Islam which made it different from anything preceding it and gave it a specific character all of its own. One of them, Islam's roots in Arabia, has already been discussed. Islam was understood by us as part and parcel of that largely linguistic and literary process which gave rise to the Arab nation. With equal right it could be said that Islam represents the self-assertion of its founder. The Koran has been called "the most human of the books of revelation". It is indeed a first rate source for the psychology of genius. Genuine concern for the well-being and salvation of others is mingled with intensive preoccupation of the author with himself. Just as the Arabs succeeded in transmitting their enthusiasm for their beautiful language to the peoples subjected by them, so Muhammad imbued his followers with the same solicitude for himself which engaged his own mind. "He who loves me, loves God"—we are in no position to know whether this and similar sayings ascribed to Muhammad in the *Ḥadīth* are authentic. They are however in full conformity with the testimony of the Koran itself. "If you love God, follow me; then God will love you and forgive your sins"[1] comes already very near to the *ḥadīth* just quoted and expresses in general the attitude expected by Muhammad from the true believers and so does "Obey God and the Messenger", this standing formula of the Medinese period. In the Muslim declaration of faith "There is no god besides God and Muhammad is the messenger of God", the

[1] Koran 3:31/29.

second part always carried most weight, since it differentiated Islam from other faiths. In addition, by assuming the role of intercessor for his flock on the Day of Judgment Muhammad became far more than the bearer of revelation. He assumed the image of the father, the protector, who saves each individual Muslim from perdition.[1] By declaring himself an example to be followed, he grew to be the archetype of the perfect man, with each generation, including our own, giving this ideal new content.[2] Finally, mysticism transformed the bearer of God's light into a lightlike hypostasis through which divinity itself can be perceived.[3] All in all, Muhammad's position in Islam holds somehow the middle ground between Moses, who was merely "the Teacher" in Judaism and the Savior in Christianity.

For reasons we shall presently have opportunity to discuss, the veneration of Muhammad has not decreased but has become even more pronounced in our own century. This is evident, first of all, in the literary production of our Muslim contemporaries. As representative of the first quarter of this century I would single out the elated mysticism of the Indian Muslim poet and thinker Iqbāl. His intimate knowledge of modern philosophy and his own sophisticated theorems did not impede him from indulging in rapturous love of the Prophet.

"With God I talk in veils, with thee (Muhammad) openly". And: "By love of him (Muhammad) the heart is made strong".

"All our glory is from the name of Muhammad".[4]

Typical of the second quarter of the century is a whole plethora of essay-like books on the Prophet in which the best Muslim writers

1 Cf. p. 78. A Yemenite Arab proverb says: "Once a Jew leaves the boundary of Judaism, he is out of it", cf. my *Jemenica* (see below p. 434), p. 177, no. 1379. When, on hearing this saying, I asked, "And the Muslims?", I was given the following answer: "Whatever a Muslim does, they say, Muhammad will intercede for him." This little piece of popular religiosity is certainly illustrative of a characteristic difference.

2 Koran 33:21. The *imitatio Dei*, the imitation of God, that great principle of philosophic and religious ethics, assumed in Islam largely the form of the imitation of the Messenger of God.

3 *Ibid.*, 42:52 etc. "The book of Moses" and the Gospel are also described in the Koran as a light for mankind, cf. p. 152. The development of the ideas about the personality of Muhammad in Islamic religious belief and doctrine has been admirably described by Tor Andrae, *Die Person Muhammads in Glauben und Lehre seiner Gemeinde*, Stockholm 1918.

4 The quotations are taken from A. Schimmel, "The Place of the Prophet in Islam in Iqbāl's Thought," *Islamic Studies*, Karachi 1, 4 (December 1962), pp. 116-117. Note that the very name Muhammad is believed to have mystical power.

tried to make the life of the founder of their religion meaningful for themselves and their readers. Practically all the veteran Muslim authors of Egypt have felt the urge to write such a book, so much so that sometimes even a certain criticism of this literary trend and a warning against clericalism was voiced. The present generation is characterized by the serious endeavor of approaching the history of the Prophet scientifically. The very extensive biography of Muhammad by M. Hamīdullāh, a renowned scholar of Indian origin, may serve as an example.[1] For us, the scientific value of this massive book is limited by the strict orthodoxy of the author which forces him to accept as literal truth reports of an obviously legendary character. For the believing Muslim, the guidance of a scholar who is versed in many European languages and familiar with both the methods and the results of modern research is certainly an illumination.

The attitude of the rank and file of the contemporary Muslim intelligentsia towards the Prophet is also significant. Experience shows that even young men with an entirely secular outlook on life are very sensitive in this respect. They would be offended by any remark smelling of criticism. This deep-seated feeling is to be understood as one, and certainly very characteristic, aspect of the present state of Islam in general.

As to the popular cult of Muhammad, we have to remember that, in addition to the purely religious and psychological element which we have characterized as father image, the very biography of the Prophet, both the real and the legendary, forms a most attractive narrative. On the one hand, it is a success story. Muhammad died after having vanquished most of his enemies, obtained all his goals and being beloved by many and honored by all. What can one wish more for one's hero? However, "admiration", as Gotthold Ephraim Lessing wrote two hundred years ago, "is a cold affect". The Prophet's biography contains also many elements which appeal to the emotions of apprehension and compassion. He knew times of anguish, despair and dangers, and the popular biographies indulge in exaggerated accounts of the persecutions suffered by him in Mecca. Then came the Flight from his native city, described as a deft and miraculous sneaking out of a state of siege. This story is embellished by romantic details such as the hiding in a cave over the entrance of which a spider spun its web, so that the persecutors did not suspect

[1] Muhammed Hamidullah, *Le prophète de l'Islam*, Paris, 1959. I. Sa vie. II. Son oeuvre.

any one of having entered it (a motif found e.g. in the stories of David fleeing Saul). Finally, phantasy finds rich nourishment in the many supernatural legends about the Prophet, in particular his ascent to Heaven on a chimeric steed, so often depicted in Persian miniatures. The term "popular" used at the beginning of this paragraph is to be understood with a grain of salt. As is natural, even sophisticated persons would cherish the emotionally rich childhood recollections of the cult of the Prophet.

Arabism and the person of Muhammad may appear as natural specifiers of Islam. There was, however, another element in Islam seemingly the opposite of anything specific, which formed the foundation of a very particular development. We are referring to what we have described above as the pristine universalism of Muhammad, his belief that God has sent messengers with one and the same mission to many peoples. Certainly, Muhammad ended by declaring Islam the only true religion, but he never renounced his original concept entirely. Whether this was done for practical or other reasons, at any event the consequences were tremendous. We do not refer here to the tolerance in principle of other monotheistic religions, important as it is, but to the pliability and adaptability of Islam acquired through its aboriginal latitude of approach to other peoples. The very fact that most of the stories of the Koran are devoted to persons and events outside Arabia induced the Muslims "to seek knowledge and were it in China". The *Ḥadīth*, the oral lore ascribed to Muhammad, is a treasure house of the most variegated provenance, harboring, in addition to the *sunna*, "the way of life", i.e. the example of the Prophet and the experience of his community, copious Jewish and Christian traditions as well as Greek and Oriental popular wisdom. The dictum put into the Prophet's mouth: "everything good which is said, has been said by me", although perhaps being itself modeled after a talmudic aphorism about Moses,[1] poignantly expresses the spiritual attitude of Islam.

This innate adaptability of Islam bore rich fruit after the great conquests. Iraq, where the greatest number of Arabs and their best minds settled first, was also the center of Judaism and the seat of its ecumenical academies. Both the *Ḥadīth* and Muslim law show that

[1] I. Goldziher, *Vorlesungen über den Islam*, Heidelberg 1910, pp. 47 and 74. The talmudic aphorism, which is transmitted in different variations, says that whatever a good scholar teaches has already been said (by God) to Moses on Mount Sinai.

there must have been vivid contacts.[1] The ubiquitous encounter with the highly developed Christian theology compelled the Muslims to rethink and to formulate their own faith. Once the impetus was given, Islamic theology developed independently into an immensely ramified science, somewhat neglected by the Muslims today, but perhaps destined to a revival in the future.[2] Similarly, the Christian hermits and monks, already referred to in the Koran, deeply impressed the religiously minded followers of the new faith. To be sure, celibacy was never acceptable to Islam. The ideals of poverty and obedience, however, propagated also by the example of the Buddhist itinerant beggars, struck home. Arabic *fakir* and Persian *dervish*, both meaning "poor", have become even in most European languages designations for Muslim pious men. The pietist and mystic movements in Islam are known under the general name of Sufism, derived from *ṣūf*, wool, which was the garb of the poor. These movements, fortified by a philosophical substructure derived from Neoplatonism[3] represent perhaps the most original contribution of Islam to the phenomenon of religion. "They meant highest exaltation for the select few and an elixir of life for the masses. To renounce the world, to wipe out one's own small personality and to find oneself again in the allembracing unity of God—this was the ultimate goal of Sufism. It could be reached only in the rapture of ecstasy, after passing through many "stations" on a "way" to ever higher perfection". The "way" could be found only under the spiritual guidance of a saintly man, who had himself attained the goal, and in the company of brethren of similar bent. This explains the excessive spread of the cult of saints in Islam, as well as that of religious orders and brotherhoods, mostly comprising both professional dervishes and lay members.[4]

[1] Cf. S. D. Goitein, *Jews and Arabs, Their Contacts through the Ages*, New York 1964, pp. 46ff. and 177ff.

[2] A succinct and lucid presentation of this difficult subject is to be found in W. Montgomery Watt, *Islamic Philosophy and Theology*, Islamic Surveys I, Edinburgh 1962. Cf. the present writer's appreciation in *Muslim World* 33 (1963), p. 332.

[3] See below, p. 63.

[4] Cf. A. J. Arberry, *Sufism, An Account of the Mystics of Islam*, London 1950, and *An Introduction to the History of Sufism* (actually an account of the history of the study of Sufism), London 1942, which are short, but authoritative. A penetrating analysis of the movement is contained in the work of two Catholic scholars, G.-C. Anawati and Louis Gardet, *Mystique musulmane*, Paris 1961. The quotation is taken from the book quoted in Note 1, p. 148ff., where Jewish and Islamic mysticism are compared.

Sufism, the flower and most intensive expression of Islam, decayed in the course of time and fell into utmost disrepute among the Muslims themselves. In particular the superstitious belief in the miracle working power of "saints" of dubious quality acted as an element of degradation. Neither did the other "sciences of Islam", such as the study of *Ḥadīth*, law and theology, escape the natural fate of decline after many centuries of efflorescence. It would be a mistake to assume that it was the impact of the modern scientific and technological civilization which shattered Islam. Islam is a great religion which has hallowed and ennobled the life of countless millions. However, by the beginning of the nineteenth century, after a long period of stagnation, it had exhausted itself. The fountains of inner rejuvenation had dried up. The Wahhabi movement originating in Arabia during the eighteenth century was a last revival, but it pointed backward, not forward, and is petering out in our own time and can no longer be called a spiritual force.

This decline of Islam is nothing exceptional. As far as recorded history goes, all creations of the human spirit have suffered a similar fate. In view of this, the contact with the new western civilization was not a curse for Islam, but a blessing. It forced the Muslim intellectuals to rediscover their own religion and to reformulate it in terms acceptable to themselves and respected by everyone. Before this endeavor can achieve full fruition, however, a challenge of far greater magnitude is to be met by Islam. In the second half of the twentieth century it is not only the intellectuals, but the broad masses, which are brought into contact with Western culture, at least its outward manifestations. What is the outcome of this confrontation? How is Islam faring today?

Everyone who knows how presumptuous and hazardous it is to answer such a question with regard to one's own religion, will despair of the possibility of arriving at definite conclusions with respect to a religion so far away, so expanded and so unstable as Islam is today. However, some general observations can legitimately be made.

It seems to be generally assumed that the broad masses of the lower classes are still faithful to Islam both in belief and observance. This assumption needs some qualification. While it may apply to certain areas such as Saudi Arabia and Yemen or parts of Pakistan and Turkey, it cannot be accepted with certainty as being true in general. In the past, peasants and the urban proletariat often made poor Muslims, both out of ignorance and indolence and because of strong resentment against their oppressors and exploiters who passed as good Muslims. Yet Islam was the only spiritual content of life and as such dominated the mind of the masses even when they did not make much use of it. In these days, when radio, television and other modern means of communication provide knowledge about many things other than religion and when political, social and economic problems of immediate concern and greatest magnitude occupy the scene, religion has lost its monopoly and most of its meaning. It is not doubt in the truth of Islam, but lack of interest which undermines its position.

On the other hand, the present population explosion, which is the outcome of the application of modern science, indirectly strengthens Islam. For an area which had a few years ago, say ten millions of observant Muslims, now has twenty. The mere weight of the mass is favorable to the preservation of Islam. In many places the spread of modern education does not keep pace with the increase of the population, which has the result that traditional beliefs are preserved or even gather strength. All in all, it is proper to say that Islam has a large reserve army to draw upon, if and when the general spiritual constellation on this globe should favor a revival of religion.

In the higher and more intellectual circles the various attitudes toward Islam are even more disparate. If we ignore the agnostics who profess Islam outwardly for reasons of expediency or out of consideration for their family and environment, three basic trends may be discerned, although the demarkation lines are naturally fluid. There are persons with a good knowledge of European languages and scientific training who are orthodox and extremist Muslims, both in belief and observance. Everyone personally acquainted with such members of the Muslim intelligentsia will agree that they are sincere. One may, however, sometimes doubt whether they really have a modern mind, despite the mass of information they have acquired. This group usually is rather vociferous.

At the opposite end there are intellectuals who nourish a grudge, if not hate, towards historical Islam, because they regard it as the source of their peoples' decline and see in the traditional forms of religion an impediment to progress. The very fact that many Muslim states have abolished or changed Islamic institutions and customs, such as the veiling of women, polygamy, the one-sided right of the husband to dismiss his wife, and other family laws, the laws of inheritance and of the so-called pious foundations, shows the direction of such complaints. However, even in these circles, if the present writer is not mistaken, disbelief in the literal truth of the holy scriptures or criticism of the theoretical foundations of religion so important in the moulding of Christian and Jewish modernism, play no role whatsoever, or, at least, have found no literary expression. One is simply indifferent towards religion and wants to be let alone by it as far as possible. The question of the ultimate truth is of no interest.

There are others who have lost, or never possessed, the belief in a personal god in the traditional sense, but still keep some of the more conspicuous observances of Islam, not out of regard to their environment—we are not concerned here with this type of agnostics—but out of the sincere belief that Islam as a system of ethics, as a moral way of life has its values and should be preserved and developed in one form or another. This attitude towards religion, which is widespread in our days amongst Protestants and Jews, has not yet found appropriate literary expression in contemporary Islam, but seems to be gaining ground.

The statement made in the preceding paragraph needs perhaps some modification. Persons standing at the parting of the ways, or rather living simultaneously in two cultures may oscillate between the belief in a personal god and other concepts of religion, without being fully aware themselves of the situation. Muhammad ʿAbduh (1849—1905), the father of Islamic modernism in Egypt and occupying, at the end of his life, the position of grand mufti, which was the highest religious dignity in that country, was of course a strictly orthodox Muslim.[1] Yet Lord Cromer, the "British Agent and Counsel-General" and actual ruler of Egypt for a quarter of a century, a shrewd observer, wrote about him: "I suspect that my friend Abdu, although he would have resented the appellation being applied to him, was in reality an Agnostic".[2] At first glance, this remark seems preposterous. The very fact, however, that ʿAbduh could make such an impression is highly significant.[3] Since ʿAbduh's death, over two

[1] There exists a whole literature about this man in European languages. The best introduction to his life and work is contained in the article "Muhammed ʿAbduh" in the *Encyclopaedia of Islam* (by Joseph Schacht). It seems to the present writer that the reform of the Arab language was to ʿAbduh at least as strong a concern as the reform of Islam.

[2] The Earl of Cromer, *Modern Egypt*, London, New York 1908, II, p. 180.

[3] May I illustrate the baffling statement of Cromer by an experience of my own. The only religious genius with whom I had close personal contact during my life was rabbi Nehemia Nobel of Frankfort a/Main (died 1922). He was

generations have passed, unprecedented changes have affected the Muslim world and the grip of tradition has become weaker and weaker. However, precisely because the belief in a personal god has been sapped by other, seemingly more plausible explanations of the universe, or by sheer indifference, Islam has gained in importance as a haven for uncertain minds. Wilfred Cantwell Smith has drawn attention to the fact that while the word Allāh (God) occurs in the Koran 2697 times and the term Islam only 8 times, at the International Islamic Colloquium held in Lahore, Pakistan, in 1958, the ratio was roughly inverted. There was much talk about Islam, but very little about God. This is rightly explained by Smith as follows: "As faith in God has weakened, there has grown a compensatory faith, or hope for faith, in a religion".[1]

This trust in an established religion rather than in the object of worship has in Islam a specific undertone. Already in Muhammad's time the Muslims formed an *umma*, or nation in the political sense of the word, and although the state of the Caliphs, the successors of the Prophet, soon disintegrated, Muslim religious law knows only of one Muslim state, one Muslim treasury, called "the money of the Muslims" or "the money of God", and of one type of war—the war against infidels. In the following, we shall try to pursue the development of this concept and to understand its meaning for the Muslims of our own day.

III

The nature of the *umma*,[2] or Muslim community, finds its explanation in the lifework of Muhammad, just as we have found that all

a real mystic, a great talmudist and at the same time an expert and profound expounder of Goethe. His sermons were not addresses given to a congregation, but dialogues with God in the presence of an audience. Still his disciple, the well-known German Jewish philosopher Franz Rosenzweig said of him that he must have had sometimes doubts as to the very existence of a personal God. To this I may add that, once on the pulpit, he made comments on the concluding verses of Goethe's Faust: "Alles Vergängliche ist nur ein Gleichnis" (All things transitory are but symbols). Suddenly he added: "Alles Unvergängliche ist auch nur ein Gleichnis" (The eternal things also are merely a simile), which seems to confirm Rosenzweig's testimony.

[1] W. C. Smith, "The Comparative Study of Religion etc.", in *Colloque sur la sociologie musulmane, Actes*, 11-14 Septembre 1961, Brussels, p. 230.

[2] The word obviously is related to *umm*, mother. However, whatever notions of matriarchate may have been originally connected with the term *umma*, they are for Islam "pre-historical". I do not quite understand why

the essentials of Muslim religion go back to its founder. The rise of the *umma* commonly is explained as follows: When Muhammad's prophetical message had only a very limited success in his native city of Mecca and its environs, he moved to Medina, where he founded a community of warriors for God's sake. In due course, he achieved with political and military means what he had been unable to obtain by way of preaching and persuasion. The more he expanded his sphere of influence, the more it became evident that the observance of religion could not be enforced except by a strong central authority. Thus the Muslim state became the seemingly indispensable corollary of the Muslim religion.

In this, as in many other respects, modern historiography developed ideas first pronounced by the great Tunisian philosopher of history Ibn Khaldun in his *Muqaddima*, or Prolegomena to his World history (written in 1377). Chapter two, section six of the *Muqaddima* undertakes to prove that no religious propaganda can have permanent success unless backed by political power. Ibn Khaldun strengthens his argument by a saying attributed to Muhammad and incorporated in the canonical collections of *Ḥadīth*: "God never sends a prophet without military support provided by his (the Prophet's) people".[1]

While this theory about the origin of the *umma* is generally correct, it needs modification in detail. The turning point in Muhammad's career was not the emigration to Medina itself, but the new insights which let such a step appear to him as unavoidable. Originally, we have seen, Muhammad believed that all messengers sent by God preached essentially the same truth. Therefore, he could rightly expect that the Possessors of the Book would hail him as one of theirs or at least as an ally in their fight against paganism. This assumption was not entirely mistaken. There are indications in the Koran that Muhammad received at certain periods recognition and even encouragement on the part of adherents of the older religions. "Believe in it (the message) or not"—he says to his compatriots—"those who have received the Knowledge before you fall down on their chins in prostration when it is read out to them and say: Praise to our Lord, the promise of our Lord has come true".[2] This does not

J. Horovitz, *HUCA* 2 (1925), p. 190, and A. Jeffery, *The Foreign Vocabulary of the Qur'an*, Baroda 1938, p. 69, assume that the word was borrowed from the Jews. For the idea of the *umma* cf. C. A. O. van Nieuwenhuijze, "The Ummah—An Analytic Approach", *Studia Islamica* 10 (1959), pp. 5-22.

[1] For details cf. Franz Rosenthal's English translation.

[2] Koran 17:107-108/109-110.

mean that the Jews or Christians referred to became "Muslims", a term probably not yet conceived at the time of that verse, but that they were moved by the success of their missionary endeavors. "If you are uncertain concerning what We sent down to you", says the Koran, "ask those who read the Book before you. Truth has come to you from your Lord; therefore, be not among the doubters".[1] This and similar verses sound as if Muhammad was confirmed in his belief by his mentors, when he himself had periods of weakness.

However, when Muhammad, in his effort to widen his knowledge, made contacts with members of different denominations, he was shocked to find opposition to his role of messenger as bitter as that of the Meccans, and matched only by the enmity nourished by one denomination against the other. This discussion between "the children of Israel" or "the Possessors of the Book" was a great stumbling block for the Prophet and constitutes one of the main themes of the Koran during the later years of his Meccan period. How could it be that the Book of Moses—and later on also the message of Jesus—by bringing enlightenment, caused also friction? To this tantalizing question Muhammad gives the same two seemingly contradictory answers with which he had explained before the obstinate opposition of the pagans: it was human wickedness on one hand and an inscrutable decree of God on the other, which brought about that unfortunate situation. "We gave Moses the Book, but there was dissension about it. Had it not been for a previous decree of your Lord, the dissension would have been decided".[2] "We gave the Children of Israel the Book, the Wisdom and the Prophecy[3] ... They dissented only after Knowledge had come to them, wronging each other. Your Lord will judge between them on the Day of Resurrection".[4] "Had God wished, he would have made them all one religious community (*umma*). However he encompasses with his mercy whomever he likes, but the evildoers have no friend and no helper".[5] "All mankind formed one *umma*. Then they dissented. Had it not been for a previous

[1] *Ibid.*, 10:94. Cf. also 11:17.

[2] *Ibid.*, 11:110/112 and 41:45. Similar passages are found throughout that period.

[3] It is likely that Muhammad had heard about the tripartition of the Old Testament into the Law, or books of Moses, the Prophets and the Writings of Wisdom.

[4] Koran 45:16-17/15-16. With exactly the same words reference is made to what happened after the appearance of Jesus, 42:13/14.

[5] *Ibid.*, 42:8/6. 11:118/120.

decree of your Lord, their dissension would have been decided".[1]

The discovery of the acute discord between the various monotheistic religions and denominations was not only a great affliction from the theological point of view. It taught Muhammad that he had to remodel his own message. If it was decreed by God that humanity should remain disunited until the Day of Judgment and that there should be different *ummas*, then the only thing to do for the prophet of the Arabs was to form an *umma* for himself. The recognition of this necessity dawned upon Muhammad quite slowly. From many passages of the Koran it is evident that he was asked by his monotheistic interlocutors to join their own faith and that he had periods of doubt in this respect. However, he overcame such hesitancy and began to organize a separate religious community. "Preach", he feels God say to him, "and remain steadfast, as you were told, and do not follow their partisanships and say: I believe in all the books sent down by God and am commanded not to discriminate between you. God is our Lord and your Lord. We have our works and you have your works. There is no dispute between us. God will confront us and to him leads the way.[2] And those who dispute with regard to God after what has been granted to him[3]—their argument is void, God's wrath comes upon them and theirs is terrible punishment".[4] The testimony of this and numerous similar passages is unmistakable: long before the end of his Meccan period Muhammad had clearly recognized that he had to fight on two fronts: against the pagans in order to bring them within the orbit of ethical monotheism; and against the monotheists in order to assert the authenticity of his own mission.

It was necessary to describe in some detail how the idea of a Muslim *umma* grew organically out of Muhammad's religious thought, because it seems to be generally assumed by Western scholarship that it was the opposition experienced with the Jews of Medina which turned Islam into a separate, pronouncedly Arabic, religious community. "It is interesting to speculate", says the latest biographer of Muhammad, "what might have happened had the Jews come to terms with Muhammad instead of opposing him. ... They might have become partners in the Arab empire and Islam a sect of Jewry. How

[1] *Ibid.*, 10:19. Cf. also 43:33/32.

[2] I.e., each community will be judged according to its own merits, for all will appear before God on the Day of Judgment.

[3] I.e., to Muhammad.

[4] Koran 42:15-16/14-15.

different the face of the world would be now had that happened! In the early months at Medina the seeds were sown of a great tragedy; a great opportunity was lost".[1]

This concept, though captivating, is wrong on three counts: (1) Muhammad's followers formed a distinct religious community, differing from and opposing the other monotheistic denominations, Christian as well as Jewish, during the later years of the Prophet's activities in Mecca. (2) There is not a single passage in the suras published in Medina which implies that Muhammad was prepared to come to terms with the Jews, except of course on condition that they enter the new community formed by himself. (3) A trustworthy historical source states unequivocally that long before Muhammad set his foot on the soil of Medina, it was clear both to him and the Medinese who invited him that his coming to their town inevitably entailed a break between themselves and their Jewish confederates of old.[2] The example of the Jews of Medina certainly was important for the elaboration of the details which were to regulate the life of the new Muslim communtity. The community itself had been organized long before this contact.

Muhammad's failure in Mecca was a blessing in disguise. Had he succeeded in his endeavor to convert his co-citizens, the Quraysh, his religion could have born the stamp of tribal narrowness. Being forced to fight his own tribe with a band of warriors consisting mostly of foreigners and held together solely by a religious belief and allegiance to himself, Muhammad saw his new community becoming essentially supra-tribal and based on an idea rather than on kinship. On the other hand, the war with Quraysh did not last long enough to cause permanent alienation. The shrewd sons of the caravan city quickly realized the enormous economic advantages provided by their sanctuaries becoming the center of the new religion (advantages

[1] W. Montgomery Watt, *Muhammad, Prophet and Statesman*, Oxford 1961, p. 191. This comparatively short book is a summary and development of two larger works on the same subject.

[2] Before moving to Medina, Muhammad concluded a formal pact with representatives of the two Arab tribes which were paramount in that oasis. An account describing the meeting in which that pact was made, lets a Medinese address Muhammad with the following question: "Oh Messenger of God, between us and the people you know—meaning the Jews—there exist bonds which we are now going to break. When, after we have done so, God gives you victory, will you go back to your own people and forsake us?" Ibn Hishām's *Biography of the Prophet*, Göttingen 1858, I, p. 298, Cairo 1936, II, p. 85. Trsl. A. Guillaume, Oxford University Press 1955, p. 203.

repeatedly underlined in the Koran itself). According to Arab notions, the Quraysh obtained the leadership of the new empire, a fact finding later its theoretical sanction in Muslim law, cf. p. 8. Muhammad himself, after conquering his native city, retained Medina as his capital, emphasizing herewith that religion and not the tribe formed the basis of his community.

This concept was operative in another most decisive feature of the Muslim state as it developed during the concluding years of Muhammad's life. The principle that politics is the art of doing the possible was understood and applied by none better than himself. When settling in Medina, where not only the Jews but large sections of the pagan population did not recognize him as messenger of God, he organized the community on a loose local basis, declaring the area of the town a *ḥaram*, or sacred conclave.[1] By this, according to well established Arab custom, certain obligations became incumbent on all inhabitants without forcing them to accept the Prophet's specific claims and without coercing him to give them all the privileges of true believers. When, after his military successes against the Meccans and others, Muhammad's power became paramount in Medina, the pagans were forced to accept Islam and the Jews were either expelled or killed, with only a few insignificant remnants staying on. Likewise, the expansion of Muhammad's sway over large parts of Arabia first took the form of loose confederations recognizing the political supremacy of Medina. After Mecca was taken and no one in Arabia able to withstand him, Muhammad left the Arab tribes only the choice between acceptance of his faith and the sword. Hence Muslim law fixed the rule that non-monotheists must be forced to embrace Islam. The application of this rule, as was later experienced with regard to India, was not always possible.[2]

The existence of an old established settlement of Jews in Medina was regarded by the Muslim historians as providential, inasmuch as

[1] This aspect of the early Medinese *umma* is well illustrated through parallels from contemporary South Arabia in R. B. Sergeant, "Haram and Hawtah, the Sacred Enclave in Arabia", *Mélanges Taha Husain*, Damascus 1962, pp. 41-58.

[2] It was out of the question to convert the multitudes of Hindus by force. However, the toleration by Islam of the obviously polytheist Indian religion always remained somewhat uneasy, a situation, which led, in the middle of the twentieth century, to the formation of a separate Muslim state, Pakistan. The well-known Pakistan religious leader Maudūdī, in his *Islamic Law and Constitution*, Lahore 1960, does not say explicitly that the Hindus are of the Possessors of the Book.

the contact with them was considered as a preparation of the Medinese for the understanding and acceptance of the religion of Islam. Muhammad's encounter with another and perhaps even more numerous colony of Jews in Arabia, that of Khaybar, set the example for the future position of monotheistic non-Muslims within the Muslim community. In this respect, too, Muhammad proved himself as a master in the art of the possible. As soon as he felt his power, his aim was to supress all opposition. At the very first occasion, he tried to liquidate one of the Jewish tribes of Medina, but gave in, when their Medinese confederates stood firm. In a second case, too, he had to be satisfied with expulsion. A third time, when he succeeded in convincing a dying chieftain that Paradise was more important than the keeping of the bonds of an old confederacy, the remaining Jews were forsaken by their allies and killed on Muhammad's command to the last man. In the case of Khaybar, neither liquidation nor expulsion were practicable. For, as the sources dryly remark, there was no one other than the Jews to look after the invaluable date plantations of that oasis. Thus they were left on their soil, but had to pay a heavy tribute to the Muslims, an arrangement which was to form a precedent for the future position of non-Muslims, although the details varied widely with time and place.

Muhammad's flexibility in his attitude towards the non-Muslim monotheists is well reflected in the Koran. On the one hand he equated them with those who associate with God another god, the polytheists, who have to be fought until they accept Islam. "The Jews say: ʿUzayr is the son of God; the Christians say: the Messiah is the son of God ... In this they resemble the unbelievers ... They take their scholars and monks and the Messiah the son of Mary as lords[1] besides God, while they have been ordered to worship only one God".[2] One clearly sees how Muhammad was groping to find a theoretical basis for an all-out war against Christians and Jews. The Jewish son of God, ʿUzayr, is a puzzle to modern scholars as it was to the Muslims who tried to identify him and the denouncing of the reverence for the Jewish rabbis and Christian monks as polytheism sounds rather odd. We are here in the last year of Muhammad's life, when his power was at its peak. In an earlier period at Medina,

[1] One has to remember that *rabbī*, meaning "my lord" in both Hebrew and Arabic, has in the latter language the connotation of 'God'. In order to avoid this coincidence, the Jews formerly living in Yemen call their rabbi *mōrī*, which also means "my lord", but has no equivalent in Arabic.

[2] Koran 9:30-31.

when most of Arabia was still pagan, we hear another voice: "Those who believe (i.e. the Muslims), the Jews and the Christians and the Sabians,[1] who believe in God and the Last Day and act righteously will receive their reward from their Lord. They have nothing to fear nor to grieve".[2]

Thus the prophet of Islam left to his followers a heritage of universalism and confessionalism, of tolerance and bellicosity and both trends found continuation. Fortunately, during the first two formative centuries in which Muslim law took shape, the conditions favored an attitude of tolerance. The very numbers of the subjected peoples, as has been pointed out before, their economic importance for the Muslim state and their comparatively high technical and educational standards made religious persecution an impracticable proposition. Moreover, the Muslims were preoccupied with wars of conquest and colonization. Thus the universalistic bent in Muhammad's message got the upper hand. Muslim law, in contradistinction to the traditional law of the Church, recognizes the right of existence of other monotheistic religions, and their recognition in principle had many important consequences in practice.[3] The comparatively high standard of civilization in the countries of Islam during the "middle" Middle Ages was certainly due in part to the liberality of its law.

On the other hand, the fabulous successes of the Muslim armies during the one and a half centuries following Muhammad's death had an adverse effect on what could be called Islamic international law. The conquest of the whole world seemed not to be out of reach. Thus the exhortations of the Koran to fight the pagans "until the religion is entirely God's"[4] and the Jews and Christians until they were subjected to Islam,[5] were taken literally. The Muslim jurists

[1] The Muslim exegetes had no idea what religion was meant by this term, nor do we know, cf. A. Jeffery, *Foreign Vocabulary* (see page 31), pp. 191-2. Since the Koran does not refer to it with a single descriptive word, Muhammad himself probably knew little more about it than the name.

[2] Koran 2:62/59. 5:69/73.

[3] Cf. the article "Dhimma" (by Cl. Cahen) in the second edition of the Encyclopaedia of Islam, where the literature on the subject up to 1961 is found. Cf. also the present writer's "Evidence on the Muslim Poll Tax from Non-Muslim sources", *JESHO* 6 (1963), pp. 218 ff., "The Muslim Government as seen by its Non-Muslim Subjects", *Journal of the Pakistan Historical Society* 12 (1964), pp. 1-12.

[4] I.e., until all pagans accept Islam, Koran 8:39/40.

[5] Ibid., 9:29. Cf. also the dictum "The religion in God's sight is Islam" 3:19/17, which, as the context shows, is directed against the Possessors of the Book.

divided the world into two areas, one to be called "the Area (literally: House) of Islam", where only Muslims were full citizens, while Christians and Jews were tributaries to the Muslim state, and "the Area of War", the rest of the world, against which permanent war was obligatory. According to Islamic law no Muslim state is allowed to make peace with a non-Muslim power. Only the conclusion of an armistice is permitted, and this, too, solely for a limited period of one, two, or, according to one school, at most ten years.[1]

This claim on world domination by Islam was renewed in our own times by the Muslim brotherhood, a fundamentalist movement founded in Egypt in 1928 and capable of attracting in the course of about twenty years the majority of the urban lower middle class and the masses.[2] In the pamphlets published by the leadership of this movement during the thirties and forties, the king of Egypt is admonished in glowing terms to live up to the duties of the Muslim ruler, to renew the glory of the Muslim arms, namely to wage war against the infidels until the ultimate goal of Islam would be reached. Such old-fashioned slogans are no longer used by the youngish modern minded officers who rule Egypt today. But Islamic propaganda is carried on by them most vigorously as a means of political expansion.

We have seen how the Muslim *umma* came into being under the pressure of the opposition encountered by Muhammad in his own tribe as well as in the wake of the exclusiveness exhibited to him by the older religions. The response to this double challenge largely moulded the character of the new body politic, especially in its relationship to the world outside itself. As far as its inner structure is concerned, the sources of Islam, i.e. the Koran and the Oral Tradition, contain much concerning the duties of the individual towards the community, but next to nothing on the organization of the community itself. It is a matter of speculation why Muhammad failed to leave any instructions as to the future form of government of the state which he created. Whatever the reasons, the absence of such instructions was a gift from heaven. It spared Islam from being burdened with a fixed system in matters which by their very nature are subject to continuous change. To be sure, the jurists abstracted

[1] Cf. Majid Khadduri, *War and Peace in the Law of Islam*, Baltimore 1955.

[2] Cf. Ishaq Musa Husaini, *The Moslem Brethren*, Beirut 1956. This is the expanded English translation of an Arabic book written before the movement was crushed by the present regime. For further literature see EI [2] s.v. "al-Bannā' " (the founder of the movement, murdered in February 1949) written by J. M. B. Jones.

laws about the Muslim state from the experience made by it during the first centuries of its existence. The only form of government the Muslim knew was that of the absolute ruler. The theories developed by the doctors of law were in accordance with this experience, but, lacking support from the Koran, carried no great weight. Consequently the experiments made by the Muslim states in modern times such as representative governments and parliaments or republican constitutions did meet only halfhearted or no opposition on the part of the official bearers of religion.

If the Koran is reticent about the constitution of the *umma* it is most outspoken with regard to its aim and general character and the position of the individual within it. The state was founded for religion's sake. It is not a goal in itself, but has its *raison d'être* in helping the Muslim to keep and to spread his faith. In other words, it is the perfection of the individual which matters most. This basic principle goes a long way toward explaining the Muslim's attitude towards government discussed in another section of this book.[1]

Thus the driving idea behind Muhammad's *umma* was religion. However, the only practical example of a community according to which he could model it was the Arab tribe. The tribe was constituted not only by a real or alleged common ancestry, but largely through the admittance of members adopted by covenants of various types. Similarly, the Muslims were "brothers through religion",[2] with all the consequences following from such a tribal brotherhood. Each individual had to be prepared to spend his life and his possessions for the defense of his fellow brothers, strict obedience to those in authority was demanded, and above all, internal disputes had to be settled henceforth not by vendetta, the most favorite pastime of the pre-Islamic Arabs, but by orderly legal procedure. War between Muslims was prohibited or, one might rather say, unimaginable.

When, within one generation, the monotheistic state of Medina waxed into a complex empire, these originally appropriate principles had to give way to the natural conflict of power groups each of which pretended to represent true Islam. Medina itself became the scene of a civil war, in which the third successor of Muhammad was murdered, and bloody revolts, justified by religion, albeit under different slogans, continued throughout the Umayyad period (660—750 A.D.). However, precisely during this period there developed the

[1] Cf. Chapter X.
[2] Koran 9:11/12. 33:5. 49:10.

beginnings of Muslim law which did not recognize any state except the Muslim *umma*, and when we read attentively the excellent accounts of the internecine wars under the Umayyads we realize that these wars sharpened rather than dimmed the sense of unity. An opposition which strives to take over the government presupposes the continued existence of the state in its completeness.

Similarly, the Abbasid empire fell apart into its natural geographical areas owing to the ambitions of secular usurpers or religious pretenders. This process was completed around 970 A.D. However, it was exactly at that time that it became habitual to speak about *mamlakat al-islam*, "the realm of Islam", which was not a mere concept, but a tangible reality. Rulers and dynasties changed incessantly with the consequence that the citizen of a Muslim state felt little allegiance to the local ruler, but regarded himself as belonging everywhere under Islam, in particular since educated people had Arabic as a common means of intercourse. This attitude was strengthened by the fact that the medieval Muslims were great travellers. Reference has been made before to the importance of the Holy Pilgrimage, one of the five "pillars" of Islam, and of the keen international trade which was partly connected with it. Of equal importance were inter-Islamic migrations, population shifts which were made possible through the unity of the Muslim realm and in turn increased its cohesive power. Thus the breaking up of the Abbasid caliphate and its subsequent parcelling into ever changing political units did not do away with the basic feeling of the average Muslim of being a citizen of the kingdom of Islam.

This awareness was significantly strengthened when, in the fifteenth and sixteenth centuries great Muslim empires were formed which were constantly at war with the infidels. The Ottoman Turkish state comprised besides its heartland Anatolia (present-day Turkey) almost the whole Arabic world as well as large sections of south-eastern Europe. The Ottomans did not call themselves by that name. They referred to the territories of their empire as "the lands of Islam" and to their armies as "the soldiers of Islam".[1] It is true that the Ottomans were as constantly at war with the Muslim Persians at the eastern border of their empire as with the Christians of Europe. However, the struggle with the latter was far more extended and more spectacular, while the conflicts with the former were also tinged with religion, since the inhabitants of the Ottoman empire belonged al-

[1] Cf. B. Lewis in the article quoted above page 7, p. 47.

most exclusively to the main stream of Muslims, the Sunnites, while the Persians were the protagonists of Shiʿism. In the eastern half of the Muslim world the glory of Islam manifested itself in the Mogul empire of India. Constantly occupied with keeping down a huge non-Muslim majority, the Mogul emperors symbolized Islamic ascendancy as did the Ottoman Sultans of Istanbul. In any case, although harrassed by corrupt administrations and affected by economic misery and cultural decay, until approximately the end of the eighteenth century the Muslims everywhere could feel themselves as the sons of a great (and for them the greatest) power on earth.

At that time, the onslaught of the West, prepared during long centuries of spiritual and technical revolutions, became paramount and gathered new strength with every decade. By 1900, Islam lay prostrate before Christian Europe. The latter dominated most of the Muslim territories directly and exercised an all-penetrating political and economic influence on the rest. With this fate, Islam was not alone. China, once a mighty empire with a claim on world domination not less pronounced than that of Islam, found itself in a similar situation. Still the Muslims regarded their predicament as a specific disaster. Since the whole realm of Islam was afflicted, they rightly asked themselves whether Islamic religion or debasement of religion were at the root of the evil. Thus the very eclipse of Islam acted as a new incentive to Muslim unity. The incarnation of supranational Islamic modernism was Djamāl al-Dīn al-Afghānī (died 1897) who may rightly be regarded as the father of both Islamic anti-colonialism and of the reassertion of Islam as a counterweight against "Western materialism".[1] He was active in his native country of Afghanistan, in India and above all in Egypt, Persia and Turkey, while frequently using Paris and London as platforms of agitation. However, while his anti-colonialism was in accordance with the general trends of the period, his pan-Islamic ideas found little support in theory and even less in practice. In World War I Indian Muslims and Arabs fought against the Ottoman caliph, the situation was similar in World War II and in these days we find Turkey, Iran and Pakistan allied with the West, while Egypt and Indonesia are neutralist, entertaining strong relations with the Communist block.

Causes as complex as those accounting for Europe's ascendancy

[1] Cf. the article devoted to him in both the first edition of the Encylopaedia of Islam (by I. Goldziher) and in the second (revised by J. Jomier).

were responsible for the termination of colonial rule. With insignificant exceptions, all the countries of Islam today form independent states. However, as has often been emphasized, liberation from the West and successful competition with it could be achieved only by the adoption of Western techniques and ideas. Thus the independence of the Muslim peoples was bought at the price of the diversion of all intellectual and spiritual forces towards non-religious goals and the corresponding weakening of the Islamic substance.[1] De-islamization made quicker progress in the national states than it had made in the colonial and semi-colonial areas. Islam as a body politic, however, depends on the intensity of religious awareness of the individual Muslim, and in particular the intellectuals. Today national, ideological and regional aspirations, such as national socialism, Arab neutralism and African revival are competing with Islam. The idea of the community of Islam, whose significant history we tried to sketch in this chapter, can no longer be regarded as a political force. This does not exclude however, the possibility that it will become one in the future, although the prospects for such a development seem to be slight at present.

IV

The basic traits of Islamic religion and the Muslim community, and, naturally, the Arab heritage embedded in them, were already present, as we have seen, in the Prophet's time. Developed Islam differed from its original as a grown up man from a child. However, just as childhood predestines the future adult, so did Muhammad's creation shape later Islam in all its essentials. Therefore, we were forced in the preceding pages again and again to take up the life story of Muhammad and to quote the Koran, the most authentic source for his work and thought. It may be also noted in passing that the modern Muslims, too, are more familiar with the origins of Islam than with its more complex phases.

Religion and community life are certainly two prominent elements in any civilization, particularly in one based on religion like Islam.

[1] While writing these lines, I have on my desk No. 1 of Vol. 1 of *Afāq* ("Horizons"), the new journal of the Association of Arabic writers of the Maghrib, published March 1963 in Casablanca. The editors wish their people "a flourishing economy, a vigorous culture, an open mind and participation in all fields of human progress". Success in the field of religion and the fulfillment of the commandments of God, which in olden times would come first among any good wishes, is not even mentioned.

Therefore it is of course true that the beginnings of Islamic civilization are to be sought in Mecca and Medina. Yet most of its other components, such as the ways of daily life and almost all manual occupations, the arts and the esthetic values, the sciences and their application, philosophical abstraction and its influence on behavioral patterns—all these had their roots outside Arabia and in peoples other than the Arabs. However, before we are able to say anything about the character and development of these components, we are compelled to define more specifically the terms we are using here.

In modern historical writings the term civilization comprises all aspects of life of a period, a nation or a group of peoples. Thus the first detailed account of Islamic civilization, that of Alfred von Kremer, contains the following chapters: The Development of the Muslim State. The Army. Administration and Finance. Law. Religious Cult. The Capital of the Caliphate. Marriage and Family Life. Population (the racial composition of the caliphal empire). Society (classes and occupations). National Character. Commerce and Industry. Poetry, Science and Literature. Reasons of Decay.[1]

A glance at this long list, which is by no means complete,[2] immediately raises the methodical question: how many and which components are essential for making a civilization an organic and clearly identifiable unit? For example, it is entirely feasible to assume that industrial techniques, laws, practices of the religious cult, and even forms of poetical expression may be transferred from one civilization to another without having much influence on its general character. Everything depends on how closely each aspect of civilization is related to its core, the answer it provides to the question of what makes life worth living.

Alfred von Kremer defined his subject solely by area and time: "Orient" which corresponds approximately to what we call today Middle East (then including Muslim Spain), and "under the caliphs", by which he meant mainly the ninth through twelfth centuries. Kremer refrained from labelling this civilization with any epithet.

[1] Alfred von Kremer, *Culturgeschichte des Orients unter den Chalifen*, Vienna vol. I, 1875; vol. II, 1877. Cf. also Shaikh Inayatullah, *Islamic Culture*, a Paper presented at the International Islamic Colloquium at Lahore 1957, p. 10-15, where the various components and contributing factors are enumerated.

[2] E.g., no special chapter is devoted to Islamic art, although the author deals with the subject under other headings.

"Arabic", as another of its great interpreters has said,[1] would express a linguistic prejudice. The fact that most of its representative literary creations are written in that language is counterbalanced by our knowledge that its contents essentially grew outside Arabia and its bearers were mostly non-Arabs. "Islamic" is also not a very propitious name, since many of its elements were not specifically Islamic and some even opposed to Islam. Consider philosophy. The Muslims themselves called philosophy and the sciences *ʿulūm al-awāʾil*, "the sciences of the ancients" and were even more conscious of the foreign origin of the arts. Moreover, non-Muslims had a very great share in the making of this civilization, especially as translators and men of science on the one hand and as artisans on the other hand. All in all, "the medieval civilization of the Middle East", clumsy as it is, would be a more appropriate name, with the understanding, of course, that for most of the countries concerned the Middle Ages continued well into the nineteenth century.

The above notwithstanding, the term "Islamic civilization" has become generally accepted, and rightly so, because its territory was under the sway of Islam and the spirit of Islamic religion was its soul. There is no harm in a term being in some respects a little too wide and in others a little too narrow, provided that those who use it are not mislead by its wording. This necessary precaution, however, is not always taken nowadays, "Islamic civilization" is being used loosely designating everything connected with a country having a majority of Muslim inhabitants.

In order to keep the term as a meaningful and valid instrument of cultural history we must realize first that this medieval civilization of the Middle East is by now a matter of the past. It is stone dead. There is no artisan who could make a real piece of art in the spirit of that civilization, no one speculates on philosophy or science in the way it was done by medieval Muslims, and despite the use of ancient literary forms, literature in the Middle East today, as far as it is literature, receives its inspiration and much of its very imagery and terminology from sources other than "Islamic civilization". A Maghribī or Persian architect may occasionally succeed in imitating the exquisite ancient examples of architecture found in his country (especially when inspired by a Frenchman or a German enthusiastic about Islamic art), but this is conscious stylization, coming after two

[1] C. H. Becker, "Der Islam als Problem", *Islamstudien*, Leipzig 1924, pp. 1-23.

or three generations of builders who unhesitatingly and indiscriminately transplanted European patterns to Eastern cities. A modern Muslim thinker may try to prove the truth of certain medieval Islamic doctrines or the superiority of Islam in general. But while doing so, his yardstick would be that specific modern creed (liberalism, fascism, national socialism etc.) which had captivated the mind of his generation. What he really believes in is the contemporary shibboleth; the Islamic sources serve him as mere matter.

This evanescence of Islamic civilization is nothing peculiar. No European is able today to create in the spirit of Gothic, Renaissance or Baroque, or of scholasticism or minstrelsy, although most penetrating studies are being written on all these subjects. The confusion with regard to Islam is due to the different "timing of history", to the fact, already emphasized, that the stage of stagnation and darkness fell in the East into a later period than in Europe. This created in the Europeans visiting the countries of Islam the false impression of "the immovable East", while the Muslim intellectuals, discovering to their dismay that their peoples had as yet contributed little to present world culture, identified themselves with their past in a degree incommensurate with the true facts of their own spirituality. In these days, when almost all Muslim countries form independent states and are beginning to make noteworthy contributions in various fields, there is no need for pretension.

Once it is established that Islamic civilization is a matter of the past, one may still ask whether the term is not too comprehensive for serving a useful purpose in the understanding of cultural history. In the following paper[1] a plea is made for the periodization of Islamic history and for singling out of what we have called the *Intermediate Civilization*, approximately the centuries between 850 and 1250 A.D. The economy and society, and above all the general spirit of this period are so different from those of the centuries preceding and, in particular, following it that despite the common Islamic background it deserves a name by itself. Awareness of the specific character of the Intermediate Civilization will also sharpen our understanding and heighten our appreciation of the subsequent period, that of *national cultures within Islam*. After a time of transition, in which the eastern half of the Muslim world was turned upside down in the wake

[1] See below, pp. 54-55 and the present writer's paper "A Plea for the Periodization of Islamic History", read at the Congress of Arabic and Islamic Studies, Cambridge 1964.

of the Mongol invasions, great states were founded in Persia, Ottoman Turkey and Mogul India, each developing special traits in administration and military organization, possessed of very characteristic literatures and reaching a high degree of perfection in architecture and the minor arts. Persia and India excelled also in the art of painting. Egypt and parts of Syria, which were spared the terrors of the Mongol visitation, witnessed a kind of territorial euphoria, at least during the first half of the rule of the Mamluks, a soldier caste formed by imported slaves of Turkish language (1250—1517). This "Turkish Government", as it was called by its Arabic speaking subjects, was at times of very remarkable vigor and splendor and, although the period was in general one of stagnation and decline, it showed considerable attainments in Islamic scholarship (such as Islamic religious sciences and historiography) and sheer excellence in architecture, as well as in metal and glass work. Most of the Islamic buildings admired by the present-day visitor of Cairo date from this period.

The tripartition of the long stretch of Muslim history into the epoch of colonization and religious consolidation (620—850), the Intermediate Civilization (850—1250) and the period of national cultures followed by decay (1250—1850) gives us a clearer vision and a deeper understanding of both the parts and the whole. There is, however, also another prerequisite for the study of Islamic civilization, the opposite method, namely trying to comprehend its nature through looking beyond its boundaries in both time and space. While doing so, we avoid the pitfall of regarding as typically Islamic what is indeed the common feature of a wider area and a whole epoch.

Thus, Islamic art is renowned for its abstract and ornamental character. This trait is not exclusively Islamic. From the fourth century A.D. on, we find that the grossly figurative and illustrative late Hellenistic and Roman art becomes replaced by an inclination for abstraction and symbolized representation. Concerning one of the most beautiful pieces of early Islamic art, the magnificent floral designs on the outer walls of the desert castle of Mshatta, a controversy raged for decades as to whether it was really Islamic or pre-Islamic.[1] Islam developed the tendency of abstraction in an unpre-

[1] The earlier experts put the origin of that marvellous piece of art somehow between 400 and 614 A.D. (the date of the Persian conquest of Palestine and Transjordan, where that castle is situated). A new and ingenious plea for

cedented and unparalleled measure. But it shared with Byzantine and early Western art this common tradition of late antiquity.

In philosophy and the sciences, the Muslims were the pupils of the Greeks, so much so that they regarded the books of the Greek masters as fixed systems laid down once for all as the final truth. To us, the most reliable knowledge in science and medecine is that attained latest. To them it was the one established by the most renowned authorities of antiquity. It would be entirely erroneous to see in this attitude an expression of the insecurity of barbarians who had no confidence in their own capacities. The concept of complete and authoritative canons of science was developed centuries prior to Islam when these systems of knowledge were organized in the form of textbooks in the schools of Alexandria, Antioch and other Near Eastern seats of learning. It prevailed for many centuries in Western Europe as well. Soon the Muslims developed with regard to their own religious sciences the theory that only the old masters were supposed to expound authoritatively the sources of divine or prophetical teachings (Koran and Ḥadīth), while for the later generations, as with regard to the Greek sciences, commentaries, glosses and systematic arrangements of the material were left. We remember, of course, that Muhammad, although confident to be in direct communication with God, purported to teach only that which was contained also "in the writings of the ancients".

What, then, is specifically Islamic? What makes the original stamp of this civilization? Obviously the way in which the various elements composing it were blended into an essentially new and unique creation. The old controversy whether or not Islam has ever succeeded in being a harmonious and consistent system of values and thoughts may be settled as follows:

Many elements admitted but not digested were eliminated in the course of time and thus did not permanently impair the integration of Islamic culture. The main religious science of Islam, the Ḥadīth, may well serve as an illustration. Only a fraction of the countless sayings attributed to the Prophet were incorporated in the canonical collections and thus became the permanent and generally accepted heritage of Islam. Bukhārī, the most authoritative editor of the Ḥadīth, is said to have known six hundred thousand traditions, but

dating the building in the Umayyad period (660-750) is made by Oleg Grabar, "Al-Mushatta, Baghdād and Wāsit", *The World of Islam*, 1959, pp. 99-108. Beautiful illustrations in EI² s.v. Architecture.

admitted to his collections, which became a classic, less than three thousand.[1]

Attention must also be paid to social stratification. Many of the superstitions, beliefs and practices rampant in Muslim countries cannot be regarded as elements of Islamic civilization. They are remnants of a pre-civilization stage, often of an ubiquitous character, or continue inveterate pre-Islamic local custom.

Likewise, the apparent incongruity of the various elements of Islamic civilization disappears, if more attention is paid to the periodization of Islamic history postulated in these pages. During the time of what we have called the Intermediate Civilization it was perfectly consistent with the office of a religious scholar to be versed in the Greek sciences. This was the case not only with regard to propagators of secular knowledge such as the great Muslim philosopher Ibn Rushd (Averroes, died 1198 A.D.), who served as *cadi*, or religious judge in his native city of Cordova, Spain (or his Jewish contemporary and co-citizen Maimonides, who likewise excelled both in secular and sacred studies and became the religious head of the Jews of Egypt; died 1204). The same applied to those condemning the Greek sciences, such as "the renewer of Islam" Ghazālī, of whom we have spoken above, p. 19 (or his younger Jewish contemporary, the poet, physician and theologian Judah ha-Levi, the greatest writer of Hebrew religious poetry after the Bible; died 1141). It would be a grave mistake to regard the Hellenic elements in the Intermediate Civilization of Islam as foreign and incongruous. On the contrary, they constituted its very character. The fact that the Greek sciences were largely abandoned in the following period proves only, that they had fulfilled their task and exhausted themselves, but not without having left an indelible imprint on the Muslim mind, as we shall presently see.

Our knowledge of Islamic civilization and understanding of its specific character have considerably increased since von Kremer's trial of a first general description. Many new insights are to be found in G. E. von Grunebaum's *Medieval Islam*,[2] followed up by a series of highly instructive complementary studies by the same author. Since Islamics has grown into a widely diffused subject of study, it has become customary of late to arrange symposiums, in which specialists unite to elucidate, each from his particular vantage

[1] See EI² s.v. al-Bukhārī (J. Robson).
[2] Chicago 1946, second edition, 1954.

point, one or another aspects. An outstanding example is the volume *Unity and Variety in Muslim Civilization*, edited by von Grunebaum.[1] Other such symposiums as well as pertinent contributions by single scholars are registered in Claude Cahen, *Introduction à l'Histoire de l'Orient Musulman*, an English version of which has just appeared.[2]

To characterize Islamic civilization in a nutshell, it might be best to take its art as an illustration. It is the one field to which the layman has immediate access, for, as one of its most competent interpreters has rightly remarked, "the unique character of Muslim art... is experienced even by people who know hardly anything about this civilization."[3] Choice examples are available in our museums and many telling reproductions are to be found in books. Finally, art is perhaps the most original and most impressive contribution of Islamic civilization to world culture. At least, as we presently shall try to show, it combined all the various elements contained in this civilization by almost unconsciously creating works bearing its specific mark.[4]

We have already had opportunity to mention one aspect of Islamic art: its general leaning towards abstraction, its predilection for stylized plants, intertwined with geometrical patterns, and the allusive and symbolic rather than elaborate and realistic representation of living things. One is tempted to say that Islamic art has attained the goal which artists nearer home were striving in vain to reach: almost total freedom from the object without violating the inexorable laws of beauty, which consists in harmony and completeness. The very term "arabesque", which is of course derived from the word "Arab", is indicative. As the author of a book on the subject has explained, two aesthetic rules are scrupulously observed in the execution of the arabesque: "the rhythmical alternation of

[1] Chicago 1955.

[2] Paris 1961, Section IIC. California University Press 1965.

[3] R. Ettinghausen, "Interaction and Integration in Islamic Art", *Unity and Variety* (see Note 1), p. 107.

[4] An enormous quantity of theoretical literature has been preserved with regard to Islamic music, but the creations themselves have been lost, since the Muslims possessed no means of musical notation, cf. EI[1] s.v. Mūsīkī (by H. G. Farmer). Contrariwise, monuments of Islamic art are extant in plenty, some being as old as the first century of Islam (such as the Dome of the Rock in Jerusalem). However, apart from a few occasional remarks by historians and litterateurs, no theory of fine arts was developed at all. So much more admirable, then, is the perfection with which the better works of Islamic art express the spirit of that medieval civilization.

movement, always rendered with harmonious effect, and the desire to fill the entire surface with ornament."[1]

Painting, although far more limited in scope than the decorative arts, was by no means absent from the Arabic-speaking heartlands of Islam during its classical period. It followed similar principles. "The human figures," we read in a magnificent recent publication, "are rather shapeless, with their body structure hardly felt under the voluminous robes, but the faces are stressed, though they reproduce types, not individual persons. The portrayal of animal forms reveals a fine comprehension of the significant features of each, whether brought out in realistic or stylized versions. At the same time a remoteness from nature is shown in the treatment of vegetation and landscapes, which often are mere stylized symbols."[2]

This tendency towards abstraction and symbolism developed, as we have seen, during the concluding centuries of antiquity. However, it was Islam which brought it to unprecedented perfection, and it is not difficult to understand why this occurred. When one looks at a representative object of Islamic art created during the ninth through the thirteenth centuries—a calligraphic and decorated Koran, a carved wooden door panel, a glazed dish bordered by stylized script, the front of a building—one is immediately struck by the impression that these objects were produced by a civilization which worshipped God without an image. Islamic oral traditions are as outspoken against figurative representation as the sources of Judaism. Some Arabic sources indicate that there was even direct influence at work in this respect. In Judaism, as is well known, the natural artistic urge was during certain periods stronger than the command not to make any images. Even synagogues were at times richly decorated with mosaics and murals representing human beings. Likewise, as just stated, painting developed also in classical Islam, albeit solely for secular purposes. However the iconoclastic tendency was overwhelming. No human or even animal figures were allowed in mosques, and as soon as the Muslims introduced a coinage of their own, they banned from it all pictorial elements, using adequate artistic forms and distribution of the script as sole aesthetic ingredients.[3]

[1] EI² s.v. "Arabesque" (by E. Kühnel).

[2] R. Ettinghausen, *Arab Painting*, SKIRA, 1962, p. 186. As alluded to above, p. 46, the development of Persian and Indian painting during the period of national cultures within Islam is an entirely different phenomenon.

[3] Cf. R. Ettinghausen, "The Character of Islamic Art", *The Arab Heritage*,

The superb works of Arabic calligraphy are another indication that the prohibition of images was an incentive for artistic creation in fields other than sculpture and painting. Many types of scripts were developed, and some of their creators were as famous among the Arabs as sculptors were among the Greeks. The ancient lapidary style, the Kufic, which during the eighth through the early eleventh centuries was the most commonly used in Korans as well as on objects and buildings, is known in eight different varieties.[1] The beauty of the forms is often matched by the harmonious fitting in of a band of writing into the facade of a building or into the ornaments of an object. As the papyri from the first century of Islam show, Arabic script originally was poor and by no means more promising than the cognate Semitic scripts of that period.[2] The latter, and in particular Hebrew, shared with Arabic the prestige of particular, almost mystical sanctity. Still, Arabic calligraphy, when fully developed, produced creations of unsurpassed beauty. In Hebrew, too, magnificent works of calligraphy were executed, as the Bible codices of the ninth and tenth centuries and many pages from the Cairo Geniza prove. However, Hebrew script could not compete in the variety of forms and multitude of uses with Arabic writing, which after Latin is the most universally diffused in the world. The reason for the excellence of Arabic calligraphy is to be sought in the fact that the artistic imagination of many peoples, kindled by religious fervor, found its outlet in this field.

The aesthetic correlative to abstraction was an inexhaustible imagery in decorative detail. The basic motifs of ornamentation were comparatively limited in number, such as stylized leaves, tendrils, flowers and fruits, bodies, or parts of bodies, of animals, stars, circles and other geometrical figures. However the artists and craftsmen continuously invented new forms and unexpected combinations to attract the eye and to refresh the mind. The same aesthetic principle prevailed in Arabic poetry. The Arab poet did not see his task in the expression of a personal experience or originality in subject matter and motif. Such attempts were regarded by him as

ed. by N. A. Faris, Princeton 1944, pp. 251-267. Only neo-Muslims from outside the Middle East, such as the Mongols, sometimes had figures on their coins. The same holds true of some of the early U mayyad coins.

1 A. Grohmann, "The Origin and Early Development of Floriated Kufic", *Bulletin de l'Institut d'Égypte* 37 (1956), p. 273.

2 Cf. Franz Rosenthal, "Significant Uses of Arabic Writing", *Ars Orientalis* 4 (1961), p. 20.

burdensome for his audience and offensive to established values. His creative power was given entirely to decorative detail. An unusual word or phrase, a new metaphor or simile, an unexpected inner rhyme or other formal elements gave delight to his hearers and were the proofs of his own excellence.

G. E. von Grunebaum's study "The Aesthetic Foundation of Arabic Literature"[1] has taught us that this characteristic of Arabic poetry was by no means confined to the latter, but was found also in later Greek and seventeenth century Western European literature. For the Arabs, however, this principle was all comprising and dominated all poetical creation from pre-Islamic times down to the fading out of Islamic civilization. It also affected the literatures encompassed by this civilization, in particular Persian and medieval Hebrew poetry. No wonder then that the same taste and the same aesthetic approach pervaded also the arts in Islam whatever material they used, stone or stucco, wood or metals, ivory or textiles.

There was however another, third basic principle in Islamic art which was completely antithetical to the nature of Arabic poetry: its strictly symmetrical structure, its harmony dominated by logic. The formal poems observed a certain sequence of topics, but there was no equilibrium at all between the various parts, and no logical development. The unit shaped diligently by the poet was the single verse. Its place in the poem was so loosely defined that different versions of a poem often showed a different order, as well as omissions and additions. The opposite was the case in the fine arts. Here the decorative detail received its meaningfulness, its very life, only through its place within the general structure of the piece to which it belonged. A similar principle is discernible in the Coptic, Syrian and Persian arts, of which Islamic art is in many respects the continuation. However, the latter seems to be far more consistent in this respect. Complete harmony and symmetry, thesis and antithesis, statement and apodosis make the work of Islamic art, as soon as it becomes its own self. Logic, more than any other branch of Greek philosophy, became part and parcel of the Muslim mind.[2] While the earliest Islamic science, the Ḥadīth, is as atomistic as Arabic poetry, i.e. consists of separate short "traditions", often

[1] Published first in English in *Comparative Literature*, Eugene, Oregon 4 (1952), pp. 323-340 and then, in revised form, in the author's *Kritik und Dichtkunst, Studien zur arabischen Literaturgeschichte*, Wiesbaden 1955, pp. 130-150.

[2] See also below, p. 68.

not longer than one line, the sciences developed later are organized in works of systematic and symmetric structure, subdivided according to logical principles. The same principle of Greek logic which permeated Islamic sciences came to fruition in Islamic art.

The three components of classical Islamic art, the "Jewish", the Arab and the Greek embody the main aspects of this civilization: a fervent belief in an absolutely transcendental God expressing itself in abstraction and symbolism, a grand sense for decorativeness in rhetoric, poetry, human behavior and other matters, and strict orderliness and harmony in the arrangement of things. These three traits are not very common and not very popular in our own age. This explains the uneasiness of the modern Muslims with regard to their spiritual heritage and their widely conflicting views in their search for cultural identity.[1] We have already stated above that Islamic civilization, in the sense defined here, is a matter of the past. However, the creations of Islamic art are still extant, and so are the literary monuments of that great civilization. Both have aroused the admiration of non-Muslim students, and lured them into devoting a lifetime to their study. They are certainly destined to become to an even higher degree a source of inspiration for new, appreciative generations of Muslims, once the spiritual climate will be more favorable to such a living contact with the past.

[1] Cf. G. E. von Grunebaum's *Modern Islam, The Search for Cultural Identity*, Berkeley and Los Angeles, 1962.

CHAPTER TWO

THE INTERMEDIATE CIVILIZATION

THE HELLENIC HERITAGE IN ISLAM

Continuity and oneness are the very essence of religiosity. For the pious and unsophisticated Muslim, the thirteen and a half centuries which have passed since the inception of his religion are but a great yesterday which merges smoothly with his own life and religious experience. For him there is no question of development or of different levels of validity. The great drama of Islam unfolds before him on one single stage, on which he himself is a performer, albeit a modest one, while the Prophet and the other heroes of Islam are so near to his mind, as if they had lived in his own time and had been seen by him with his own eyes.

Religious thought and theology take a different attitude. The life of the Prophet himself was carefully periodicized by the Muslim scholars, because, according to their legal theory, laws promulgated during the earlier stages of his career as messenger of God were abrogated by those relevant to the same subject matter but decreed later. Therefore, the *asbāb al-nuzūl*, the historical circumstances accompanying the revelation of the various parts of the Koran, sometimes even of a single verse, formed the object of serious study, the results of which have been often confirmed by modern research. The oral traditions concerning the Prophet were subjected to severe scrutiny, developing into a full scale science, and one of the most important concepts of Muslim theology, *bidʿa,* or unwarranted innovation, is based on the notion of development, on the idea that an originally pure core of religion was contaminated by later accretions. The very theory of Muslim law is based on a historical concept, on periodization of Islamic history, namely on the assumption that only during the first three centuries or so of Islam, the great teachers were competent to interpret authoritatively the Book of God and the traditions of his prophet, while, since "the closing of the gate of authoritative decisions" it was left to the religious scholars only to adapt the findings of the ancient masters to the exigencies of their own time. Thus we see that the scholars of Islam—unlike those of some other great religions—viewed their faith in the light of historical development, a mental attitude which found a magnificent expression in the great Islamic historiography.

The modern historian has to go still one step further. While he reverently appreciates the spiritual forces which make for continuity and oneness in the concept of Islam, while he tries to understand the motives and methods of the Muslim scholars of the past, his business is to write history, i.e. to describe and to try to explain changes. In this respect, the present writer believes, we have not yet done enough. By using loosely the term Islamic Civilization, comprising in it everything which happened in the countries of Islam from the first revelations of the Prophet down to the constitution of Pakistan or the new Arab socialism, we have done a disservice both to the religion of Islam and to the history of the Islamic peoples. Such generalizations obscure the nature of religion and deprive the term civilization of any real content. No one would dream of characterizing the development of Italy from the arrival of the apostle Paul in Rome down to the activities of the Italian political parties calling themselves Christian as "Christian Civilization". There is no doubt some connection between the apostolate of Paul and the existence of political parties in Italy styled as Christian. But many other important forces have moulded the destinies of Italy, and consequently, its history has been broken up into periods, characterized by those forces and confided to specialists studying them. Similarly, we have to periodicize the long history of Islam in order to arrive at clear concepts of cultural entities, each possessing a social framework of its own and characterized by a coherent set of values, shared only in part with other periods.

In this paper, we are dealing with the Islamic world as it was approximately between 850 and 1250 A.D. For reasons explained on p. 59, we have described it as the INTERMEDIATE CIVILIZATION. Note: *Intermediate*, not *Intermediary*, for that civilization created its own works of the spirit and was not a mere transmitter of an ancient heritage. That period is characterized by the predominance of the middle class, which thrived on a free enterprise economy, and by the all pervading influence of Greek science in both matter and spirit. It is this latter aspect which will occupy us here.

Hellenism was to classical Greece what contemporary world civilization is to Western Culture, as it developed between 1500-1900.

In both cases, sciences and techniques, ideas and ways of life, developed by one people or by one group of peoples, were adopted, in varying degrees of intensity, by many others. Therefore, the fate of Hellenism, its quality and duration, are of great concern both to those who are the sons of this Western culture and to the citizens of a civilization which more and more is encompassing the whole human race.

In order to avoid ambiguity, I would like to start with a definition. We normally apply the term Hellenism to the period between Alexander and Augustus, between the establishment of the Macedonian empire and the final replacement of its heirs by Rome. This is Hellenism as seen from Greece and from the point of view of political history. However, from the standpoint of cultural history and the peoples affected by the Greek heritage, we have to extend this period far longer, well down to the seventh century A.D., when the study of Greek finally had come to an end in Latin Europe and when the countries of the eastern and southern shores of the Mediterranean were conquered by a new language and a new civilization, Arabic and Islam. What happened between the seventh century, the end of Hellenic studies in Western Europe, and the twelfth, the beginning of their revival?

As it is well known, Hellenism found a refuge precisely in the civilization and the language which had replaced Greek and Greek culture in most countries which they had dominated for centuries. Countless works of Greek authors were translated into Arabic and formed the basis of a new and largely secular civilization inside Islam. The combined results of these efforts, namely the translations of Greek books, and the scientific creations based on them, were made available to Latin Europe, either through direct translations or through the intermediary of Hebrew or Spanish, and both contributed substantially to the so-called renaissance of the twelfth century.[1]

[1] Most of the literature relevant to the subject of this paper is listed in J. Kraemer's *Das Problem der islamischen Kulturgeschichte*, Tübingen, 1959. I am much indebted to this short, but meaty study, although in some points I had to disagree with it. I had also an opportunity to discuss some aspects of the problem with the lamented author only a few days before he met with an untimely death on September 26, 1961.
Shorter, recent treatments of the subject are found in R. Paret, *Der Islam und das griechische Bildungsgut*, Tübingen 1950, B. Spuler, "*Hellenistisches Denken im Islam,*" *Saeculum* 5 (1954), and G. E. von Grunebaum, "Islam and Hellenism", in *Islam*, Chicago, 1955, pp. 159-167. Richard Walzer, *Greek into*

The very first book in the English language to be printed in England was the translation of a collection of sayings by Greek philosophers, compiled by a Muslim gentleman and bibliophile in 1048-9. The book was translated from Arabic into Spanish, from Spanish into Latin, from Latin into French and finally from French into English. It was first printed in 1477.[1]

However, we are concerned here not with the late, albeit fascinating history of the translations from Arabic, but with the translations into Arabic from Greek.

There was much of the paradoxical in this process. The Romans were so eager to learn the Greek language that there was no great incentive for translations into Latin. Even in the provincial towns of Gaul (present day France) and as late as the fourth century A.D., boys learned Greek and memorized its classical authors. In particular there was no need to translate scientific works, for Greek was the language of science. Galen, the great physician of the second century A.D., lived and taught most of his life in Rome, but his books are written in Greek. The same could be said of many other prominent scholars of the Roman Hellenistic period. The ultimate result of all this was, however, that in later, barbarian times, with the loss of knowledge of the Greek language in the West, knowledge of the scientific literature was lost as well. The Muslim Arabs, on the other hand, never knew a word of Greek and never made the slightest effort to learn the language, but Christian and pagan Syrians, as well as some Persians and Jews did the work of translation for them so completely, that the whole corpus of Hellenic sciences still in existence at the time of the Muslim conquests became available in Arabic.

Let me illustrate this by one example. The Nestorian Christian Ḥunayn ibn Isḥāq (John, the son of Isaac), who died in 873 A.D., wrote a treatise in which he gave detailed information about no less than one hundred and twenty-nine works of Galen alone which he had translated into Arabic, partly also into Syriac. These translations did not remain a dead letter, but became handbooks used by the medical practitioners throughout the Middle Ages. I had the good luck to find in the treasures of the so-called Cairo Geniza an

Arabic, Essays on Islamic Philosophy, Oxford 1962, contains both general articles on the legacy of the classics in the Islamic world and highly specialized studies.

[1] Cf. Franz Rosenthal, "Al-Mubashshir Ibn Fatik", *Oriens* 13-14, Leiden 1961, p. 132-158.

inventory of the library of a Jewish physician in Old Cairo, which was sold by auction in November 1190, i.e. three hundred years after Ḥunayn ibn Isḥāq's death. As Baneth's painstaking edition of the text shows, this library contained at least thirty-seven volumes of Galen's writings, of course in Arabic translation.[1]

Around 1190, we remember, the most prominent Jewish scholar in Old Cairo was Moses Maimonides, the great philosopher, who was also a renowned physician and medical writer. In medicine, Maimonides was entirely dependent on Galen. He took exception, however, to Galen's philosophical views and found it necessary to refute them in a special treatise, because he rightly assumed that Galen's overwhelming authority as physician would induce the students of his work to accept his philosophy as well.[2]

By that time, i.e. the end of the twelfth century, most of the Arabic translations of Galen had already been put into Latin, along with many of the original works of medical authors writing in Arabic, such as the famous North-African Jewish physician Isaac Israeli.

The broad outlines of this great historical process of the preservation of Greek thought through the medium of Arabic and its ultimate transmission to the Latin West is of course familiar to everyone. Many of its details, however, and particularly its evaluation still need much additional research and have formed the subject of long standing controversies, not yet terminated. Three parties are involved here: the classical scholar, the Islamist and the medievalist. Classical philology's first interest in the matter is to know which Greek writings whose originals have been lost have come down to us in Arabic translations, abridgements and adaptations. Examples are the Oikonomikos, or treatise on the management of the house, by the Neopythagorean Bryson, the Book of the Plants, an ancient Greek source, although not by Aristotle to whom it was ascribed, and in particular, writings on mathematics, astronomy, mechanics and medicine, but also a considerable number of treatises by later philosophical writers. Secondly, the Arabic translations and commentaries may be useful for the emendation and better under-

[1] D. Z. H. Baneth, "A Doctor's Library in Egypt at the Time of Maimonides", Tarbiz 30, Jerusalem 1960, p. 171-185 (in Hebrew). (English summary ib., p. VI).

[2] M. Meyerhof and J. Schacht, "Maimonides Against Galen on Philosophy and Cosmogony", Bulletin of the Faculty of Arts, University of Egypt, 5, 1939, p. 53-88.

standing of classical texts whose originals we possess. A case in point is the discussion by Richard Walzer of Aristotle's Posterior Analytics in the light of its Arabic translation.[1]

It stands to reason that quite a number of new developments will take place in this field in the near future. For long lost or altogether unknown Arabic manuscripts are making their appearance in our day all over the Middle East in libraries which had remained untapped or had not been sufficiently examined before.

The recent discovery by Arthur J. Arberry of books I-VI of the Arabic translation of the Nicomachean Ethics and that of books VII-X by D. M. Dunlop are telling examples. Both were found in the Qarawiyyīn Library in Fez, Morocco, where they are kept under the care of the learned librarian Shaykh al-ʿĀbid al-Fāsī. Since the translation is as old or older than the existing Greek manuscripts, it should certainly not be overlooked by the classicist.

The translator, possibly Ḥunayn b. Ishāq himself, most conscientiously compared a quotation from Hesiod with the Greek original of the poet, criticizing the inaccuracy of the quotation in the text of the Nicomachean Ethics.

The same Qarawiyyīn manuscript contains the Arabic translation of a hitherto unknown ethical treatise, discussed by M. C. Lyons, who ascribed it tentatively to the fourth century A.D. It is noteworthy that the author states in his introduction that he wrote the book for his daughter.[2]

In addition to these practical interests of classical philology in the adoption and transmission of the Greek heritage by the Arabs, there is a third and broader, more philosophical concern. How far was this heritage still Greek? How far did Hellas succeed in bequeathing to the world of those days a scientific culture transcending the barriers of languages, nations and religions? These questions pertain to the Latin West in the same degree as to the Arabic speaking world. However, as a student of Islam, I have to leave that field to the medievalist while confining myself to Islam, or, more exactly, to the medieval civilization of the Middle East. We have called this civilization INTERMEDIATE, because it is intermediate in *time* be-

[1] *Greek into Arabic* (cf. p. 57), p. 103 ff.

[2] A. J. Arberry, "The Nicomachean Ethics in Arabic", *BSOAS* 17, 1955, pp. 1-9. D. M. Dunlop, "The Nicomachean Ethics in Arabic books", I-VI, Oriens 15, 1962, pp. 18-34. In this article Dunlop announces his own find of Books VII-X, and discusses the merits and defects of Books I-VI. M. C. Lyons "A Greek Ethical Treatise", Oriens 13-14 (1960-61), pp. 35-57.

tween Hellenism and Renaissance, intermediate in *character* between the largely secular culture of the later Roman period and the thoroughly clerical world of Medieval Europe, and intermediate in *space* between Europe and Africa on the one hand, and India and China on the other hand, thus forming, for the first time in history, a strong cultural link between all parts of the ancient world.

In order to obtain a balanced view of the scope and quality of this "intermediate" Islamic culture as an heir and trustee of the heritage of Greece, we have to consider four interrelated questions:

1. How did Islam look before its direct contact with the Greek sciences, or, more generally speaking, what is Islam without the Greek ingredient? We are able to answer this question, because two hundred years and more elapsed between the establishment of the Muslim community by the prophet Muhammad at the beginning of the seventh century and the great period of translation around the middle of the ninth.

2. Why was Arabic Islam so much more receptive to the Greek heritage than Germanic Europe? To what extent were the general conditions in the Middle East more propitious than in Western Europe, and in what way did the very character of the new Islamic religion and society predispose them for this great cultural acquisition?

3. Which features of Hellenic civilization were adopted by Islam and which remained unknown to it or were refused admittance? Which were taken over directly and intentionally and which came to it indirectly and without being recognized as such?

4. How far and how well was the Hellenic tradition absorbed by Islam and how did it contribute to the latter's substance and permanent character? With this another question is connected, which is easy to formulate, but hard to answer: why did the Hellenic tradition decline so completely in the countries of Islam? In other words: why did these countries not witness anything comparable to the renaissance which transformed Europe?

Turning now to the first question: Islam, of course, is mainly and essentially a religion. It was founded by Muhammad, the Arab prophet, who died in 632, but it took another two hundred years, before the nucleus created by Muhammad developed into a full-fledged religious system. To all intents and purposes, this process was completed around 830, that is exactly at the time when Ḥunayn ibn Isḥāq and his school and other scholars started their great work of the translation of Greek authors. From the outset, Muhammad's message bore a remarkably universalistic character, partly, but only partly, explicable by his being the son of a caravan city which traded with peoples belonging at least to five different religions and speaking five different languages. He professed to convey to his countrymen in clear Arabic, in a language intelligible and acceptable to them, the same heavenly message which was already contained in the older monotheistic religions. This claim is fully vindicated by the basic religious and moral tenets and many of the institutions of Islam. Muhammad regarded himself as the last in a long series of messengers of God, beginning with the patriarchs and prophets of Israel and concluding with preachers of righteousness sent to the peoples of Arabia. Even a reminiscence of the story of Alexander the Great is not absent from the Koran. In the course of Muhammad's own life time, Islam became a fully autonomous denomination with many institutions peculiar to itself and with rudiments of dogmas dissociating it clearly from Christianity and Judaism. Yet, the Arabian prophet's original concept that God had revealed one and the same truth to all peoples remained alive in Islam and disposed it for eclecticism and the acceptance of the most diversified influences.[1]

In addition to this general readiness of ancient Islam to admit foreign ideas and ideals, there were a number of specific factors which made the Muslim Arabs, in contrast to the Germanic peoples of Europe, so susceptible to the impact of Hellenism.

Firstly, unlike Western Europe, the countries conquered by the Arabs were the seats of Hellenism, where the study of the Greek sciences had never been entirely discontinued. We should not forget that Alexandria had been the metropolis of Greek learning during its heyday. We need only mention the names of Euclid and Heron, the mathematicians, or Eratosthenes and Ptolemy, the astronomers and geographers, and of Plotinus, the Neo-Platonist. To be sure, by the time of the Arab conquest the school of Alexandria was no longer active. However, its tradition of learning and courses of study had remained alive in Syria, Mesopotamia and Southern Persia, precisely those countries, which formed the center of the new Muslim empire. Syriac Christians and pagans, as well as some Persians and Jews studied and practiced the ancient sciences, either with the help of the Greek originals or through translations into Syriac.

[1] Cf. above pp. 9-18.

Thus the Muslim rulers and governors had at their doors physicians who could look after their health, mathematicians who could help them with land measurement in newly conquered countries, and astronomers who could serve them as astrologers. At the beginning, it was out of practical consideration that the Arab conquerors employed the services of men trained in Greek science. However, according to the course of studies developed originally in Alexandria, medicine was closely connected with philosophy. Therefore, when one consulted a doctor, one got at the same time, a philosophical advisor.

There were other and more essential reasons which induced the Muslims to make themselves acquainted with Greek philosophy. Islam, at that time, was still in a crude state and made a comparatively poor show, if compared with the refined systems of thought prevailing in the conquered countries. The extremely developed and ramified Christian theology, as well as philosophical rationalism which denied heavenly revelation altogether, and also Iranian dualism, which was often intertwined with gnosticism—all these constituted challenges which Islam could not afford to ignore. Moreover, inside Islam itself, whether independently or set into motion by the spiritual forces just referred to, controversies with regard to essential beliefs became widespread: what was man's relationship to God? Did man possess free will, or were all his deeds predestined by the Almighty? And what was the nature of revelation? Was the Koran, the Muslim scripture, eternal and uncreated like the eternal truth it represented, or did it come into being by a special act of creation? These and other controversies were soon fought out with the means of Greek logic and dialectic, which marked the beginnings of Muslim scholasticism. The borrowings from the arsenal of Greek philosophy, however, were not confined to the technical means for disputations. Since Philo, the Jewish philosopher of Alexandria, had tried to reconcile revelation with reason, the Hebrew scriptures with Greek rationalism, many centuries had passed. Fortified by the arguments and proofs developed in Christian theology, Islam could safely undertake to formulate its creed in the terms of Greek philosophy. Above and beyond this, some Muslim thinkers, especially of Persian descent, undertook the study of Greek metaphysics and ethics for their own sake and made valuable contributions to their elucidation and systematization.

Greek thought penetrated Islam in another, less direct and more subtle way, with effects, however, which were perhaps even greater. I am referring to the very core of developed Islam, Islamic mysticism. Muhammad's religious message originally possessed a strong ascetic trend: "Renounce this world, which anyhow will come to an end very soon." However, in the course of the sweeping victories of Islam, when fabulous treasures and women of all races fell into their hands as easy prey, many Muslims became attracted by wordly riches and pleasures. This was in stark contrast to the aim of a holy war waged in the name of a religion which preached otherworldliness. It is natural that pious and thinking men abhorred this development. A genuinely Muslim movement of ascetism and pietism came into being, partly inspired perhaps by the example of the Christian monks and hermits, who were found all over the Middle East. In Iraq, there were also contacts with Jewish pietists. By the end of the second century of Islam, a new incentive was given to this pietistic movement which diverted it into the direction of mysticism. Islam is a religion of commandments. It soon assumed a legalistic and highly formalistic character, similar to its prototype, rabbinical Judaism. Pietism, which had first revolted against exaggerated worldliness, revolted again, this time against religious pedantry which, instead of sanctifying life, threatened to act as a barrier between man and his Creator. The outcome was mysticism, the strife for union or even identification with God in the rapture of ecstasy. The theory of Muslim mysticism was largely nourished by Greek thought, in particular, Neo-Platonism. In the last instance, mysticism goes back to Plato's theory of knowledge. Plato taught that in order to know a certain object, the observer himself must possess something of the nature of the object studied. This logically leads to the assumption that man cannot know God fully except by sharing God's nature, by being God. Or, as Plotinus, the great expounder of Neo-Platonism, has put it: Our endeavor is not only to be without sin, but to be God.

Thus we have seen that the legacy of Greece affected Islam in many of the most essential spheres of life: in the practical and secular sciences, in dogma and theology and also in mysticism, which in Islam, more than in any other religion, became a widespread movement encompassing almost all classes of society. We have attributed this great historical process to three causes:

a) the fact that the Greek heritage was still alive and available in the countries and the times of the Muslim conquest;

b) the general receptivity of Islam which was due to its originally universalistic and eclectic character;

c) specific spiritual situations during the first three centuries of Islam, which made the influx of Greek ideas and systems of thought both inevitable and fruitful.

To these three basic causes, two accessory, but most vital factors must be added. Unlike the Germanic peoples, who had been real barbarians, the Arabs possessed a secular culture of their own, before they experienced the impact of Judaism and Christianity. I am referring to the miracle of pre-Islamic poetry and the highly developed and extremely refined Arabic classical language which had been developed through it. The Arabs had a passion for rhetoric and eloquence, they were infatuated by their beautiful language and conveyed their enthusiasm for it to the peoples conquered by them. This had the effect that the best minds in all the countries occupied by the Arabs soon tried to express in Arabic the choicest spiritual values they themselves possessed. Thus Arabic became immensely rich and pliable, and through the work of the translators from Greek also very suitable for the expression of abstract thoughts. It was the Arabs' own cultural heritage, the devotion to their language and their inherited literature which made them so receptive to the refinements of another culture.

Secondly, Hellenic studies could flourish in Islam so profusely, because in the third, fourth and fifth centuries of Islam there developed a broad and affluent middle class, which had the means, the leisure and the ambition to acquire knowledge and with it, social status. The extraordinary role of this middle class was the outcome of a many-sided historical process which cannot be described here.[1] The courts of the caliphs and princes gave a shelter to the Greek sciences in Islam, when they were still in their infancy. Their broad diffusion, however, was due to the new middle class.

After having discussed in detail why Arabic Islam was so receptive to the Greek heritage, there is almost no need to specify which features of the latter were absorbed by it and which remained outside its pale. Homer and Sophocles, Sappho and Thucydides—Greek epic, tragedy, lyrical poetry and classical history writing left no trace in Arabic language. (Sporadic quotations from Homer or the tragedians came to the Arabs through later sources.) The Muslims had no use for the world of the pagan gods or of the Greek polity.

[1] Cf. below p. 217 ff.

It is also doubtful how much of this literature was still alive and easily accessible at the time of the advent of Islam. On the other hand, the sciences of the Greeks were taken over by the Muslims in full and the latter recognized the former frankly and gratefully as their masters. There was medicine and pharmaceutics (an enormous field, later expanded by the Muslims and in particular by Arabic speaking Jews), botany and zoology, mineralogy and metereology, mathematics, mechanics and astronomy, the theories of sound and light, music and optics (very extensively treated by the Muslims), and above all, of course, philosophy in all its branches: logic and dialectic, ethics and metaphysics. The Greek theories of rhetoric and poetics also became known to the Arabs, but did not have much influence over them, for they had their own great traditions in these fields. Of late, G. E. von Grunebaum has drawn our attention to the fact that Arabic literature has taken over not only many motives and themes from late Greek popular sources, but also much of their "patterns of presentation and conventional shades of emotion."[1]

Hellenistic influence prevailed strongly in many other aspects of civilization. It is sufficient to mention architecture and the techniques of building, arts and crafts, alchemy, law, administration, and coinage. In all these domains, the Greek heritage had undergone fusions with local traditions and with foreign influences, especially from Iran and other eastern countries. Thus the Greek share was less conspicuous in them. It was in the spiritual field, in philosophy and the sciences, in which the Muslims regarded themselves as the disciples of the Greeks.

Were they good disciples? Did they grasp the spirit of Hellas? In this respect, opinions are divided. For C. H. Becker, one of the most competent students of our problem, Islam *is* Hellenism, to be sure an Islamized Hellenism. Following him, Werner Jaeger speaks about the internationality of Greek science, accomplished through the efforts of the Islamic scholars and their colleagues in Latin Europe. There is, however, another school of thought, led by such eminent German scholars as Ernst Troeltsch and H. H. Schaeder, according to whom Islam and the Orient in general absorbed only the externals, but never the essentials of Greek culture.[2]

[1] G. E. von Grunebaum, in *Medieval Islam*, Chicago, 1946, p. 294 ff.

[2] C. H. Becker, *Islamstudien I*, Leipzig 1924, p, 24-53 and passim. Werner Jaeger, "Die Antike und das Problem der Internationalität der Geisteswissen-

I believe that we are able to arrive at a just, that is to say, historically correct solution of the problem, if we stop talking in such general terms as East and West, Orient and Occident, and even Islam and Christianity. Instead, we have to consider each historical period in its own right. As far as Islam is concerned, three periods can clearly be distinguished. The first two hundred years of Islam were given to conquest and colonization and the development of its religion. Then comes the great period, which was characterized by the preponderance of Hellenism in the cultural field and by the middle class, as far as social organization is concerned. This period lasted approximately from the middle of the ninth century to the middle of the thirteenth. As from around 1250, Islamic history was dominated by foreign soldier castes and clerical obscurantism, until the contact with the modern scientific and technological civilization brought about the profound changes which we are witnessing in our own century.

With regard to the middle, the Hellenistic, period which we have called the *Intermediate Civilization*, it is fair to say that the disciple was worthy of his master. The question how far the individual sciences and techniques were furthered during this period must be left to the specialists in the various fields. Information about this subject is found in such books as *The Legacy of Islam*, edited by Sir Thomas Arnold and Alfred Guillaume, 1931, or in George Sarton's *Introduction to the History of Science* or *A History of Technology*, edited by Charles Singer and others, Oxford 1956. We are concerned here with the problem of culture in general. How far did the Greek heritage affect the spirit of the epoch, how much did it mold the personality of the individuals?

A man of Hellenic culture is characterized by his inquisitive mind, his gift of observation, his striving for a well balanced total view of the world and by his refined, urbane behavior. We are in a position to form a well-founded opinion about the personality and attainments of a good many excellent representatives of the Intermediate Civilization, because they have left us a large body of writings. Naturally, there were great individual differences between the various authors, and some of them, including some well known

schaften", *Inter Nationes* I, Berlin, 1931, 93b. H. H. Schaeder, "Der Orient und das griechische Erbe", *Die Antike* 4, 1928, p. 226 ff. E. Troeltsch, "Der Historismus und seine Probleme", *Gesammelte Schriften* vol. 3, p. 706 ff., see J. Kraemer (above p. 56), p. 16-7.

philosophers, can hardly be regarded as having lived up to the ideal type just described. Others, however, have realized it, combining an amazing range of knowledge with a well integrated world view and a harmonious, ethical and humane personality.

In some respects, I should say, the Intermediate Civilization has surpassed its masters, the ancient Greeks and Romans. I have in mind the Islamic science of *Comparative Religion*, the like of which, to my knowledge, was not found before. We possess in Arabic comprehensive books about the tenets and beliefs of all the then known denominations, sects, philosophical schools and systems of thought, Muslim and non-Muslim, ancient and contemporary. The most famous example of this type of literature is the *Book of Religions and Beliefs*, which was completed in 1127 by Shahrastānī, a scholar from Khorāsān in Northeastern Iran. When we compare his detailed, well informed and remarkably unbiased accounts with the Greek and Latin texts related to Judaism, we have to confess that, between Tacitus and Shahrastānī, humanity has made a great step forward. All that the illustrious Roman historian knew about monotheism was that the Jews worshipped in the Temple of Jerusalem the image of a donkey. About the Sabbath, this most precious gift of Judaism to mankind, he remarked only that the Jews were the laziest of all peoples, since they took off a full day every week. In order to obtain authoritative information about Judaism, Tacitus had just to walk up one or two blocks, where he would have found educated Jews of Hellenic upbringing who could have taught him better. But he and his Greek masters, whom he copied, lacked the spirit of research and scientific responsibility needed for the task.[1] How different was Shahrastānī, who took pains to study in detail and to describe objectively such sects as the Persian dualists, the Manichaeans and the followers of Mazdak, all of whom were, of course, anathema to him from the point of view of religion.

Another illustrious example of the spirit of research alive in the Intermediate Civilization was al-Bīrūni, also an Iranian (died around 1050). He was equally great in mathematics, astronomy and the natural sciences and as an observer of foreign peoples and creeds. In India, he taught the Greek sciences to the local scholars and learned from them Sanskrit and the contents of their religion. His *Description of India* is an invaluable source for our knowledge of the

[1] Cf. Theodor Reinach, *Textes d'auteurs Grecs et Romains relatifs au judaisme*, Paris 1890, passim.

culture of that country during the eleventh century and a notable document of scientific curiosity and careful observation.

We are also able to confirm Werner Jaeger's assumption that a truly international fellowship of science existed in the days of the Intermediate Civilization. Both literary sources, such as Ibn Abī Uṣaybiʿa's *History of the Physicians*, and documentary evidence, such as the records of the Cairo Geniza, prove that in general, a spirit of tolerance and mutual esteem prevailed between the students of the Greek sciences of different races and religions.[1]

From the thirteenth century on, both the spirit of research and that of tolerance dwindled rapidly and became next to extinct by the end of the fifteenth, exactly when Europe started to make its great strides forward. There were many symptoms which accompanied this decline and perhaps were partly its causes: the rule of foreign soldier castes, already referred to, the eclipse of the middle class and the replacement of a free, mercantile economy by feudalism, to be sure: feudalism of the Oriental type, and, finally, the increasing institutionalization and organization by the state of the Muslim clergy, which, in the preceding centuries, had formed a loose brotherhood of independent religious scholars.

It is, however, fair to say that the Greek heritage never became entirely lost in the countries of Islam. Logic was taught in the Muslim religious schools of higher learning, as long as their traditional syllabus was in force, and the systematic arrangement of books, which the Muslims had learned from Greek science, remained the rule, although the ancient sources of Islamic religion, which were mainly studied in the schools, were very poorly organized.

Secondly, Arabic, which had become an efficient tool for the expression of abstract ideas owing to the translations from Greek, preserved its pliability and richness. Because of this profound influence of Greek on Arabic, and through it on Hebrew, Persian and Turkish, all these Middle Eastern languages were able to express modern thought, once it was conveyed to them, with comparative ease.

In our own day, a galaxy of Middle Eastern savants and litterateurs have taken up again the task of translation and appreciation of Greek writings, this time, not of scientific books, but of belles lettres, precisely that branch of literature which had not been touched upon by the scholars of the Intermediate Civilization.

[1] Cf. the present writer's, "The Medical Profession in the Light of the Cairo Geniza Documents", *Hebrew Union College Annual* 34 (1963), pp. 177-194.

Homer, the tragedians, the lyrics and the historians are now available in Arabic, Persian and Turkish. I have in mind translations made for the benefit of the educated general reader, not those destined for University studies, which include also the works of the philosophers. Today, a high school boy in Cairo, Istanbul or Teheran would know about classical Greece approximately as much as his peer in New York or Los Angeles. However, this interest of Islamic peoples in classical Greece does not constitute a continuation of what had happened in the times of the Intermediate Civilization. In this, as in many other respects, the contemporary Muslims act as members of the world civilization to which we all belong.[1]

The introductory words to this paper emphasized that the fate of the Greek heritage in Islam, its quality and duration, are not without concern and significance in our own day. What conclusions are we to draw from our review of the character and development of the Hellenistic period of Islam? As to its quality, I believe nothing need be added to what has already been said. The example of the Intermediate Civilization proves that real values created by one culture can successfully be transferred to another. As to the duration of the Hellenistic period of Islam, which we have described as having lasted for about 400 years, it may be compared to the Humanistic period in Europe, that is to say, the prevalence of classical studies, which was in force approximately between 1500 and 1900. Of course, I am fully aware of the difference. While the Greek heritage has become an integral, albeit not always evident part of contemporary Western culture, the same cannot be said of later Islam. The reason for this difference is that modern culture grew out of the humanism of the renaissance, while the medieval civilization of the Middle East was not, as has been defined by C. H. Becker, asiatisized Hellenism, but Hellenized Islam, since Islam was already a fully developed religious system when it experienced the impact of Hellenism. When this impact became weak and weaker, finally only Islam remained, and religion alone obviously was not strong enough to counteract the many destructive forces which were at work in the Islamic world during the last six hundred years.

[1] See S. Bencheneb, "Les humanités grecques et l'Orient arabe moderne", *Mélanges Louis Massignon*, vol. I, Damascus 1956, pp. 173-198, and Jörg Kraemer, "Der Islamische Modernismus und das griechische Erbe", *Der Islam* 38 (1962), pp. 1-27.

In our own time, the cultural process is reversed. It is not Islam which absorbs modern civilization, but modern civilization which puts itself in the place of Islam, forcing it to participate in a world culture from which there is no escape.[1] What is happening today cannot be compared in all respects to what happened eleven hundred years ago. We may learn from history, but history never repeats itself.

[1] As early as 1911 the Turkish Muslim Abdullah Çevdet wrote: "There is no second civilization. Civilization means European civilization." In 1924, Kemal Ataturk declared: "Countries vary, but civilization is one and for a nation to progress it must take part in this single civilization." See Bernard Lewis, *The Emergence of Modern Turkey*, Oxford University Press 1961, pp. 231, 263 and 287. Most Muslims would object to these statements, but this does not detract from their validity.

PART TWO

ISLAMIC RELIGIOUS AND POLITICAL INSTITUTIONS

CHAPTER THREE

PRAYER IN ISLAM

"The majority of young men in the Middle East do not pray at all." This statement is made in a posthumously published article by the Reverend John Van Ess, an American missionary who had lived in Basra, Iraq, for about forty years and was an unusually keen and sympathetic observer of the Middle Eastern scene.[1] A Moroccan Muslim writer, who belongs himself to the younger generation, voices an even stronger opinion on the subject—and this with regard to his own country, which until recently was renowned as ultra-conservative: "As regards the prayers, only the aged perform them. And even with them praying is mostly a habit or a show."[2]

It would be rash to attribute this waning of devoutness in modern Islam to the impact of "Western materialism". Observations similar to those quoted above were made at a time when European influence was practically absent. "There are comparatively few persons in Egypt," writes E. W. Lane around 1835, "who do not sometimes, or often, neglect this duty (of prayer); and there are many who scarcely ever pray."[3] It was that inner exhaustion of Islam, or of religion in general of which we have spoken above p. 42, rather than any outward factors which deprived many Muslims of the urge and the faculty to pray.

Yet prayer is the quintessence of Islam. There is no other duty which can be compared with it in scope and intensity and there is no trait which marks the true Muslim as does his sincerity in devotion.

There is hardly a page in the Koran which does not contain a reference to prayer, either directly, by exhorting and instructing the true believers, or indirectly, by providing examples of supplication, meditation and hymnal poetry.[4] The very first definition of

[1] *The Muslim World* 40 (July 1950), p. 155. His book *Meet the Arab*, New York 1943, is still worth reading.

[2] Driss Chraibi, *Le Passé simple* (Paris 1954), quoted by G. E. von Grunebaum, *Modern Islam* (California University Press, Berkeley and Los Angeles 1962), p. 284.

[3] *An Account of the Manners and Customs of the Modern Egyptians*, Chapter III, Everyman's Library, p. 73.

[4] A comprehensive study of all the different aspects of the Koranic prayer is contained in the present writer's unpublished Ph.D. thesis, cf. above p. 17,

an adherent to Muhammad's faith is "one who pronounces the name of his Lord and prays."[1] Muslims are "those who pray and are persevering in their prayers", while, in another very ancient sura, the sinners who are burning in hell-fire, when asked about their crimes, confess: "We were not of those who pray."[2]

THE ORIGIN OF INSTITUTIONAL PRAYER

The word for prayer used in these early passages, *ṣalāt*, is already the same which later became in Islam the general designation for this foremost duty of a Muslim. It is derived from the Aramaic language, where it originally meant "bowing", but had adopted the general meaning of institutional prayer both in the Synagogue and the Church long before it penetrated into Arabia and other countries. In its wide diffusion it represents a significant piece of religious history. Calling celestial powers for help or glorifying them in grateful devotion is generally human and found, in one form or another, almost anywhere in the world.[3] However, prayer as an institution, consisting of set texts to be recited with precisely fixed movements of the body at prescribed times is something specific. To be sure, formal prayer as such goes back to remote antiquity and was rather diffused. It constituted part of a ceremony of sacrifice or of a magical act. On the other hand, unaccompanied, "abstract" prayer, or, as it was called in Hebrew, "temple service with the heart" came into being under very specific historical circumstances. When, for the sake of the preservation of monotheism, sacrifice was forbidden in Israel everywhere except in the Temple of Jerusalem, and when, on the other hand, a canon of holy scriptures developed, the knowledge of which was regarded as indispensable for the acquisition of right conduct, a new type of house of worship had to be substituted for the ancient temples. *Synagogue* is the Greek translation of a Hebrew word meaning House of Assembly, and the

note 1. What is said in the Koran *about* prayer is extensively and beautifully described in "La prière selon le Coran", by le Père André d'Alverny, S.J., *Proche Orient Chrétien* 10 (1960), pp. 212-226, 303-317, 11 (1961), pp. 3-16.

[1] Koran 87:15.

[2] *Ibid.*, 70:22-23, 74:43/44.

[3] The standard work on the subject is still Friedrich Heiler, *Prayer, a Study in the History and Psychology of Religion*, transl. by Samuel McComb with the assistance of J. Edgar Park, Oxford University Press, 1932. Cf. also "Gebet" in *Religion in Geschichte und Gegenwart*, Tübingen 1958, V, pp. 1210-1235 (by F. Heiler and others).

Greek word for Church: *ecclesia*, means the same. Mosque, Arabic *masjid*, designates literally a place for prostration, but its function was the same as that of the synagogue and the ecclesia of old: formal worship, unaccompanied by sacrifice, and gatherings for religious instruction and any other activity connected with the community of faith.

Therefore, while translating *ṣalāt* as "prayer", we should always keep in mind that the reference generally is not to spontaneous devotion, but to the fulfillment of a duty, the most noble duty a man was regarded to have on earth, the service of God. "Thee do we serve" is repeated by a practicing Muslim at least twenty times a day and this is indeed the essence of the *ṣalāt*.

NAMES AND TYPES OF PRAYER IN THE KORAN

Ṣalāt and its derivatives recur in the Koran about a hundred times.[1] But it is only one of the many expressions with which Muhammad designates the act of worship. In the Koran, as in the Bible, the most common word for prayer is "calling God", while God's "answer" means favorable acceptance. Of equal importance is the phrase, already met with by us in one of the oldest suras of the Koran: "pronouncing the name of God", which means professing one's faith in him. It is used similarly in the Bible. The words describing the movements of the body which accompany the recitation of sacred texts are also used in the Koran as general designations for prayer. Thus, when Muhammad repeatedly urges non-Muslims to "bow with those who bow" or to "prostrate themselves before God and serve him" he simply wants to say that they should join the worship of the Muslim community.[2]

The Hebrew and Aramaic expressions of "praising" and "blessing" God (the latter especially in the phrase: "blessed be God" at the beginning of a benediction) were taken over by Muhammad from the older religions and used profusely. He preferred the foreign term to the indigenous Arabic word for praising because of the exclusively religious connotation of the former.[3] On the other hand,

[1] Cf. d'Alverny (cf. page 74), *Proche Orient Chrétien* 10, p. 303.

[2] Koran 77:48. Cf. 2:43/40. 53:62. Cf. Psalm 95:6, where the word translated in the Authorized Version as "worship" corresponds exactly to what has been rendered here with "prostrating oneself".

[3] Even a casual visitor to an Arab country knows the phrase *al-ḥamdu lillāh*, "Praise be to God", "Thank God". This phrase, which is Arabic, occurs

"hallowing", "sanctifying", also derived from Hebrew and Aramaic, occurs in the Koran only once as a designation of prayer, in sura 2:30/28, where it is said of the angels, as in Isaiah 6:3. The idea of sanctity, so prominent in Judaism and Christianity, somehow did not take root in Islam.[1]

A sense of guilt and contrition were the first prerequisites of that return to God which Muhammad preached to his countrymen. Therefore "asking God's forgiveness" became a major postulate of the pre-Islamic prophets, mentioned in the Koran as from the second Meccan period, as well as of Muhammad himself.[2] Soon it assumed also the general connotation of prayer: "The pious... take only little rest during the night and ask God's forgiveness in the mornings."[3]

Dread of divine judgment was only one, though the most essential element in Muhammad's original message. From the outset he also emphasized God's bounty and the ensuing duty of man to show his gratitude. "Serve God and thank him", or, "and be of those who thank him", is tantamount to a call to prayer.[4] In Medina, as in the New Testament, "giving thanks" designates the grace to be said at a meal.[5] Muhammad expressly permitted Muslims to partake of food prepared by "the Possessors of the Book".[6] Thus it most probably did not escape him that every Jewish meal was preceded by a benediction and concluded with a grace. Similarly, a Muslim, before beginning to eat, says *bi-smi-llāh* (In the name of God) and, when he has finished, *al-ḥamdu li-llāh* (Praise be to God).[7]

frequently in the Koran, especially at the beginning of chapters or passages, as was common with regard to the corresponding phrase in the Syriac liturgy. The more so is it remarkable that, with one exception, Muhammad never uses the *verb* belonging to this noun, but replaces it throughout with the loan word *sabbaḥa* (Hebrew and Aramaic *shabbeaḥ*).

[1] *Kabbara*, "to glorify", literally "to make great", has the same semantic derivation as the Hebrew *gaddel* (familiar from *yithgaddal*, the opening of the Qaddish prayer and other parts of the daily service). It may have developed independently from the phrase *Allāhu akbar*, "God is great" even in pre-Islamic times, cf. its occurrence in the ancient sura 74:3.

[2] Koran 71:10/9 (Noah). 11:54/52, 90/92 (two Arab prophets). 11:3 (Muhammad).

[3] *Ibid.*, 51:15-18.

[4] *Ibid.*, 29:17/16. 39:66. Cf. 46:15/14. 27:19 (Solomon).

[5] *Ibid.*, 2:162/167. Matthew 15:36.

[6] Koran 5:5/7.

[7] He may also use the more complete formulas: "In the name of God, the Compassionate and Merciful" and "Praise be to God, the Lord of all the beings". After the master of the house has pronounced the *bi-smi-llāh* the guest should respond with: *hanī'an* "may it be enjoyable".

Observant Muslims, like orthodox Jews, wash their hands (in certain prescribed ways) both before and after meals. Although this religious custom certainly was conducive to hygiene (since one used his fingers instead of a fork), it may originally go back to the ceremonial washings connected with sacrifice. The idea behind all this is that God, if properly served, is present at a man's table, as He is at his own altar.

A primordial and certainly pre-Islamic form of praying is "the seeking of refuge", a short and fervent invocation of God against a specified enemy or enemies. Suras 113 and 114, with which the Koran concludes, are two more elaborate examples of such an invocation. In sura 16:98/100 Muhammad receives the instruction: "When you read the Koran take refuge with God against Satan, the accursed."[1] Since then, any recitation of the holy book of Islam (or study of its oral law, the Ḥadīth) is introduced by the words "I take my refuge with God against Satan, the accursed." These words take precedence even over the formula "In the name of God, the Compassionate and Merciful", which, with one exception, prefaces all the suras of the Koran and which is said by Muslims before any undertaking of some significance. Needless to mention that the Koran readings broadcast from radio stations also open with this "seeking of refuge" from Satan.

This short survey of the names and types of prayers in the Koran would be incomplete without a note about the idea of intercession, the prayer on behalf of others which, in different forms, is very frequently referred to in the Muslim scripture. Muhammad tells us about Abraham praying for his father, Moses calling to God for Israel, the prophets in general testifying for their flock on the Day of Judgment and the angels "interceding for those for whom God gives them permission" to do so.[2] In Medina, the Prophet's prayer for his followers, for single groups and persons (alive or dead) became an indispensable element in the religious life of his community and

[1] The word *rajīm*, translated here as "accursed" is understood by the Muslims as meaning originally "pelted", cf. Koran 67:5, where the Satans (who strive to listen to the heavenly councils) are driven away by being pelted with stones. Western scholarship used to regard it as a loanword from Ethiopian *r^{e}gūm*, cursed. However, the eminent Semitologist Franz Rosenthal takes it as being derived from the root *rgm*, *rgn*, in the meaning of speaking or grumbling, which would describe Satan as a grumbler or slanderer, cf. *Joshua Starr Memorial Volume*, New York 1953, pp. 83-84.

[2] Koran 19:47/48. 2:68-69/62-63. 77:11. 53:26-27.

a bulwark of his own position of leadership.[1] In another part of this book it has been emphasized that this idea of the intercession of the Prophet for each individual Muslim is one of the strongest psychological factors in popular (and perhaps not only popular) Islamic religion.[2]

Finally, God himself is described as praying. "(The pious), from their Lord (are) prayers upon them and mercy." Since God is addressed in prayer, it seems strange that he himself should be engaged in this pious work. Therefore, *ṣalāt,* while referring to God, has been rendered in modern translations by "blessings" and similar phrases.[3] This is a misunderstanding of religious psychology. Man has always seen God in his own image. Since prayer is the most significant occupation of the pious, it is unimaginable that God should not pray himself. The Talmud, that treasure house of Jewish religious folklore, is curious to know even the text of God's prayer. It provides us with one example: "May my mercy for my creatures be stronger than my wrath."[4] The close affinity of the Koranic verse referred to at the beginning of this paragraph with the Talmudic passage is evident. The main object of God's prayer, of course, is the Prophet of Islam. "God and his angels pray upon the Prophet. O ye who believe pray upon him and give (him) the Salutation of Peace."[5] On the basis of this verse, whenever the name of Muhammad is mentioned, whether orally or in writing or in print, the eulogy "may God pray upon him and give him the Salutation of Peace" is added. This is absolutely de rigueur.[6]

Salutations, as the verse just quoted above shows, are a kind of prayer for the greeted. Therefore, the Koran (and of course also later Muslim sources) devote much attention to this formality.

[1] *Ibid.*, 48:11. 9:103. 63:5. 9:80.

[2] See above, p. 23.

[3] Koran 2:157/152, cf. the representative renderings of Richard Bell, *The Qur'ān Translated etc.*, Edinburgh 1937, p. 22, Régis Blachère, *Le Coran*, Paris 1949-51, p. 993, and Rudi Paret, *Der Koran*, Stuttgart 1963, p. 23. Cf. also André d'Alverny (see page 74), *Proche Orient Chrétien* 10, p. 314.

[4] Talmud Bab., Berakhoth fol. 7a, where the same roots for "prayer" and "mercy" are used as in the Koranic verse referred to in the preceding note.

[5] Koran 33:56.

[6] But not for non-Muslims. When the present writer studied Ḥadīth with the late Sheikh *Sa'ūd al-'Urī* in Jerusalem, the master always succeeded in preceding the disciple by the split of a second in pronouncing the eulogy over the Prophet whenever his name was mentioned. It took me some time to understand that the saying of that blessing by a non-Muslim, notwithstanding the good intention, was bad form.

"Peace be upon you", although being the common Jewish salutation, was regarded as specifically Islamic, namely in contrast to the various other forms of friendly intercourse in vogue among the pagan Arabs.[1] In many passages, the pious in Paradise are greeted with the Salām by their companions, the angels or God himself, which is paralleled by the Talmudic notion: "When the pious part to their eternal abode, it is said to them: come in peace."[2] Various instructions for the proper use of the greeting are given in the Koran, e.g. never to enter someone else's house without pronouncing first "a salutation from God" (cf. for this phrase Psalm 24:5) or to return any greeting with a more beautiful one (cf. Ruth 2:4). Both injunctions are found in Talmudic sources, but most probably were time honored and widely accepted rules of conduct in the Middle East. Strict Muslims never greet a non-Muslim with the Islamic "Peace upon you" and one should never greet a Muslim thus, unless one were sure he would like it.

INSTITUTIONAL PRAYER IN THE KORAN

We shall not attempt here to reconstruct in detail the development of the Muslim prayer service during Muhammad's lifetime, a controversial subject which by its very nature precludes exact results.[3] On the other hand, a study of the elements of this great institution as represented in the Koran is highly conducive to its proper understanding, since the Koran is its original source, and, in addition, is present in the mind of the average Muslim more than any other Islamic book.

When we open the relevant chapter in Bukhārī, the most widely accepted collection of Ḥadīth, we find the following account about the introduction of the daily prayer. When Muhammad, on his miraculous ascent to the heavenly spheres, arrived at the uppermost, seventh Heaven, he was given the instruction that his community should say fifty prayers every day. While descending and informing Moses, who dwelt in another heaven, about this injunction, the experienced leader of the older community told him to go back and

[1] I. Goldziher, *Muhammedanische Studien* I, Halle 1888, p. 264.

[2] Tanna debe Eliyahu, ch. 2. Cf. also M. Lidzbarski, "Salām und Islām", *Zeitschrift für Semitistik* I, 1, p. 90.

[3] In addition to the studies mentioned on p. 73, cf. EI[1], s.v. Ṣalāt (by A. J. Wensinck), where further literature, and J. J. Rivlin, *Gesetz im Koran*, Jerusalem 1934, pp. 90-117.

to ask for a remission, since the Muslims would be unable to meet such an obligation. This was repeated three times, until the number of the obligatory daily prayers was finally reduced to five. The narrative frame of the story is of course legendary and reminds one of Genesis 18:20-33, where Abraham argues with God, until the number of righteous men required to save sinful Sodom is reduced from fifty to ten. In its basic assumptions, however, the account of the Ḥadīth is correct and borne out by the testimony of the Koran.[1]

The latter will be more easily comprehensible, if we take notice first of the structure of Muslim prayer as it is discernible to us from the oldest post-Koranic sources and has remained in practice with little changes up to the present day. Prayer is said five times a day and consists of almost identical units called *rakʿa*, literally a bowing and bending of the body. The *rakʿa* contains the following main elements: 1. The pronouncement of the name of God (*Allāhu akbar*, "God is great") said in standing position with the hands raised on each side of the face. 2. In the same position, but with the hands placed before the body, the *Fātiḥa*, the opening sura[2] of the Koran is recited. A few other verses of the Koran are recited next, which should be different in each *rakʿa*. 3. Inclination of head and body with placing of the hands on the knees (*rukūʿ*, cf. *rakʿa*, the designation of the prayer unit). 4. Prostration, i.e. dropping upon the knees, followed by putting nose and forehead on the ground. 5. Pronouncement, in sitting posture, of "God is great" and a second prostration. With the second prostration the rakʿa is completed. Two rakʿas (which originally formed the whole prayer) are followed by the declaration of faith ("I testify that there is no God except God and that Muhammad is his servant and messenger") and the blessing upon the Prophet, cf. above p. 78, as well as upon the true believers. The whole prayer is concluded with the formula "Peace be upon you", pronounced while turning the head to the right and the left.[3]

Each prayer consists of two, three or four mandatory rakʿas, followed or preceded (or both) by others imposed "by religious

[1] Bukhārī, Book *Prayer*, first paragraph. Repeated in practically all the other canonical collections of Ḥadīth.

[2] This should not be translated as "the first sura", but as "the sura preceding the Koran" a distinction which, as we shall presently see, is not without significance.

[3] The same greeting and gesture concluded the Jewish main prayer already in Talmudic times, see Talmud Bab., Yoma, 53b.

custom", i.e. normally kept, but regarded as being of less rigor. There are slight differences between the various Muslim rites as to the number of rak'as as well as concerning the postures of the body and the formulas pronounced.[1]

Returning now to the story of the Ḥadīth about the introduction of the Muslim prayer we discern in it as its first and foremost element the idea that praying is a duty and a rather heavy one. It is not any more an occasional cry for help, or an expression of gratitude, or a confession of sins, but a permanent service encompassing the true believer's whole day.

The same idea prevails in the Koran already in its most ancient sections. In these, night time in particular was given to devotion. "Stay up during the night, except a little, half of it, or a little less or a little more, and recite the Koran[2] distinctly. Lo, We shall burden you with a heavy command. Being up at night is more impressive and more conducive to correct recitation. During day time you have many (lit. long) occupations. And pronounce the name of your Lord and devote yourself entirely to him."[3] "The servants of the Allmerciful are those who... devote the nights to their Lord, prostrating themselves and standing."[4] Two reasons are given for the preference of prayer at night. During the day everyone is busy, while during the night the mind is more receptive. To this may be added that the members of Muhammad's still small congregation could not easily disengage themselves from their environment during daytime. Thus it is natural that in the early years of the Prophet we hear almost exclusively about nightly prayer assemblies, while later on and in particular in Medina vigils became an optional work of personal piety, which character they retained in fully developed Islam.[5]

As to the contents of the earliest prayer assemblies in Islam we

[1] The most convenient and exact description of the Muslim prayer (accompanied by pictures of the various postures of the body) is contained in E. W. Lane (see page 73), pp. 77-81.

[2] "Koran" designates not only the whole book, but also any section of it. At the time of the promulgation of this sura, only a small fraction of the Koran was in existence.

[3] Koran 73:2-8. Ten other Meccan suras refer to prayers at night time, cf. also above, p. 74.

[4] *Ibid.*, 25:64/65.

[5] Vigils formed a prominent element in the devotion of the Christian ascetics, as well as in the community who left us the Dead Sea Scrolls, cf. *Manual of Discipline* VI, 7-8. In Talmudic Judaism study (but not prayer) became the regular activity of nightly devotion.

learn about the following elements: the pronouncement of the name of God, recitations from the Scripture and prosternations following the latter, accompanied by a eulogy said by the congregation. In addition to the passages quoted in the preceding pages, the two following here are illustrative: "Why do they not believe and, when the Koran is read to them, prostrate themselves?"[1] "Only those believe in our words who, when they are recited to them, fall down prostrating themselves and praise the grace of their Lord."[2] Thus the original Islamic prayer differed from its later, definite form in the readings being recited before the congregation—and in that there was no fixed text said by the participants. The first difference was conditioned by the Koran being still in the first stages of promulgation, the latter by the simple fact that such a text was not yet in existence.

This was changed however before much time had passed since the formation of a substantial fellowship of Islam. The account of the Ḥadīth on the introduction of the mandatory prayer, quoted above, connects it with Muhammad's nightly journey to Heaven, a significant detail of the Prophet's biography based on Koran 17:1. The story takes it for granted that immediately five daily prayers were introduced. This is at variance with the Koran where this number is never mentioned and where the times of the prayers, in accordance with the literary character of the Koran, are mostly indicated in a poetical, inexact manner.[3] There is however one detail in the Ḥadīth which deserves more attention by modern research than it has hitherto received, namely the assumption that prayer, in the form known to the Ḥadīth (and later) was consciously introduced at a certain time and did not simply "develop". This assumption, which is reasonable in itself, is borne out by a scrutiny of the Muslim scripture.

THE FATIHA—A DELIBERATE LITURGICAL COMPOSITION

Early in his second Meccan period Muhammad introduced a new term, borrowed, it seems, from the Syriac Church *'aqāma 'l-ṣalāt'* "to perform the prayer", and used it almost exclusively as a designation for mandatory prayer.[4] At the same time, he gave to his

[1] Koran 84:20-21.

[2] *Ibid.*, 32:15. Cf. also 25:73. 17:107-8/108.

[3] Details in EI[1] s.v. *Ṣalāt.*

[4] Cf. A. Jeffery, *The Foreign Vocabulary of the Qur'ān*, Baroda 1938, p. 198, where further literature will be found.

community a fixed liturgy: none other than the *Fātiḥa*, the sura preceding the Koran. The specific character of this sura is recognizable first in its position. The chapters of the Koran are arranged approximately according to their length. First comes sura Two with 286 verses, while the suras at the end of the book have only three to six. The Fātiḥa, the "opening" sura, contains seven verses, but still, as its name indicates, precedes the others. Furthermore, it is the only chapter in the holy book of Islam which is composed solely of words of communal prayer.[1] Finally, its very contents prove that it is a liturgical composition created deliberately for this purpose and at a comparatively early period when Muhammad was still eager to give no offense to members of the older religions who wanted to take part in the devotion of his community.[2] On the one hand, the prayer contains the main points of Muhammad's original preaching: the faith in God, the Day of Judgment and God's bounty which may avert man's doom, if he is guided along the right path. On the other hand it refrains from including any specific Islamic tenets, such as the belief in Muhammad's revelation, so prominent already in the second Meccan period, or the veneration of the "House", the Kaʿba, which became a central doctrine even before the exodus to Medina.

One may wonder why the Islamic equivalent of the Lord's Prayer is so extremely short and simple. It would be a great mistake to attribute this to a dearth of ideas and ways of expression on the part of Muhammad. A study of the prayers and hymnal passages included in the Koran betrays a great treasure of religious notions and liturgical traditions. However, we must keep in mind how utterly strange and unfamiliar most of all this material must have been to the average pagan Arab. Only by keeping the daily prayer as restricted and uncomplicated as possible could it become a practice adopted by every one. Sura Two (which is actually the first one, as we have seen), concludes as follows: "God does not charge any one with more than he has capacity for... O our Lord, do not lay upon us a burden such as you have laid upon those who were before us. O our Lord, do not load upon us what we are unable

[1] Suras 113-114 (see above p. 77) are not communal prayers.

[2] In the same sura 17, in which Muhammad refers to his nightly excursion (cf. above p. 79) he addresses the Meccans as follows: "Believe in it (the Koran) or not, those upon whom the Knowledge (i.e. a heavenly revelation) has previously been given, when it (the Koran) is recited to them, fall down on their chins in prostration." (verses 107-8/108).

to bear." Muhammad knew his people. He confined himself to the barest essentials and by doing so succeeded in making full participation in the service possible even for the uninitiated.

NUMBER, TIMES AND OTHER EXTERNALIA OF THE DAILY PRAYER

It stands to reason that because of its extreme shortness the *Fātiḥa,* which forms the main content of the Islamic congregational prayer, was repeated several times during one service. In other words, from its institution at the beginning of the second Meccan period Islamic prayer bore essentially the same character as we know it today. This assumption explains also another aspect of the Muslim service whose Koranic references have given much trouble to both Muslim and modern scholars: the number and the times of the daily prayers. Since a service consisted in a number of more or less identical units, it lent itself easily to being split into two or three different services. In many places in the Koran, morning and evening, the natural hours for devotion before and after a day's work, are recommended as times for prayer. However, we read also: "Praise be to God in the evening and the morning... early at night and at noon"[1] and "Keep the prayers (in the plural, not in the dual!) and the middle prayer."[2] This makes a minimum of five daily services. Thus it may well be that this number which is unanimously attested to by the traditions of Islam had become mandatory already during the lifetime of the Prophet.

Why five? The various answers to this question offered thus far cannot be regarded as satisfactory. It is possible that this number was reached in the course of the development of the Muslim service and was finally fixed for no particular reason. On the other hand, it is not excluded that this choice was not quite fortuitous. Seeing that the liturgical elements contained in the Koran are almost in their entirety derived from the services of the Eastern Church and the Synagogue, it is feasible to seek an answer to our question in Muhammad's relationship to the two older monotheistic religions.

The Psalms offer two choices for the number of daily prayers,

[1] Koran 30:17/16. "Early at night" translates *'ashiyyan.*

[2] *Ibid.,* 2:238/239. The "middle prayer" is according to the most accepted opinion the afternoon prayer which in Islam obtained specific significance similar to that which it had before in Judaism, cf. I. Goldziher, *Die Richtungen der Islamischen Koranauslegung,* Leiden 1952 (Reprint), pp. 14-15.

three in Psalm 55:18/17[1] ("Evening, morning and at noon shall I pray") and *seven* in Psalm 119:164 ("Seven times a day shall I praise you"). The first became the rule for the Jewish prayer, cf. already Daniel 6:11/10[2], the second was the model for the *horae canonicae*, the seven "hours" of the (Syriac) monks.[3] While the Muslims had daily dealings with a populous Jewish community, they were familiar with Christian monks and hermits, frequently referred to both in pre-Islamic poetry and in the Koran. It is thus highly probable that Muhammad was well aware of the times of daily prayer kept by the two religious bodies. Now, in a Koranic passage dealing with institutional prayer, albeit an aspect of it different from that dealt with here, the Muslims are told that they form a community "in the middle, witnessing for mankind (to what is right)".[4] In view of such a role, the choice of five daily prayers as a reasonable median between the seven "hours" of the Christian monks and the three services of the Synagogue becomes rather plausible.

The verse just referred to is taken from a lengthy passage in sura Two dealing with the *qibla*, or direction to which the Muslims should turn in prayer. This was a moot point between the various denominations and also between different views within one and the same religious community. No wonder, then, that this question occupied Muhammad's mind already in Mecca,[5] while sura 2:142-150/136-145 shows that he was wavering a long time until he was "given" the qibla which satisfied him, the direction towards the sanctuary of his native city. An attentive reading of the passages in question reveals four stages of development. At first, any sanctuary was regarded as a proper direction for the prayer; then Muhammad shared the qibla with another community (according to the unanimous opinion of the tradition, that to Jerusalem); thirdly, while wishing to dissociate himself from this connection, other directions were tried ("We see how you turn your face to and fro" 2:144/139); finally the true direction, i.e. the one in conformity with the new confessional

[1] The first number refers to the numeration in the Hebrew text, the second to that generally followed in the English translations.

[2] See preceding note.

[3] Cf. E. A. W. Budge, The Book of Governors, London 1893, Introduction, p. LV. The eight horae of the Greek church are particular to it and possibly of later origin.

[4] Koran 2:143/137.

[5] *Ibid.*, 10:87. 7:29/28.

conception of Islam, the direction towards Mecca, was chosen. The present writer does not concur with the generally accepted theory that the turning towards Jerusalem was a political move destined to win over the Jews of Medina. In addition to the reasons given above p. 34, it must be emphasized that Jerusalem in those days was as holy for Christians as for Jews.

The final acceptance of the qibla towards Mecca was of great impact on the religious consciousness of the Muslims all over the world. It should be noted, however, that Muhammad was well aware of the fact that "To God belong the East and the West; wherever you turn to there is the face of God".[1] True belief and moral conduct were more important than such technical details of the rites.[2] It is interesting to note that the Talmudic passage dealing with the direction of prayer also utters the opinion that God's presence is everywhere.[3]

In Medina, detailed instructions were promulgated for another characteristic of Muslim prayer, the mandatory washing of the face, the hands and the arms up to the elbows, as well as of the feet. That physical cleanliness was conducive to the purity of the mind was recognized already by the most ancient civilizations of the Middle East and the state of ritual purity was a foremost concern of most of its religions. By requiring it for every believer five times a day Islam has exercised a great educational influence. As may be noted in passing, this prerequisite has affected also genuine Muslim attire everywhere (shoes which can easily be removed, wide sleeves which can be pushed back above the elbow, etc.).

THE ENIGMA OF MUSLIM PRAYER

Our study of Muslim prayer has shown that it is extremely short, simple and repetitive. To this should be added that it lacks variation. The same prayers are said in the morning and in the evening, although the Koran is most eloquent about the change of day and night and God's wondrous ways in bringing about that change. There are no special prayers for Friday, the weekly day of communal worship, nor for the various holidays.

[1] *Ibid.*, 2:115/109.

[2] *Ibid.*, 2:177/172 "Piety is not that you turn towards East or West, but belief in God and the Last Day... and spending lovingly your possessions for relatives, orphans etc."

[3] Baba Bathra 25a.

We tried to understand why Muhammad kept his liturgical creation so short and simple and why he composed only one and not several formal prayers to be used by his community. We have emphasized that this was not due to any shortcomings on the side of the Prophet, but was done purposely out of consideration for the limited capacity of many of his followers. However what was recommendable during the early years of Islam did not apply to its later stages. How was it possible that prayer, this most central institution of the new religion, did not develop at all? Why did the Arab genius, so prolific in secular poetry, not turn the Muslim service into a grand performance, where ever new poetical creations expressed the eternal religious truths, as well as the specific moods and notions connected with the various times of the day and the night, and the weekly and yearly holidays?

Such questions are suggested by the story of liturgy in the sister religions. When we open a book on Hebrew medieval literature we find as the first and foremost item: religious poetry, and the situation was similar in Greek and Latin letters of that age. Brockelmann's most detailed *Geschichte der arabischen Literatur* does not even contain a chapter about this subject. The Jewish liturgy is usually contained in six volumes, one for the regular service and the other five for the holidays. The Oriental mass, the western Catholic missal, the Protestant prayer books are voluminous creations. The Arab language, one of the richest on earth, does not even have a proper word for (Muslim) "prayer book".

How is this discrepancy between the importance of prayer in Islam and the absence of a liturgy worth speaking of to be explained? As in the case of Muhammad himself we cannot attribute this state to any constitutional deficiency. The Islamic mind was so rich in religious creativeness that it would not have failed to bring forth a new liturgy—had the Muslims craved to do so.

Why was there no urge in Islam to develop a liturgy? Three possible explanations immediately present themselves to the mind. Islamic institutional prayer was complete in all essentials at a very early stage, as we have suggested, already in the Prophet's lifetime. Therefore no one dared to make substantial changes.

Secondly, some of the conditions which induced Muhammad to give to his community such an extremely basic prayertext persisted during the creative centuries of Islam. Millions of new converts unfamiliar with Arabic entered Islam, and since the language-minded Arabs could not imagine that God could properly be addressed except in pure Arabic, a heavy price had to be paid: prayer had to be reduced to a bare minimum of a few sentences which could be easily memorized by non-Arabs.

Thirdly, the Koran itself is the prayer book of Islam. It was intended to be so from the outset (we remember what we have found concerning the prayer assemblies during Muhammad's first Meccan period) and it has remained so ever since. Formally, the Koran is the word of God addressed to man, but it contains many hymnical elements and a considerable number of prayers, either put into the mouth of the prophets mentioned, or spoken by Muhammad (introduced by "Say!" or otherwise), or unconnected with the frame of the Koran as a book of revelation.[1] Thus the reading of the Koran is to a certain extent tantamount to the recitation of a liturgy.

Personal piety, as well as sectarian and popular religious movements in Islam partly sought expression in the composition of prayers and religious poetry. This is particularly true of the pietist and mystical movement of Sufism which is to be credited with some of the most perfect poetical embodiments of religious feelings found in any language. None, however, has been admitted to the official Islamic service, as has happened to outstanding individual creations of poetry in other religions.

In the introductory paragraph to this study testimonies have been quoted to the effect that in modern times, even in Islam, prayer has largely become a habit or a mere show, or has been discontinued altogether. Such "modern times" have occurred previously in human history, in particular in late classical antiquity. The Arabs of the sixth century A.D. were the late heirs of that world, which has been characterized by one of its recent students as "a secularized world despite its abundance of denominations."[2] One of the oldest suras of the Koran speaking of prayer denounces "those who are careless of their prayers and make only a show."[3] As the context indicates, the reference is to the pagan co-citizens of Muhammad and to whatever religious service they held at their holy shrines.[4] Pre-Islamic and early Islamic poetry, the Koran and the biography

[1] As the prayer at the end of sura Two mentioned above, p. 83.

[2] Carl Schneider, *Geistesgeschichte des antiken Christentums*, München 1954, II, p. 311.

[3] Koran 107:4-6.

[4] Cf. *ibid.*, 108:2, where a *ṣalāt*, i.e. a prayer service, is connected with the sacrifice (at the pilgrimage).

of the Prophet prove that it was not a strong religious belief which had to be shattered by the new faith but an almost insuperable wall of indifference and worldliness. Such a wall is going up again and a great circle seems to be nearing completion. Will there be another turn of the wheel?

CHAPTER FOUR

RAMADAN, THE MUSLIM MONTH OF FASTING

The total or partial abstinence from food during certain periods, coupled or not with voluntary self-denial of sexual pleasures, is a practice common to many religions. Even a cursory reader of the Old and New Testaments is aware of the fact how widespread fasting was in ancient Israel, and how many different notions were associated with this custom. Moses, Elijah and Jesus are described as having fasted forty days in preparation for a supernatural apparition.[1] Abstainment from food, or "practicing self-denial", as the new Philadelphia Bible translation has it, was above all regarded as a work of repentance, contrition and atonement.[2] As such it was believed to enhance the efficacy of prayer, and, like any other sacrifice, to ward off evil.[3] Therefore, in times of calamity, public fasts were proclaimed, coupled with prayers for forgiveness and intercession for help.[4] It was also common to fast as a sign of mourning, both for relatives or public leaders, or in commemoration of national disasters.[5]

In the later centuries of the Second Temple, when intense religious feeling had taken possession of large sections of the population, voluntary, supererogatory fasting, freed from whatever magic shackles had been attached to the practice before, was observed by individuals as an act of pure devotion. It is with regard to this form of private fasting that Jesus enjoins that it should not be advertised, but kept secretly, known only to the One for whose sake it was undertaken.[6]

The same and additional motifs for fasting are apparent in post-biblical Judaism and in later Christianity. Public fasting and supplication in times of drought were so common a feature in

[1] Deuteronomy 9:9-10. 1 Kings 19:8. Matthew 4:2.

[2] Leviticus 16:29. *The Torah, A New Translation of the Holy Scriptures*, Jewish Publication Society, Philadelphia, 1962, p. 212.

[3] Jonah 3:7-8. Ezra 8:21. Daniel 9:3. Psalm 35:13.

[4] Jeremiah 36:9. Cf. ibid. 14:11-12.

[5] 1 Samuel 31:13. 2 Samuel 1:12. ibid. 3:35. ibid. 12:20-23. Zechariah 7:3-5. Matthew 9:14-15.

[6] Matthew 6:16-18. A similar Jewish injunction in Shulḥan ʿArukh, Oraḥ Hayyim 565, para. 6.

Palestine that a whole book of the Talmud is devoted to this practice—paralleled by the extensive treatment given by Muslim scholars to the same subject (*istisqā'*). When a famous rabbi wished to be blessed with an apparition of the everliving Prophet Elijah, he fasted for many days, and similar practices were widespread among the Christian monks and saints contemporary with him. The abstention from food in preparation of the holy communion is a general Christian observance, while Lent, or the period of forty weekdays (quadragesima) before Easter combines the ideas of mourning for Christ, of penitence and of preparation for the holiday. Fasts of preparation were also held by various Christian churches before other holidays.[1]

In order to illustrate the great variety of popular beliefs connected with fasting, two other instances are adduced here, one repeatedly referred to in the Talmud and one characteristic of later, mystically inclined, Judaism. Fasting after an ominous dream was regarded as so essential for the dreamer's peace of mind that it was permitted even on the Sabbath, on which, with the exception of the Day of Atonement falling on the Sabbath, no fasting is allowed. Pious people used to celebrate the anniversary of their wedding day by fasting. Since marrying for God's sake was to be rewarded by the forgiveness of one's sins, the wedding day was properly commemorated by an act of penitence.[2]

Outside the two ancient monotheistic religions the emphasis on the various aspects of fasting was different, but most of the types themselves were there. The Babylonians and the Egyptians, the Greeks and the Romans, Brahmans and Jains all practiced fasting, albeit for different reasons and purposes; mourning, atonement, preparation for an apparition or a sacrifice, and in Jainism self-mortification bordering on suicide.[3] The gnostic and astral religions

[1] Cf. E. A. Westermark, "The Principles of Fasting", *Folklore* 18 (1907). Peter Gerlitz, "Das Fasten im religionsgeschichtlichen Vergleich", *Zeitschrift für Religions- und Geistesgeschichte* 7 (1955), pp. 116-126. This article is a summary of a Ph.D. thesis bearing the same title, submitted to the University of Erlangen in 1954. Cf. also "Fasting" in J. Hastings, *Encyclopedia of Religion and Ethics* V, New York, 1951, pp. 759-771 (rich, but antiquated); "Fasten", *Die Religion in Geschichte und Gegenwart II* (1958), pp. 881-886 (modern approach).

[2] Shulḥan 'Arukh, Even ha-'Ezer 61, para. 1, glosses of R. M. Isserles. One has to bear in mind that according to Jewish custom, still observed by the religious, bride and bridegroom fast on the wedding day itself.

[3] Cf. the sources given in Note 1.

of the Manichaeans and the Harranians had a fast in honor of the moon lasting thirty days, but beginning on the eighth, not the first, of a certain month. It is natural that because of its duration this fast has been likened to the Muslim month of Ramadan, which forms the subject of this study.[1]

Comparative religion is certainly to be thanked for providing us with so many examples of the practice and motivation for fasting. It is, however, the concern of the Islamist to define as exactly as possible the specific circumstances under which the great institution of Ramadan came into being as well as to try to find the particular meaning originally given to it by the Prophet and his followers.

FASTING IN PRE-ISLAMIC ARABIA

For this purpose it would be of great value to know whether the Arabs had been familiar with the practice of fasting before Muhammad. Any attempt to answer this question is hampered by the fact that, with the exception of the Koran, all information about the pre-Islamic Arabs is contained in sources committed to writing one hundred and twenty years and more after the advent of Islam. The real picture might have been blurred not only by time, but also by the natural inclination of the traditionists to paint the past in colors congruent with their own ideas. After careful weighing of the evidence available the following facts emerge.

The whole rhythm of life of the pre-Islamic Arabs was regulated by the institution of holy months. Blood feuds, the normal pastime of the bedouin, were prohibited during these months. At the same time, pilgrimages to great sanctuaries, often connected with fairs, provided an outlet for religious feelings and the satisfaction of economic and social needs. The holy months are attested to in the Koran, which takes for granted that the prohibition of fighting for the time of their duration was as valid in Islam as it was in paganism.[2] Many trustworthy references to them are found in pre-Islamic poetry and in the ancient traditions. The holy month called Rajab was kept in spring and three others were observed in the autumn, when the great pilgrimage to the sanctuaries situated in

[1] The literature about this comparison is assembled in Frants Buhl, *Das Leben Muhammeds*, p. 227, notes 71-73.

[2] Koran 9:36. This institution, however, became obsolete in Islam, since war between Muslims is theoretically prohibited altogether, while non-Muslims have to be fought eternally until the world will be dominated by Islam.

the proximity of Mecca took place.[1] There is less certitude concerning an alleged custom of the inhabitants of Mecca to devote one month to solitude and ascetic practices, including almsgiving, although the strange term *taḥannuth* used for it suggests some ancient tradition.[2] In any event, the idea of a holy month was most familiar to the pre-Islamic Arabs (who, by the way, did not have the notion of a week). No foreign model is to be sought for the introduction into Islam of a period of special religious devotion lasting a full month.

As to fasting in pre-Islamic Arabia, the most plausible traditions are those which report that this was done during Rajab, the holy month of the spring. There were still people who observed it during the reign of the second caliph ʿOmar and the latter had those "Rajab-fasters" flogged and coerced them to eat in order that "Rajab should not be like Ramadan."[3] The ancient Arabs, like the ancient Babylonians and Israelites, had two New Years, one in the spring and one in the fall, and, as in Babylonia, the spring month served as a period of purification and penance. As is well known, the prophet Ezekiel wanted to introduce this practice also to the Israelite cult, but was not successful.[4]

Whatever the historical value of these traditions about the pre-

[1] A lunar year consisting of twelve months amounts to approximately 354 days, while the solar year, on which the seasons depend, comprises about 365 days. In order to adapt the lunar to the solar year, from time to time a month has to be added ("intercalated") to the calendar. The Jews do this seven times during nineteen years. The pre-Islamic Arabs had a similar arrangement, but by the time of Muhammad their calendar had become so confused that Muhammad abolished intercalation (Koran 9:37). Spring and Autumn mentioned here refer therefore to the original calendar of the pre-Islamic Arabs, not to its state in the days of the Prophet.

[2] *Ibn Hishām*, ed. Wüstenfeld, p. 152, ed. Cairo 1936, I, p. 251. Critical discussion of this tradition in L. Caetani, *Annali dell'Islam*, Introduzione, Milano, 1905, para. 208-9. The derivation of *taḥannuth* ("abstention from sin") from Hebrew *teḥinnōth*, "private prayers", suggested by H. Hirschfeld, *New Researches etc.*, London, 1902, p. 10, unlikely in itself, is impossible, since the Hebrew word was used in that technical sense only in far later times. The suggestion is mentioned here only because it was revived by W. Montgomery Watt, *Muhammad at Mecca*, Oxford, 1953, p. 44.

[3] Cf. the traditions in Ṭurṭūshī, *al-Ḥawādith wal-Bidaʿ*, ed. M. al-Ṭālibī, Tunis 1959, pp. 129-130, and M. J. Kister's review of this book in *Journal of Semitic Studies* 6 (1961), pp. 139-140, where further sources about the subject are indicated.

[4] Ezekiel 45:18 and 20. Cf. the stimulating essay of A. J. Wensinck, "The Semitic New Year and the Origin of Eschatology", *Acta Orientalia* I (1923), pp. 158-199.

Islamic celebration of the month of Rajab may be, there is little doubt that fasting was widely practiced. Vows of abstinence (from wine, sexual pleasures, and washing and cutting one's hair) were commonplace, and abstention from food was only another form of self-denial. Of particular importance are a number of verses in the Koran in which individual fasting is recommended as a substitute for the non-fulfillment of certain obligations or as a partial atonement for grave sins. A man unable to make the pilgrimage to Mecca owing to illness should 'redeem' the lost opportunity by fasting.[1] Unintentional manslaughter of a person belonging to a tribe with whom the Muslims had a peace treaty should be expiated by a fast of two months.[2] Fasting is prescribed for killing game while being in the sacred state of a pilgrim.[3] A man who had sworn a solemn oath—the so-called *ẓihār*—not to touch his wife, but wished to break it (as recommended by Islam) was given the choice between a fast of two consecutive months and other means of expiation.[4]

These strange provisions found little or no application in later Islam. They are clearly remnants of pre-Islamic practices slightly varied by the spirit of the new religion. The very fact that in two cases: unintentional manslaughter and repudiation of one's wife by the use of a certain oath, a fast of two months was recommended, indicates that the idea of a month of fasting had been familiar to the Arabs.

It is against this background that we have to evaluate the testimony of the Koran and the oral tradition, the Ḥadīth, concerning the establishment of the Ramadanfast.

THE ORAL TRADITIONS ABOUT THE ESTABLISHMENT OF THE RAMADAN

The sections of the Koran which reflect the Prophet's activities in his native city of Mecca do not contain a single provision concerning fasts. This does not necessarily imply that the institution as

[1] Koran 2:196/2. The pre-Islamic word *fidya*, redemption, is used here.
[2] *Ibid.*, 4:92/94. Again *fidya* is used.
[3] *Ibid.*, 5:89/91.
[4] *Ibid.*, 58:4/5. The name of this oath is derived from the formula "you are (unapproachable) like the back (*ẓahr*, i.e. body) of my mother". Islamic law regarded this form of repudiation of one's wife as illegal, cf. J. Schacht, *An Introduction to Islamic Law*, Oxford 1964, p. 165.

such was unknown to Muhammad and his followers. It only means, that, unlike prayer, which manifested adherence to the new faith, fasting was not regarded as anything specifically Islamic and, therefore, did not require legislation promulgated through heavenly message.[1] One early Meccan verse in which an oath is pronounced "by the ten nights" (Koran 89:2) might refer to the ten days of fasting and sexual abstention, the *iʿtikāf*, cf. below.

Things changed when Muhammad came to Medina and found there a large monotheistic community which observed fasting as an act of piety in fulfillment of a written command of God. Now we read in the Koran, Sūra 2:183/179:

"O you true believers, fasting has been written down (as obligatory) upon you, as it was upon those before you, so that you may be pious."

"Written" is to be understood literally, as a comparison with Sura 5:45/49, where Exodus 21:24 is quoted, proves. Fasting was no longer an exercise in personal asceticism, but a deed prescribed by God's law. The word translated as "pious" originally meant "(God) fearing", but had already in pre-Islamic times assumed the general idea of "religious".[2] Thus, the first and foremost motivation of fasting was a precept of God imposed on all those to whom he revealed his will. Consequently, its observance was conducive to the cultivation of a general attitude of religiosity.

The allusion in the Koran to "those before you" is expanded in a great number of oral traditions, which describe how the Prophet originally had commanded his disciples to fast on the day of ʿĀshūrā', observed by the Jews. "When the Prophet came to Medina, he found that the Jews fasted on the ʿĀ. day. (Addition in another version: He said: 'This is a very solemn day'). They were asked about it and replied: this is the day on which God gave Moses and the Children of Israel victory over Pharaoh. Therefore we celebrate it in honor of Moses. (According to a variant: 'Moses fasted on it in gratitude to God'). Upon this the Prophet said: 'I am closer to (or: I have more rights on) Moses than you' and ordered that a

[1] At least in the early years of the prophet's message Muhammad and his flock may well have kept any fasts his countrymen observed just as they did with regard to other religious practices such as sacrifices and the holy pilgrimage.

[2] Cf. H. Ringgren, "Die Gottesfurcht im Koran", *Orientalia Suecana* 2 (1954), pp. 121 and 124, and M. M. Bravmann, "Heroic Motives in Early Arabic Literature", *Der Islam* 36 (1960) pp. 30-1.

fast should be held on that day."[1] A shorter version states: "The Jews kept 'Ā. as a holiday. Said the Prophet: So you too fast on it."[2]

'Āshūrā', Hebrew-Aramaic 'Āsōrā, "the tenth", has rightly been identified with the Jewish day of Atonement, which is observed on the tenth of the month of Tishri, cf. Leviticus 16:29, where the same word is used. It must be remarked, however, that this Biblical designation was not common in post-Biblical, pre-Islamic, Hebrew and Aramaic literature. The term probably owed its revival to the widely attested, and therefore presumably widely diffused custom of fasting during all the "ten days of penitence", beginning with the New Year's day falling on the first of Tishri. Therefore, the Day of Atonement, on which not only "the pious" or "the elected", but everyone fasted, rightly resumed its ancient name of the Tenth.[3]

According to another, also often repeated tradition, attributed to Muhammad's wife 'Ā'isha, "the Quraysh (i.e. the citizens of Mecca) used to fast on the day of 'Āshūrā', and the Prophet did likewise in the Time of Ignorance (i.e. before he received a revelation). Then, when he came to Medina, he fasted on that day and ordered that a fast should be held on it."[4] It has been suggested that this version was invented to refute the traditions mentioned before, in which Muhammad was reported to have followed the model of the Jews. Taken at face value, however, there is no contradiction between the two series of traditions. Both state the basic fact that fasting, as a religious obligation, was introduced into Islam when Muhammad came to Medina.

Two elements stand out in these Muslim traditions about the Jewish 'Āshūrā'. It was a solemn day, a holiday, in other words it was an impressive celebration which did not escape the attention of the followers of the new religion. Secondly, it was associated with Moses, so much so that this very connection justified its acceptance as a Muslim holiday as well.

[1] Bukhārī 30, 69 (ed. Krehl, I, Leiden 1862, p. 498). *Ibid.*, 60, 24 (ed Krehl, II, p. 354). *Ibid.*, 63, 52 (ed. Krehl, III, p. 51) and innumerable parallels. All these traditions are ascribed to 'Abdallah b. 'Abbās, the Prophet's cousin. Cf. Nöldeke-Schwally, *Geschichte des Qorāns* I, Leipzig 1909, p. 179, n. 1. W. M. Watt, *Muhammad at Medina*, Oxford 1956, pp. 199 and 203.

[2] Bukhārī 30, 69. In the name of Abū Mūsā (al-Ash'arī).

[3] About the fasting of the *keshērīm* or *yeḥīdīm* during the first decade of Tishri cf. Leviticus Rabba ch. 30, para. 7, Koheleth Rabba on verse 9:7, Tanhūma Emor 22, Pesiqta, ed. S. Buber, p. 183, Note 91.

[4] Bukhārī 30, 69 (ed. Krehl, I, p. 497, line 8 ff.).

Now any Jew of the seventh century A.D. asked about the meaning of the Day of Atonement would have answered: "This is the day on which Moses completed his second stay of forty days on Mount Sinai and descended, bringing with him the new tables, after having been granted remission and forgiveness for his people in a special manifestation of God. In commemoration of this day, the Fast of the Tenth was instituted."[1] The theophany described in Exodus 34:6-7, where God manifests himself as the compassionate and merciful, forms the nucleus of the penitential prayers (Selīḥōt) which are the most characteristic part of the liturgy of the Day of Atonement.[2]

We remember, of course, that, in the ḥadīth quoted above, another motivation for the Jewish ʿAshūrā was given: Moses' deliverance from and victory over Pharaoh. However, anyone familiar with the technique of the Muslim traditions derived from Jews or Christians is aware of the fact that they more often than not contain fanciful accretions to an authentic core. Muhammad's dictum connected with the ʿA.: "We are closer to (or: have more right to) Moses than you" may well have been genuine and remembered by some of his adherents. The explanation provided for the saying is manifestly spurious.

MOSES, THE DAY OF ATONEMENT AND MUHAMMAD

The Koran itself, however, provides a full and authentic commentary on the claim of Muhammad to be in a particularly close relationship with Moses and the specific connection of Moses with the Day of Atonement. From the very first phase of his prophetic career, when he still used the enigmatic language of the Arabian soothsayers, Muhammad regarded himself as the direct successor of Moses. Suras 52 and 95 begin with an oath by Mount Sinai and the sanctuary of Mecca, the scene of Muhammad's own activity. In two other Meccan suras we read: "Before it (the Koran) there was the book of Moses, given as a guide and an act of mercy, and this is a book confirming it in the Arabic language."[3] The true believers are quoted as testifying about the Koran: "We have heard of a book coming

[1] Cf. Talmud Taʿanith 30b. Baba Bathra 129a. Seder ʿOlam, ch. 6. Pirqē de-Rabbi Eliezer ch. 46.

[2] Cf. I. Elbogen, *Der Jüdische Gottesdienst*, pp. 153 and 222.

[3] Koran 11:17, 46:12.

down from Heaven after the book of Moses."[1] Correspondingly Muhammad's opponents lump the Israelite and Arab prophet together and are reputed to have said: "Two imposters who assist one another; verily, we reject them both." To which Muhammad retorts: "Let them produce a book containing better guidance than these two."[2]

In the chapters of the Koran promulgated in Mecca, Moses is mentioned no less than one hundred and eight times and many of the Biblical accounts about him are reproduced. In the Medinese sura 2, the same that contains the promulgation of the fast of Ramadan, the motifs of the Moses story connected with the Day of Atonement constitute a main topic. Moses' stay on Mount Sinai, the sin of the golden calf, God's forgiving and bestowal of the Book (in this sequence), although recounted already in Mecca extensively,[3] are repeated in sura 2 with much emphasis and with many details betraying familiarity with the Jewish legends embellishing these events.[4] In the following verses, the "Children of Israel" are addressed and they are reminded of all the favors granted to them by God. "And when we called Moses to Us for forty nights[5]; then, after he was away, you made the calf, by which you did wrong. Then We forgave you afterwards, so that you might be grateful. And when We gave Moses the Book and the *furqān* (see below) so that you might be guided. And when Moses said to his people: you have wronged yourselves by making the calf. Therefore, return unto your Creator and slay your own kin.[6] That will be better for you in your Creator's eyes. Then He returned unto you, verily, He is the one who returns, the allmerciful."[7] In this passage, the combina-

[1] *Ibid.*, 46:30.

[2] *Ibid.*, 28:48-49.

[3] Cf., in particular, *ibid.*, 7:142/138-154/153, where the ideas of repentance and forgiveness are very much emphasized.

[4] Cf. Heinrich Speyer, *Die biblischen Erzählungen im Qoran*, Hildesheim 1961, pp. 298-9 and 303-4.

[5] "Nights" in the language of the ancient Arabs includes the days, just as when we say—"ten days" we tacitly include the nights.

[6] Literally: "Your souls". This strange expression, which caused the Muslim commentators great difficulty, finds its explanation in Exodus 32:26-29, where the members of the tribe of Levi slay their own relatives who had worshipped the golden calf.

[7] Koran 2:51/48-54/51. The Arabic word translated here as "return" is taken over from the Aramaic. The phrase as a whole is a replica of Malachi 3:7 and parallel biblical passages: "Return unto Me and I will return unto you." The ten days of penance, culminating in the Day of Atonement, are called "the days of return".

tion of the acts of forgiving and revelation and those of human repentance and God's mercy is clearly evident.

We are now prepared for a discussion of the only, albeit very much involved, section of the Koran dealing with the introduction of Ramadan. For the convenience of the reader, the lengthy section is subdivided into paragraphs and the introductory verse, already quoted above, is repeated here.

Koran 2:183/179 (a) O you true believers, fasting has been written down (as obligatory) upon you, as it was upon those before you, so that you may be pious.

184/180 (b) (Fast) numbered days. (c) If any one of you be sick or on travel, then a number of other days. (d) Those who are able to fast (but do not), may expiate by feeding a poor man. (e) But doing good voluntarily is better and it is better for you to fast, having understanding.

185/181 (f) The month of Ramadan (shall you fast) in which the Koran was sent down as a guidance for the people and as demonstrations of guidance and of the *furqān* (see below). (g) So whoever of you is at home during the month let him fast in it; but whoever is sick or on travel, may fast a number of other days. God wishes to make it easy for you and not hard. So complete the number (of days) and glorify God for his guidance so that you may be grateful.

186/182 (h) And if My servants ask you about Me, verily I am near to answer the call of the caller when he calls upon Me. So may they respond to Me and believe in Me so that they may be on the right way."

The following, very lengthy verse 187/183 contains regulations concerning sexual abstinence during the holy month, to which we shall come back later.

THE MOTIVATION OF THE FAST: FORGIVENESS OF SINS, REVELATION, AND GOD'S DECISION ABOUT MEN'S FATE

As to the motivation of the fast, one is immediately struck by the similarity of Koran 2:186/182 to Isaiah 55:6, which, incidentally, opens the section from the Prophets on Jewish fasts: "Seek the Lord, since he is to be found, *call* upon him, since he is *near*." Litanies in which each line begins with the words "*Answer us*" were repeated endlessly on the Day of Atonement and on other fasts. Behind all this is the idea that the state of self-castigation is best suited for intercession and for the seeking of God's pardon. This concept is echoed in widely different traditions found in most of the canonical collections of Ḥadīth and is well known to the average Muslim even today: "All previous sins are forgiven to one who keeps Ramadan in faith and for God's sake".[1] The value of prayer during the time of fasting is emphasized in an equally popular tradition which becomes fully understandable only in the light of its parallels or antecedents in more ancient monotheistic literature: "When Ramadan comes, the gates of Heaven (or: of Paradise) are opened and the gates of Hell are closed and the Satans are chained".[2]

The notion of the gates of Heaven or of Paradise has a long history. It goes back to the time of the Temple, when prayer used to be said as long as the gates of the Temple stood open, namely in daytime. Hence the solemn prayer at the end of the Day of Atonement: "Open us the gate at the time when the gate is being closed." Thus the idea of the gates of Heaven being open originally means: it is a propitious time for the acceptance of prayer. This is stated expressly with regard to the Ten Days of Penitence, referred to on p. 96: "On the New Year's Day I give judgment... If you do repentance before Me, I shall judge you with mercy, for the gates of Heaven are open and I hear your prayers before signing the judgment on the Day of Atonement."[3] On the Day of Atonement, Satan is not allowed to exercise his usual office of prosecutor.[4] Similarly, according to the Ḥadīth, as we have seen, during Ramadan the Satans are chained. It is a time when prayers for forgiveness have unimpeded access.

The reason for the fixation of the period of fasting during Ramadan was its being the month "in which the Koran was sent down", cf. the passage quoted above (f). To be sure, the Koran, the book designated by this name, was promulgated in the course of twenty years or more. Here, however, no doubt the reference is to Muhammad's first revelation, the month of whose occurrence he remembered, but not the day. Definite allusions to this unique event are found in other parts of the Koran, as we shall presently see.

[1] Bukhārī 30,6 and 31,1. Nasā'ī 22, 39. Tirmidhī 6,1. Cf. A. J. Wensinck, *Handbook of Early Muhammadan Tradition*, Leiden 1927, p. 202b under "fasting (and praying) in R(amadan) causes forgiveness of sins."

The translation "for God's sake" renders *iḥtisāban*, doing something for no other purposes except in anticipation of God's reward.

[2] Bukhārī 30,5 and 59,11. Muslim 3, 121. Tirmidhī 6,1.

[3] Pesiqta, ed. S. Buber, ch. 24, p. 156b.

[4] *Ibid.*, ch. 27, p. 176a. Talmud Yoma, 20a.

The institution of a fast in commemoration of the "coming down" of the heavenly Book seems strange in itself, but finds its full explanation in Muhammad's claim on his close relationship with Moses, made in connection with the ʿĀshūrā, cf. p. 95. The Day of Atonement, the solemn day of fasting, which made such an impression on the Muslims arriving in Medina, was dedicated to Moses' descending from Mount Sinai with the tables. There was a direct link between the fast and the tables. The fast commemorated the theophany in which God manifested his grace and mercy. Only after Israel's sin of the golden calf was remitted, was it ready and worthy to receive the word of God. Once this association between revelation and fast was established, it was not unnatural to transfer it to another religion.

In both the passages about the Ramadan (Koran 2:185/1) and in the story of Moses (*ibid.*, verse 53/50; also 21:49/48) the book sent from Heaven is characterized as *furqān*, a term which has given much trouble to the ancient Muslim and even more to the modern scholars. The latter were inclined to derive at least some of its supposed meanings from the Hebrew and Aramaic *purqān*, redemption, delivery or *pirqīn*, study of the Holy Scripture or both.[1] While it is probable that the term *purqān*, redemption, which was so common among Christians and Jews, entered the language of the Arabs at some time, Muhammad himself clearly understood it in the general sense of something bestowed by God and as derived from the Arabic root *frq*, to distinguish, to discern.[2] He uses this root in an important testimony about his prophetical experience which is apt to throw additional light on the origin of Ramadan and its nature.

In four passages of the Koran the Prophet alludes to the unique experience which marked the beginning of his prophetic mission. In two suras, 44 and 97, it happened on a particularly blessed night;

[1] In words taken over from a foreign language, Arabic, which has no *p*, replaces this sound by *f*. Detailed, but inconclusive discussion of *furqān* in J. Horovitz, "Jewish Proper Names and Derivatives in the Koran," *Hebrew Union College Annual II* (1925), pp. 216-218, and A. Jeffery, *The Foreign Vocabulary of the Qur'an*, Baroda 1938, pp. 225-229. J. J. Rivlin, "Al-furqān in the Q':", *Tarbiz* 23 (1952), pp. 160-169, regards the word as purely Arabic.

The blessing for the scholars, repeated in the Qaddīsh prayer of the synagogue at least twice every day, concludes with the request for *purqānā*, redemption.

[2] Namely between truth and falsehood or the just and their adversaries, cf. Jeffery (see preceding note), p. 226.

in a third, 81:23, the angel transmitting the revelation was seen "on the clear horizon", obviously at the dawn following that night, while the fourth, 53:1-11, which opens with an oath "by the setting star" and describes the angel as standing "on the highest horizon", reflects the same vision.

Sura 44 begins as follows: "By the clear Book! We sent it down in a blessed night... in which every determined thing is discerned (or: decided, *yufraq*) as an order from Us. We are sending prophets as an act of mercy." We have here the ancient Middle Eastern idea that on a certain date in the year (usually on New Year) God decrees life or death for all his creatures and writes this decision down in a heavenly book. There existed another book in Heaven containing God's commandments and teachings, communicated through the prophets to mankind. According to his own testimony, Muhammad started his mission on the night of God's decrees and, throughout the Koran, the two ideas of the Book of Decrees and the Book of Teachings are combined (or confused). The connection between the two is evident even in the rather mysterious and abrupt passage translated above: the revelation of God's laws is an act of mercy, since their observance might change his decree to the good. Thus, the idea that Moses' descent from Mount Sinai with the tables should have coincided with the Day of Atonement when God's judgments are signed and sealed, which Muhammad seems to have learned when he arrived in Medina, was essentially nothing new to him. The novelty was only that such an event should be commemorated by fasting. Consequently, Muhammad's first receiving of a portion of the heavenly book of teachings which coincided with the night of the decisions was to be celebrated in the same way.

The Koran thus contins two indications as to the time of "the descent of the Book": the month of Ramadan and the blessed night of God's decrees, but gives no additional specification as to the exact date. As a matter of fact, there is no absolute consensus among the Muslims as to which night of the Ramadan was meant, although preference is given to one of the nights of the last ten days. It is almost certain that in pre-Islamic times the same situation prevailed, namely that popular belief did not fix the night of the decrees on a specific date, but ascribed it to the month of Ramadan in general, or as the Muslims later on did, to one of its three thirds, preferably the last.

THE I'TIKĀF AND THE "NUMBERED DAYS"

The singling out of a certain period within Ramadan as particularly holy must be pre-Islamic, since the Koran refers to it as already existent and with a technical term. Sura 2:187/183 permits sexual relations during the nights of Ramadan with exception of the time *wa'antum 'ākifūna fi 'l-masājidi*, "when you practice seclusion in the mosques." The verb *'kf* is frequently used in the Koran as a designation for a kind of worship practiced by idolators before their graven images, and also with reference to the adoration of the Ka'ba of Mecca.[1] In ancient Arabic poetry it occurs in connection with the presence of the worshippers at a sacrifice or at the ceremony of "standing" on the holy Mount 'Arafāt.[2] The original meaning of the word is "to be and to remain in the proximity of someone" as a horse standing over a dead man[3] or birds of prey circling around him.[4] Islam has no visible symbols of the presence of God except mosques. Therefore, seclusion in a mosque replaced pre-Islamic "staying with one's idol". This seclusion, called *I'tikāf* (from *'kf*), usually lasts ten days and is mostly observed during the last third of Ramadan, although ancient traditions state that it was originally held in the first, or, according to others, in the second.[5] The *I'tikāf* was finally established during the last third of Ramadan because the Night of the Decrees was supposed to occur in that period, although opinion differed on this point too, some authorities maintaining that it could fall on any night of the holy month.[6]

In addition to a month and a day we have thus a lapse of ten days as another period of particular holiness. This may be pre-Islamic,

1 Koran 7:138/134. 21:52/53. 26:71. With reference to the golden calf: 20:91/93, to the Ka'ba: 2:125/119.

2 Cf. Yāqūt, *Geographical Dictionary*, ed. Wüstenfeld III, p. 182, 1. 2, Kumait, ed. J. Horovitz, Leiden 1904, No. 3, verse 48. Naķā'id, ed. A. A. Bevan, Leiden 1905, p. 62, 1. 30.

3 'Abīd b. al-Abras, ed. Ch. Lyall, No. 4, v. 10 and 14. Aghānī[1] IV, p. 148, l.4.

4 Ṭarafa, No. 14, v. 22. Imru 'ul-qays No. 62, v. 5, both in W. Ahlwardt, *Six Ancient Poets*, London 1870. Naķā'id (see Note 2) 62, l. 35. I owe the references in Notes 2-4 to the Concordance of Ancient Arabic Poetry, prepared by the Institute for Asian and African Studies of the Hebrew University, Jerusalem.

5 Bukhārī 10, 135. 32,2. 33,1c. 9, 13. So most of the traditions noted in Wensinck, *Handbook* (see p. 100), p. 202b: "Prayer and ascetism in the last (ten) nights of Ramadan", *ibid.*, 206b: "Retreat of Muhammad in R.". For the date of the Night of the Decrees see also Bukhārī 32, 3-4 and 2, 36.

6 Tabarī, *Tafsīr* XXX, p. 167, and others.

since an early sura of the Koran opens with an oath by the ten nights, cf. above, p. 95, and since in a provision regarding the originally pagan ceremony of the pilgrimage a fast totalling ten days is prescribed as a substitute for the obligatory sacrifice.[1] Attention is also drawn to a most remarkable statement made in sura 7:132/138 with regard to Moses' stay on Mount Sinai: "We called Moses to us for thirty nights and completed them by ten others, thus the meeting with his lord lasted altogether forty nights." This sounds as if Muhammad wanted to make plausible the duration of the theophany granted to Moses as a combination of two holy periods with which he and his compatriots were familiar. The concept of Moses' stay on Mount Sinai as a period of thirty plus ten days is suggested of course also by the Jewish month of Elul, which is followed by the ten days of penance, during which, as stated on p. 96, pious people used to fast. To this should be added that particularly devout Jews fasted during the whole period of forty days from the first of Elul to the Day of Atonement during which Moses was believed to have abstained from food.[2]

These facts and considerations are apt to throw light on the enigmatic verse 2:184/180, which contains the first precept about fasting in Islam, cf. p. 99. "Numbered days" may mean "a few days" as the Muslim commentators observe, but the verse certainly does not imply that the number itself was left to the choice of each individual. For the detailed injunctions for the replacement of fast days missed, (ibid., paragraphs *c-e*), which are partly repeated in verse 185/181 after the institution of the Ramadan, indicate that a certain period was observed in common by all Muslims. It is quite likely that this was a period of ten days, for which the ten days of penance of the Jews and most probably also pre-Islamic Arab customs formed a precedent, and which lived on in Islam in the rite of the *Iʿtikāf*.

[1] Koran 2:196/192. This is, by the way, a beautiful illustration of the ancient idea that fasting ("diminishing one's flesh and blood", as the Hebrew phrase goes) fulfills the same task of self-denial as a sacrifice.

[2] Elia Zutta, ed. M. Friedman, Vienna 1901, IV, 180. Cf. also L. Zunz, *Die Synagogale Poesie des Mittelalters*, Frankfurt 1920, p. 82. In Morocco and Bukhara (Central Asia) this fast of forty days was kept by pious old people even in this century.

THE CHRONOLOGY OF THE INTRODUCTION OF THE RAMADAN

The various stages of the early development of obligatory fasting in Islam fit well into the chronological scheme of Muhammad's activities after his "flight" from his native city of Mecca. At the time of his arrival in Medina in September 622, the Jews celebrated their Day of Atonement, and after learning about its motivation he ordered his followers to keep the day.[1] This order is recorded in the Muslim oral tradition, but not in the Koran for the simple reason that Muhammad did not regard it as a word of God and consequently did not include it in the book from Heaven. He became, however, convinced that the commandment of fasting belonged to a revealed religion and ordered for his community a fast during "a few days", most probably ten. The number was not stated expressly in the Koran, because Muhammad did not yet have the prophetic certainty as to the details. This second step might have occurred at any time during the first or in the early months of the second year of his stay in Medina. We have here the same state of wavering which is to be observed with regard to the *qibla*, or the point toward which Muslims should turn during prayer. Then, "one month after the change of the *qibla* (from Jerusalem or elsewhere to Mecca), eighteen months after the Flight",[2] came the illumination, the absolute certitude. Like all other observances of Islam, fasting had to be related to something specifically Arabic and Muhammadan. The definitely

[1] The Muslim sources seem to be unanimous in assuming that Muhammad arrived in Medina in the month of Rabīʿ I, which began on September 13 (or 12), but disagree with regard to the day (the second, eighth and twelfth respectively are mentioned.) The twelfth of Rabīʿ I was the date of Muhammad's death. According to a motif found also in Jewish legend, in particular with regard to Moses (see L. Ginzberg, *The Legends of the Jews*, Philadelphia 1925, III, p. 397, Note 44) the righteous die on the anniversary of their birth day. Correspondingly, Rabīʿ I, 12 was regarded as the Prophet's day of birth, and according to some also of the two decisive events in his life, the beginning of his prophetical message and of his "Flight". The Jewish Day of Atonement fell in September 622 A.D.

When the great Muslim chronologist Birūnī (died approximately 1050) states that Muhammad arrived in Medina at the time when the Jews celebrated their Day of Atonement, he explained the tradition quoted above, p. 95 in the light of his astronomical calculation. For the sources cf. EI[1], s.v. "Hidjra" (by B. Carra de Vaux).

[2] Ibn Saʿd, ed. Sachau *et al.*, I, part II (Leiden 1917), p. 8. While we have of course no means to check the exactitude of Ibn Saʿd's date, it certainly conforms with the sequence of events suggested by the Koran and the trustworthy traditions.

fixed fast was not to commemorate Moses but Muhammad, and it was extended to a month, the unit of a period of holiness most familiar to the Arabs.

RAMADAN IN SAUDI ARABIA OF 1918

What Ramadan means to the Muslim could best be observed by an outsider in Arabia itself and at a time when the impact of modern scientific and technical civilization was not yet felt. In his *Arabia of the Wahhabis*,[1] H. St. J. B. Philby gives an excellent picture of the Muslim month of fasting as it was celebrated in the capital of Saudi Arabia in the summer of 1918. In that year, Ramadan coincided with the hottest, driest and dustiest season of the year and required abstinence from food and drink during a full fifteen and a half hours every day. The nights were not passed in feasting and popular amusements as was the case in many other cities of Islam even during the Middle Ages, but in prayer and recitations from the Koran. The last ten days were observed with particular solemnity because they were believed to be the choicest section of the month, containing the "Night of Glory, which releases from Hell". During these nights a further item was added to the usual exercises, the *Qiyām*,[2] consisting of genuflections and prostrations terribly prolonged, often for as long as a quarter of an hour at a time and so exhausting that human frailty had to be supported in the intervals between each set by coffee and tea actually served within the precincts of the mosque. In general, it was explained to Philby, bodily abstinence was regarded as a means of purification of the soul for admission to Paradise.

RAMADAN IN CAIRO, 1836, 1956 AND 1963

Turning from the heartland of Arabia to Cairo, the most westernized of the great capitals of the Islamic world, we find as early as 1836, E. W. Lane making the following remarkable statement in his classic *The Modern Egyptians*: "The modern Muslims seem to regard the fast of Ramadan as of more importance than any other religious

[1] London 1928, pp. 3-7, 11-13.

[2] *Qiyām* is a common term for night prayer during Ramadan, found in the Ḥadīth and other religious writings. Philby translates "Resurrection prayer". It is not clear whether this explanation was given to him by a Muslim friend or is his own (and wrong) interpretation.

act, for many of them keep the fast who neglect their daily prayers; and even those who break the fast, with very few exceptions, pretend to keep it."[1]

The same observation was made one hundred and twenty years later in the detailed and meritorious analysis of Ramadan as it was celebrated in the capital of Egypt in the spring of 1956, written by J. Jomier and J. Corbin.[2] The authors quote copiously from broadcasts and newspapers, as well as from articles in journals and lectures, and register their own observations and those conveyed to them by others. On the negative side they note a complete absence of the feelings of contrition and penitence. The fast is definitely not regarded as an act of atonement.[3] Its main motivation seemed to be that Ramadan is a commandment of God given to his true believers and that its keeping, requiring great will power, constituted a victory of the spirit over the body. "It is a month of collective pride."[4] Since it is the time of the revelation of the Koran, the reading of the holy book was highly recommended, which found its expression e.g. in the fact that radio Cairo devoted two hours and a half every day to Koran readings (as against one hour during the rest of the year). Similarly, religious questions in general were discussed more frequently than at other times. Since fasting united the whole Islamic world, "from Dakar to Jakarta", Ramadan also offered an opportunity for the manifestation of the unity of Islam and the commemoration of its victories on the battlefield over the unbelievers during that month. On the other hand, the *Iʿtikāf*, the seclusion and continence which used to be practiced during the last ten days of Ramadan, seemed to have fallen into desuetude entirely.

The great dilemma facing a modern society trying to keep Ramadan is the impossibility to carry out—quantitatively and qualitatively—a full work load while fasting. In Cairo in 1956, the government officials worked only four hours per day, from 10 a.m. to 2 p.m. The factories, too, started work late, trying to make good the lost hours by overtime in the subsequent month.[5] However the calls for

[1] Ch. III, p. 93-4, in Everyman's Library No. 315. The description of the Ramadan itself is included in Ch. XXV, pp. 478-486.

[2] "Le Ramadan, au Caire, en 1956", *Institut Dominicain d'Études Orientales, Mélanges* 3, 1956, pp. 1-74.

[3] Cf. especially *ibid.*, pp. 14 and 38-40.

[4] *Ibid.*, p. 26.

[5] *Ibid.*, p. 19. The fasters used to sleep after the breakfast, which must be taken before dawn, as well as in the afternoon. Thus only the hours around noon, albeit unsuitable because of the heat, remain for work.

reform, published by a professor of Al-Azhar University in 1955 and 1956 (and a few years later by the President of Tunisia, Bourguiba) made little headway. Many sections of the population of Cairo, especially of the richer quarter of the city, disregard Ramadan in practice, but would not care or dare to fight against it in theory. For the time being, the fast of Ramadan is firmly entrenched. Precisely because of its interference with the normal course of life it manifests most conspicuously the might of religion.

It is, however, natural that the men of religion themselves should feel most poignantly the unsatisfactory state of fasting as it is celebrated today. Aḥmad Ḥasan al-Zayyāt, the editor of the magazine of Al-Azhar University in Cairo, makes the following bitter comments in an editorial devoted to the Ramadan of 1963. We do not have any more thirty days of fasting, but thirty days of breaking the fast. For people nowadays spend the nights at the table and daytime in bed. Fasting is being kept not out of religiosity, but as sheer habit.[1] The writer then recalls with nostalgia how once people used to fast in the villages of Egypt and concludes with a cry of despair: "Only God knows what the capitalist civilization and scientific materialism have in store for the spirituality which reveals itself in fasting and for the religious fervor which is embodied in the faster."[2]

Summary

Our study of this great institution has brought out the following main points:

1. The pre-Islamic Arabs were familiar with the idea of holy months as well as with fasting. Certain passages in the Koran and some Muslim oral traditions make it likely that even the practice of fasting during a whole month was known to the ancient Arabs.

2. Muhammad may have kept some fasts even before his exodus from Mecca, just as he observed other religious practices customary to his native city.

3. His arrival in Medina in September 622 coincided with the Jewish Day of Atonement, which was a solemn and impressive affair. It was explained to him as the day of Moses. According to

[1] The same term *taqwā* is used as that discussed above p. 95. Habit translates *taqlīd*.

[2] *Majallat al-Azhar* 1963, pp. 757-760.

Jewish religious lore, Moses descended on the Day of Atonement from Mount Sinai with the new tables after having obtained forgiveness for the sin of the golden calf.

4. The story of Moses' stay on Mount Sinai during thirty plus ten days, his receiving of the Torah and intercession for the Children of Israel, forms a main topic in sura 2, the same that contains the passage about the introduction of the Ramadan.

5. Three motivations for the fast emerge from that passage: it is commanded by God and obligatory for the Muslims as it was "for those preceding you"; the month of Ramadan is the period in which the Koran was revealed: God "is near, answering the call of the callers when he calls", a phrase reminiscent of Isaiah 55:6, which opens the section from the Prophets on the Jewish days of fast. The idea of forgiveness, which is implied in the phrase of the answering God, is expressly combined with Ramadan in Muslim oral tradition.

6. In the first, formative year in Medina, a fast of "a few days" was instituted, presumably of ten, which lived on in the *I'tikāf*, the ten days of seclusion practiced by the pious during Ramadan. This *I'tikāf* has pre-Islamic antecedents, but possibly had some connection with the Jewish ten days of penance culminating in the Day of Atonement, which was called in the Muslim oral tradition by the Hebrew-Aramaic term '*'Āshurā*', "the tenth".

7. Muhammad certainly remembered that he had his first revelation in Ramadan. By establishing Ramadan as the fast, he adopted the pattern of the Jewish Day of Atonement which combined the ideas of the "descent" of the tables and God's forgiveness with the obligation of fasting.

8. Throughout the Koran, the revelation of God's message to men is regarded as an act of mercy and, consequently, in Muslim oral tradition, Ramadan, "when the gates of Heaven stand open", is the appropriate time for intercession.

9. It is natural that the motivation and practices of fasting should change with changes in the religious climate. While in Arabia of 1918 the basic attitude toward Ramadan and its observance seem to have been much the same as those apparent in the ancient sources, the ideas and customs connected with the fast as reported in Cairo in 1956 were tangibly different. Still, Ramadan was more generally kept than prayer—and the same observation was made by E. W. Lane already in 1836. Prayer requires a personal relationship to God to a far higher degree than abstention from food, which may be

motivated and rationalized in many different ways. Therefore, in a period in which religious fervor has been on the wane, the Ramadan, which is mentioned only in one single passage of the Koran, has remained far more popular with the modern Muslims than prayer, although the latter pervades the holy scripture of Islam from beginning to end.

CHAPTER FIVE

THE ORIGIN AND NATURE OF THE MUSLIM FRIDAY WORSHIP

The idea of a weekly day of rest is taken for granted by modern man. It appears to him so natural that he is hardly aware of the fact that it was largely founded on essentially religious, rather than rational, conceptions; that it took hundreds of years of severe, sometimes abstruse, practices to put it into effect even within the Jewish community, in which it originated; and that this legacy of Judaism in Christianity was adopted by the major part of humanity only in the wake of modern social legislation.

Likewise, it is not always realized that Friday, the Muslim weekly holy day, is essentially different from the Jewish Sabbath or the Christian Sunday. It is not at all a day of rest, but one of obligatory public worship, held at noon, the most characteristic part of which is a sermon consisting of two sections.[1]

Therefore, on inquiring into the origin and nature of the Muslim Friday worship, it would not be correct to assume that the founder of Islam merely followed the example of the other religions, although it was certainly natural for him and his successors to do so with

[1] Recently, various Muslim states have made Friday an official day of rest. However, this was done in response to the exigencies of modern life and in imitation of Western precedent. It is significant to note in this respect that Kemal Atatürk's Turkish republic made Sunday, and not Friday, its official weekly day of rest, cf. also below p. 125. To be sure, sporadic cases of closing the Government offices on Friday occurred also in the times of the Caliphs. Thus the Caliph al-Muʿtadid is reported to have ordered to close the offices on Friday and on Tuesday, "on Friday, because it was the day of prayer and because he loved that day, since his tutor used to free him on Friday from his lessons; and on Tuesday, so that the officials would have time to rest and to look after their own affairs." A. Mez, *Die Renaissance des Islams*, Heidelberg 1922, p. 79. Al-Jahshiyārī, *Kitāb al-Wuzarā* p. 141, reports that the Government offices were closed on Thursday and Friday.

A query submitted to Moses Maimonides around 1190 speaks of Jewish and Muslim silversmiths and glassmakers forming partnerships. The Muslims received the gains made on Saturday and the Jews those made on Friday, obviously because the Muslims did not work on that day; cf. below p. 270.

It is most characteristic for the Muslim conception of the weekly day of worship that out of these ancient usages there developed no general day of rest.

regard to certain aspects of the holiday. Thus an ancient tradition has the Muslims say: "The Jews have every seventh day a day when they get together (for prayer), and so do the Christians; therefore, let us do the same."[1]

As might be expected, there exists no authentic and complete account of the establishment of this most important institution of Islam in the ancient sources. The only passage of the Koran which refers to it (see below), supposes it to be already in existence. On the other hand, the various reports about its beginnings by Muhammad's Muslim biographers, such as Ibn Sa'd and Ibn Hishām, or found in the compilations of Ḥadīth, or oral tradition, are only too patently tendentious and highly contradictory.[2]

Nevertheless, a number of facts about the origin of the Friday service emerge clearly from those accounts: (1) There was no Friday service in Mecca, the caravan city in which Muhammad began his prophetic career. Ṭabarī, in his *Annals*, part 1, p. 1256, l. 20, says so expressly, while all the other sources confirm this fact by implication.[3] (2) Public worship was held by the new Muslims, at their own initiative, in Medina even before Muhammad arrived there in 622 and made it his permanent domicile, but it was Muhammad who ordered that it should be held regularly on Friday. (3) Some sort of address (rather than sermon) used to be made at that gathering, although the ancient sources do not contain any reliable information as to the regularity and contents of those speeches.[4] (4) The ancient accounts of the establishment of the Muslim weekly holiday indicate only one connection between it and that of the preceding religions: the instruction given by Muhammad to his representative in Medina

[1] Al-Qasṭallānī II, 176, ult., quoted by A. J. Wensinck, *Mohammed en de Joden te Medina*, Leiden 1908, CXII. The part of Wensinck's study which deals with the borrowings of the Muslim from the Jewish cult has been translated from Dutch into French by G. H. Bousquet and G. W. Bousquet-Mirandolle, under the title "L'influence juive sur les origins du culte musulman" in *Revue Africaine* 98 (1954), 85-112.

[2] These reports have been studied by Wensinck in his thesis, quoted in the previous note and discussed thoroughly by C. H. Becker in his study of the development of the Muslim worship, *Islamstudien* I, 476 ff. (published previously in *Der Islam* 3 (1912), 374-399). Cf. also Franz Buhl, *Das Leben Muhammeds*, Leipzig 1930, 214-5, and W. Montgomery Watt, *Muhammad at Medina*, Oxford 1956, 198.

[3] That a late author should depict Muhammad as preaching to his tribesmen in Mecca, on that day, of course, is of no consequence. Cf. *Lisān al-'Arab*, 1300 H, II, 82-83 s.v. *'rb*. See also below page 117.

[4] The material about this question has been collected and discussed by A. J. Wensinck in the article *Khuṭba* in EI[1].

to hold the public service on the day when the Jews bought their provisions for their Sabbath.[1]

The key to an understanding of the question which occupies us is the right interpretation of the reference to the Jewish Sabbath made in Muhammad's instruction. The authors mentioned above, page 112, Wensinck, Becker, Buhl and Watt, see in it a general dependence of the Prophet on the Jewish example. Others, like the Nestor of the French orientalists, in his new book on Muhammad, explain it as just another indication of his endeavors to win the Jews over, and assume that Muhammad intended originally to hold the weekly worship on Saturday itself.[2] Contrariwise, some regard the choice of Friday as a deliberate act of opposition to the older religions.[3]

However, unbiased reading of the passage under discussion[4] shows that it betrays neither a polemical tendency against the Jews nor dependence on them. The day was chosen for the simple reason that on it, "the Jews bought their provisions for their Sabbath," i.e., it was the weekly market-day of the oasis of Medina; everybody was present, and it was, thus, a natural occasion for bringing people together for the purpose of prayer and admonition.

That Friday was the weekly Jewish market-day everywhere, except in big cities, is known from Talmudic sources.[5] It is indeed

[1] Ibn Sa'd, III, part 1 (not part 2, as is printed erroneously in C. H. Becker, *Islamstudien* 1, 477, note 3, following Wensinck, *Moh. en de Joden*, 111 sq., where the same misprint occurs), p. 83, has *yajharu*, which means "make public". The Jews used to blow the shōfār horn on Friday afternoon in order to call everybody's attention to the approaching Sabbath (which begins on Friday afternoon, approximately an hour before nightfall). Cf. Talmud Babli, Hullin fol. 26b. A later source (*Kāshānī, Badā'i al-ṣanā'ī*, Cairo, 1327/8, 1, 268, cf. Becker, l.c.) reads here *yatajahhazu*, "buy provisions". Whatever the original reading, the meaning is one: on the eve of Sabbath. It is, however, almost sure that Ibn Sa'd, too, had originally *yatajahhazu*, as Becker suggests, or rather *tajahhazu* (Franz Rosenthal in a letter to the present writer).

[2] M. Gaudefroy-Demombynes, *Mahomet*, Paris 1957, 522. The late author was ninety-four, when he published this voluminous book.

[3] D. S. Margoliouth: "Since the Christians had seized the day after the Saturday, he had no choice (!) but to take the day before it", *Mohammed*, London-NewYork 1905, 248-9. Such argumentation reminds one of medieval polemics, such as actually found in Simon b. Zemah Duran's (1361-1444) writings on Islam, or in the lines of the famous Hebrew poet, Judah ha-Levi: "Like ladies-in-waiting, who surround their queen, Friday precedes and Sunday follows queen Sabbath." *Diwān*, vol. IV (Berlin 1930), p. 3.

[4] Ibn Sa'd, III, part 1, p. 83 and parallels, see above note 1.

[5] Tosefta, *Baba Meṣi'a*, ch. 3 para. 20; ed. Zuckermandel, page 377, line 30: The market (Hebrew shūq, Arab. sūq) is held in smaller towns on Friday.

natural that people should do their marketing on the eve of the weekly holiday. A striking parallel to this phenomenon is the present day Muslim Thursday market in that part of Arabia which is least touched by foreign influences: the borderland between Ḥijāz and Yemen. Of that country, we possess a detailed description in H. St. J. B. Philby's masterly *Arabian Highlands* (Cornell University Press 1952), in which one may count no less than six such Thursday markets.[1]

In one district, the famous Najran oasis, they have two weekly market-days, one on Monday and the other on Thursday. However, the latter, Philby, l.c. 274, says "was always more lively... because it was the custom here as elsewhere for families to have their week-end joints on Friday (the Muslim holy day and holiday) and the Thursday market provided excellent opportunities of laying in the necessary stores and also of collecting guests, if desired. At any rate, it seemed on this Thursday as if the whole population of Najran must be gathered here in the enormous space over which the multifarious activities of the market were spread."

The Jewish Friday market possibly had behind it a longer history. For it is reported[2] that Friday was the weekly market-day in the great Phoenician mercantile center of Sidon. In any case, it lies in the nature of the eve of a holiday that no special religious service was connected with it. There were, however, in antiquity other Jewish market-days which were used for public prayer and scripture readings, and which form, thus, a telling illustration and parallel of Muhammad's creation. In the large, fortified cities, markets were held on Mondays and Thursdays; people from all over the country

Further literature in S. Krauss, *Talmudische Archaeologie*, Leipzig 1911, II, p. 690, note 340. Cf. also G. Allon, Tarbiz 4 (1934), 290, to which Dr. E. Urbach kindly drew my attention.

[1] In Nimran, p. 36; Najran, p. 233, 238, 274-5; Mushait, p. 130; Dhahran, p. 387; ʿAiban, 485-7; Khauba, 597. In Yemen, of course, there exist numerous Thursday markets. One, the Sūq al-Khamīs, on the highroad between the Red Sea and the capital (between Manākha and Sanʿā) has developed into a fullfledged town bearing that name. The weekly market-days of Yemen are discussed best in E. Brauer, *Ethnologie der Jemenitischen Juden*, Heidelberg 1934, 255-258.

[2] Talmud Babli, *Pesaḥim*, 50b, at the bottom of the page. Quoted by Krauss, l.c. It may well be, however, that there is no connection between these Phoenician and the Jewish market-days. As may be remarked in passing, it is a remainder of the ancient custom that in Western countries, where women usually do the shopping, pious Jews would go on Friday, immediately after the morning prayer, and buy at least some of the food for the Sabbath .g. a fish).

streamed into the cities to buy and sell, as well as for any other business restricted to the provincial or district capital, such as visiting government offices. Therefore, the Jewish courts of law used to meet on Mondays and Thursdays—a custom observed in the East almost down to the end of the Middle Ages, which is proved by many legal deeds and court records preserved in the Cairo Geniza and made out on those days of the week.[1]

The Jewish legislator seized this opportunity for taking hold of the population of the open country and for providing it with religious education. Public services, in which a portion of the scripture was read, were held on Mondays and Thursdays, and these days were also recommended for—of course, non-obligatory—fasting.[2] Many hundreds of years after these days had ceased to be market-days, they retained their religious character as days of public readings from the Pentateuch and of facultative fasting, and, in the East, as we have seen, also of the meeting of the rabbinical courts.

It is significant—although it may be a mere coincidence—that in the oasis of Najran, where Jews had been living from ancient times up till 1949, when they emigrated to Israel—the weekly markets were being held on Monday and Thursday, see above p. 114. It is even more interesting, from the sociological point of view, that judgments were given there on these days. Let us hear Philby again:

"Market days were always busy occasions for the Amir, who sat all the morning in public audience as a court of summary jurisdiction to hear the plaints and claims of anybody who cared to avail himself of such facilities."[3]

Philby's descriptions of the market-days in Najran serve, thus, as a vivid illustration of the Jewish market-days of old, as they were held in the capitals of districts or provinces. These days are a striking example of originally secular gatherings which began to be used, in time, for worship and instruction and, finally, became a purely religious institution. As such—it may be mentioned in pass-

[1] Cf. S. D. Goitein, *Jews and Arabs, their Contacts through the Ages*, New York, Schocken Books, 1964, p. 179 f.

[2] The combination of fasting with the market-day is old. On days of public fasting, people from all over the country gathered in the capital, Jeremiah 36:9. Isaiah's famous speech about the fast in chap. 58, in particular, verses 3-4, can be understood only from this aspect; "On the day of your fast you pursue business and exact money from needy debtors."

[3] *Arabian Highlands*, pp. 312-313.

ing—they were adopted by Islam, where Monday and Thursday were recommended as days for supererogatory fasting and on which pious or bigot rulers, such as the famous Saladin or the Mamluk Sultan al-Malik al-Nāṣir, held public courts of justice in person.

If, as we have concluded from Ibn Sa'd's account, Friday was chosen by Muhammad as the weekly day of worship, because it was the market-day of the oasis of Medina, one may ask, why does the account not say so expressly and, instead, speaks of the day on which the Jews buy their provisions for the Sabbath? This brings us to a topic treated at length by the Muslim antiquarians and often referred to in modern books on Arab literature and history: the pre-Islamic fairs and markets of the Arabs. Lately, Robert Brunschvig has dealt with it in the broader context of the history of the Islamic fairs in general.[1]

Our sources are full of accounts of yearly fairs taking place around sanctuaries and during holy months, in which no blood was shed and which alone safeguarded the peaceful intercourse of the Arab tribes, normally at loggerheads with each other. On the other hand, weekly market-days were not a practical proposition for the majority of the population of North Arabia, which consisted either of bedouin or of merchants. The distances were too great and the products handled not of the perishable type of small consumer goods. It was, therefore, quite natural for Muhammad, the son of the merchants' city of Mecca, not to use the word *sūq*, which carried the connotation of the great yearly fairs, for the Friday market of Medina, a conglomerate of agricultural settlements, but to circumscribe it clumsily as the day when the Jews bought their provisions for their Sabbath. One has also to bear in mind that, in those times, the sūq of the Jewish "tribe" of the Banū Qainuqā' served as the market for the whole oasis of Medina, cf. J. Wellhausen, *Medina vor dem Islam*, Berlin 1889, p. 10, note 4.

There are, indeed, other indications of the fact that Arabs of pre-Islamic times held markets in connection with Jewish settlements. The *Kitāb al-Aghānī* says so expressly with regard to Al-Ablaq, the famous castle of Al-Samaw'al,[2] the Jewish lord of the

[1] "Coup d'oeil sur l'histoire des foires a travers l'Islam" in *Recueils de la Société Jean Bodin*, vol. V, Brussels 1953. Other literature on the subject in the article "Sūḳ" in the supplementary volume to *EI*[1].

[2] XIX, p. 98, line 3 from the bottom: 'The Arabs used to alight at his place, whereupon he extended to them his hospitality and they took provisions from his castle and established markets there." Modern scholars, both Western

ancient oasis of Taimā, northeast of Medina. Even more significant is the fact that the Arabs took over the Aramaic word for Friday: *ʿarūba*[1] which means: Eve (of Saturday), certainly because it played some role in their life; for otherwise, the Arabs had no week before Islam; the passing of the weeks was indicated to them by their Christian and Jewish neighbors. *ʿArūba*, was to them a market-day, as may be gathered from a verse, preserved in Al-Shāfiʿī's *Kitāb al-Umm*[2]: "May my soul be a ransom for men who heaped,[3] on the day of *ʿArūba*, provisions on provisions."

It is highly probable that in Medina, and perhaps also elsewhere, the Friday market bore, in addition to its foreign name: *ʿArūba*, another, Arabic designation: none other than *Yawm al-Jumʿa*, the Day of the Assembly or Gathering.

There exist, indeed, various accounts of ancient Muslim scholars to the effect that this expression was known before Islam. Yaʿqūbī, in his *Historiae*, (ed. Houtsma, Leiden 1883, p. 272), says of Kaʿb ibn Lu'ayy, one of the ancestors of Quraysh, the inhabitants of Mecca, that he was the first to call Friday by that name, because he used to assemble his people on that day and address them on the vanity and futility of human life.[4] In the *Tāj al-ʿArūs*, we read[5] that the first to call Friday by that name were the Medinans, because they held on that day public worship, before Muhammad emigrated to their town.

Needless to say, these accounts of the ancient Muslim scholars

and Muslim, have devoted a considerable amount of discussion to the personality and religion of Al-Samaw'al. For the purpose of this paper, it is enough to state that the account in which the above-mentioned passage occurs describes him expressly as Jewish, and more especially, as a Kohen.

1 Cf. A. Fischer, "Die altarabischen Namen der sieben Wochentage", *Zeitschrift der Deutschen Morgenländischen Gesellschaft*, 50, p. 224, where much literature is quoted, but none related to the subject of this study.

2 ed. Būlāq 1321H, I, p. 167.

3 Literally: "mixed". The poet obviously praises people who, on the market-day, bestowed on him many of the provisions acquired there.

4 Similar statements are made in the commentaries to the Koran, Sura 62:9, e.g., Baiḍāwī. There can be no doubt that in early Islamic times, this Kaʿb ibn Lu'ayy was regarded as the ancestor of a prominent group of families in Mecca. Ṭabarī, *Annals*, part 1, 1153, lines 3-4, and Yaʿqūbī, l.c., say that the Arabs used to count their years as from his death. However, no authentic tradition about him could have survived so many generations. His sermon, recorded at length by Yaʿqūbī, both in rhymed prose and in verses, is not more historical than the elegy composed by Adam on his son Abel, which is faithfully quoted by Ṭabarī.

5 I, p. 373, s.v. *ʿrb*.

do not represent a living tradition, but are learned conjectures. They are quoted here only to show that it was by no means strange for learned Muslims to assume that the name *Yawm al-Jum'a*, Day of Assembly, was in use before Muhammad.

We have, indeed, reason to believe that this assumption is true—however with the important modification that the name originally did not denote a day of common worship, but the market-day, when the people all over the oasis of Medina and its environment came together at one place. For *yawm al-jum'a* is nothing but the Arabic equivalent of Hebrew *yōm hak-kenīsa*, "The Day of the Assembly," which was the name of the two weekly market-days, Monday and Thursday, described above.[1] After the failure of the Bar Kokhba revolt (135 A.D.), these gatherings in the provincial capitals fell into disuse[2] and there remained only one "Day of Assembly," the eve of Sabbath. It is highly probable that the Jews of Medina themselves used the Arabic, and not the Hebrew (or Aramaic), form of the term.

The explanation of the original meaning of *Yawm al-Jum'a*, suggested here, is supported by the very wording of the only passage in the Koran, where it occurs. We turn now to the discussion of these often-quoted verses (Sura 62:9-11):

(9) O true believers, when you are called to prayer on the day of the assembly, hasten to the commemoration of God and cease trading. This is better for you, if you have understanding.

(10) Only when prayer is ended, scatter in the country and seek the bounty of God: commemorate God frequently, so that you may prosper.

(11) However, when they see any business or amusement, they flock there and leave you[3] standing. Say: that which is with God is better than amusement and business; and God is the best supplier.

It is evident that if the term *jum'a* had been coined originally for denoting a gathering for worship,[4] the wording of verse 9 would

[1] Cf. *Mishna Megilla*, I, I. *Tosefta* ib. 1, 2. For *kenīsa* in the sense of 'assembly', cf. *Bereshit Rabba*, ch. 49, para. 2 (Ed. J. Theodor, Berlin 1912, p. 514, 1.6).

[2] For details see G. Allon in the article quoted above, p. 114.

[3] The Prophet is addressed. As everywhere in the Koran, God is the speaker.

[4] As it is generally assumed. Consequently, Josef J. Rivlin, *Das Gesetz im Koran*, Jerusalem 1934, p. 19, proposes, although hesitantly, Hebrew-Aramaic *keneset*, *kenishtā*, "congregation" as the prototype for *jum'a*.

have to be quite different; not "when you are called to prayer *on the day of* the assembly," but "to the prayer of the Assembly." Therefore, *yawm al-jumʿa* means here nothing but Friday, the day when people gather for the market. It is highly significant that the Koran text of the famous Ibn Ubayy did not read *yawm al-jumʿa* at all, but *yawm al-ʿarūba al-kubrā*, "the day of the great *ʿArūba*", i.e., the common pre-Islamic name for Friday.[1]

Furthermore, the whole tenor of the passage quoted clearly indicates that it was said against the background of a market-day. The people of Medina were mainly farmers; buying and selling were not their normal occupations. Therefore, if Muhammad simply intended to say: "Leave your work and come to prayer", he had to talk about going to the mosque from the fields, rather than about leaving business. Likewise, the double reference to *lahw*, "amusement", suggests the market-day. All over the world, fairs and markets are accompanied by popular entertainments provided by professionals. We know this with regard to the great yearly fairs in pre-Islamic Arabia, as well as for the weekly market-days in Yemen today, and the situation certainly was not different in Medina.

The connection of the Muslim Friday service with the weekly market-day of Medina is brought out by one of its features which has puzzled both ancient and modern observers: the fact that it is held at noon,[2] a most impracticable time in the hot climate of Arabia and, indeed, the climate of most Muslim countries. No wonder that already the ancient books of Muslim law are full of details about the faithful who fall asleep during the sermon[3] or even faint at the

[1] See A. Jeffery, *Materials for the History of the Text of the Qur'ān*, Leiden 1937, p. 170. R. Blachère, *Le Coran*, Paris 1950, p. 825.

Ibn Ubayy's reading is remarkable also for the epithet, "the great" given to ʿArūba. This is certainly to be connected with a similar attribute of it occurring in a verse quoted in the Jamhara of Ibn Doreid, cf. S. Fraenkel, *Die Aramäischen Fremdwörter im Arabischen*, Leipzig, 1886, 277: "A day like the long drawn (mutaṭāwil) day of ʿArūba". Perhaps there were two types of Friday markets, one short and of a more local character, and another catering for a whole environment, which continued well into the afternoon. The authenticity of Ibn Ubayy's readings has been confirmed conspicuously by the discovery of an Umayyad inscription bearing a quotation from the Koran not in the textus receptus, but in Ibn Ubayy's reading (oral communication by the late Professor A. Jeffery).

[2] According to some, it is permissable to hold it also in the early afternoon. In practice, it is held all over the Muslim world at noon.

[3] This occurs, of course, also in more merciful climates and at better hours of the day. However, the Muslim sermon, as a rule, is very short and consists mostly of a fixed set of a few religious sayings.

service. The reason for this inconvenient arrangement is to be found in the circumstances accompanying the creation of the Muslim weekly day of worship. The market in Arabia breaks up soon after noon, so that everybody attending it is able to reach his home before nightfall.[1] To hold public worship early in the morning was out of the question, for at that time everyone was eager to do business, as the proverb has it: "When the dust (from the way to the market) is still on your feet, sell your merchandise."[2] Neither was it feasible to do so when the sūq was "standing", as the Arabs say, i.e., when it was in full force. Therefore, the proper time for the public worship was at noon, shortly before people dispersed to get to their homes, and thus it has remained until the present day.

However, verse 10 of sura 62: "When prayer is ended, scatter in the country and seek the bounty of God (i.e. do business, cf. 2:198/4") should not be pressed as meaning that immediately after prayer every one was supposed to leave the city ("scatter in the country"). The verse intends only to emphasize that any business may be attended to after prayer but not during the time reserved for the service.

There are other characteristics of the Muslim Friday service which may have had their origin in its relation to the Medinan market-day. The preacher delivers the sermon from a *Minbar* (originally a platform, or, rather, a chair, not a pulpit), while carrying in his hand a rod, or a sword, or a lance. C. H. Becker has shown how probable it was that these were originally the insignia of the judge.[3] Now, as we have seen above, the courts of justice or the judges both in Israel and in Arabia used to sit on market-days. However, this point should not be pressed. For, if the present writer is not mistaken, the many references in ancient Muslim literature to Muhammad's activity as judge do not connect it expressly with the Friday service, at least not as a rule.

For the same reason, it is more than doubtful whether the controversy about the sitting of the preacher at the Friday service had anything to do with the office of the magistrate. An enormous

[1] See E. Brauer, *Die Enthnologie der Jemenitischen Juden*, p. 257, Philby, *Arabian Highlands*, 234: "By the midday prayer the (Monday) Sūq usually came to an end," and passim.

[2] S. D. Goitein, *Jemenica, Sprichwörter und Redensarten aus Zentral-Jemen*, Leipzig 1934, p. 46, no. 249. There exist numerous other proverbs to the same effect.

[3] *Islamstudien*, I, p. 463 ff.

amount of discussion on this question is to be found in Muslim religious literature. The practice finally adopted is this: the preacher sits at the beginning of the service, stands up for the first section of his sermon, sits down again, but stands while delivering the second part. This is clearly a compromise. The original practice most probably was that related in the name of Abū Saʿīd al-Khuḍrī, by Al-Bukhārī, (Chapter II (Jumʿa), para. 28, ed. Krehl, Leiden 1862, I, 233): "The Prophet sat on the *Minbar* and we sat around him". For us, it is the most natural thing that a preacher should stand up while delivering his sermon. However, in ancient Hebrew literature, we have invariably the same picture as that given for Muhammad in the Ḥadīth just quoted: *ḥākhām yōshēv wedōrēsh,* the scholar who expounded the Scripture was seated on a platform, while his audience 'sat at his feet', either on the floor or on benches, and the same was the case in the ancient Christian church.[1] The heated controversies[2] in Islam, whether the preacher should stand up or not certainly had something to do with its turbulent inner development; for, originally, the caliphs and the provincial governors addressed the congregation, which was identified with the political community, in person. However, these disputations reflect a later stage in the history of the Friday service and lie outside the scope of this paper.

There remains, however, one aspect of the discussion of the Muslim scholars on the Friday service which has a significant bearing on the origin and nature of this institution—the question, in which place, and for whom that service was obligatory. At the end, a generally accepted consensus was worked out, according to which the service should be held wherever forty male, adult, free Muslims had their permanent domicile, and were it even in a village. The compromise reached was a regulation for the fulfillment of a religious duty. The differences of opinion preceding it showed that the Friday service had, from its inception, a far wider scope, to the discussion of which we now turn.

It was stated at the beginning of this study, that, according to the commonly accepted Muslim tradition, no Friday service had

[1] Zunz, *Die gottesdienstlichen Vorträge der Juden,* Frankfurt a.M. 1892, 350, note kk; 358, note d; 359, note b.

[2] As against the Ḥadīth, quoted above, describing the Prophet usually as addressing the congregation while seated on a platform, another states: "Whoever tells you that the Prophet preached while seated is a liar," Al-Bayhaqī 3, 197, quoting Muslim (7, 33-35).

been held in Mecca. It goes without saying that in Mecca, too, Muhammad's followers met for common prayer. However, the Friday meetings introduced in Medina at the suggestion of Muhammad's missionaries served a purpose wider than mere devotion. They were rallies which manifested who adhered to the new religion and who failed to do so. They had, from the outset, the character of a socio-political gathering. Therefore, attendance was (and remained) obligatory for everybody[1] and, thus, it was long believed that they should be held only in provincial capitals, where a representative of the Government had his seat, and not in villages,[2] also only in one main mosque, not in several in one town, of whatever size they were.[3] The prayer for the ruler, expressed in the Friday sermon, had its Jewish and Christian antecedents. However, the immense practical importance attached to it in Islam was in conformity with the original concept that the attendance of the Friday service was essentially an act of showing one's allegiance.

As we have seen, in his practical wisdom, Muhammad fixed the day of public worship on the weekly market-day, because then the people of the oasis of Medina and its environment were assembled in one place anyhow.[4] This day happend to be the eve of Sabbath, because the Jews, who formed a very considerable part of the population of the oasis, bought on it the necessary stores for their holy day, when no work, including buying and selling, was permitted. However Muhammad had not the slightest reason to adopt the Sabbath itself. First of all, as has been said in the introductory passage of this study, the idea of a weekly day of rest was foreign in general to the majority of mankind up to the threshold of modern times. In addition, for most of Muhammad's followers a weekly day of rest would not have been a practical proposition. For the Meccans, whose main occupation was the long distance transit-trade between

[1] Women excepted, which also shows that the Friday service was more than religious worship. For from the religious point of view, according to ancient Islam, woman was equal to man; she was obliged to observe the daily prayers and even to study the religious law. However, she did not belong to the body politic, in which only free men, bearing arms, were members.

[2] Al-Shāfiʿī, *Kitāb al-Umm*, 1321H; I, 169, line 10.

[3] Ibid., 171, l. 4.

[4] The following ruling of Al-Shāfiʿī, ib. 170, line 8 from bottom, shows the natural link between marketing and the Friday service: "If a village which has a Friday service is surrounded by others bordering on it, and these do most of their marketing there, I do not allow a single one (of those villagers) not to attend the service (in the central village, where the market is held)."

the Mediterranean and Yemen, such an institution would have been a serious impediment, rather than a blessing, while the Bedouin had no need for such a day, as they did not do regular work anyhow.[1]

Muhammad knew, of course, that the institution of the Sabbath formed part of the heavenly revelation,[2] but succeeded in solving the theological problem: how one and the same God could give different laws to different peoples, at least to the satisfaction of his own followers.[3] It is evident from Sura 62, 9-11, quoted above, that Muhammad did not regard it as incompatible with the holiness of the weekly day of worship for it to be also one of flourishing business[4] —a conception which is the more plausible if we consider that that day originally was the one set aside for commerce in an otherwise agricultural environment. Similarly, the Koran[5] and popular belief[6] regard the yearly pilgrimage to the Holy Places in the environment

[1] Except such routine work as milking the camels, which anyhow had to be done every day. Cf. J. Wellhausen, *Reste arabischen Heidentums*, Berlin 1897, p. 87; S. D. Goitein, *Jews and Arabs*, New York 1964, 39-40.

[2] "We (God is speaking, see above, p. 118) lifted the mountain (of Sinai) over them (the Children of Israel), while we concluded with them the covenant and said... Transgress not on the Sabbath day. And we received from them a strong covenant." Sura 4:154/153. The Koran relates also legends not found in this form in Jewish sources, about desecrators of the Sabbath, who were converted into apes (2:65/61; 4:47/50) and about fish which used to come to a certain village on the seashore only when its inhabitants kept the Sabbath, 7, 163, see H. Speier, *Die biblischen Erzählungen im Qor'ān*, p. 313.

These quotations show that the idea of the Sabbath occupied Muhammad's mind to a certain degree. It is also natural that his believers, seeing that the Sabbath was so important a feature in a monotheistic religion next door to them, wondered whether God had not a similar command in store for them. In reply to such queries, Muhammad declared: "The Sabbath was enjoined only on those that disagreed with regard to it"—obviously Jews and Christians—"your Lord will judge between them on the day of Resurrection about their differences" 16:124/123. See next note.

[3] Cf. the present writer's "The Controversies of the Banū Isrā'īl, a Quranic Study", *Tarbiz* 3 (1932), 410-422, and the article "Banū Isrā'īl" in EI[2].

[4] It is useful to remember that in many Christian countries markets used to be held on Sundays. The little town of Sūq al-Aḥad ("Sunday-market") in Northern Mesopotamia, described by Ibn Hauqal, p. 217, obviously was also originally Christian, cf. R. Brunschvig, *Histoire des foires a travers l'Islam*, p. 49

In biblical times, as we learn from the book of Nehemiah, chap. 13:15-21, Sabbath was the market-day in Jerusalem, both for local agricultural products and for fish imported by Phoenician traders. It was Nehemiah, who stopped that usage by force, thus "robbing the population of their natural day of marketing," as a prominent historian caustically remarked.

[5] Sura 2:198/194, where the same expression, "ask for the bounty of God" is used as in the passage on the Friday service in Sura 62, see above, p. 118.

[6] A man participating in the holy pilgrimage is blessed with the wish: *ḥajj mabrūr watijāra lā tabūr*, "May your pilgrimage be accepted by God and

of Mecca as an appropriate occasion for prosperous business—again in conformity with the fact that in pagan times the yearly pilgrimages were also the season of the yearly fair. It may even be that an ancient epithet for Friday, *yawm al-mazīd*, the day of God's special bounty, may have something to do with this practical aspect of the weekly day of worship.[1]

However, although Islam did not enhance the holiness of Friday by forbidding on it wordly business, it succeeded in conveying to its believers, both by the solemnity of the service and by a number of accessory means,[2] the feeling of a specially blessed day. There is no better way of putting this sociological study into its proper religious context than by quoting a description of the Friday service written by a sympathetic, but not uncritical, European observer at a time when Islam was almost untouched by foreign intrusions:[3]

> "The utmost solemnity and decorum are observed in the public worship of the Muslims. Their looks and behavior in the mosque are not those of enthusiastic devotion, but of calm and modest piety. Never are they guilty of a designedly irregular word or action during their prayers. The pride and fanaticism which they exhibit in common life, in intercourse with persons of their own, or of a different faith, seem to be dropped on their entering the mosque, and they appear wholly absorbed in the adoration of their Creator..."

The main findings of this inquiry may be summarized as follows:

1. The expression *yawm al-jumʿa* is pre-Islamic and designated the market-day, just as its Hebrew (and Aramaic) equivalent *yōm hak-kenīsa*.

2. The market-day was held in the oasis of Medina on Friday, the day, "when the Jews bought their provisions for the Sabbath."

3. For *yawm al-jumʿa* in Sura 62:9, Ibn Ubayy read *yawm al-ʿarūba al-kubrā*, the word for Friday derived from Aramaic. This, together with the very wording of that verse, indicates that *yawm al-jumʿa* there means simply Friday.

your merchandise may not remain unsold." An expanded variant of this wish is quoted, further on.

[1] Cf. S. D. Goitein, "Beholding God on Friday", *Islamic Culture* 34 (1960), pp. 163-168.

[2] Such as the provisions that people should bathe and perfume themselves, put on their best clothes and eat choice food, etc.

[3] E. W. Lane, *Manners and Customs of the Modern Egyptians*, London (Dent) 1936, p. 85 (ch. III). The same author stresses the fact that "the Muslim does not abstain from wordly business on Friday except during the time of prayer", ib., p. 81.

4. Muhammad chose Friday as a day of public worship, because on that day the people of Medina gathered anyhow to do their shopping. There was no intention of polemics against the older religions.

5. A striking parallel to the institution of public service on a market day is that of the ancient Jewish service on Mondays and Thursdays, originally the days when the villagers came to town, but which remained days of public prayer, as well as of fasting and sittings of the courts, long after the Monday and Thursday markets had been abolished.

6. This origin explains why the Friday prayer was fixed at noon, a very inconvenient time in a hot country: the Arab markets used to break up early in the afternoon. In view of this, the choice of noon was very practicable.

7. The reference to "business and amusement" in Sura 62:11 (which was promulgated in Medina) fits a community of farmers only if understood as describing a fair with public entertainment.

8. From the outset, the Friday service was of more than religious significance. Participation in it demonstrated the participants' adhesion to the Muslim community. This socio-political character was never given up entirely and has left many traces in the details prescribed for its celebration by Muslim law. However, in the consciousness of the average Muslim, the purely religious aspect certainly prevails over the others.

9. The adoption, in 1935, of Sunday as weekly holiday by the Turkish republic was not anti-Islamic, but dictated by practical considerations, partly connected with the very character of the Muslim Friday. Since the latter provided the natural market day, there was no point in converting it into an official day of rest, while Sunday, being international, had great economic advantages, consider e.g. the closure of banks.[1]

[1] Thursday, "as religiously neutral", was borrowed by the Turks from the French in the twenties of the nineteenth century as the day of closure of the Government offices, cf. Bernard Lewis, *The Emergence of Modern Turkey*, Oxford University Press 1961, p. 101.

CHAPTER SIX

THE BIRTH-HOUR OF MUSLIM LAW

AN ESSAY IN EXEGESIS

Islamic religion is characterized by the prominence of legal conceptions in its system: The Sharīʿa, or holy law, is its very essence, and Fiqh, or religious jurisprudence, is its science (*ʿilm*) par excellence. The minute observation of many commandments is its most conspicuous practical aspect; the free fellowship of religious scholars, who do not need authorization by any government to interpret, develop, and apply its law, is its most representative body, and even the purely legal sections of the Fiqh are studied reverently as an act of worship.

All these features are so familiar to the student of Islam that they seem to be natural and need no explanation of their provenance. In fact, however, their origin and early formation are far from being fully known and may partly elude our knowledge forever. There is, of course, a striking resemblance between early Islam and Judaism in all the aspects mentioned above. However, as many of these seem to originate from parallel developments rather than from borrowing, the similarity between the two religions poses problems rather than solves them.

There has been a considerable amount of discussion on this question of the origin and early development of Muslim law. At the third international congress of Comparative Law, held in London in August 1950, Professor Joseph Schacht surveyed the problem in a paper entitled "Foreign Elements in Ancient Islamic Law", which stressed in particular the parallels between Islamic and Roman Law.[1] Shortly afterwards, Professor S. Vesey Fitzgerald of London published an article the very name of which ("The Alleged Debt of Islamic to Roman Law") betrays the author's opinion that Islamic jurisprudence was not influenced by Roman legal science.[2] It is not surprising, therefore, that Professor Bousquet of Algiers speaks

[1] *Journal of Comparative Legislation*, 1950, nos. 3-4, 9-16.
[2] *Law Quarterly Journal*, January 1951, pp. 81-102.

about the mystery surrounding the genesis of Muhammadan legal science.[1]

The present paper is not concerned with the origin of Fiqh, the science of Muslim Jurisprudence, but with that of Muslim law itself, i.e. the legal parts of the Sharīʿa. As is well known, the Sharīʿa does not differentiate between purely legal matters, such as contracts or the laws of inheritance, and religious duties, such as prayers and fasting; all alike are part of the Holy Law. Through detailed interpretation of a significant passage in the Koran, this paper tries to answer the question whether this particular character of the Sharīʿa goes back to the founder of Islam himself, and if so, at what juncture of his activities did a tendency towards it become evident.

It has often been stressed that the Koran contains comparatively little legal matter and that the little it contains is entirely unsystematic and haphazard; or as an article on the subject put it: "It is evident that Muhammad himself made no attempt to work out any comprehensive legal system, a task for which he seems to have been singularly ill-suited; instead, he contended himself with what went little beyond 'ad hoc' amendments to the existing customary law".[2] A number of modern authors on Muslim Law have repeated a statement, obviously going back to Count Ostorog's book *The Angora Reform*, p. 19, that of the 6236 verses of the Koran, no more than about five hundred, less than one-twelfth, could be considered as having legal import.

However, these statements need some qualification. The average length of a verse in the Koran varies from one to three lines (in the Egyptian edition), while those of legal content usually comprise three to six, and some are considerably longer, e.g. verse 282 of the second Sura, which stretches over fifteen lines. Thus, from the purely arithmetical point of view, legal matters occupy a far larger part of the holy book of Islam than assumed by the aforesaid estimate. And there is another very important point to be considered. As is well known, the Koran teems with repetitions; the same thing seems to be said many times, often in the same words; in legal matters, however, repetitions are rare, and when they occur, they usually contain some progress in legislation. According to the view of the Muslim theologians, expressed for instance by Ghazālī in his *Jawāhir*

[1] "Le mystère de la formation et des origines du Fiqh", *Revue Algérienne ... de Législation et de Jurisprudence*, Algiers, 1947, pp. 66-80.

[2] J. N. D. Anderson, *The Muslim World*, Vol. 40 (1950), p. 245.

al-Qur'ān, strictly speaking, no repetitions occur in the holy book of Islam. In any case, if one condenses its subject matter to its mere essence, under the five main headings of preaching, polemics, stories, allusions to the Prophet's life, and legislation, one will reach the conclusion that proportionately the Koran does contain legal material not less than the Pentateuch, the Torah, which is known in world literature as "The Law".

The accepted view of Muhammad's career as a law-giver seems to be that, while in Mecca, he acted solely as preacher and prophet, whereas in Medina the requirements of an ever-growing community forced him to give legal decisions from time to time. This view is based on the fact that Muhammad sincerely and most vehemently believed that the Last Judgment and the end of the known physical world were imminent. What purpose was there, then, in expounding an elaborate legal system, when all human beings were to come to an end soon? It is true that even the earliest parts of the Koran are not devoid of legal matters; for instance, when Muhammad enjoins the true believers to keep to their pledges and contracts, to stand by their testimony (70:32-33) and to be just in measure and weight (83:1-3), or when he objects from the outset to usury, i.e. the taking of interest (30:39). However, these prescriptions are religious and moral commandments rather then pieces of formal legislation.

On the other hand, Tor Andrae has rightly shown[1] that even in Mecca Muhammad conceived the religious community as a social and even political unit, *umma*—a concept which no doubt has to account for the astonishing fact that soon after his arrival at Medina, he was able to organize the whole population of the town, Muslims and non-Muslims, as one body politic, called *umma*[2]. Muhammad's biographer, Ibn Isḥāq, has preserved the document constituting this *umma*, and even the most critical minds do not cast doubt on its authenticity. This document, which contains forty seven paragraphs, betrays a highly legalistic and even formalistic mind—a fact which is not surprising in the son of a flourishing city of merchants. The same holds true of the many treaties contracted by him with Arab tribes, discussed in special studies by Julius Wellhausen[3],

[1] *Muhammad, The Man and his Faith*, Chapter 6.

[2] W. Montgomery Watt, *Muhammad at Medina*, Oxford 1956, p. 227, assumes that "the Constitution"—as he calls the document under discussion—was promulgated after year 5 of the Hijrah. For many reasons, which cannot be discussed here, this surmise is unacceptable.

[3] *Skizzen und Vorarbeiten* IV, Berlin 1889.

Jacob Sperber[1], and in the well known books of Muhammad Ḥamīdullāh.[2]

In contrast with this, one has to concede that many Medinese Suras, which are contemporary with the deeds just referred to, contain little or no legal material, while it is abundantly clear from the testimony of *Ḥadīth, Sīrah* and *Tafsīr* (the oral traditions, the biographies of the Prophet and the commentaries on the Koran), as well as from inner evidence, that many legal questions must have been brought before Muhammad and decided by him at that time. For according to the Arab as well as the old Israelite conception, law is not a fixed order imposed and exercised by the power of an organized community and need not be created by a king or a legal assembly. Law is a truth, which exists forever and which has only to be discovered by a wise man; the judge in pre-Islamic Arabia was called *al-ḥakam*, cf. Hebrew *ḥākhām*, the wise man who possesses divinely inspired power. The vast literature on Arab tribal customs shows that in many cases the judges were not the chiefs of the tribes or other persons of authority, but wise men, often from some distant locale, who were famous for their inspiration and experience.

To this may be added the astonishing fact that, during a prolonged study of the language and life of the Jews in Yemen, the writer came across quite a number of cases where, in out-of-the-way areas, the Jewish *ʿāqil*, i.e. the headman of the local community, was approached by Arab tribesmen to settle minor disputes of theirs. Similarly, Kaʿb ibn al-Ashraf, one of the prominent Jews of Medina, used to serve as a judge to non-Jews. However, Muhammad was the outstanding spiritual authority in the town, and according to Arabic conceptions, it was only natural that he should act as a *ḥakam* not only for Muslims, but also, as we shall see, for unbelievers, including Jews, although these had, as the Koran reports, their own *rabbāniyyūn* and *aḥbār* (in Hebrew, *rabbānīm* and *ḥavērīm*), rabbis and scholars, who guided them in legal matters.

Why, then, were so few of these legal decisions incorporated in the many Suras of the early Medinese period? To my mind, the only answer to this question can be that it occurred to Muhammad only at a relatively late period that even strictly legal matters were not

[1] *Die Sendschreiben Muḥammads an die Stämme Arabiens*, Berlin (Seminar f. Orientalische Sprachen) 1916.

[2] *Documents sur la diplomatie musulmane a l'époque du Prophète* etc., Paris 1935 (also in Arabic).

religiously irrelevant, but were part and parcel of the divine revelation and were included in the heavenly book, which was the source of all religions. I believe that we have an exact account of this most fateful development in the Prophet's career in a lengthy koranic passage, namely Sura 5:42-51, to the discussion of which the rest of this study will be devoted.

In verses 42-43, Muhammad expresses his astonishment that the Jews of Medina applied to him as judge, although they were in the possession of a divinely revealed law. God says to Muhammad: "When they come to you, you may act as a judge between them or you may turn away from them; ... (43) But why should they make you their judge, seeing that in their hand is the Torah, containing the judgment of God? ... (44) Verily, we have sent down the Torah containing guidance and light, by it the prophets ... gave judgment for the Jews, as likewise did the rabbis and the scholars by such portion of the Book of God, as they were entrusted with; ...[1] (45) Therein We have prescribed for them: A life (verbally soul) for a life, an eye for an eye, etc.; ...[2] (46) In their footsteps we caused Jesus, son of Mary, to follow, confirming the Torah which was before him, and we gave him the Gospel, wherein is guidance and light; ... (47) Let the people of the Gospel judge by that which God has sent down therein. Whoso do not judge by what God has sent down, such are evil doers. (48) And unto you we have sent down the Book with the Truth, confirming whatever Book was before, and as a watcher over it; so judge between them by what God has sent down and do not follow their inclinations away from the truth which has come to you. For each one we have made a fixed way and an open road." After this there follows again an admonishment to judge only according to the divine law, and the passage concludes with the exclamation (50): "Do they then desire the (mode of) judgment of the Time of Ignorance? But who is better than God in judgment to a people who have certainty in their belief?"

The import of these lines seems evident. Some members of the Jewish community of Medina had applied to Muhammad's court, but there arose difficulties; perhaps one party refused to accept his decision. As may be learned from the end of the passage, and from

[1] By that time, Muhammad was well aware of the fact that in addition to the *Tawrāt* or Bible, the Jewish scholars used other books which they believed to contain God's commandments.

[2] An allusion to the well-known passages of the Pentateuch which deal with the law of retaliation (Exodus 21:23-25. Deuteronomy 19:21).

other verses of the Koran, in particular from the eighth Sura, and from various stories reported by the *Ḥadīth,* among the Muslims too, there were some who had *ahwā'*, "bad inclinations", i.e. took a critical attitude towards the Prophet's judgments. Owing to the close connection between spiritual leadership and the role of a judge such an attitude was dangerous. Hitherto, according to our hypothesis, Muhammad had not regarded his judicial activities as part of his prophetic office. This was now to change. From that time onward, *ḥukm al-Jāhiliyya,* the mode of judgment of the Time of Ignorance, had to be given up. The decision of legal questions was now a matter of one's religion, exactly as were the beliefs about God or resurrection or Muhammad's prophetic mission. That is why this passage is followed by another one, in which the true believers are enjoined not to take Jews or Christians as their patrons (*awliyā'*), as had frequently been the case before, because each community was now to be regarded as a completely separate entity in itself. Religion had become totalitarian, comprising all departments of life, including the hitherto neutral aspect of law. Muhammad regrets this fact; "If God had wished," he says, "he would have made all mankind one community" (Sura 5:4a). But for the time being, such was God's will, and humanity was bound to comply with it.

It would, of course, be extremely useful if we knew exactly when these verses were first promulgated. As usual, the Muslim commentators and other authors dealing with the *asbāb al-nuzūl,* the occasions for the promulgation of parts of the Koran, differ widely on this point. Some make the whole fifth Sura the last of the Prophet's utterances, and in this they are followed, e.g., by Professor Blachère in his chronologically arranged, French translation, though he states that the various parts of this Sura seem to belong to considerably different times.[1] Another widely diffused traditional view connects our passage with a contest of nobility between two Jewish tribes, which would indicate a comparatively early date. My own opinion is that the repeated references to the Jewish rabbis and scholars can only fit a time when there still remained a considerable number of Jews in Medina, i.e. before the end of the fifth year of the Hijrah, while the complete confessional segregation of Christians, Jews, and Muslims, here advocated, points to a rather developed stage of Muhammad's activities. The most suitable date for this passage would therefore be the fifth year of the Hijrah, five years before Muhammad's death, a date suggested, for other reasons of course, by such eminent Muslim authors as Zuhrī, Wāqidī, and Ṭabarī.[1]

It would hardly be an exaggeration to say that this passage indicates the birth-hour of Muslim law. As has been shown here, more legal material is contained in later parts of the Koran than is usually believed. But this is not the decisive point. What matters is the attitude which regards everything, including, seemingly, religiously irrelevant legal matters, as emanating from God through His true prophet. This attitude, as we believe, was first clearly conceived and expressed in the passage just discussed, approximately halfway through the ten years which Muhammad passed in Medina.

There remains the question whether this concept of the heavenly origin of law came to Muhammad from outside or was developed by him independently. Here the historian may meet the theologian halfway. According to the tenets of the predominant Muslim theology, the Koran, like God himself, is eternally pre-existent. The historian may find that ideas which at a certain date found expression in the Koran were pre-existent in Muhammad's original preaching, as is to be found in the early chapters of the holy book of Islam. This is indeed the case with the idea of the Sharīʿa. It is contained in Muhammad's original view of the religious *umma* as a social and even political entity, in his early idea of the prophets as lawgivers and in his own first attempts at the codification of basic socio-religious duties, contained in Suras 17:23-28 and 6:151-152, which Thaʿālibī in his *Kitāb al-ʿArāʾis* already recognized as a replica of the Biblical Ten Commandments.[2] However, it is a far cry from these early beginnings to the concept of Islam as a separate denomination exacting all-embracing duties, as expressed in the passage from Sura 5 discussed above. For this elaborate address clearly indicates a complete change of attitude, a turning point, in the Prophet's thoughts on the relation between law and religion. As was usual with Muhammad, a thorough pragmatist, the change came about in the wake of some practical problem which he had to solve. Some Jews had come to litigate before him and something went wrong

[1] Cf. T. Noeldeke-F. Schwally, *Geschichte des Qorans*, I, p. 231, note 1.

[2] H. Hirschfeld, *New Researches into the Composition and Exegesis of the Qoran*, London 1902, p. 81. H. Grimme, *Mohammed*, II, Münster 1895, pp. 115-118.

with the case. God then gives His prophet the permission to refuse to act as a judge for non-Muslims, if he chose to do so. This particular incident, however, served as an occasion for a far wider ruling: the Muslims and the adherents of other religions had to have different laws altogether, for law was a part of the prophetic message, with the consequence that the followers of different prophets could be properly judged only by those who believed in their respective revelations. In pagan times, people did not care what religion their judges had, as long as they were competent and inspired men. With Islam—according to the new conception—law, even civil law, had become part of the message which was contained in one heavenly Book, but was sent in different forms to different peoples.

The emphatic and detailed exposition of the new idea in the passage under discussion; the repeated references in Sura 5 to the Jewish rabbis and scholars who gave judgments according to the Law revealed by God; the quotation from the Pentateuch, which deals not with theological matters, but with questions of criminal law; and, finally the very occasion which gave rise to the promulgation of Sura 5:42-51, suggest that Muhammad, at a certain stage of his prophetical and political career in Medina, suddenly became aware of the fact that the scriptures revealed before him contained not only religious and moral injunctions, but also detailed laws concerning matters which were religiously irrelevant. This new knowledge, together with some difficulties incurred in practice, created in him the belief—which was well in line with his original idea of religion as a constitution for a body politic—that he, too, had to recognize the details of civil law as inseparable constituents of God's message. In other words, the idea of the Sharīʿa was not the result of post-Koranic developments, but was formulated by Muhammad himself.

The results obtained here seem to be at variance with the conclusions of Joseph Schacht's penetrating study *The Origins of Muhammedan Jurisprudence*, Oxford, 1950. Schacht assumes that, during the first century of the Hijrah, law still fell outside the sphere of religion and was brought into its orbit only during the second century, when Muslim jurisprudence, properly speaking, came into being.

There is, however, no basic contradiction between the two views. As Goldziher in the first chapter of his *Muhammedan Studies*, called *Dīn and Muruwwa*, has shown, it took generations until the Muslim spirit of "religion" replaced the pagan concept of "virtue" as the essential quality of a man.[1] In the same way, it is only natural that *ḥukm al-Jāhiliyyah,* judgment according to arbitrary opinion or established local practice, did not disappear immediately and altogether after Muhammad denounced it, but was replaced only gradually—and, as is well-known, never completely—by a legal system worked out on religious lines. However, it seems to emerge clearly from our analysis of the lengthy passage in Sura 5 that it was Muhammad himself who envisaged law as part of divine revelation.

[1] *Muhammedanische Studien,* Halle 1888 (reprint Hildesheim 1961), I pp. 1-39.

CHAPTER SEVEN

THE SANCTITY OF JERUSALEM AND PALESTINE IN EARLY ISLAM

In a famous passage of his Muhammedanische Studien,[1] I. Goldziher expounds in great detail the theory that the Umayyad caliph ʿAbd al-Malik, by erecting the Dome of the Rock in Jerusalem, intended to outdo his rival ʿAbdallah b. Zubayr, who exploited the holiness of Mecca, his capital, for his own political ends. The Ḥajj, the Muslim pilgrimage, was to be diverted from the Kaʿba to the new temple of Jerusalem, a procedure which was to be justified by sayings attributed to the Prophet or some of his Companions. According to this thesis, the numerous holy traditions supporting or opposing the religious importance of Jerusalem and its sanctuary were but weapons in the war between the two competitors for the caliphate. As we shall presently see, Goldziher's thesis could rely on certain passages in Arabic sources, but its elaborate exposition was due to the master's methodical endeavor to make the contradictory sayings of the Ḥadīth intelligible in the light of contemporary history. In any case, this theory about the motives for the erection of the Dome of the Rock has been generally accepted and invariably appears in historical textbooks dealing with the period. ʿAbd al-Malik was nicknamed a second Jeroboam[2] and even the circular ground plan of the magnificent building was explained as intended for the ceremony of the Ṭawāf, the circumambulation of the sanctuary.[3]

However, a thorough study of the sources and a careful weighing of the historical circumstances show that the erection of the Dome of the Rock could not have been intended to divert the Ḥajj from Mecca to Jerusalem, while the contradictory traditions concerning the holiness of the latter could not have had their origin exclusively, or even mainly, in the short period between the beginning of the erection of the Qubbat al-Ṣakhra (about 66 A.H.) and Ibn Zubayr's

[1] Muhammedanische Studien, II, pp. 35-37.

[2] Cf. 2 Kings 12:26-33.

[3] Abel et Vincent, *Jéruzalem*, 933 b. As is well known, the Kaʿba itself is a rectangular, and not a circular, building.

death (73 A.H.). To begin with: the great Muslim historians of the third century, who deal with the conflict between the Umayyads and Ibn Zubayr in the utmost detail,[1] as well as all the earlier geographers, including al-Maqdisī, a native of Jerusalem, never make the slightest allusion to ʿAbd al-Malik's alleged intention of making Jerusalem instead of Mecca the center of Islam. On the contrary, for the year 68, Ṭabarī (part 2, pp. 781-3) reports[2] that four camps—those of ʿAbd al-Malik, Ibn Zubayr, Najda the Kharidjite, and Ibn al-Ḥanafiyya, the representative of the Shiʿa, took part jointly in the Ḥajj. This report stresses only the strange fact that FOUR different parties joined together at one time in the performance of the rites of the pilgrimage. It takes for granted the fact that men from Syria performed the Ḥajj also at other times during those crucial years. *Ta'rīkh al Khamīs*, using an older source, states (vol. 2, p. 339, ll. 17-18) that ʿAbd al-Malik asked people proceeding to Mecca to renew their oath of allegiance to him. Even during the very siege of Mecca by al-Ḥajjāj, the Syrians were eager to make the Ṭawāf, a request which Ibn Zubayr naturally had to refuse.[3]

It appears that only two older sources mention the allegation that ʿAbd al-Malik, in putting up the Qubbat al-Ṣakhra, intended to divert the Ḥajj to Jerusalem: Yaʿqūbī, who was an outspoken partisan of the Shiʿites, and Eutychius, the well-known Christian chronographer; but both append to this allegation other statements which invalidate it by their obvious untruth. Eutychius (Ibn Batrīq, ed. Cheikho, vol. 2, p. 39) says that ʿAbd al-Malik and al-Walīd—who reigned long after Ibn Zubayr was dead—forbade the pilgrimage to Mecca, while Yaʿqūbī (vol. 2, p. 311) extends this accusation to all the Umayyads, which is clearly in contradiction to trustworthy traditions about the pilgrimage of these caliphs to Mecca.

It is true that a number of later authors[4] repeat Yaʿqūbī's account, but everyone versed in the technique of Arabic historio-

[1] In particular Ṭabarī (and the sources dependent on him) and Balādhurī, Ansāb al-Ashrāf, V, Jerusalem 1936, pp. 255-378.

[2] For other sources about this event cf. Caetani, Chronographia, annum 68, part. 20.

[3] Ansāb al-Ashrāf V, p. 360, ll. 6-7. Cf. also Ṭabarī part. 2, p. 830, l. 18.

[4] E.g. Ibn Taghribirdī, al-Nujūm al-Ẓāhira I, p. 207. Ibn Kathīr VIII, p. 280; Ta'rīkh al-Khamīs II, p. 339. Mujīr al-Dīn, al-Uns al-Jalīl bita'rīkh al-Quds wal-Khalīl I, p. 240-243. Cf. Caetani, Chronographia, annum 66, par. 18.

graphy knows that once a story has been incorporated into the mass of historical traditions, it appears again and again in later compilations. The account given by Ya'qūbī and Eutychius has its origin partly in anti-Umayyad tendencies[1] and partly reflects a certain religious usage, to be discussed presently, which, however, was by no means restricted to Jerusalem. When the Muslims spread all over the Middle East, they were of course unable to attend the yearly pilgrimage, as many of them had been accustomed to do in the early days of Islam. In order to compensate the faithful, certain rites of the Ḥajj, in particular the most holy Wuqūf, the standing in the presence of God, was observed in the great provincial capitals, a procedure called *'arraf* (*Ta'rīf*) after the Mount of 'Arafāt near Mecca, where the original Wuqūf takes place. 'Abdallah b. 'Abbās is reported to have introduced that rite when he occupied the position of an Amir at Basra, while 'Abd al-'Azīz b. Merwān followed this example during his administration of Egypt for his brother 'Abd al-Malik in Fusṭāṭ.[2] A passage from Nāṣir-i-Khosraw's Persian 'Book of Travel', which has sometimes been quoted as a corroboration of Goldziher's above-mentioned thesis, is to be explained in the light of this custom. Nāṣir-i-Khosraw[3] says that those who are unable to make the Ḥajj come to Jerusalem *vebimōqif biīstand* 'and perform the Wuqūf'... sometimes over 20,000 persons[4] assembled in Jerusalem for that purpose. Clearly the Persian traveler speaks of the custom of the Ta'rīf, described above, and not of the Ṭawāf, as performed at the Ka'ba. But these yearly assemblies in Jerusalem at the time of the Ḥajj—although, as we have seen, they

[1] Of the same genre is the allegation that Mu'āwiya intended to declare Saturday instead of Friday as the Muslim day of prayer. Ibn 'Asākir, Ta'rīkh Dimashq, I, p. 80, l. 12, toils much on refuting it.

[2] Ibn Taghribirdī I, p. 207. Similar substitutes are found in other religions. Maqrīzī, Khiṭaṭ II, p. 465, relates that the Jews of Egypt used to visit the old synagogue of Dammūh (near giza, dedicated to Moses) on a certain feast, instead of making the pilgrimage to Jerusalem.

[3] ed. Kaviani, p. 28. Nāṣir-i-Khosraw visited Jerusalem in A.D. 1047. The custom persisted in later centuries too. Cf. Ibn Athīr XII, p. 14, l. 5-7, where Ṣalāḥ al-Dīn is reported to have proceeded from Safad to Jerusalem expressly for that purpose.

[4] This must not be taken too literally. 20,000 is used by Nāṣir-i-Khosraw and other writers as a round sum. Thus he gives that number as the total of the population of Jerusalem (p. 29), as well as of Tripoli in Syria (p. 18), while a source quoted by Ibn Kathīr XI, p. 20, alleges that the followers of the heretical doctrines of Ibn Karrām in Jerusalem alone amounted to the same number.

were not confined to that town—helped to give a semblance of truth to the calumnious reports of Ya'qūbī and Eutychius.[1]

Thus far our examination of the sources has shown that nothing in them justifies the assumption that the Dome of the Rock was originally conceived to replace the Ka'ba. This testimony of the sources may be corroborated by some general historical considerations. It seems obvious that 'Abd al-Malik could not endanger his position more than by trying to divert the Ḥajj from the Holy Places most solemnly proclaimed as such in the Qur'ān. The very incorporation of the rites of the pre-Islamic sanctuaries in and around Mecca into the Islamic religion constituted the decisive step by which Islam made itself independent of the older monotheistic religions. By violating so basic a commandment, 'Abd al-Malik would have marked himself as a Kāfīr, against whom the Holy War was obligatory. Moreover, Rajā' b. Ḥaywā', the official in charge of the erection of the Qubbat al-Ṣakhrā,[2] was an intimate friend of the pious caliph 'Omar b. 'Abd al-'Azīz as well as a famous theologian, who could never have given his consent to such a flagrant break with the koranic Ḥajj, one of the five pillars of Islam, and according to all we know, 'Abd al-Malik himself was an orthodox and observant Muslim. All this taken together compels us to discard the notion that the Umayyad caliph intended to replace the chief sanctuary of Islam by another building.[3]

It is, however, not difficult to understand the historical conditions which favored the erection of the Dome of the Rock. The first generation of Muslims, accustomed to the simplicity of the Prophet's own mosque in Medina, was content with that primitive wooden structure on the Ḥaram al-Sharīf of Jerusalem which served as a building

[1] Many historians, e.g. Ṭabarī, part 3, p. 2128, Abu-l-Fidā, II, p. 58, l. 23, Ibn Khaldūn, III, p. 336, l. 7, ascribe—under the year 278—to the Isma'īlī Qarmaṭs of Kufa the custom of turning in prayer to Jerusalem instead of Mecca and also of making the pilgrimage thither. These reports seem to be of the same value as the allegation that this esoterical sect practiced communal property of women.

[2] Mujīr al-Dīn I, p. 241 and other sources.

[3] Already J. Wellhausen doubted whether 'Abd al-Malik really had the intention of substituting Jerusalem for Mecca (Die Absicht, Jerusalem anstelle von Mekka zu setzen, *wenn er sie je gehabt hat, ...*), *Arabisches Reich*, p. 133.

On the other hand, Mu'āwiya's endeavor, repeated by al-Walīd (Ṭabarī, part 2, p. 92), to transfer the *minbar* of the Prophet from Medina to Syria was quite a different matter. The pulpit belonged to the insignia of the ruler; thus it was only natural that the Umayyad caliphs tried to gain possession of the Prophet's own pulpit.

of worship in Mu'āwiya's times, as described by the French traveler Arculf about 670 A.D. But the gorgeous splendor of the Christian churches of Jerusalem, Lydda, Damascus, Edessa (Urfa), and other towns of Syria, could not have failed to make a deep impression on the second generation, which had already grown up in the newly conquered countries and become imbued with aesthetic feelings and a more refined taste. In a well-known passage of his Book of Geography (second edition, p. 159, ll. 4-11) al-Maqdisī tells us how his uncle excused 'Abd al-Malik and al-Walīd for spending so much good Muslim money on buildings: They intended to remove the *fitna*, the 'annoyance', constituted by the existence of the many fine buildings of worship of other religions. The very form of a rotunda, given to the Qubbat al-Ṣakhra, although it was foreign to Islam, was destined to rival the many Christian domes. The inscriptions decorating the interior[1] clearly display a spirit of polemic against Christianity, while stressing at the same time the koranic doctrine that Jesus Christ was a true prophet. The formula *lā sharīka lahu* 'God has no companion' is repeated five times, the verses from Sura 19:34-37, which strongly deny Jesus' sonship to God, are quoted together with the remarkable prayer: *allāhumma ṣallī* (with *yā* for the more grammatical *ṣalli* without *yā*) *'alā rasūlika wa'abdika 'Īsā b. Maryam* 'Pray for your Prophet and Servant (not Son, of course) Jesus.' All this shows that rivalry with Christendom, together with the spirit of Islamic mission to the Christians, was at work at the creation of the famous Dome.

There remains the question why 'Abd al-Malik engaged in so vast an undertaking as the construction of the Qubbat al-Ṣakhra—which cost him seven years of revenue from Egypt, his richest province[2]—at a time when he waged war against Ibn Zubayr. Unfortunately, the authentic old reports about the erection of the Dome of the Rock are as scanty as those about the war with Ibn Zubayr are copious. While we possess, therefore, excellent knowledge of the details of the conflict, we can only conjecture what were 'Abd al-Malik's personal intentions or those of his entourage concerning that building, in addition to the general trends of the epoch discussed in the previous paragraph. As a matter of fact, the war with Ibn Zubayr, once the attack on Palestine was repulsed in the second battle of

[1] Cf. *Corpus Inscriptionum Arabicarum* II, p. 214. *Répertoire d'épigraphie arabe* 7-10.

[2] Mujīr al-Dīn I, p. 241, line 11.

Ajnādayn,[1] did not constitute a heavy burden for the Umayyads. For Ibn Zubayr himself, who took refuge in the Ḥaram of Mecca, was unable to assume the initiative, while his mighty brother, Muṣʿab, who acted as viceroy of Iraq, wasted his resources in many years of civil war with Shiʿites and Kharijites. With typical Umayyad patience, ʿAbd al-Malik waited until the Zubayri provinces fell into his hands one after another without any serious fighting. During these years of suspense, the Umayyad ruler had sufficient leisure for the construction of the magnificent Dome of the Rock, by which deed he was able to prove that HE was the real protagonist of Islam and not Ibn Zubayr, who timidly 'stuck his tail in the Ḥaram.'[2] This, if any, is the only connection between the history of the Qubbat as-Ṣakhra and the Zubayri contest for the caliphate.

Finally, we have to consider the fact, rightly observed by Goldziher, that the holiness of Jerusalem and of Palestine in general formed the object of a vivid controversy, which found its expression in many sayings and stories. The examples adduced by Goldziher could easily be augmented by a great many other instances selected from writers of different periods. This alone shows that the cause of the controversy could not have been a political crisis of transient importance. The earliest polemic against the Ṣakhra is contained in the often repeated story[3] according to which Kaʿb al-Aḥbār, the learned Jew converted to Islam, proposed to the caliph ʿOmar that the place of prayer in Jerusalem should be fixed north of the Ṣakhra, so that the Muslims should turn during their prayers towards the Holy Rock and the Kaʿba at one and the same time; to which ʿOmar replied "you want to adapt yourself to Jewish usage, but we were not told to pray towards the Ṣakhra, but towards the Kaʿba alone." Of ʿOmar's son ʿAbdallah it was said that he prayed in the

[1] The first battle of Ajnādayn was fought in July 634, when Khālid b. al-Walīd defeated and dispersed the Byzantines. Miednikoff, the Russian historian, suggested the reading of that name as Jannabatain, which was accepted by Caetani, Becker and others. But a verse composed by a Kalbī poet on the occasion of the second battle at that place, when ʿAbd al-Malik, at the beginning of his reign, routed Ibn Zubayr's followers, proves that the true reading can only be al-Ajnādayn, which is actually given in all Arabic sources. Balādhurī, Ansāb al-Ashrāf V, p. 158, l. 20. Masʿūdī, Murūj al-Dhabab V, p. 225.

[2] Ansāb al-Ashrāf V, p. 348, l. 13.

[3] Ibn ʿAsākir, Ta'rīkh Dimashq I, p. 176. Bakrī, Muʿjam, p. 600. Mujīr al-Dīn I, p. 227.

al-Aqṣa mosque without even paying a visit to the Dome of the Rock.[1] Al-Awzāʿī, the famous Faqīh, prayed with his back towards the Ṣakhra *walam ya'ti shay'an min almazārāt* 'and did not go to any of the holy places usually visited."[2] The same was reported of Wakīʿ b. al-Jarrāḥ.[3] There exists a vast mass of literature on the *faḍā'il al-Quds*, the religious importance of Jerusalem and Palestine, which was handed down partly in special compilations or was incorporated in books of different types,[4] but at the same time the validity of the material included was often a matter of controversy. Referring to the well-known popular belief that Jerusalem would be the scene of the Resurrection, Muṭahhar b. Ṭāhir al-Maqdisī remarks in his *Kitāb al-Bad' wal-Ta'rīkh*[5] (vol. 2, p. 230-1): "The Muslims say that the dead will be quickened and assembled in Jerusalem and a tradition to this effect is attributed to the Prophet. Many Jews share the same belief. But I have heard someone say that this was one of the inventions[6] of the people of Syria and that Allah would resurrect the dead wherever it pleased him." In the same way Ibn Kathīr (died 774 A.H./1373 A.D.) characterizes the stories about the Last Judgment, which was to take place in Jerusalem, as inventions intended to attract visitors to the Holy City[7] and the great theologian Ibn Taymiyya (died 682 A.H./1283 A.D.) devoted a special treatise to the refutation of the exaggerated claims of Palestine.[8]

It is evident from the character of this polemic as well as from that of the persons quoted[9] that its source was purely religious, namely strict adherence to authoritative Muhammedan tradition, the endeavor to avoid any *bidʿa*, or innovation, and to discard popular beliefs, especially those borrowed from non-Muslims. Even a comparatively liberal man like Muṭahhar b. Ṭāhir, who, relying

[1] Shihāb al-Dīn al-Maqdisī, Muthīr al-Gharām ilā Ziyārat al-Quds wal-Shām (edited 1946 by Aḥmad Sāmiḥ al-Khālidī), p. 13.

[2] Ibid., p. 52. Mujīr al-Dīn I, p. 259.

[3] Muthīr al-Gharām p. 54.

[4] E.g. Ibn Faqīh's book of geography, pp. 93-97 ,or Nuwayrī's encyclopedia, Nihāyat al-arab I, pp. 325-339.

[5] Written 355 A.H. (A.D. 966).

[6] *Mawḍūʿ*, which is the technical term for a forged *ḥadīth*.

[7] K. al-Bidāya wal-Nihāya, VIII, p. 280, l. 24.

[8] *Qāʿida fī ziyārat Bayt al-Maqdis*, ed. Ch. D. Mathews, *JAOS* 56, pp. 1-21.

[9] About Muṭahhar b. Ṭāhir al-Maqdisī, who is little known today, but whose above-quoted book was widely read in the eastern countries of Islam, where it was simply called Ta'rīkh-i-Maqdisī, see Cl. Huart, Journal asiatique 18, pp. 16-21 (1901), and J. Goldziher, ZDMG, 55, p. 702 sq.

on the saying of the Prophet, *ḥaddithū ʿan Banī Isrāʾīl walā ḥaraj* "Relate in the name of the Israelites without scruples,"[1] quoted Christian, Jewish and other sources copiously, and who compared them freely to Muslim beliefs, could not but realize that most of the traditions about Jerusalem and its sanctuary were local and largely of foreign origin and had no foundation in the old Muhammedan stock. For this reason, the great Faqīhs had their own ideas about the matter.

On the other hand, there existed a large group of Muslims who were fervent champions of the particular sanctity of Jerusalem and Palestine in general; these were the ascetics and mystics, later to be known as Sufis. Almost all of the great early mystics—although originating mostly in Iran and other Eastern countries—such as Sufyān al-Thawrī, Ibrāhīm b. Adham, Bāyazīd Bisṭāmī, Bishr al-Ḥāfī, Sarī al-Saqaṭī, are reported to have visited Jerusalem.[2] The greatest pleasure in life according to Sufyān al-Thawrī was to eat bananas in the shadow of the Qubbat al-Ṣakhra (Mujīr al-Dīn, I, p. 259), while Bishr contented himself with lying down on his side under the heaven in the same place (ibid., p. 261). Bananas, it may be remarked in passing, were a novelty at that time. They were grown in the Jordan valley and brought from there to Jerusalem.

The examples of the early mystics was followed by their pupils, above all the great Ghazālī, whose seclusion in the sanctuary of Jerusalem in the year 1095, described by himself in his *Munqidh* (edition 1329, p. 30) was reported by the chronicles as a remarkable historical event.[3] Kāzirūnī, the Persian saint (died A.D. 1034), ate only bread made of grain grown from seeds coming from Jerusalem, because only there, he believed, was food *ḥalāl*, free from religious taint.[4] Even Abū Saʿīd b. Abi 'l-Khayr, the most "freethinking" of the mystics, knows how to tell a story of the appearance of Khidr

[1] K.al-Badʾ wal-Taʾrīkh, III, p. 95, l. 8. About this saying of the Prophet cf. Goldziher, ZDMG 58, p. 926, REJ 44, p. 64.

[2] Cf. Mujīr al-Dīn I, 251-258 and the relevant biographies in ʿAṭṭār's Tezkiret el-Evliya, Abū Nuʿaym's Ḥilyat al-awliyāʾ, Ibn ʿAsākir's Taʾrīkh Dimashq, Ibn Saʿd's Ṭabaqāt, al-Qushayri's Risāla, al-Sarrāj's Lumaʿ etc.

[3] Ibn al-Athīr, X, p. 172, Al-Yāfiʿī, Mirʾāt al-Janān III, p. 146. Ibn Kathīr, XII, p. 149. In Jerusalem he wrote a part of his classic, the Iḥyā ʿUlūm al-Dīn, at least the epitome of the Muslim creed, called al-Risāla al-Qudsīya 'The Epistle from Jerusalem', included in the first section of the book (cf. vol. I, p. 93, l. 4 of the edition of 1352/1933).

[4] ʿAṭṭār, Tezkire, II, p. 293, l. 23.

(the Muslim equivalent of the prophet Elijah) in Jerusalem.[1] Abu 'l-Najīb al-Suhrawardī, the first of a long series of famous mystics of this name, set out on a pilgrimage to Jerusalem in 1163.[2] The same attitude towards Jerusalem is to be observed in the writings of the greatest of the later mystics, Sha'rānī[3] (died 973/1565).

As in many other matters, the mystics only developed and expanded ideas which originated in early Islam. The Koran itself calls Palestine the *Holy Land*, when it lets Moses say to the Children of Israel: "My people, enter the Holy Land, which God has destined for you."[4] The term is quite common in ancient Muslim literature, although it was dropped later on and replaced by Sha'm (Shām), a term comprising Palestine, Lebanon, and Syria. A Jewish religious scholar predicted to the caliph 'Omar that "the governor of the Holy Land," that is to say Mu'āwiya, would at one point take his place as ruler of Islam.[5] A canonical collection of traditions about the Prophet reports the following story in the name of Ibn Ḥawāla one of his younger companions: "The Messenger of God put his hand on my head and said: when the (caliphate) will fix its place in the Holy Land, earthquakes and other tribulations will occur and the Hour (of the Last Judgment) will be nearer than my hand is now to your head."[6] Speaking about the Jewish custom of transporting the dead to Palestine to inter them in the sacred soil, 'Urwa b. Zubayr, 'Abdallah's brother, uses the term the Holy Land.[7] It may be remarked in passing that this custom, which is related to the belief, referred to above, that the Last Judgment and Resurrection will take place in Jerusalem, was later adopted by many prominent Muslims.

Palestine was holy, because it was the homeland of prophecy and of God's revelation. "I heard," one of Muhammad's companions is credited as saying, "that nowhere a messenger was sent by God except in Sha'm, and when he was not from Sha'm, he was at least

[1] R. A. Nicholson, Studies in Islamic Mysticism, p. 66.

[2] A. J. Arberry, An Introduction to the History of Sufism, p. 68.

[3] Cf. his books Laṭā'if al-Minan I, p. 289, l. 26-30; Durar al-Ghawwāṣ fī Fatāwi 'Alī 'al-Khawwāṣ, 1277, p. 76; Lawāqiḥ al-Anwār al-Qudsiyya, II, p. 109.

[4] Sura 5: 21: *al-arḍ al-muqaddasa*, which goes back in the last instance to Zechariah 2:12 (in the Hebrew text verse 16) and similar sources. In Sura 17: 7, the Temple of Jerusalem is referred to as *the* Mosque.

[5] Ṭabarī, part 1, pp. 3251-2.

[6] Sunan Abū Dā'ūd, book 15, par. 33.

[7] Ṭabarī, part 1, p. 486, l. 12.

carried there in a nightly apparition (like Muhammad or Ezekiel)." This statement is at variance with the many stories of the Koran about prophets acting in ancient times in various parts of Arabia, but reflects the well known rabbinic theory that God's spirit rests upon men solely in the Holy Land.[1]

Furthermore, "Sha'm was the mine of the ascetics and servants of God (i.e. holy men)"[2] and in particular of the forty "just"[3]—a Hebrew term, which is rarely used—or the *abdāl*, "the substitutes", whose righteousness protects humanity from drought and other calamities. They were called "substitutes", because God in his mercy always sees to it that a new righteous man arises in the Holy Land when another dies, because otherwise the world would perish.[4] A goodly number of Muslim traditions to this effect is acsribed to Kaʿb al-Aḥbār, the Jewish convert to Islam, which in itself is of course no proof of their Jewish origin. There can be, however, no doubt that some relationship must exist between the idea of the *abdāl* and the rabbinical theory of the thirty-six (or thirty, or forty-five) hidden "just", who through their piety save the world. It is also noteworthy that in the ancient texts the *abdāl* appear exclusively in the plural. Thus, it seems, the notion was taken over as a whole and did not develop, as in Judaism, from the belief in the world saving power even of one righteous man.[5]

Exhortations to live in Palestine are found in ancient Muslim literature in a wording which is strangely reminiscent of pre-Islamic Hebrew sayings. When the above mentioned Ibn Ḥawāla was reluctant to take up residence in Sha'm, the Prophet allegedly conveyed to him the following pronouncement of God: "It is the choicest of all my countries, therefore I place there the best of my servants," cf. the similar statement put into God's mouth in a midrash: "The Holy Land is dear to me and Israel is dear to me. Therefore I let the latter dwell in the former."[6] This idea is connected in both literatures

[1] Saying of Ḍamra b. Rabīʿa, quoted by Ibn ʿAsākir I, p. 36. The rabbinic theory cf.e.g. Louis Ginzberg, The Legends of the Jews, 5, p. 301, vol. 6, p. 411.

[2] Al-Nuwayrī, Nihāyat al-arab I, p. 340.

[3] Ibn ʿAsākir I, p. 62, ascribed to Ḥasan al-Baṣrī.

[4] Cf. EI[2], 94-95, s.v. Abdāl (by I. Goldziher), and Ibn ʿAsākir I, pp. 59-62, which gives many versions of this tradition.

[5] For the Jewish 30, 36, or 45 "just" and their connection with Palestine see Ḥullin 92a and the sources discussed in C.G. Montefiore and H. Loewe, *Rabbinical Anthology*, Meridian Books, pp. 231-2.

[6] Ibn ʿAsākir I, p. 33, l. 3, and the sources quoted there. Bamidbar Rabba ch. 23.

with the migration of the patriarch Abraham to Palestine. Migration to a place to which duty calls, *hijra,* was a title of honor in Islam since Muhammad's followers emigrated at his command from Mecca to Medina. "The best of all men are those who migrate to a place to which Abraham migrated"—so goes a saying attributed to the Muslim prophet, to which the following midrash should be compared: "When Abraham wandered around in Mesopotamia, he saw its people carousing and leading a frivolous life, whereupon he said: 'I should hate to live in this country'. When he passed into Palestine and observed its inhabitants working all day, weeding at the time of weeding and hoeing at the time of hoeing, he exclaimed: 'may this country be my lot'."[1]

In both literatures, the frugality and purity of life in the Holy Land are extolled. The midrash just quoted is a case in point. "Dry bread consumed in peace...," says another midrash with reference to Proverbs 17:1, "this is the Land of Israel, where a man may have nothing but bread and salt every day, but will partake of eternal life—is better than a house full of meat-courses, but also of strife—this is life abroad, where wrongdoing and rapacity prevail."[2] Similarly the Muslim mystics emigrating to the Holy Land, or, Sha'm, are depicted as being satisfied there with the lowest of manual occupations and enjoying their life of privation and austerity.[3] "I have emigrated to Sha'm in order to eat there food free from religious taint," says Ibrahīm b. Adham, the former prince who earned his frugal livelihood in the Holy Land as a porter or watchman.[4] Finally, as proved by the story of the Persian saint Kāzirūnī, quoted above p. 142, the very soil of "Jerusalem"[5] was regarded as producing immaculate food, unsoiled by any tinge of injustice.

In view of the close connections between certain circles of the early Muslim pietists with their Jewish counterparts, which were

[1] Sunan Abū Dā'ūd, book 15, par. 3. Ibn 'Asākir I, p. 54 and parallels. Bereshith Rabba ch. 39, ed. Theodor-Albeck, p. 371.

[2] Yalquṭ Shim'oni, Proverbs 17:1.

[3] The term Holy Land is used in this connection with regard to Abū Muslim al-Khawlānī, one of the earliest pietists, who left his native town of Basra for Palestine, cf. Ḥilyat al-Awliyā' 2, p. 125, l. 7 and Ibn Sa'd, Ṭabaqāt 7, part 2, p. 157, l. 22.

[4] Cf. the sources indicated above page 142, note 3 and EI[1] s.v. Ibrāhīm b. Adham (by R. A. Nicholson).

[5] Both the Arabic and the Hebrew names of Jerusalem were used occasionally to designate also the Holy Land in general. The Syriac Christians had the same usage.

in fact a direct continuation of similar relationships at the time of the Prophet and his companions, it is not surprising that some notions about the sanctity of Jerusalem and Palestine attested in Jewish sources should have found their way into Islam. It seems, however, to the present writer that an equally strong, if not stronger, influence was exercised in this respect by the example of the Christian monks and hermits. Even after the conquest of Jerusalem by the Muslims, the city remained predominantly Christian for many years, and the barren hills of Judea and the forests of Mount Lebanon teemed with recluses of Christian anchorites. It was these from whom the fledgling Muslim pietists sought instruction in the mysteries of a saintly life. "I asked a monk in Jerusalem", or "I learned from a monk at the gate of Jerusalem", are stereotypes found in Muslim literature with regard to teachings about the Holy City or the Holy Land.[1] It is instructive in this respect to compare the stories of Ibrāhīm b. Adham's solitary life on the mountains of Palestine or Lebanon with the report of an early Muslim historian about a deacon from Alexandria, who travelled to Jerusalem to pray there in the Church of the Holy Sepulchre and then to rove for a month over the hills of Judea. The extension of the term The Holy Land to cover the whole of Sha'm, i.e. including Lebanon and Syria, might have had its origin not only in pre-Islamic usage, which conceived the fertile area north of Arabia as one region, but in the fact that some of the main centers of Christian monastic and hermit life were found outside Palestine.

Another factor too most probably contributed to this broadening of the term "The Holy Land" and its application to the whole country stretching along the eastern shores of the Mediterranean. It was this part of the Muslim realm which, during the first century of Islām, bore the brunt of the battle in the prolonged contest with Byzantium. While the very idea of a sacred soil, expressed already in the Koran, was originally and essentially religious, it is only natural that it was used to attract volunteers for the perpetual war against the unbelievers on the Syrian front. Ibrahīm b. Adham, the Iranian saint, whom we have repeatedly met as a fervent devotee to the holiness of Sha'm, died on an expedition against Byzantine forces. Again during Crusader times there was a revival of Muslim literature on the religious merits of Sha'm. Similarly, in Judaism,

[1] Muthīr al-Gharām (see above page 141), pp. 57 and 58, and Mujīr al-Dīn I, p. 256, ll. 1 and 6.

the overemphasis on the mystical powers of the soil of the Holy Land was not without practical motifs. When during the wars of 67-70 and 132-135 A.D. Palestine was terribly devastated, it became difficult to make a livelihood there, and many people sought shelter in more prosperous countries. Under these circumstances, the Jewish sages insisted that full salvation in this world and in particular in the world to come was possible only through life in the Holy Land.

In view of the complicated and controversial problems dealt with in this paper, a summary may be appropriate.

1. Early Islamic literature contains a great many sayings either recommending or censuring the notion of the particular sanctity of Palestine, Jerusalem and the Dome of the Rock. The assumption that this vast material should have been created during the short years of the contest for the caliphate between ʿAbd al-Malik and Ibn Zubayr (approximately 66-73 A.H.) is extremely unlikely and is refuted by the fact that the ancient sources which provide a most detailed account of this war, make not the slightest allusion to such a controversy.

2. In particular there is no foundation to the surmise that the Dome of the Rock in Jerusalem was erected in order to divert the Muslim pilgrimage from the holy sites of Islam to those of Judaism and Christianity. It is high time for this Shiʿite fable to disappear from our textbooks.

3. The erection of the Dome of the Rock was prompted by the cultural needs of the second generation of Muslims. It was intended —as proved by its inscriptions—as a means of rivalry with the Christians and as an appeal to them to join the new religion, which, so to say, incorporated their own. Finally, it was apt to show to the Muslims that ʿAbd al-Malik and not Ibn Zubayr was the real champion of Islam.

4. The ancient, but later discontinued, custom of assemblies of Muslims in Jerusalem during the days of the pilgrimage was not particular to that city and did not originate there. We hear about it first in Basra, Iraq, then with regard to Fusṭāṭ, the ancient capital of Egypt, and only very much later with respect to Jerusalem.

5. The veneration for the Holy Land was particularly cultivated by Islamic pietists and ascetics. Some of these must have been in close contact with congenial Jewish circles, as may be concluded from the many reminiscences on the subject from rabbinical literature found in early Islamic writings. It seems, however, that the

movement received its main impetus from the example of the Christian monks and anchorites of Palestine and Lebanon.

6. The opposition of Muslim religious scholars to the over-emphasis of the holiness of Palestine, Jerusalem and the Dome of the Rock had its origin not in transient political, but intrinsic religious motives. They were well aware of the foreign and un-canonical character of most of the sayings or usages ascribed to the Prophet or his Companions in this matter.

7. Sayings about the holiness of al-Sha'm, i.e. the region encompassing Palestine, Lebanon and Syria, and the merit of visiting or even living there, became widely popular when that territory was threatened by the enemies of Islam, as by the Byzantines in early Islamic times and by the Crusaders in later centuries. In short, it was not inner-Islamic political rivalries which originated the dissension over the significance of the Holy Land for Islam, but differing religious attitudes. In later medieval times the mystical and legalistic trends in Islam merged and, under additional pressure from outside, the same happened with the contrasting ideas about the sanctity of Jerusalem and Palestine.[1]

[1] On the spiritual and artistic background of the erection of the Dome of the Rock see also Oleg Grabar, "The Umayyad Dome of the Rock in Jerusalem", *Ars Orientalis* 3 (1959), pp. 33-62. On the place of Jerusalem in Islamic religion cf. also the literature indicated in J. Prawer, The Latin Kingdom of Jerusalem, Jerusalem 1963 (in Hebrew), I, p. 142.

CHAPTER EIGHT

A TURNING POINT IN THE HISTORY OF THE MUSLIM STATE

(Apropos of the Kitāb al-Ṣaḥāba of Ibn al-Muqaffaʿ)

It is generally admitted that the transition of the caliphate from the Umayyads to the Abbasids (750 A.D.), as well as the shifting of its seat from Syria to Iraq, marked a change in the whole structure of the Muslim state: an essentially secular "Kingdom", it is believed, was replaced by the "Imamat", which emphasized the religious character of the highest office of the state. A bureaucratic system of administration took the place of a haphazardly governing aristocracy, and an army composed of mercenaries came instead of one consisting mainly of tribesmen. The national preponderance of the Arabs was superseded by the growing influence of other nationalities, in particular the Iranian, which is believed to have been mainly responsible for the new order of things.

However, the changes that took place in the inner constitution of the Muslim state at that time were much more complicated than is generally assumed. There are many questions which still await a satisfactory solution. What were the limits of the caliph's religious authority in theory and practice? How much was Muslim law, which was the law of the state, affected by it? By what means was the ruler able to control the army, after the old idea of a caste of warriors, exploiting for their common interest the *misera contribuens plebs* (the mass of people paying taxes) was abandoned[1]? What was the

[1] It has often occurred to the present writer that the fabric of the original Muslim state, as it was formed approximately in ʿOmar's time, bore a strange resemblance to the various strata of the ideal state conceived by Plato in his *Politeia*. The Companions (*aṣḥāb*), or rather the small circle of noble Meccans, who, or whose parents, had been closely connected with the Prophet, correspond to the Rulers (*archontes*) or the Perfect Guardians (*phylakes panteleis*). The mass of tribesmen, who, by leaving Arabia, became recognized as the warriors of Allah (*muhājirūn fī sabīl Allāh*) and were registered in fixed dīwāns, resemble Plato's "Guardians" (*phylakes*), while the rest of the population, the non-Muslims, who contributed the means of subsistence to the former two classes, may be compared with Plato's Employers and Maintainers (*misthodotai, tropheis*). The designation of the non-Muslims as *māddat al-muslimīn*, Helpers of the Muslims (Yaḥyā b. Ādam, *K. al-Kharāj*, p. 27 and else-

origin of the new system of administration? Were the people introducing it themselves aware of the changes they effected? Since the early Abbasid period saw the formation and formulation of Islamic law, a satisfactory answer to the questions raised above may further the understanding of an important phase of Islamic religious and constitutional history.

Fortunately, we possess a document of unique value from the first days of the Abbasid caliphate which shows us this regime as witnessed by a shrewd observer, the *Kitāb al-Ṣaḥāba* of Ibn al-Muqaffaʿ.[1] Every sentence in this remarkable memorandum on government bears the mark of strict authenticity and acute observation. Ibn al-Muqaffaʿ was a man of the type and calibre of Ibn Khaldūn and Niccolo Machiavelli, who, although gifted with deep insight in political matters, were barred from occupying leading positions in active politics during the most creative periods of their lives.

This personal tragedy was, in the case of Ibn al-Muqaffaʿ, enhanced by his being a Mawla, a non-Arab. Neither his superior knowledge of Arabic and his general erudition, nor his great wealth or his intimate relations with the highest Arab aristocracy, could save him from a most cruel death, perpetrated, with the connivance of the caliph, by an amir who was unable to retaliate Ibn al-Muqaffaʿ's witty insults except by physical brutality.[2] Although he passed the greater

where) is strangely reminiscent of the terms used by Plato. Two further instances of resemblance are the facts that the Muslims used to live together in special camp-cities, separated from the rest of the population, and that a serious attempt was made at preventing them from holding or cultivating land. As is well known, Plato's Guardians were supposed to live in closed communities and not to possess private property. It is needless to say that the Muslim state came into being without any connection with Plato's theories. The nearest historical parallel was the Sassanid empire, where the nobility, the gentry, the priests, the scribes and all other "Servants of the King" were exempted from the poll-tax. The Sassanid poll tax was graded according to the capacity of the tax-payer and so was the jizya paid by non-Muslims to the caliph's treasurer. (Cf. Nöldeke, *Geschichte der Perser, etc.*, 1879, pp. 246-7).

[1] Included in Abū Ṭāhir Ṭaifūr's (died 280/893) Anthology, the *Kitāb al-Manthūr wal-Manẓūm*, manuscripts of which have been preserved at the British Museum and at Cairo, cf. Brockelmann, *Geschichte der Arabischen Literatur*, vol. I, pp. 138 and 151, Supplement I, pp. 210 and 236. Published by M. Kurd ʿAli in his *Rasā'il al-Bulaghā'*, pp. 120-131. The title ("On the Entourage of the Caliph") refers to the passage on pp. 127-129, which will be discussed later on.

[2] Both the historical accounts and the dirges composed on Ibn al-Muqaffaʿ after his death—which remained unrevenged—show that his deplorable end

part of his life as a non-Muslim,[1] Ibn al-Muqaffaʿ received, owing to the foresight of his father, a very careful training in Arabic, both in the circles of the savants of Basra and under the guidance of two eloquent Bedouins; as a result, his Arabic prose has been regarded as an unsurpassed model up to the present day.[2] His zeal for the preservation of the purity of the Arabic language was almost proverbial[3]. With the arrogance characteristic of a man of wit living

was possible only because in those early days the murder of a mawla was still looked upon lightly, cf. al-Balādhurī, Ansāb al-Ashrāf, fol. 319 b.

[1] Probably not a Zoroastrian, but a Manichaean, since he was charged with crypto-Manichaean tendencies, cf. M. Guidi, *La lotta tra l'Islam e il Manicheismo*, Roma, 1927.

H. S. Nyberg, *Orientalistische Literaturzeitung* 1929, p. 432, seems to believe that Ibn al-Muqaffaʿ did not adopt Islam at all. A. Christensen, *L'Iran sous les Sassanides*, 1936, p. 54, calls him "Person zoroastrien". But the content of the Kitāb al-Ṣaḥāba—see especially below p. 157-164—as well as the story given below (and many other anecdotes from his life) clearly show that he was a Muslim convert. It is also possible that before his conversion he professed the official Persian religion, Zoroastrianism of Sassanid brand, but belonged at the same time to some Manichaean sect. Al-Balādhurī reports the following anecdote about his conversion: In the early days of the Abbāsids (*lamma jā'at al-dawla*), he came to ʿIsā b. ʿAlī, a relative of the caliph, whom he served as a scribe and informed him one evening of his intention to embrace Islam on the following morning. When asked to dinner, he first refused (as indeed a Manichaean or Zoroastrian would have done with regard to a Muslim invitation), but finally accepted—murmuring his prayers before serving himself. When ʿIsā expressed his astonishment that a man who was about to become a Muslim recited Manichaean prayers (*zamzama*), Ibn al-Muqaffaʿ replied: "I dislike the idea of passing a night without having a religion" (*Ansāb al-Ashrāf* ms., fol. 318 b).

This story, which bears the stamp of authenticity, shows—to my mind—not so much Ibn al-Muqaffaʿ's religiosity, as his conviction that any positive religion had only relative value, a conviction disclosed in the Introduction to Kalīla wa-Dimna, cf. the admirable paper of Paul Kraus, "Burzōē's Einleitung zu Kalīla wa-Dimna" in *Rivista degli Studi Orientali*, vol. 14, 1934, pp. 16-18. Kraus thinks that Burzōē, King Anūshirwān's physician, himself already had doubts as to the objective truth of the various religious tenets; cf. A. Christensen, *Acta Orientalia*, vol. 8, 1929, pp. 81 sq.

[2] It is generally believed that Arabic was adopted by the conquered nations as the language of the ruling religion. This is only partially true. As Ibn al-Muqaffaʿ's example shows, members of the subject population studied Arabic most eagerly long before they thought of embracing Islam. In addition to the practical value of knowing Arabic, it was the unique expressiveness and structural lucidity of this language which exercised a spell on the speakers of Middle-Persian or Aramaic.

[3] This gave rise to anecdotes showing the futility of the endeavors to correct linguistic mistakes. Thus, after he had succeeded in teaching his attendant to pronounce *dukhān* "smoke" with one *kh* instead of two (as it is pronounced in colloquial Arabic up till the present day) he was discouraged when hearing him after some days saying *dukān* "shop" (with one *k*), instead

on the border-line between two races he used to correct the mistakes in speech made by the Arab aristocrats (for example, by the amir who afterwards put him to death). In general he was unable to suppress his poignant sarcasm when confronted by people of consequence but little intelligence. He adopted the social ideals of Arab high society most diligently and surpassed it by lavishing stupendous sums on poets and singers, helping friends in distress and by rescuing complete strangers who applied to him for assistance. He also taught the Arabs the fine manners of the Persian nobles; thus, his Arab guests were surprised, when at the beginning of a meal his butler announced the exact sequence of dishes, "so that everyone could save his appetite for the dish he liked best", or when they were given alcali (ushnān) for washing their hands after the meal.[1] Although his books are among the earliest specimens of Arabic prose, he himself regarded his own time as one of late epigones; thus he declared in the introduction to his Kitāb al-Ādāb al-Kabīr[2] that everything of importance had already been said in the works of the previous generations, while for the contemporary author nothing was left but "some fine distinctions and subtle notions, derived from the more substantial sayings of the ancients"—an attitude well suited to a writer whose greatest merit was the translation—in its highest meaning—of Middle-Persian literature into Arabic.

It has been necessary to demonstrate the complex character of Ibn al-Muqaffaʿ in order to put the content of the Kitāb al-Ṣaḥāba into its true perspective, nor is it simple to define the exact nature of that little book itself. It is not a "Mirror for Princes" (a book on the virtues and vices of the rulers), a kind of literature much in vogue in the Middle Ages, for which Ibn al-Muqaffaʿ himself set the model in his Ādāb al-Kabīr and—to a certain extent— in Kalīla wa Dimna.[3] For that type of literature describes the duties of, and provides advice for the rulers in a general way, while the Kitāb al-Ṣaḥāba speaks of a definite historical situation, for which it suggests

of *dukkān*. Or when he had taught a young man of the caliph's family that "black", if referring to a mule, should be rendered with *adham*, not *aswad*, it was exasperating for him to hear the young nobleman applying this adjective also to his black coat (*Ansāb al-Ashrāf*, fol. 318-319).

[1] *Ansāb*, loc. cit.

[2] *Rasā'il al-Bulaghā'*, pp. 55-6. Quoted also by Aḥmad Amīn, *Ḍuḥa 'l-Islām*, vol. I, p. 200.

[3] Cf. Gustav Richter, *Studien zur Geschichte der älteren arabischen Fürstenspiegel*, 1932, pp. 4-32.

definite solutions.[1] On the other hand, it cannot be compared with the Kitāb al-Kharāj of Abū Yūsuf, to which it bears some resemblance. The latter is a compendium of religious law on many questions connected with the conduct of the state on which the caliph Hārūn al-Rashīd asked the advice of his cadi. Ibn al-Muqaffaʿ, however, had no religious authority and obviously was not invited at all to give his opinion on the matters he dealt with. It has been suggested[2] that the Kitāb al-Ṣaḥāba was written to the order of some of the caliph's relatives, to whom Ibn al-Muqaffaʿ had occasionally rendered the services of a scribe. But nothing in the book itself bears out this suggestion. On the contrary, the introduction clearly indicates that Ibn al-Muqaffaʿ wrote the book of his own accord. For, after having described the caliph[3] as austere, open to advice, and living in expectation of future life, as becoming a true Muslim, he continues by saying that these traits encourage a man with ideas to put forward to the caliph suggestions which, it may be assumed, no one had ever made to him before.

[1] Of a somewhat similar character is an epistle addressed by ʿAbd al-Ḥamīd, the famous Umayyad scribe, in the name of his father, to Abdallah, the son of Marwān II, when the latter was away on a military expedition against the Khawārij (*Rasā'il al-Bulaghā'*, pp. 139-164). The second part of that epistle is very interesting for the history of the art of war, while the first part lies midway between the generalities of a "Mirror for Princes" and the concrete advice of an experienced statesman. Of particular interest is ʿAbd al-Ḥamīd's urgent entreaty that no one should be received by the crown-prince, and no request dealt with by him, before the matter had been scrutinized by and discussed with his secretary or his chamberlain, who should, in the appropriate cases, also provide the answers or receive the applicants (*Ras. Bul.*, p. 145). Only fifty years later the caliph had become separated from his subjects to such a degree that Abū Yūsuf had to admonish Hārūn al-Rashīd to be accessible to everybody, "and were it only for one day in the whole year, not in a month." (*K. al-Kharāj*, Cairo 1346, p. 134, l. 8).

In any case, ʿAbd al-Ḥamīd's epistle passed as having been issued by the caliph and was not a private communication as Ibn al-Muqaffaʿ's Kitāb al-Ṣaḥāba, cf. also Goldziher, *Muhammedanische Studien*, vol. 2, p. 67.

[2] C. Brockelmann, *Geschichte der Arabischen Literatur*, Supplement I, p. 236.

[3] The name of the caliph is not mentioned expressly. But as al-Saffāḥ is referred to as dead, (p. 128, l. 1) the caliph addressed must be al-Manṣūr and therefore the epistle was written between 136/754, the year of al-Manṣūr's accession to the throne, and 142/759, the year of Ibn al-Muqaffaʿ's death, cf. F. Gabrieli, "L'opera di Ibn al-Muqaffaʿ", *Rivista degli Studi Orientali*, vol. 13, 1931, p. 231. The repeated references to the fact that Allah had rid the caliph of the man who shared with him the highest authority (e.g. 121, l. 10), seems to indicate that ʿAbdallah b. ʿAlī, Manṣūr's uncle, was already crushed and Abū Muslim, the almighty leader of the Khorasanians, already dead (137/755). The description of the caliph as austere and strong is in conformity with what is known about al-Manṣūr's character.

It is extremely difficult to understand how the Persian nobleman dared to submit to the Arab caliph a complete political program, especially at a time when such eminent Iranians as Abū Muslim and Sunbādh were put to death because of their prominent interference in the affairs of the Muslim state. We may not be far from the truth if we assume that our memorandum, although composed out of serious concern for the well-being of the caliphate, contributed to the arousal of al-Manṣūr's suspicions and ultimately lead to the author's death. Indeed, while reading the long and rather strained captatio benevolentiae at the beginning of the book, one can hardly fail to observe that Ibn al-Muqaffaʿ himself felt that this step was very unusual, and in direct contradiction to his own advice given in the Ādāb al-Kabīr to avoid as far as possible any intercourse with the rulers. Only a strong and genuine interest in political matters could have induced the experienced courtier to disregard the counsel of caution and to put himself, in a manner of speaking, in the place of the ruler of the empire, despite his position as a member of a subject race. To the historian, of course, this attitude only enhances the value of the Kitāb al-Ṣaḥāba.

The first and main subject dealt with by Ibn al-Muqaffaʿ was the army. For the Muslim empire was essentially a military state, whose concern was the upkeep of an army and the raising of funds necessary for its continued maintenance.[1] In later Umayyad times the Arab army had already ceased to be a national all-embracing unit, but consisted of two entirely different parts; the main and more efficient contingent, the imperial guards, had to ensure the caliph's rule over his territories. On the other hand, local corps were used mainly for the Jihād, the war with Byzantium and other foreign states, which was of little moment at the time when Ibn al-Muqaffaʿ wrote. During the Umayyad period the imperial army consisted mainly of Syrian contingents which lived in the other provinces of the empire at the expense of the local population and were for the

[1] To a generation like ours, which is accustomed to the fact that the state affects each and every department of life, the old military state, whose professed aim was mainly the protection of life and property of the law-abiding citizen, seems somewhat crude. But let us remember that some of the most enlightened men of all times, such as Wilhelm von Humboldt (cf. his book on the Limits of the State, 1792), believed that it was precisely that limitation which made the good state. As a matter of fact, the caliph's state left a great measure of freedom to the religious and other minorities. For reasons which will presently be explained, the Abbasid state was soon forced to interfere with the beliefs of its Muslim subjects.

most part stationed in separate quarters or camp-towns (e.g., Wāsiṭ in Iraq). The Umayyad state disintegrated when the Syrian army lost its esprit de corps owing to tribal and other internal friction. The imperial guards of the early Abbasids consisted of Khorasanians, warriors coming from the north-eastern march of Iran who brought with them a great military tradition owing to the incessant border warfare with the peoples of Central Asia. These Khorasanians were by no means pure Iranians. Most of the commanders and many of the men were Arabs, who, however, had mixed with the Iranians and often adopted Persian costume as well as Persian speech and modes of thought. Ibn al-Muqaffaʿ speaks in the highest terms of the discipline and the obedience of these troops, who showed a respect for the life, property and honor of the civilian population a thing quite unheard of in Islam before.[1] There was however one basic difference between the Syrian army of the Umayyads and the Khorasanian troops of the first Abbasids: While the former had been attached to their rulers by natural and traditional ties, the Khorasanians had become the vanguard of the Abbasids owing to religious propaganda. There was no other bond between the caliph and his army besides religious conviction. It was for this reason that "right belief"[2] became most important at that time, a fact clearly recognized by Ibn al-Muqaffaʿ, who made it the cornerstone of his political program.

Despite the enormous mass of information concerning the political and military events which led to the rise of the Abbasids, we have very little exact knowledge about the contents of their secret propaganda. It has been rightly assumed that there was some

[1] This praise could not be due to national pride. First, as we have seen, the Khorasanians were of mixed race. Furthermore, Ibn al-Muqaffaʿ originated from Fārs in South-West Iran (Ansāb 318 a), grew up in Iraq and seemed to have had a strong bias for the ʿIrāqis. See p. 159 ff.

[2] It had already been of some political importance in the later Umayyad period. The Qadarites, who taught freedom of the will, were the favorites of the usurper Yazīd III b. Walīd (Wellhausen, Das arabische Reich, p. 229), but were persecuted by rulers like Hishām (Ṭabarī part 2, p. 1777 and 1733) or Marwān II. Most significant is the speech made by the unsuccessful pretender ʿAmr b. Saʿīd al-Ashdaq after his conquest of Damascus (as early as A.H. 70/A.D. 710, Ṭabarī part 2, 784, 18). However, it must be stated that despite the obvious bearing on politics of a religious belief which taught that man should not suffer a tyrannous rule like a heavenly decree, the sources do not expressly state that the persecution of the Qadarites by Hishām or Marwān II had political undertones. In any case, during the Umayyad rule, these persecutions were on a very small scale and are mentioned only incidentally.

connection between the Abbasids and the sect of the Muʿtazila, which is not surprising, as the theory of the free-will, which the Muʿtazilites took over from the Qadarites, was always favored by revolutionary movements.[1] But although the sources deliberately obscure it, there is little doubt that the Abbasids employed the most extreme theories of divine kingship and possibly even of outright libertinism. This is evident from the numerous extremist religious upheavals subsequently connected with Abū Muslim, the Abbasid chief of propaganda (Sunbādh, Muqannaʿ, Khurramiya, Pāpak), but also from what is to be inferred from direct testimony such as the Kitāb al-Ṣaḥāba. After having stressed the necessity of "putting straight the hands, the thought and the words"[2] of the Khorasanians, Ibn al-Muqaffaʿ ascribes to their officers the belief that if the caliph ordered the mountains to move they would obey, or if he ordered that in prayer one should turn one's back to the Kaʿba of Mecca his will would be done. In order to understand the full import of these words, one has only to recall the well-known Rawendiya Corps incident[3] in which these troops declared Manṣūr their God (*rabb*) and tried to kill him when he was unwilling to accept their devotion. Balādhurī reports that once when al-Manṣūr was late for the Ḥajj, he was even advised to change the obligatory dates for the annual pilgrimage.[4] Ibn al-Muqaffaʿ thought that troops whose officers held such beliefs were a most dangerous instrument in the hands of their rulers, "as if a man wanted to frighten

[1] Cf. H. S. Nyberg, EI[1] s.v. Muʿtazila, vol. 3, p. 852 a. The manuscript of the Ansāb al-Ashrāf contains (fol. 309 a) some interesting details about the relations between ʿAmr b. ʿUbayd, the Muʿtazili leader, and al-Manṣūr, which were partly copied by later sources, e.g. al-Maqrīzī, published in ZDMG, vol. 2, p. 225-6.

[2] I do not remember having read this threefold expression in earlier Arabic literature. But it is found in the Ghatas in the Awesta, cf. H. Oldenberg, "Die iranische Religion," *Die Kultur der Gegenwart* I, III, 1 p. 96.

[3] Reported by Ṭabarī part 3, 129, al-Fakhrī and many others. It is significant that the rebellion was quelled by the noble, but cruel Bedouin chieftain Maʿn b. Zā'ida, who certainly had little understanding for the Khorasanians' religious fervor.

[4] *Ansāb al-Ashrāf*, fol. 311 a. - ʿAbdallah al-Qaṣrī, the Umayyad viceroy of Iraq, is reported to have said that he was prepared to pull down the Kaʿba stone by stone, if he were ordered to do so by his caliph, for rulers were more important in the eyes of God than prophets (*Aghānī*, vol. 19, p. 60, I. II, cf. Wellhausen, *Das arabische Reich* 133, note 3, where the quotation as well as the explanation of the passage is somewhat inexact.). The saying attributed to the Umayyad viceroy is meant to demonstrate his heathen mind, while Ibn al-Muqaffaʿ's Khorasanians believed that the caliph was free to make the most basic changes in Muslim religious law.

people by riding on a lion, while the rider himself was frightened of it more than anyone else."[1]

In order to overcome this danger, Ibn al-Muqaffaʿ suggested that the caliph issue a short but complete catechism[2] clearly defining the beliefs to be held by the officers and men of the imperial army and containing the proofs supporting these articles of belief (p. 122). Officers and men should be given instruction in the Koran and the Oral Tradition, as well as in the basic religious tenets, and be bound to lead an austere life according to the example set by the caliph (p. 124). Ibn al-Muqaffaʿ deals at length with the central question of this catechism: the extent and nature of the religious authority of the caliph. After refuting the old formula of Muslim dissidents that "man owes no obedience to rulers who disobey God", as well as the opposite belief that man is bound to obey his superiors without having resource to the judgment of his own conscience, he explains that all matters for which the Koran and the Oral Tradition had no explicit injunctions were left to the discretion of the caliph. The religious law did not embrace all life, and left adequate room for free decision (*ra'y*). This was the domain of the ruler, while the rest of the Muslims were permitted to express their opinion only when asked.

It is a well-known fact that orthodox Islam has not adopted this theory. The place assigned by Ibn al-Muqaffaʿ to the *ra'y* of the ruler was taken in later theory by the *ijmāʿ*: not the decision of the caliph, but the consensus of the competent religious scholars was to solve the questions for which Scripture and Tradition had no answer. But at the time when Ibn al-Muqaffaʿ wrote—a few years after the overwhelming victory of Abbasid propaganda—it seemed only natural that the caliph should be regarded as the highest religious authority. At that time, the Byzantine Emperor was the absolute ruler of the Church, convoked the assemblies of the bishops, led their discussions and decided theological disputes. Abū Yūsuf himself uses *ra'y* a great deal, but in many cases he lays before the caliph the various possibilities, leaving to him the decision; for, although he was more critical of his own caliph (Hārūn al Rashīd), than Ibn al-Muqaffaʿ was of his, he stood in religious awe of the caliph's office itself.[3]

[1] A favorite simile of Ibn al-Muqaffaʿ, cf. *Rasā'il al-Bulaghā'*, p. 65, l. 5.

[2] 'Amān (p. 122, l. 1, cf. 'amāna, p. 124, 2). The meaning of the word seems to be "safeguard" (which protects its bearer from false creeds), cf. the context of p. 124, l. 2.

[3] *Fakhudh bi'ayyi l-qawlayn, fa'inna dhālika muwassaʿun ʿalayka,* "Choose

Furthermore, it is not necessary to explain in detail that the first Abbasid caliphs—even more than the later Umayyads—often meddled in theological discussions. The Mu'tazilite *miḥna* or persecution of the opponents of the Mu'tazila under al-Ma'mūn and the orthodox reaction under al-Mutawakkil are only the most famous examples of a general practice. We never hear, however, about an official catechism composed by the order of a caliph for the use of his army. Many books were written on the Muslim creed in later times, but these were free compositions by individual authors belonging to different schools. In this respect, too, orthodox Islam, although it often invoked the assistance of the rulers for the imposition of certain doctrines, refrained from too close a connection between religion and state.

In one respect, however, Ibn al-Muqaffa' seems to have foreshadowed later developments. We do not know how far al-Manṣūr followed his advice to discipline his guards through systematic religious education. But later on, from the Samānids, whose efficient training was admired by Nizām al-Mulk in his *Siyāset Nāma*, down to the Egyptian Mamluks and the Ottoman Janizaries, religious education formed an important part of the preparation of choice troops for their task.[1]

Of no small historical interest are also the remarks of Ibn al-Muqaffa' about the administrative aspects of the maintenance of the imperial guards. He strongly advises the caliph not to allow them to deal with the collection of the land-tax, which according to him was detrimental to their morale, incompatible with the dignity of the military profession and a danger to the security of the civil population. Between the lines we read the reason for this unfavorable development (p. 123): even at that very early period the payment of the guards seems to have been neither very regular nor sufficient owing to the high prices of cereals and fodder in Iraq (p. 124). By entrusting them with the collection of the land-tax, the administration seems to have tried to overcome these difficulties.

whichever of the two opinions you prefer, for it is up to you to decide." Ed. 1346, p. 22, 63, 69, etc., Abū Yūsuf quotes freely the decisions of earlier caliphs, p. 48, even of Umayyads, e.g., 'Abd al-Malik, p. 49, Mu'āwiya, p. 179 (and even of their viceroy al-Ḥajjāj p. 69), but the matters concerned in those passages are more of an administrative than a legal or religious nature.

[1] The Mamluk Military Schools were studied in detail by Dr. D. Neustadt, *Bulletin of the Jewish Palestine Exploration Society*, vol. 12, pp. 132-140, the study being a chapter of a comprehensive book on the Mamluk army of Egypt.

But the combination of military command with fiscal power over land marked the beginnings of Muslim feudalism, which was destined to shape the social structure of the Middle East down to the end of the eighteenth century. However, it seems that the symptoms so eagerly watched by Ibn al-Muqaffaʿ developed slowly, particularly at the time when the Khorasanians had been replaced by Turkish slaves. Abū Yūsuf, who deals with the question of the collection of taxes at great length, although objecting to the farming of taxes in general (*taqbīl*),[1] apparently never mentions that the publicans came partly from the imperial guards. C. H. Becker, who gives an excellent summary of the research into the history of early Muslim feudalism, also puts its beginnings a century or so after Ibn al-Muqaffaʿ.[2] Still, it is interesting to discover its traces in the first decade of the Abbasid caliphate, as observed in these passages of the Kitāb al-Ṣaḥāba.

Ibn al-Muqaffaʿ concludes his exposition of the state of the Imperial Guard with the typically Iranian advice that the caliph should organize an efficient intelligence service to keep him informed about all that was going on among his troops in Khorasan, where they were recruited, as well as at the seat of the government and in the outlying garrisons. A state which, as we have seen, was based on the convictions and the religious belief of the imperial guards, certainly needed such supervision.

From the Khorasanian guards Ibn al-Muqaffaʿ turns to Iraq, which, being the focus of Arab colonization as well as of Muslim religious learning, gives him the opportunity to discuss a number of most important questions. At that time, Bagdad was not yet in existence; the towns mentioned were al-Miṣrān, i.e. Kufa and Basra, and Ḥīra. The Khorasanian Arabs themselves, as Ibn al-Muqaffaʿ points out, had originally come from Iraq. Therefore, they were expected to mix easily with the local population, while Iraq in general was the ideal place where the various peoples, in particular

[1] *Kitāb al-Kharāj*, p. 125 sq. Instead of publicans, officials with fixed salary paid by the imperial Treasury should be entrusted with the collection of taxes. The qualifications of these officials should be that of a faqīh able to serve as a judge (p. 127). This may be compared with Ṭabarī's report that in the Sassanid empire the judges were charged with the supervision of the collection of taxes; e.g. reductions had to be granted by them, part 1, pp. 962-3; cf. A. Christensen, *L'Iran sous les Sassanides*, p. 362.

[2] C. H. Becker, *Islamstudien*, vol. I, 241; cf. also A. N. Poliak, "La Féodalité islamique", *Revue des Études Islamiques*, 1936, p. 247-265; idem, *Feudalism in Egypt, Syria*, etc., London 1939, which deal with later developments.

Arabs and Iranians, were able to amalgamate and constitute one united nation. In those days, the mixture of races had become an ideal, just as up to that time purity of race had been almost an article of faith among both the Arabs and the Persians.[1] Ibn al-Muqaffaʿ seems to have been one of the first who expressed the new attitude, which was only natural to a non-Arab, who saw in the Khorasanian blend of Arabs and Iranians the backbone of the empire.

The mixing of the Khorasanians with the Iraqian population so eagerly desired by Ibn al-Muqaffaʿ actually took place, but it was precisely this process which made them unfit to remain the military force on which the Caliphs could rely; before long they were replaced by foreign mercenaries, whose sole or main allegiance to the ruler was the pay they received.

The unsatisfactory position of the Iraqis with regard to employment in the service of the Abbasid government gives Ibn al-Muqaffaʿ the opportunity to discuss the main topic of his book: the *Ṣaḥāba*, the "companions" (of the caliph)[2] and in this connection, the service of the state in general. Owing to their linguistic and religious characteristics as well as to their noble origin, the Iraqis, according to Ibn al-Muqaffaʿ, should occupy the most prominent positions at the court of the Abbasids, in their army and in their administration. In fact, however, they were deprived of their natural prerogative (p. 125) by people "who were neither educated nor of noble birth,

[1] For a detailed exposition of the new attitude cf. e.g., al-Tawḥīdī, *Kitāb al-Imtāʿ wal-Mu'ānasa*, vol. I, pp. 90-95 who corroborates it by a comparison with the successful crossing of various breeds of cattle. Ibn Khaldūn, Muqaddima, part 2, par. 9, maliciously remarks that only very primitive tribes are racially pure. In his polemical treatise "Against the Christians" *al-Radd ʿala'l-Naṣāra*, p. 16, al-Jāḥiz incidentally describes the Jews of his time as rude and incapable of philosophical thinking, "because an Israelite never marries any but a Jewish woman, which inbreeding leads to stupidity, *masākha*." Concerning the historical correctness of these allegations cf. J. Finkel, JAOS, 47, p. 320.

[2] The notion of the "Companion" or "Friend" of the Ruler is very old, cf. the Hebrew title rēʿa ha-melekh "the Friend of the King" (II Samuel, 15:37, 16:16. I Kings, 4:5. I Chronicles 27:33) and its parallels from the Ancient East, to which the *philos* of the Hellenistic kingdoms obviously was but a continuation. However, it seems that Ibn al-Muqaffaʿ had a particularly high opinion of his task: Friendship with the best men of the state appeared to him as the foremost virtue of the ruler. It is obviously for this reason that he devotes the third part of his Ādāb al-Kabīr, which deals with the conduct of state, to the idea of friendship in general. A similar attitude prevails in Kalīla wa-Dimna, cf. G. Richter, *Fürstenspiegel*, pp. 18 and 31.

persons of poor intelligence, well known for their crimes, without merit in either peace or war and—most shocking of all—persons who had passed most of their lives as laborers, having done manual work." Such people had succeeded in obtaining access to the caliph and precedence over the old Muslim aristocracy (Muhājirūn and Anṣār), the scions of noble Arab houses which included the caliph's own family. In addition, those parvenus were in receipt of substantial grants without having qualified for them by literary refinement,[1] religious knowledge or military service. Their only importance was that they served as scribes or doorkeepers (chamberlains)[2] and used these offices to acquire power (p. 128). Ibn al-Muqaffaʿ recounts that when he, together with a party of noblemen from Basra, went to see Abu 'l-'Abbās, the first Abbasid caliph, most of the company broke away before the meeting, because the entourage of the caliph was composed of people who the noblemen believed were beneath their dignity to meet. Ibn al-Muqaffaʿ explains to his sovereign in very strong terms that a ruler was not in the same position as a private man who could promote or neglect any of his freedmen according to his own whims. In the service of the state, only the qualifications and the usefulness of each person to the community should guide the ruler's choice. There were three types of men suited for the service of the state, or, as Ibn al-Muqaffaʿ calls it, the Companionship (of the caliph):

(a) Deserving officers "who should be promoted from the military service to the Companionship",

(b) Faqīhs, whose religious knowledge would be beneficial to the community,

(c) Prominent men of noble birth.

People serving as scribes or chamberlains should have neither executive power, nor the honor of the caliph's company, but should be content with receiving an adequate remuneration for their services (p. 129).

These eloquent passages from the *Kitāb al-Ṣaḥāba* demonstrate what is indeed indicated in many an old source, but not yet fully realized by the historians of Islam, namely that the rise of the Abbasids marks not only the beginning of a new dynasty and a new system of state, but also a great social and economic upheaval. This

[1] The most conspicuous requirements of the Persian *debīr* and the Muslim *kātib* ("scribe").

[2] Cf. above page 153.

in turn had a considerable effect on the organization of the empire. As this question will be dealt with in a separate paper, we confine ourselves here to the remark that the new system was very far from that of the Sassanid state, of which it is the supposed continuation. The Sassanid state was essentially aristocratic, being based on the leadership of the great families and the gentry whose sons formed the nucleus of the royal army, as well as the mobeds, the caste of priests. The recommendations of Ibn al-Muqaffaʿ just mentioned were in conformity with the Persian tradition; his inclinations were indeed intrinsically aristocratic, as may be learnt from many a passage in his books.[1] But the reality of the new Abbasid state, so vividly described in the pages of the *Kitāb al-Ṣaḥāba* summarized above,[2] was very remote from these ideals: the *wuzarā'*[3] and *ʿummāl,* the officials of the central and district administration, chose their staff from their own environment, having themselves come from very mixed origins (p. 125).

Even more astonishing than the plea of Ibn al-Muqaffaʿ for the rights of the Arab nobility is his detailed treatment of the necessary reforms of Muslim law—considering that he was a new convert who had embraced Islam only very late in life. But there is no doubt that his advice was completely sincere, for his chief object was to secure the good conduct of the state, which could not be achieved except by a properly functioning system of law. At that early period, Muslim law was in theory as well as in practice the law of the state, but it was in itself still very rudimentary and ill-defined. Ibn al-Muqaffaʿ vividly describes the dissensions about most basic questions with regard to both civil and criminal law which prevailed not only between two such cities as Kufa and Ḥīra, but also between various parts of Kufa itself, and there was, of course, a far-reaching discord between the two main "schools" of Iraq and Ḥijāz. Where

[1] E.g., *Rasā'il al-Bulaghā'* 61. 62. 66-67. The ruler is advised to meet the needs of the noblemen, but to suppress the plebeians.

[2] Some allowance must be made for a certain degree of exaggeration, quite natural to a man in the position of Ibn al-Muqaffa.ʿ

[3] It should be noted that Ibn al-Muqaffaʿ usually speaks of the *viziers* of a ruler in the plural: e.g., *Rasā'il al-Bulaghā'* 66,7 (together with *quranā',* companions) 77, 12. 80, 11 (together with *dukhalā'* "those that are admitted to the presence of the caliph") 125, 10. 17 (together with *ʿummāl*). This shows that in the early days of the Abbasid caliphate, wazīr "helper" was a general term denoting those employed in the caliph's immediate service—another instance that proves the thesis of the gradual development of the vizierate, cf. below Chapter IX.

decisions were based on traditions (*sunna*), authority for such traditions was often very weak, or relied on precedent, not set by the Prophet or the Righteous Caliphs,[1] but by an Umayyad like ʿAbd al-Malik or a simple amir.[2] But where judgment was given on the basis of free reasoning, *ra'y*, it tended to become quite arbitrary, and the judge did not care whether he was alone in his decision or not.

In view of such confusion, Ibn al-Muqaffaʿ entreats the caliph to take the administration of law into his own hands by creating a Code—to be properly amended by his successors—based on (a) precedents and usage (*siyar*), (b) tradition and analogy (c) his own decisions. Of the traditions only those whose authenticity was attested by good authority and which were themselves reasonable should be included, while for free judgment not so much logical analogy (*qiyās*) as public welfare and equity (*mustaḥsan, maʿrūf*) were to be the true measurement.

It may be asked from which sources did Ibn al-Muqaffaʿ derive this idea of codification by the ruler? Aḥmad Amīn, in his study of the *Kitāb al-Ṣaḥāba* (*Ḍuḥa 'l-Islam*, vol. I. p. 215-6) takes it for granted that *taqnīn qānūn*, codification, was a traditional feature of the Persian empire and as such familiar to Ibn al-Muqaffaʿ. However, as far as it is known, the Sassanids possessed no authorized code of law. The legal sources for that period, whether preserved in Pehlevi or in Syriac versions, were private collections of laws and judgments made by legal scholars.[3] Nor is it reasonable to assume that the example of the Roman legal codes had any influence on our author. It is true that Roman law contributed to a certain extent to the formation of Muslim legal conceptions, although it was not the codes (whose very existence seems not to have come to the knowledge of

[1] *A'immat al-hudā*, meaning probably the first four Caliphs and Umar II b. ʿAbd al-ʿAzīz. In his review of David Santillana's Compendium of Maliki Law (*Instituzioni di diritto musulmano malichita*, Roma, 1926), G. Bergstraesser stresses the fact that many authentic rulings of these caliphs have been preserved, in particular by the *Kanz al-ʿUmmāl*, the well-known collection of traditions. Cf. *Orientalistische Literaturzeitung*, 1929, p. 278.

[2] As we have seen above, p. 158, Abū Yūsuf, Harūn al-Rashīd's Chief Justice, was much less scrupulous in this respect than Ibn al-Muqaffaʿ.

[3] In Pehlevi: the Madhighān i hazār dādhistān, "The Account of the thousand Decisions", written by one Farrukhmard. The Syriac collection was made by a Christian of the eighth century, cf. Christensen, *L'Iran sous les Sassanides*, pp. 51-2. So far no Manichaean code of laws has become known, cf. H. J. Polotsky, "Manichaeismus", *Pauly-Wissowa, Real Encyclopaedie*, Suppl. VI, p. 263-4.

the Arabs) but the practice of law as they found it in the provinces conquered by them, that influenced them.

There remains only one explanation for the ideas of Ibn al-Muqaffaʿ about the codification of Muslim law and belief by the Caliph: they were suggested to him by an acute observation of the Muslim state and religion themselves. Both had arrived at the crossroads where their mutual relationship had to be defined. State control over religion and law—as envisaged by Ibn al-Muqaffaʿ—was one possibility; divorce of the state from religious law with the consequence that the latter would largely become theoretical, while the state developed a secular jurisdiction of its own—was the other. Orthodox Islam chose the second alternative, opening the way for the development of numerous "schools" of religious law which were finally condensed into the official four *madhāhib*. But it is significant that exactly in those years the Christian church codified its own law, the so-called Dionysio-Hadriana (774), which was officially authorized by Charlemagne in 802.[1]

The *Kitāb al-Ṣaḥāba* deals with a number of other questions, of which the section on the treatment of the newly-conquered population of Syria reveals a particularly high degree of political wisdom. But we need not dwell on this chapter nor on others which reflect contemporary history rather than the development of the Muslim state. There remains only the short, but highly interesting, paragraph on the collection of the land tax, the main source of income of the caliphate, which is to be considered here. Ibn al-Muqaffaʿ denounces the tax collectors' arbitrariness and cruelty which have the effect that the landowners who let their fields lie fallow are rewarded for their laziness, while the industrious husbandmen are penalized for their zeal. He suggests that the sums to be paid for

[1] A well-known story, retold, e.g., by Ghazālī, *Iḥyā ʿUlūm al-Dīn*, 1352 vol. I, 24-25, lets Hārūn al-Rashīd (or al-Manṣūr) say to Mālik b. Anas, the founder of the Mālikī madhhab: "I am prepared to make your compendium of religious law (the *Muwaṭṭa*) obligatory for all Muslims in the same way as the caliph ʿUthmān has made his edition of the Koran officially recognized throughout the Muslim empire. Mālik refused to accept this offer, saying: The various provincial capitals have already adopted different usages and the Prophet himself has said: 'the dissensions in my community are an act of grace'" (a ḥadīth, declared as "weak" by Ghazālī). The story itself may be without historical foundation (other sources for it are quoted in *Ḍuḥa 'l-Islām*, pp. 210-211), but it shows, like Ibn al-Muqaffaʿ's suggestions, that the Muslims were well aware of the two possibilities referred to above. The Shiʿite theories of state, and in particular those of the Zaydiyya, deserve a separate study in this connection.

each particular stretch of land be fixed once and for all; everyone should know exactly what was due from him, otherwise no one would put much work into his farm, knowing that the tax collector would rob him of the fruit of his labor.

The system recommended by Ibn al-Muqaffaʿ was not new. It was first put into practice under the Sassanid king Kavādh at the beginning of the sixth century,[1] taken over by the Muslim conqueror in Iraq and introduced under Abd al-Malik even in northern Mesopotamia and in Syria.[2] However, owing to considerable changes in the economic structure of the Muslim empire, it fell into decay in the early days of the Abbasid era,[3] and, a generation after Ibn al-Muqaffaʿ, Abū Yūsuf recommended its replacement by the more primitive system of the *muqāsama*, according to which the state received a certain percentage of the yearly crop.[4] It is significant that Ibn al-Muqaffaʿ insists on the strict application of the Sassanid system, which, if it works well, is of course more conducive to the stability of both the state's and the land-owners' budget than the yearly fluctuating *muqāsama*. As everywhere else, Ibn al-Muqaffaʿ aims at stability and rigid control by the state.

The importance of the *Kitāb al-Ṣaḥāba* lies in the fact that its author, besides being a shrewd observer who was able to make full use of his close connections with the caliph's family, had a very definite attitude regarding most of the problems facing the Muslim empire in those days. That attitude was by no means one-sided; for although he was a Persian aristocrat of Manichaean inclinations, he was fully aware of the benefits of the integration of Persians and Arabs within the Islamic state guided by an established religion.[5] He saw a remedy for many shortcomings of the Abbasid administration in the return to, or stricter application of, the Sassanid system of government. But in other instances his recommendations were suggested to him by a close observation of the inner state of the Muslim religion and empire and were quite contrary to the Sassanian tradition. In a number of cases he foresaw later developments, e.g.,

[1] Ṭabarī, part 1, 960-3. Cf. Christensen, *L'Iran sous les Sassanides*, pp. 361-2.

[2] Abū Yūsuf, *Kitāb al-Kharāj*, p. 49.

[3] The farmers who were unable to pay the tax were compelled to leave their land altogether. Abū Yūsuf, p. 101.

[4] Abū Yūsuf, passim, especially pp. 57 sq. and pp. 100 sq. About *muqāsama* under al-Ma'mūn, cf., e.g., al-Fakhrī, ed. Derenbourg, p. 218.

[5] If the fervently anti-Islamic treatise ascribed to him (see above p. 151), really was his, it might have been written at an earlier period of his life.

the beginnings of Islamic military feudalism, or the introduction of religious education for the imperial guards, emphasized by him again in the closing paragraph of his treatise, where he says that guidance to correct conduct and beliefs (*taqwīm ādābihim wa-ṭarā'iqihim*) was more important for a people than the provision of food (p. 130). In many cases, however, the subsequent development went counter to the ways recommended by Ibn al-Muqaffaʿ. But this fact detracts nothing from the importance of the author nor diminishes the historical value of his statements, for these reveal to us certain tendencies of historical developments which otherwise might have escaped our attention.

As we have seen, Ibn al-Muqaffaʿ expected the caliph to become the ultimate authority in religious matters, as well as the codifier of Muslim law and creed. The Sassanian kings had not occupied a similar position, nor could the model of the Byzantine emperor or the Roman Pope have had any influence on our author.[1] His suggestions reflect the expectations of the generation which witnessed the sweeping victory of the Abbasids and believed that the caliphs from the Prophet's own family would enjoy an authority comparable almost to that of the founder of Islam itself. But although some of the earlier Abbasid caliphs meddled in theological and legal matters, Ibn al-Muqaffaʿ's ideas of a rigid control by the state of the religion of its subjects never materialized. The result was that the state became weak while religion gained what the state had lost: it enjoyed a degree of freedom and a variety of possibilities of development which under strict control of the state it would never have attained.

We shall arrive at similar conclusions if we consider the second main point made by Ibn al-Muqaffaʿ in his Kitāb al-Ṣaḥāba. In his days, a new form of bureaucracy was coming into existence, which was neither Arab nor Sassanian. In accordance with Sassanian tradition, Ibn al-Muqaffaʿ believed that the candidates for the higher offices of the state should be recruited from either the military

[1] Cf. p. 163. The Sassanid king was a half-god, "an immortal man amongst the Gods and a resplendent God amongst men" (Theophylactes IV, 8. Christensen, p. 225, note 4); he was often addressed as mōbedh "priest" (in Firdawsī's *Shāhnameh*), and there are famous instances of founders of religious systems trying to win over the ruling monarch (Māni: Shapūr I, in 242, Mazdak: Kavādh I, about 500). But he was not the head of the Zoroastrian church—this was the mōbedhan mōbedh, the high-priest—nor did he act as codifier of law or religion.

or the nobility, but in reality they were enlisted from the personal entourage of the rulers, mostly people with experience in economic life. This fact is explained both by economic and social developments in general and by the role played by the newly converted merchants and industrialists who were instrumental in the Abbasid rise to power. In any case, Ibn al-Muqaffaʿ was right in deploring this situation. Because of it, the Muslim empire lost its traditional aristocracy and failed to develop a new ruling class, a deficiency which no doubt contributed to the rapid disintegration of the caliphate. But the Muslim religion, instead of becoming the interest of a limited clique—as Zoroastrianism was—became the concern of a vast middle class, and while the Persian religion almost disappeared with the downfall of the Sassanid empire, the dismemberment of the Muslim state had an opposite effect on Muslim religion. The plea of Ibn al-Muqaffaʿ for the closest connection between state and religion was in full accord with the tendencies prevailing at the very beginning of the Abbasid era. Subsequent history showed that this connection was not insoluble.

CHAPTER NINE

THE ORIGIN OF THE VIZIERATE AND ITS TRUE CHARACTER

This paper was written twenty-five years ago, but no substantial changes were made in it, because it is repeatedly referred to in a two volume book devoted to the same subject, Dominique Sourdel's *Le Vizirat ʿAbbaside*, Damascus 1959-60. Despite Sourdel's extensive study, the material presented here for the first time has retained its value and the conclusions drawn from it are valid. Moreover, this chapter is perhaps better suited as an introduction to the historical problems involved than an extremely detailed book. However, in order to enable the reader to form his own judgment, the article is printed here in its original form.

The vizierate is so typical an institution of the Muslim state that the very term vizier has come to be internationally accepted in the sense of an oriental prime minister with unrestricted powers. Nevertheless, we are still far from a correct historical conception of the origin and the true character of this important office. *The Encyclopaedia of Islam* s.v. *Wazīr* (Franz Babinger) takes it for granted that both the word and the institution were borrowed from the Sassanian empire. Philip K. Hitti simply speaks of "... the vizir (wazir), whose office was of Persian origin."[1] In his *L'Iran sous les Sassanides*, which appeared in 1936, Arthur Christensen still adheres to the opinion, expressed thirty years before in his *L'Empire des Sassanides*, p. 33, that "la charge de grand vezir... est un emprunt direct (!) de l'État Sassanide."[2] But when he comes to describe the office of the Sassanian *vuzurg framādhār*, the alleged prototype of the vizierate, his lack of material is so considerable that he must take recourse to the description of the vizierate by Māwardī, the eleventh century Muslim lawyer. In fact, so far, no one has indicated the channels through which the Muslims borrowed the office of vizier, which came into existence more than a hundred years after

[1] *History of the Arabs* (2nd edition) 1940, p. 318.

[2] The list of authors holding the same opinion could be easily extended. In this connection I should like to mention one book especially devoted to the question, i.e., Harold Bowen, *The Life and Times of ʿAlī Ibn ʿIsā, 'the Good Vizier'*, Cambridge, 1928. Bowen says on p. 14: "The designation Vizier, of Persian origin, had been introduced by the Abbasids, who had modelled their Court procedure as closely as possible on that of the Sassanians."

the destruction of the Sassanid empire. As a matter of fact, no sources have been adduced to corroborate the assumption that it *was* actually borrowed. This theory is, indeed, nothing but a mere generalization based on the fact that many Iranians, and above all the famous Barmecides, held the post of vizier in the Abbasid government, and that books and sayings on Sassanid statecraft in general profoundly impressed Muslim writers. But there were many viziers of non-Iranian origin. Furthermore, the Barmecides were not the first viziers, and, above all, their forefathers were Buddhists, not Zoroastrians, and consequently had no connection with the fanatically Zoroastrian Sassanid administration. For the Muslim writers the vizierate was not typically or solely Sassanid. As far as they were concerned, there had also been viziers in the Greek (Byzantine), Roman, Indian and Chinese empires, as well as in the pre-Islamic Arabic kingdoms.[1] It is true that Buzurgmihr, the vizier of the Sassanid King Khusrō Anūsharvān, is the prototype of the wise minister in Muslim literature. However, it was observed by Th. Noeldeke[2] long ago that Buzurgmihr does not appear in strictly historical tradition, but only in the rhetorical and moralist writings of the Muslims, from which the late Russian Orientalist W. Barthold[3] very ingeniously inferred that it was not the historical Buzurgmihr who had influenced the Abbasid viziers, but the picture of a legendary Buzurgmihr which had been modelled after the prototypes of the Barmecides and other great Muslim viziers.

As we see, the Persian origin of the vizierate is far from an established fact. Thus far, the whole question has been treated in a very general way and has, moreover, been based mainly on juridical literature and books of *Adab*, while the historical narratives and sources especially devoted to the subject, like Ibn ʿAbdūs al-Jahshiyārī's *Book of the Viziers and Scribes*,[4] have been neglected. In the following pages an attempt is made to understand the origin and

[1] Cf., e.g., Masʿūdī, *Tanbīh*, pp. 339-40.

[2] *Geschichte der Perser und Araber zur Zeit der Sasaniden*, 1879, p. 251, note I.

[3] "*Die Persische Shuubija und die moderne Wissenschaft*" (The Persian Shuubiya and Modern Research). *Zeitschrift für Assyriologie*, 1912. We shall have occasion to come back to this important article.

[4] Published in facsimile by V. Mzik, 1926. The fact that this most valuable source was published in facsimile and not in print may be the reason why it was used less widely than it deserves to be. It is only recently that the book has been published in print, and this time by two rival Egyptian editors in the course of one year.

character of the Abbasid vizierate from a close study of its beginnings, and to trace the development of both the term and the office step by step until they acquire the meaning we now commonly attach to them.

We need not dwell on the alleged Persian origin of the word vizier. This question has been treated by Professor M. Sprengling of Chicago in a chapter of his article *From Persian to Arabic*[1]. Sprengling discusses the Persian root from which wazīr might be derived. His conclusion is that with the material at hand clear precision is perhaps unattainable. The Pahlavī word "vicir" means "a legal document" or "decision", but is not used to designate an office, rank, or man; the root is also found in the Persian loan-word *gezirpat*, which is used in the Babylonian Talmud as the title of a village official of low rank. The Muslims, although admitting the possibility of loan-words in the Koran, unanimously consider wazīr to be an Arabic word. The eminent Dutch orientalist De Goeje also expresses the opinion that the word is Arabic.[2]

In contrast to the obscurity prevailing around the alleged Persian origin of the word, we have perfect lucidity with regard to its Arabic derivation. The root *wzr* means "to help somebody" and *wazīr* is the "helper". In this meaning the word occurs in the Koran, where Aaron is twice called "the helper" of Moses, and is very often found in poems contemporaneous with Muḥammad, both by poets serving the case of Islam like Ḥassān b. Thābit (Ibn-Hishām, 629, 19)[3], Ka'b b. Mālik (ib. 659, 4) 'Abbās b. Mirdās (ib. 860, 16), and, others who had no connection with it (Ibn-Qutayba, *Shi'r*, 414, I, a Hudhaylit). The word was in common use during the Umayyad period; e.g., Hind b. Zaid, a woman poet, says of Ziyād, the viceroy of Mu'āwiya in Iraq *"lahu min sharri ummatihi wazīru"*, "He (Mu'āwiya) has a helper chosen from the worst people of his nation" (Cheikho, *Khansa*, 187, 10 — Ṭabarī, part 2, p. 146, l. 16), while another poet, Ḥāritha b. Badr, says, addressing the same man:

[1] *American Journal of Semitic Languages and Literatures*, 56 (1939), pp. 331-336, quoting Noeldeke, Ṭabarī 53 and 444 sq., Bartholomae, *Sitzungsberichte der Akademie der Wissenschaften, Heidelberg*, 1920, v. 18, pp. 39 sq. and others.

[2] In a note to R. A. Nicholson's *Literary History of the Arabs*, Cambridge, 1957, p. 256.

[3] I owe this and a number of the following quotations to the card-index of the *Concordance of Pre-Islamic and Early Islamic Poetry*, prepared by the Institute of Asian and African Studies of the Hebrew University, Jerusalem.

"You (Ziyād) are his helper—and what an excellent helper you are!"[1] (ibid., 2, p. 146, l. 15). The word was also used in later Umayyad times (ibid., 2, p. 778, l. 2) and, what is of special interest to us (see below, p. 172), in Khorāsān, immediately before the rise of the Abbasids, (ibid., 2, 1936, II), ʿAlī, the son of the famous Kirmānī, being called the wazīr of his brother.

At this point it may be fitting to leave the history of the word and return to the origin of the institution. When we open Zambaur's *Manuel de genealogie et de chronologie pour l'histoire de l'Islam*, p. 6, *sq.*, or similar books, we get the impression that an uninterrupted line of viziers following each other started with the reign of the first Abbasid caliph. In reality, things were quite different. It is true that we have a man termed vizier even before Abu 'l-ʿAbbās, the first Abbasid, had been recognized as caliph. But it took a long time before the office of the plenipotentiary minister came to be regarded as a permanent and indispensable institution in the Muslim state.

The vizierate originated in the days when the relatives of the Prophet, the Abbasids, were, previous to their rise to power, busy organizing secret propaganda in many parts of the Muslim empire. The Abbasids lived at al-Ḥumayma, a lonely village in the desert south-east of Palestine, and were unable to lead their cause in person. They kept a chief of propaganda in Iraq, whom an old source clumsily styles "*kāna yaktubu ʿala 'l-duʿāt*," "the man who did the work of chief scribe to the secret agents." When this man died, his son-in-law, Abū Salama Ḥafṣ b. Sulaymān, was made chief of Abbasid propaganda at his request and sent to Khorāsān, the north-eastern province of Iran, where the most vigorous Muslim soldiers were found outside Syria. There he was soon recognized by the troops rebelling in favor of the Abbasids, and a fifth part of all booty was secretly sent to him—the most conspicuous privilege of a Muslim ruler at that time (Jahshiyārī, 84-85). When, under the leadership of the extraordinarily gifted Abū Muslim, the revolt finally succeeded, the Khorasanians hailed Abū Salama as the legitimate representative of the House of Muḥammad. However, they stood before a constitutional puzzle: the Arabs did not owe allegiance to a state or even to a ruling family: the *bayʿa* (oath of allegiance) was

[1] It is, of course, incorrect to say, as Wellhausen, *Arabisches Reich*, p. 81, note 1, does with regard to this verse: "the title (vizier) is found here for the first time." Here, as in the other quotations, wazīr is used not in a technical sense, but in the general meaning of "helper". It is however,, significant that the viceroy of the caliph is given this epithet by two poets.

strictly personal and expired with the death of the ruler.[1] At that time, no Abbasid had yet been elected caliph, and anything other than personal rule could not be imagined by the Muslims. In this perplexity, "they publicly recognized Abū Salama and turned over the leadership to him, calling him "the Helper" (wazīr) of the House of Muḥammad. He took over the government and proclaimed the Hāshimite Imamate (caliphate) without nominating anyone as caliph. Abū Muslim used to address him in his letters as follows: "To the Amīr Ḥafṣ... the Helper (wazīr) of the House of Muhammad from... the Amīr[2] of the House of Muhammad" (Jahshiyārī, 85-7).[3] Shortly afterwards, Abū Salama went down to Iraq, where he was also recognized, with the result that when the Abbasids subsequently appeared there he showed no sign of willingness to relinquish his powers to them. It was only with the help of another Khorasani, Abu' l-Jahm, that they succeeded in proclaiming one of themselves caliph and in murdering Abū Salama.[4]

The preceding account clearly indicates the circumstances in which the word wazīr was first applied to the designation of an office. The position held by Abū Salama was something unheard of, and a new word had to be found to describe it. The word wazīr, "helper of one's case in his struggle against another", was very appropriate and, as we saw above, p. 171, in vogue in Khorāsān. How strange and novel the title sounded to Muslim ears at that time may be concluded from a famous stanza composed on the occasion of Abū Salama's murder:

"Lo! the Helper (wazīr), the Helper of the House of Muḥammad has perished. Thus the man who hates you was Helper!"[5]

[1] Even a judgment passed by a caliph became void at his death, unless expressly confirmed by his successor.

[2] According to the majority of the other sources: the Amīn, the trustee, cf., especially *Fragmenta Historicorum Arabicorum*, ed. De Goeje, p. 221, 1. 4-6.

[3] Similar narratives are found in other ancient sources, e.g. Ṭabarī, part 2, pp. 1916-17, and Mas'ūdī, *Murūj*, ed. 1346, Vol. II, p. 222, but they do not give the constitutional point of view so clearly as Jahshiyārī. For Abū Salama's title, cf. al-Ṭabarī, part 3, p. 16, l. 14, and p. 20, l. 14.

[4] It is extremely significant that a later source, the famous Fakhrī, which had such a great influence on the European conception of Muslim history, describes these events with a slight, but very important difference: Abu 'l-'Abbās nominated Abū Salama vizier *after* his coronation and *then* Abū Salama was called "the helper (wazīr) of the House of Muḥammad." Fakhrī was obviously copying Jahshiyārī, but for the sake of uniformity he changed his original. He could not imagine a self-made vizier *preceding* his own caliph.

[5] Ṭabarī, part 3, p. 60, l. 18. Mas'ūdī, Jahshiyārī, etc.

There can be no doubt that the threefold repetition of the word "wazīr" and the ironical assertion that a man who hated the Abbasids was their "helper", prove that the poet and his contemporaries found it curious that "wazīr" should designate an office. At the same time it shows that it was the original meaning of the word, "helper", which was intended and which was familiar to everyone. In the whole matter I can see Iranian influence in only one respect. Their predilection for pompous titles may have inspired the deeply Iranized Arabs of Khorāsān, whereas the Arabs in general at that time, were slow in giving *epitheta ornantia.*

Now we must not imagine that immediately after the fall of Abū Salama another "vizier" was appointed by the caliph. Nothing of the sort is reported in the reliable old sources. Even the comparatively late Fakhrī, who cannot imagine an Abbasid caliph without a vizier, admits that there is a controversy as to who was Abū Salama's successor, and mentions that according to one tradition 'no one' assumed this title because of the bad omen adhering to it after Abū Salama's murder. Some, he says, mention Abu 'l-Jahm[1] (cf. above). Others, like Ṣūlī, prefer Khālid b. Barmak.[2] Concerning the latter, however, we have the more detailed statement of Jahshiyārī, pp. 90-91, which says that he gradually succeeded in uniting various offices in his hand (e.g., the supervision of tax collection and military pay-rolls), until he was *like* a vizier (*ḥall maḥall al-wazīr*, p. 91, 1), which can only mean that in those days there existed no established institution officially called by that name.

This conclusion corresponds exactly to what is known to us about the inner policy of the early Abbasids. Far from consenting to govern by deputy, they murdered, one by one, Abū Salama, Abū Muslim and Abu'l-Jahm, the able men who had paved their way to power. As people born and bred in Arabia, they conceived the same form of government as the Marwānid Umayyads, coming fresh from Arabia, tried to establish: *family*-rule, by which the majority of the importtant posts were held by the brothers, uncles and cousins of the ruling caliph.[3] This is what we find under Abu'l-'Abbās and for some time

[1] Jahshiyārī, p. 156, 2, calls him, in an informal way, the vizier of Abu 'l-'Abbās. Cf. also the list in Ṭabarī, 3, 88, 11, who, however, mentions Abu 'l-Jahm's appointment nowhere in his historical account. For other sources, cf. L. Caetani, *Cronografia Generale del Bacino Mediterraneo e dell' Oriente Musulmano*, 1923, pp. 82-4 (A.H. 136).

[2] Mentioned in Ṭabari, 2, 840, 3, as the *Kātib* of Abu 'l-'Abbās.

[3] According to al-Haytham b. 'Adī, al-Manṣūr says the following to his

after him. When he died, his cousin ʿIsā b. Mūsā, saw to it that the successor designated by him safely assumed authority, a delicate operation, normally carried out in a later period by a vizier or chamberlain. Al-Manṣūr, the second of the Abbasids and the real founder of their administration, was such an autocrat that Noeldeke[1] in his detailed biography of him does not even mention the question of the vizierate under his rule. In this omission Noeldeke's description reflects the old sources, so carefully studied by him. There is even some evidence that al-Manṣūr complained of his lack of a competent collaborator or representative. In three places in his *Ansāb al-Ashrāf*, Balādhurī[2] quotes the following words of al-Manṣūr: "Each of the great Umayyad caliphs had a man who did their work (Kāfiya),[3] but I have no one of this description" (*wa'anā walā kafiyā lī*). These words of al-Manṣūr refer to the three famous viceroys of Iraq under Umayyad rule.[4] There is another saying of al-Manṣūr which shows his want of a competent minister even more directly. Jahshiyārī, p. 81, makes him say: "I envy the Umayyads their scribe, ʿAbd al-Ḥamīd b. Yaḥyā." ʿAbd al-Ḥamīd was the chancellor of Marwān, the last Umayyad, and had a function similar to that held by the later Abbasid viziers. For Marwān was fighting throughout his reign and had no time for the administration of his vast empire. ʿAbd al-Ḥamīd seems to have been a man of ability and character, and some of his sayings are quoted in Muslim writings on statecraft. As we have seen, al-Manṣūr complained of not having found an assistant of this caliber. It is, therefore, not surprising to find that the *Ansāb al-Ashrāf* of Balādhurī, which often represents the oldest tradition known to us, does not mention viziers under al-Manṣūr, and, in a special chapter devoted to him, calls Abū Ayyūb al-Mūryānī, the most conspicuous of al-Manṣūr's servants

son and heir in his political testament: "... Give precedence to the members of your family, overwhelm them with benefits... and appoint them to the important posts, for their being honored is an honor to you" (Ṭabari 3, 444, 7-10). The system, however, proved to be of little success, most probably because the members of the ruling family, like most of the caliphs themselves, were not gifted for administrative work. With regard to this state of affairs al-Haytham makes al-Manṣūr add to this part of his political testament to his son the following statement: "But I am sure you will not follow my advice."

[1] In his book *Orientalische Skizzen*, translated into English under the title *Sketches from Eastern History*, London 1892.

[2] MS. fol. 311b, 583a, 585a.

[3] According to Masʿūdī, *Tanbīh*, p. 339, last line, *kāfī* was the title of the viziers of the pre-Islamic Arabic kings.

[4] Cf. also Masʿūdī, *Murūj*, ed. 1346, II, p. 239, l. 22.

who are styled *vizier* by other sources, simply as *kātib amīr al-mu'minīn*, "the scribe of the caliph" (*Ansāb al-Ashrāf*, fol. 325a).[1] The same is done by Ibn-Kathīr in his *al-Bidāya wal-Nihāya*, X, p. 111, while reporting Abū Ayyūb's fall in 154 A.H., where he had special reason to call him by his official title. Even Ṭabarī, who very often refers to Abū Ayyūb, never speaks of him as vizier. On the other hand, Jahshiyārī mentions viziers under Abu'l-'Abbās, and so does Mas'ūdī,[2] giving a list of viziers under al-Manṣūr, which is expanded by *Kitāb al-'Uyūn, Fragmenta Historicorum Arabicorum*, 268-9. As we have seen, the name of a vizier appears in Ṭabarī in a list of officers under the first caliph.

But we must not attach too much importance to the occasional mentioning of the title of vizier at this early period or to its occurrence in schematic lists. All the historical records of the Muslims which have come down to us were compiled at a time when the vizierate had long been a well-established institution. It is no more astonishing to find writers of the third or fourth centuries of the Hijra ascribing the title of vizier to persons who may never have borne it, than to find historians of the fifth or sixth centuries speaking of the first Umayyads in Spain as caliphs,[3] although they were still far from assuming that dignity. What we have to look for are definite statements concerning the official use of the word vizier, and details about the origin, rise, and particularly, the activities of the more important men who were known as viziers in the earlier days of the Abbasid caliphate.

The first[4] man who deserves our attention in this respect is Abū Ayyūb al-Mūryānī, of whom we have already had occasion to observe that he is called a "scribe" and not a "vizier" in good sources.[5]

[1] In Balādhurī's *Futūḥ al-Buldān*, p. 465, l. 4, in a note copied from Madā'inī, Abū Ayyūb is called vizier. The note deals with the materials used in connection with the government stationery.

[2] *Murūj*, II, p. 231, l. 4 (Paris 1871, VI, pp. 165-6).

[3] E.g., in *Fragmenta Historicorum Arabicorum*, p. 225, l. 11.

[4] In the places quoted above, Mas'ūdī and *Kitāb al-'Uyūn* reckon Ibn 'Aṭiyya al-Bāhilī, who is better known under the name Abu 'l-Jahm (cf. above), as the first of al-Manṣūr's viziers. There exists a famous anecdote about his poisoning by the ruthless caliph (related by al-Fakhrī and others; the original in *Ansāb al-Ashrāf*, fol. 311a), but nothing indicates that he held a position similar to that of a vizier with al-Manṣūr. Possibly there is a confusion with Abu 'l-Jahm's service to Abu 'l-'Abbās, cf. above.

[5] The *Ṭabaqāt al-Shu'arā* of Ibn al-Mu'tazz, ed. A. Eghbal, 1939, p. 17, l. 16 calls him 'the treasurer', obviously in connection with the story reported of him in that book.

Mūryānī came from Khūzistān in south-west Iran and served as secretary to one of the Umayyad governors. In this capacity he saved the later caliph al-Manṣūr from corporal punishment which was to be inflicted on him for participation in a Hāshimite conspiracy (Jahshiyārī, 103). Notwithstanding this, after the victory of the Abbasids he needed the recommendation of a noble Kindite to be taken by al-Manṣūr into his personal service (*Ansāb al-Ashrāf*, fol. 325a). Al-Mūryānī said of himself that he was well versed in alchemy, medicine, astrology, arithmetic and sorcery,[1] but not in Muslim law (Jahshiyārī, 101). At first he served as an assistant to al-Manṣūr's secretary, 'Abd al-Malik b. Ḥumayd al-Ḥarrānī,[2] and the two must have acted jointly during many years, for they often appear together as the advisers of al-Manṣūr in administrative and other public matters (Ṭabarī, part 3, p. 273 and 291).

Abū Ayyūb was of a more sociable character than this superior.[3] When the latter fell ill, he acted as his substitute and finally replaced him. The scope of Abū Ayyūb's powers may be gathered from the appointments made by al-Manṣūr after his overthrow. Three persons were engaged in Abū Ayyūb's place, one for the seal, another for the caliph's general and confidential correspondence, and a third for the royal estates (Jahshiyārī, 139). From this and some occasional remarks of the historians, we may infer that Abū Ayyūb did not supervise tax collection and military pay-rolls, which was regarded as being so important an office as to make its holder "like a vizier" (cf. above p. 173). His was essentially the *personal service of the caliph*, including (a) the attendance on the caliph on public occasions (often mentioned in historical accounts), (b) service as his counsellor, (c) the conducting of the caliph's correspondence, and, last but not least, (d) the administration of the royal estates,[4] a very important office, as the revenue from them

[1] It should, of course, not surprise us to find alchemy and sorcery mentioned in the same category as medicine and arithmetic. On the other hand, it is worth noting that the writer describes his erudition as *strictly secular*.

[2] Of Ḥarrān, the town of the 'star-worshippers'. Converts from this center of secular learning and emporium of international traffic gave to Islam some illustrious scholars and men of affairs.

[3] The smoothness of his character became proverbial. One writer speaks of "Abū Ayyūb's Ointment", which is explained literally: he used to anoint his face with a certain oil before entering al-Manṣūr's presence, cf. his statement concerning his proficiency in sorcery, noted above.

[4] Created by the confiscation of the lands belonging to the last Umayyad caliph and his followers, cf. Jahshiyārī, 92.

seems to have been at that time one of the chief pillars on which the caliph's power rested. It is in connection with this part of Abū Ayyūb's duties that the sources explain his success as due to his suppleness and personal charm.

Al-Rabīʿ, the next man regarded as al-Manṣūr's vizier by many sources, appears as the caliph's personal attendant even more than Abū Ayyūb. His origin was quite different from that of his predecessor. While Abū Ayyūb came from Iran and had formerly served in the Umayyad administration, al-Rabīʿ was a slave and a descendant of freedmen,[1] who had lived for several generations in Medina. An uncle of the first Abbasid caliph bought him, and then gave him to his nephew, who was greatly pleased with his service (*fakhadamahū wakhaffa ʿalā qalbihi*). After the death of Abū 'l-ʿAbbās, al-Manṣūr made al-Rabīʿ his chamberlain (*ḥājib*), under which title he is generally known in Arabic historiography. Some time after Abū Ayyūb's fall, al-Manṣūr entrusted him with the supervision of the royal household (*nafaqatuhu*)[2] and with *ʿarḍ alayhi*, i.e., the act of submitting state affairs to the caliph.[3] These services were called "vizierate" by Jahshiyārī, cf. p. 140, l. 4, 10 and 16.

The origin of the vizierate from the *personal service of the caliph* can be seen clearly from the way by which, under the caliphs following al-Manṣūr, many viziers arrived at their position. When al-Manṣūr appointed his son and heir al-Mahdī governor of the eastern provinces, he "joined to him" (*ḍamma ilayhi*, Jahshiyārī, 141, l. 8) Abū ʿUbaidallah Muʿāwiya b. ʿAbdallah as his scribe, with full liberty to dispose of public revenue (ib. 143, 4), since the heir-apparent was then very young—about seventeen. Muʿāwiya's appointment was regarded as permanent. Khālid b. Barmak says to him, (ib. 143, 9): "You prepare yourself for governing the caliphate" (*turashshiḥu nafsaka litadbīri 'l-khilāfati*). As soon as al-Mahdī became caliph, he appointed Abū ʿUbaidallah to the vizierate. In the same way, al-Mahdī gave a special advisor[4] to his son and

[1] For this origin, cf. Jahshiyārī, p. 140, and especially the lengthy exposition of the matter in al-Fakhrī.

[2] According to *Ansāb al-Ashrāf*, fol. 329b, for sometime also with his correspondence; cf. Abū Ayyūb's office described above.

[3] Al-Rabīʿ shared this part of his office with another, less famous freedman, Jahshiyārī, 153, 7-8. Both appear together on public occasions as the caliph's attendants, ib. 157, 7.

[4] Ibrahīm b. Dhakwān al-Ḥarrānī, again a man originating from Ḥarrān.

successor al-Hādī (*khuṣṣa bi-Mūsā*, ib. 198, 4). This man afterwards became vizier to his young ward (ib. 197, 10). For his second son and successor Hārūn al-Rashīd, on the occasion of his being made governor-general of the western part of the empire, he appointed the famous secretary Khālid b. Barmak as plenipotentiary advisor (*Wa-amara kātibahu Khālidan bitawallī dhālika kullihi wa-tadbīrihi*). Hārūn al-Rashīd followed the same course with his two sons and successors.[1] He gave al-Amīn to the charge of his subsequent vizier al-Faḍl b. Yaḥya (Jahshiyārī 234), while al-Ma'mūn, having at first been the ward of Ja'far the Barmecide (ib. p. 258), received al-Faḍl b. Sahl as secretary and administrator of all his affairs (*'alā kitābatihi wa-amrihi kullihi*). The same al-Faḍl afterwards became his first and most famous vizier (ib. p. 337).[2] And what the fathers did for their sons, brothers did for brothers. After the death of Khālid b. Barmak, al-Hādī nominated the latter's son Yaḥyā b. Khālid to be administrator of all the provinces of his brother Hārūn and to be his kātib (ib. 200). The vizier of al-Mu'taṣim was the man who served as his secretary during the caliphate of his brother al-Ma'mūn (Mas'ūdī, *Tanbīh*, p. 356).

The material adduced clearly shows that here, as in many other matters, al-Manṣūr laid the foundations for a very important institution of the early Abbasid administration whereby the young heir-apparents were, as a rule, given experienced men of affairs, freedmen of the caliph, as instructors, when they were appointed to governorships or other public offices. These men introduced them into the business of a highly complicated governmental machine, and served them, after their assumption of office, as more or less plenipotentiary ministers. In addition, these men were most probably used by the ruling caliphs for the purpose of supervising the crown-princes.[3]

[1] As al-Ma'mūn was born in 170/786 and Ja'far was killed by Hārūn in 187/803, the crown-prince must have been almost a child when he received his prospective vizier as tutor.

[2] In later times we find the acting vizier charged with the education of the heir-apparent. Al-Mu'tazz was under the care (*fī ḥajr*) of 'Ubaydallah b. Yaḥya, his father's vizier. Mas'ūdī, *Tanbīh*, p. 362.

[3] It seems, however, from a poem by Abū Dulāma quoted by Balādhurī, *Ansāb al-Ashrāf*, fol. 318a, that Abū 'Ubaydallah tried to give his ward an independent position by proposing that he should reside in al-Rāfiqa (near Raqqa), and not in Bagdad under the eyes of his father. Al-Manṣūr turned this proposal down after agreeing to it temporarily. The heir-apparents, when given governorships, remained as a rule in Bagdad and did not reside in the capitals of their provinces.

From where did al-Manṣūr take the model for this important institution?

We know from Ṭabarī, part I, p. 855 sq., that Khusrō Anūsharvān, the great Sassanian king, entrusted the education of his son and heir Vahrām to al-Mundhir, king of Ḥīra. In his *Shāh-Nāma*, Firdawsī describes Sīyāvūsh, son of king Kā'ūs, as being brought up by Rustam, the famous hero and ruler of Zābūlistān. But these examples, if not exceptional in themselves,[1] are fundamentally different from the practice of the early Abbasid caliphs mentioned above. The Iranian princes were sent to the courts of other, semi-independent rulers.

This procedure is often found in the education of royal princes elsewhere.[2] In contrast to this, al-Manṣūr and his successors selected from their own household a man whose task it was to educate the heir-apparent, and to serve him afterwards when he became crown-prince and later caliph. These men did not belong to the nobility nor were they free Arabs. They were exclusively freedmen or ex-slaves. The origin of this system can be easily derived from Arabic tribal custom. In Arabia, as in Israel, the slave was a member of the family to which he belonged. Even after his emancipation, the ex-slave remained the follower of his former lord and bore the name of his tribe.[3] Very often the slave or freedman was the confidant of his lord and "ruled over all that he had" (cf. Genesis 24:1). The education of the children was entrusted to him. This custom remained in force well into the twentieth century. "The little sons of the chiefs", says A. Musil, "are brought up by the slaves; they make friends with the slaves' sons and everything that they do is on the advice of the

[1] I do not know of another case of a Sassanian prince being brought up like Vahrām V. Concerning the legendary kings, I may note that Firdawsī's contemporary Tha'ālibī gives a special reason why Sīyāvūsh was sent to Rustam, in his *Ghurar Akhbār Mulūk al-Furs*, ed. Zotenberg, 1900, which, as is well known, is a more faithful reproduction of the original Iranian saga than Firdawsī's epic. The reason given is that Sīyāvūsh's mother died immediately after his birth. That Firdawsī's treatment of the subject is much more poetical, is, of course, quite another matter.—For the education of the royal princes in Sassanian times in general, see A. Christensen, *L'Iran sous les Sassanides*, p. 411-13.

[2] Vahrām's case, if I am not mistaken, has been—or, at all events, may be—compared with the practice of the Egyptian Khedīvs, who let their sons be brought up by noble Bedouin Sheikhs in the desert east of Trans-Jordan.

[3] Thus, the Mawālī, the freedmen of the House of Muḥammad, enjoyed in the Abbasid state the same financial prerogatives as the genuine members of the House.

slaves and with their assistance. The slave... is often the real guardian of his master's orphans, whom he also assists to regain their power and property."[1] Sometimes, a slave child is suckled by the same woman who suckles the son of his lord, in order to constitute between the children a "milk-relationship", which, according to Arab custom and Islamic law, is a bond almost as strong as blood. Al-Manṣūr himself had been brought up in the same way. Yaḥyā, a freedman of his family, was his foster-brother and therefore he entrusted him with a highly responsible task at the most critical period of his career, when, at the very beginning of his reign, the caliphate was contested by his powerful uncle ʿAbdallāh (Balādhurī, *Ansāb al-Ashrāf*, fol. 314a).[2] It is also a well-known fact that Hārūn al-Rashīd was suckled by a woman of the Barmak family whose members were, legally speaking, freedmen,—while al-Faḍl the Barmecide was fostered by the future caliph's mother.[3]

To sum up, we may say that al-Manṣūr, while retaining the system of family-rule brought over from Arabia (see above p. 173), initiated at the same time the rise of the vizierate by transferring an important feature of the household of the Arabic chieftain to the administration of the Abbasid empire. The vizierate thus initiated came into blossom during the reign of al-Manṣūr's son and successor, al-Mahdī, the first caliph to be tutored as crown-prince by his future prime minister.

So far we have studied a very important aspect of the vizierate at the period of its full development from al-Mahdī, the third, to al-Ma'mūn, the seventh Abbasid caliph. We must now turn back and consider in some detail a number of administrations in order to define the scope of this office with more precision.

Abū ʿUbaydallāh, the tutor and subsequent first vizier of al-Mahdī, did not come from Iran, Arabia or Ḥarrān, but from Palestine, where his family had served in the Umayyad administration. His father had been secretary to the quartermaster-general of the second Syrian Army Corps (*Jund Urdunn*) which had its

[1] *The Manners and Customs of the Rwala Bedouins*, 1928, p. 277.

[2] Yaḥyā, however, took ʿAbdallāh's side, and after al-Manṣūr's victory was cruelly put to death for his particularly culpable treachery.

[3] This is, of course, nothing but an intensified form of the original procedure, by which future friends are suckled by the same woman. And the poet Marwān b. Abī-Ḥafṣa is right when addressing al-Faḍl with the words "you and the caliph were suckled at the same breast," Fakhrī, ed. Derenbourg, p. 276. An earlier example of "milk-relationship" between Abbasids and Barmecides is noted by Ṭabarī, part 2, p. 840.

headquarters in Tiberias, hence Abū 'Ubaydallah's *nisba* Ṭabarānī.[1] Fakhrī has preserved two very important notes about this man, probably from Ṣūlī's *Book of Viziers*, which, for the time being, must be regarded as lost. Abū 'Ubaydallah, he says, introduced the system of *muqāsama*, by which taxes were paid not in lump sums for definite areas of cultivable land—the system prevailing in the Sassanian empire for many years—but in percentages from the annual yield of the fields.[2] Furthermore, adds Fakhrī (ed. Derenbourg, p. 247), Abū 'Ubaydallāh was the first to compile a book on Land-tax, *Kitāb al-Kharāj*. These facts show that Abū 'Ubaydallāh's powers were much greater than those of the viziers during al-Manṣūr's caliphate. Indeed, Jahshiyārī says, p. 161, l. 2, that al-Mahdī appointed him to his vizierate *and* ministries (dawāwīn, a general name for the central offices of the caliph's administration). We may infer from this that, as a rule, the office of vizier at the time did *not* include the supreme direction of the general administration.

The first unmistakable literary evidence for the official use of the title vizier is found in connection with Abū 'Ubaydallāh's successor, Ya'qūb b. Dā'ūd. His father, too, had served the Umayyads (as secretary to their famous governor of Khorāsān, Naṣr b. Sayyār). Ya'qūb went over to the 'Alids and finally took service with al-Mahdī. Al-Mahdī was so pleased with him that "he called him *his brother in God and helper* (*wazīr*) and published this in official letters which were set down in the government papers," Jahshiyārī, p. 181, l. 12.[3] We remember at once that "brother and helper" (wazīr) appear connected both in the Koran and in poetry down to the end of the Umayyad period,[4] and we appreciate the official use of the phrase as a further evidence for the definition of this office as one of personal service to the ruler with whom its bearer was bound by ties sanctified through old tribal custom.

In this connection, attention must be drawn to a list of the scribes and viziers of the Muslim rulers from Muḥammad down to Hārūn al-Rashīd, which is quoted by Ṭabarī, part 2, pp. 836-843. In this

[1] Mas'ūdī, *Tanbīh*, p. 343, l. 11.

[2] Abū-Yūsuf, Hārūn al-Rashīd's cadi, recommends this system to his master in his *Kitāb al-Kharāj*, cf. above p. 165.

[3] This fact is alluded to in Mas'ūdī, *Murūj*, ed. 1346, II, p. 248, l. 13, and in al-Fakhrī, who only mentions, however, that Ya'qūb was called the caliph's brother—most probably because later generations could not imagine that the title 'wazīr' was also a novelty.

[4] See above pp. 170 ff.

list no mention is made of viziers before Ya'qūb b. Dā'ūd, whereas beginning with him down to Ja'far the Barmecide, a number of viziers are mentioned by name. It would be erroneous to assume that Ya'qūb is here expressly mentioned as vizier on account of his being the first *scribe* promoted to this office (Abū 'Ubaydallāh also appears in this list, but only as a scribe). For the time being, we do not venture to conclude from the combined testimonies of Jahshiyārī and Ṭabarī[1] that Ya'qūb was actually the first vizier officially addressed by this title (after Abū Salama, cf. above p. 172). But, the possibility that this was the case must be taken into account.

It seems that al-Mahdī, who loved the humanities, music and pleasure more than statecraft, left to Ya'qūb the whole administration of his empire, a state of affairs which was denounced by the blind poet Bashshār b. Burd in the famous lines: "The caliph is Ya'qūb b. Dā'ūd..., while Allāh's caliphate is found between the wine-skin and the lute."[2] But this powerful position did not preserve Ya'qūb from a cruel downfall any more than it did his predecessor. He was replaced by Fayḍ b. Shērōē, who originated from a Christian family of Nīsābūr in Khorāsān. It is again characteristic of the personal nature of the vizierate that with the death of al-Mahdī, Fayḍ ceased to hold public office.

The "vizierate", or, as we should say more exactly, government by deputy, reached its apogee in the times of Hārūn al-Rashīd. Jahshiyārī, p. 211,[3] makes Hārūn say the following words to Yaḥyā the Barmecide: "I delegate to you the responsibility for my subjects. You may pass judgments as you like, appoint whom you like, and spend money as you like, for I shall not occupy myself with these matters together with you." Indeed we hear that Yaḥyā and two of his sons acted as judges in the caliph's place, a hitherto unheard of renunciation of the caliph's most sacred rights. Even Hārūn's unworthy brother al-Hādī did not allow more than three days to pass without "sitting" for public audience in the dār al-maẓālim (Office of Complaints), cf. Ṭabarī, part 3, p. 582, l. 19. The pleasure-loving al-Ma'mūn did so every Sunday, whereas it may be safely concluded from more than one passage in Abū Yūsuf's *Book of the*

[1] Corroborated by Fakhrī's well-known statement quoted above that after Abū Salama's death nobody bore the title of vizier because of the bad omen attached to it.

[2] *Ṭabaqāt al-Shu'arā* by Ibn al-Mu'tazz, p. 3, *Aghānī*, ed. 1347, III, p. 245.

[3] Almost the same words are found also in Ṭabarī, 3, 603, 1, 1959, under the year 170.

Land-tax, mentioned above, that Hārūn actually neglected this supreme duty of every Muslim ruler.[1] Abū Yūsuf most humbly entreats the caliph to seek Allāh's favor by holding at least one public audience every one or two months or even once a year (ed. 1346, pp. 133-4, cf. also the Introduction). Furthermore, Jahshiyārī, p. 212, 3, informs us that in *addition* to the vizierate, Yaḥyā was entrusted with the supervision of all government departments and after some time was also given the Royal Seal.[2] Moreover, we hear that he was the first vizier with the rank of an Amīr—a very important innovation, which more than anything else was apt to make the vizier a deputy of the caliph. In a state in which the ruler's official title was "Commander-in-Chief of the True-believers", a man without military rank could hardly exercise the highest authority.

Indeed, it was a position like that of Yaḥyā the Barmecide which created the idea of the plenipotentiary vizier so popular both in the East and the West. But it must be borne in mind that Yaḥyā's case was quite exceptional. Hārūn was a young man of twenty when made caliph, and he owed his throne, most probably also his life, to the sagacity of his fatherly tutor. Even as caliph he used to address Yaḥyā with the words "My father",[3] and, above all, Hārūn lacked both the talent and the inclination for public affairs.[4] Moreover, the wording of the sources clearly shows that Yaḥyā's powers were not regarded as belonging to the competence of a vizier, but as being accessory to it. In addition to Jahshiyārī, who expressly says so (see above), we may adduce Ṭabarī, who remarks, p. 606, 3, "in this way Yaḥyā combined the *two* vizierates",[5] when he was given the

[1] It was regarded as such down to our own times. Compare the descriptions of a day in the life of the late King 'Abd al-'Azīz of Saudi Arabia or of the late Imām Yaḥyā of Yemen.

[2] Previously, the official correspondence went out under Yaḥyā's name, while another dignitary was entrusted with the Seal, Jahshiyārī, 213, 1-8, and especially Ṭabarī part 3, 606.

[3] Down to the present day, the slave or ex-slave who has educated a boy is addressed in such a way by his ward, cf. Snouck Hurgronje, *Mekka*, Vol. 2, *passim*.

[4] Cf. Mas'ūdī, *Tanbīh*, p. 346, 10: "After the fall of the Barmecides, the government became disorderly and Hārūn's incapacity for administration and his lack of statesmanship became evident to everybody." Hārūn's fame is based on other merits—on his ceaseless prosecution of the Holy War and his ostentatious religiosity. That he himself sought his fame in these matters is shown, e.g., by a report preserved by Ṭabarī 3, 709 (*anno* 190), that Hārūn adopted the custom of wearing a top-hat (*qalansuwa*) with the inscription *Ghāzī Ḥājj*, "Conqueror and Pilgrim."

[5] By characterizing Yaḥyā's office in such a way, Ṭabarī may have been

Royal Seal in 171.[1] We find however that it was not until the year 178 (p. 631) that al-Rashīd handed over to Yaḥyā all the affairs of his empire. And even at that time, when the Barmecide rule was at its height, there was no complete continuity. In 173, after the death of the caliph's mother, who exercised a sort of guardianship over him, al-Faḍl b. al-Rabīʿ, the son of al-Manṣūr's chamberlain and great antagonist of the Barmecides, was given the Royal Seal,[2] with which Yaḥyā had meanwhile entrusted his son Jaʿfar (Ṭab. 609, 17). It is possible that it returned to the Barmecides in 178, for we find Jaʿfar again in possession of it in 180, Ṭabarī, p. 644. Very significant for the character of the vizierate is also the fact that Jaʿfar b. Yaḥyā obviously bore the title of vizier at the same time as his father, as may be concluded from various sources.

In the above-mentioned list of scribes and viziers quoted by Ṭabarī (*Anno* 72, part 2, p. 813), Jaʿfar is called Hārūn's vizier. Abū Nuwās also calls him vizier in a well-known stanza,[3] and so does the poet Marwān b. Abī Ḥafṣa.[4] After the Barmecides' disgrace, the famous Abu 'l-ʿAtāhiya says with reference to Yaḥyā and Jaʿfar, in a lengthy poem devoted to this event, "They have been

influenced by the title Dhu'l-wizāratayn borne by a vizier of his own times (see below p. 189). Tornberg, *Numi Cufici*, Upsala, 1848, p. 57, no. 214, notes a coin bearing this title under the year 190. Assuming a slight misreading we could arrive at 170. But it is out of the question that Yaḥyā did *not* bear this title and, without doubt, 270 instead of 190 is to be read. I owe this information to my lamented colleague Professor L. A. Mayer, the eminent numismatist.

[1] Ṭab. 604, 1, mentions this event also for the year 170 H. But the passage there quoted contains a general remark about Yaḥyā's powers and is not meant to be chronologically exact.

[2] G. Weil, *Geschichte der Chalifen*, V. II, pp. 135-36, is, however, mistaken when he identifies the holder of this office with the vizier. The handing over of the Royal Seal to the plenipotentiary minister is known to us from many courts of the ancient East (cf. Joseph and Haman) and of later times (cf. the Ottoman grand vizier), but, as we have seen above on various occasions, in early Abbasid times the holding of the Royal Seal was only one office among many others. Weil was obviously influenced by his authority Ibn al-Athīr (Tornberg's edition VI, pp. 82, 100 and 104), who mainly copies Ṭabarī, but whose wording may mislead.

[3] Jahshiyārī, p. 264. Instead of al-wazīr, the *Dīwān* (ed. 1898, p. 173, ed. 1937, p. 304) has al-amīr, possibly because the compiler found it strange that Ja'far should share the vizierate with his father. On the other hand, I do not remember that Ja'far was given the title of an amīr. The poet could, however, use it informally.

[4] *Ṭabaqāt al-Shuʿarā'*, by Ibn al-Mu'tazz, 1939, p. 12. The verse reads as follows: "If anything befalls the caliph, he (Ja'far), as vizier, suggests the orders to be given by the caliph."

the two viziers of Allāh's caliph" (Ṭabarī, part 3, p. 687).[1] The testimony so far given is corroborated by the evidence gathered from coins. During the years 177-186, coins from places so distant from each other as Zerenj, Kirmān, Muḥammadiya (Ray), Baghdād, Rāfiqa, bear the name of Ja'far[2] in addition to that of the caliph. As far as I can see, no dignitary before Ja'far was given this honor,[3] and, with the exception of Faḍl b. Sahl Dhu 'l-Ri'āsatayn, to be discussed presently, nobody after him, at least in the period under consideration. In accordance with this, Jahshiyārī, p. 249, reports that Hārūn officially called Ja'far his brother,[4] entrusting him with the royal mints in all provinces.[5] There is, therefore, nothing surprising in Abu 'l-'Atāhiya's statement, corroborated by other poets, that Ja'far shared the vizierate with his father. In later times, the Buwayhids actually made the experiment of dividing this office between two men,[6] but I do not think that this happened in the case of Yaḥyā and Ja'far. The latter was the caliph's favorite, but was himself not particularly suited for administrative work. He could be called vizier, because this title, although increasingly becoming the designation of a public office, still had much of its original meaning of personal confidant and "helper" of the ruler.

After the fall of the Barmecides, their rival, al-Faḍl b. al-Rabī' was made vizier, as is commonly assumed, although the old sources, like Jahshiyārī and Ṭabarī, do not state so expressly. At all events he was far from being plenipotentiary prime minister.[7] The great

[1] Fakhrī (Derenbourg, p. 281) reports that al-Faḍl was nicknamed "the little vizier" and so was Ja'far, after having been made "maitre du Palais". The Persian Ṭabarī, translated by Zotenberg, Vol. 4, p. 463, says that Faḍl replaced his father for some time, in which position he was afterwards followed by his brother, see L. Bouvat, *Les Barmecides*, Paris, 1912, p. 49. Ja'far must have been known in the East under the title vizier, for Niẓām al-Mulk, in his famous *Siyāsat Nāma*, p. 151, sq. makes him even vizier of the Umayyad caliph Sulayman!

[2] Cf. Tornberg, *Numi Cufici*, p. 41 foll., *Katalog d. Orientalischen Münzen*, Berlin I, no. 1020-1164 *passim*.

[3] The name of the governor as the *local* representative of the caliph often appears on coins. But it is quite exceptional to find this prerogative of the ruling monarch shared by one of his servants in a number of mints in different provinces.

[4] Most probably the title was "his brother and helper, *wazīr*", cf. above p. 181.

[5] *Kuwar*, a name for the provinces of the eastern part of the empire. The coins bearing Ja'far's name actually originate from Rāfiqa (near Raqqa on the Euphrates) eastwards.

[6] Cf., e.g., Ibn al-Athīr, *anno* 382, IX, p. 67, l. 3, and Mez, *Die Renaissance des Islams*, p. 86.

[7] Zambour, *Manuel... de Chronologie... de l'Islam*, p.6 , ascribes coins to

departments of Land-tax and the caliph's correspondence (Jahshiyārī, 325), as well as those of the royal estates and the secret correspondence (ib. 337), were under the supervision of Ismāʿīl b. Ṣubayḥ. This is why al-Yaʿqūbī, *Taʾrīkh*, II, says that after the Barmecides' disgrace al-Faḍl b. al-Rabīʿ and Ismāʿīl shared the supreme power. But there were other high offices formerly united in Barmecide hands which, after their fall, were given to other than the two above-mentioned dignitaries. The most important office of the post and the secret reports (*al-barīd wal-akhbār*), which according to al-Manṣūr was one of the four pillars of the state (Ṭabarī, part 3, p. 398, Anno 158), was given to Masrūr, the black slave and ill-famed executioner, and after him to another slave of the Palace. They did their work well: after Hārūn's death it was found that four thousand bags with official despatches (*kharāʾiṭ*) had been left unopened (Jahshiyārī, pp. 249 and 336).

Under circumstances similar to those prevailing during the greater part of Hārūn's caliphate we find a vizier with very extensive powers at the beginning of al-Maʾmūn's reign. Al-Maʾmūn was a young man of twenty on coming to power and was used to the guidance of his foster-father al-Faḍl b. Sahl, who, by the way, had embraced Islam "through him" (*ʿalā yadihi*) only a few years before (*anno* 190, Ṭabarī, part 3, 709, l. 3). Moreover, it was only al-Faḍl's firmness and persistence which secured the throne for al-Maʾmūn. Al-Maʾmūn evinced his gratitude by making him the highest civil and military authority (*riʾāsat al-ḥarb wa-riʾāsat al-tadbīr*) and bestowing on him the title of Dhūl-Riʾāsatayn, "the man with the two powers". This was inscribed on a standard[2] borne before him on official occasions and on the coins struck throughout that part of the Muslim empire which was under al-Maʾmūn's sway, both when he was crown-prince and when he became caliph[3] (Jahshiyārī, p. 387).

The aspiration to military rank by a vizier who had not made

him, both in the time of Hārūn and in that of his successor al-Amīn. But as far as I am able to judge from the catalogue of coins of the British Museum, and from the Berlin and Swedish catalogues, all the coins bearing the name al-Faḍl from A.H. 190-197 were struck in the name of al-Faḍl b. Sahl, the vizier of the crown prince al-Maʾmūn, and not in that of al-Faḍl b. al-Rabīʿ, see below p. 189.

[2] The standard was the mark of distinction of the military commander.

[3] The *Katalog der Orientalischen Münzen*, Berlin, 1898, vol. I, enumerates about sixty coins of this type coming from the eastern part of the empire, including Iraq. In addition, the *Catalogue of Oriental Coins in the British Museum*, vol. I, registers two coins bearing this title which were struck in

himself known by achievements in the conduct of war is fully comprehensible in view of the martial character of the Muslim state (cf. our remarks in connection with Yaḥyā the Barmecide's Amīrate). But it may also be that these Iranians were led in this case by the example of the Sassanian Vuzurg Framādhār, who, like the major-domo of the Frankish kings,[1] was military commander as well as head of the civil administration. This conjecture is however open to objections, for the great days of the Vuzurg Framādhārs had come to an end many years before the downfall of the Sassanian empire. Whether this office had been abolished altogether, as Barthold assumes, or reduced to insignificance, as Christensen, *L'Empire des Sassanides*, p. 519 *sq.*, tries to show, there hardly remained a living tradition about the major-domo with full powers, and, if I am not mistaken, even Buzurgmihr, the prototype of the Sassanian vizier in Muslim literature, does not appear as a military commander. It is, however, possible that Yaḥyā and Faḍl b. Sahl were guided by descriptions of the office of the Vuzurg Framādhār, read by them in Pehlevī books which are lost to us, since faint reminiscences of it are discernible in the books of Muslim historians.

Al-Faḍl suffered the same fate as Jaʿfar.[2] But, unlike that of the Barmecide, his family was spared and his brother Ḥasan became his successor—although not with all his powers—while the latter's daughter Būrān was married to the caliph.[3]

the West (Egypt) in A.H. 199 and 202. The two last coins also bear, together with the honorific surname of the vizier mentioned, his name al-Faḍl. In the East, the two names appear separately. From A.H. 194 to 196, i.e., from Hārūn's death to the decisive victories of al-Ma'mūn's armies over those of his brother al-Amīn, the name al-Faḍl occurs on coins from Bukhāra, Balkh, Samarqand, al-Ray, Marv, Nīsābūr and Herāt, while, beginning with 196 (Samarqand, *Catalogue, Berlin*, no. 1361, Nīsābūr and al-Ray, Tornberg, *Numi Cufici, passim*), but more frequently in the following years, the title Dhu 'l-Ri'āsatayn is used alone. Tornberg, no. 233, notes a coin bearing this title for as early as A.H. 193, but this must be a misreading. It is very interesting to note that here, as in a later case (see p. 189, note 4), a military commander was given an honorific title in dual form at the same time as the vizier. And this title (Dhu 'l-Yamīnayn of Ṭāhir) also appears on some coins, cf. the catalogues of the British and Berlin Museums.

[1] Cf. Barthold's article quoted above p. 169, note 3. According to him, the office of the Vuzurg framādhār is as typical of the chivalrous state of the Sassanians as that of the vizier is of the urban civilization of the Abbasid empire.

[2] For the circumstances leading to his murder, Fr. Gabrieli, *al-Ma'mūn e gli 'Alidi*, 1929, may be consulted.

[3] In Umayyad times this would have been an unheard of honor. The Abbasids, however, were less particular in the selection of their wives and,

Ḥasan soon retired from office. Four other ministers served after him. In some sources they are called by the title of viziers, while in others they are not. Masʿūdī, in his *Tanbīh*, p. 352, expressly remarks that after al-Faḍl's death, al-Ma'mūn did not give full powers to any of his officers, "because he did not consider that he was in need of a vizier who would share government with him; no minister was called vizier in his presence and nobody was addressed so in writing." Therefore, adds Masʿūdī, many of those who compiled books on the history of the vizierate, like Ṣūlī and Jahshiyārī,[1] disagree as to whether or not those ministers who served after al-Faḍl should be called viziers.

With al-Faḍl's administration, the second instance of the vizierate at its highest development, we appropriately conclude our enquiry into the origin of this office. We should add that following the precedent of al-Faḍl and of Yaḥyā the Barmecide, adduced above p. 187, who were both given military rank, at a later time, which was more inclined to etiquette, the vizier was made supreme to all other officials including the highest military commanders.[2] Most probably this also gave rise to a *ḥadīth*, ascribed to the Prophet, saying that Allāh created the world for the sword and the pen, *subordinating* the former to the latter.[3] However, the caliph's vizier continued to be an officer of the civil administration. It was quite unusual for a vizier to be charged with a military function. We hear of such a case under the troublesome reign of al-Mutawakkil (232/847-247/861). When this caliph tried to counterbalance the Turkish guards made too powerful by his father, al-Muʿtaṣim, "he put some twelve thousand bedouins, desperadoes (*ṣaʿālik*) and other people under the authority of his vizier ʿUbaydallāh b. Yaḥyā b. Khāqān (*ḍamma ilaihi*), the nominal commander being prince al-Muʿtazz, who was under the care (*fī ḥajr*) of the vizier," (see Masʿūdī, *Tanbīh*, p. 362).

The permanent holding of military command by a vizier was regarded as exceptional, and was recorded as such by the historians. Thus Fakhrī, ed. Derenbourg, p. 345, l. 2, says with reference to

as is well known, almost all of them were sons of slave-girls. Nevertheless, the pompous wedding of Būrān in 210 (825/6) may be regarded as the most conspicuous demonstration of the importance of the vizierate in early Abbasid times.

[1] The later part of this most valuable source is unfortunately lost.

[2] Mez, *Die Renaissance des Islams*, p. 80.

[3] Māwardī, *Ādāb al-Wazīr*, 1348/1929, p. 10.

Ismā'īl b. Bulbul, a vizier of al-Mu'tamid (256/870-279/892), that he held both civil and military authority (*jumi'a lahu al-sayfu wal-qalamu*). Fakhrī's statement, however, refers not to Ismā'īl, the vizier of the caliph, but to Ṣā'id b. Makhlad, the prime minister[1] of al-Muwaffaq, the caliph's almighty brother and deputy.[2] For Ṭabarī, part 3, p. 2083 under the year 269 relates that Ṣā'id was given the title Dhu'l-Wizāratayn, "the man with the two vizierates", and there is also other literary evidence[3] that Ṣā'id b. Makhlad, not Ismā'īl, bore that title. The title of Dhu'l-Wizāratayn also appears on coins struck in the year 270 in al-Ahwāz, Hamadān, Shirāz, Sāmarrā, Baghdād and Baṣra, and in 271 in Sāmarrā, cf. the catalogues of the British Museum,[4] of the Berlin Museums and of Tornberg. As in the case of Faḍl b. Sahl Dhu 'l-Ri'āsatayn, the vizier of al-Ma'mūn, the exceptional position and title of Ṣā'id were commemorated by coins struck in different parts of the empire.

[1] If I am not mistaken, he is exclusively called *kātib*, not *wazīr* by Ṭabarī, cf. especially part 3, pp. 1930 and 2079. Mas'ūdī, VIII, p. 39, who makes him the caliph's prime minister, naturally calls him vizier.

[2] Owing to the fact that both the caliph and his brother had prime ministers, much confusion prevails regarding the vizierate at the time of al-Mu'tamid, in the sources as well as in the works written by European scholars (cf. also the preceding note). Fakhrī makes Ismā'īl b. Bulbul bear the title Dhu 'l-Wizāratayn, because he was the caliph's vizier during the years in which this title was used (A.H. 269-272). But we have already seen that Fakhrī is mistaken; besides, no military exploits are reported of Ismā'īl, while Ṣā'id was a great general (cf. Ṭabarī, pp. 1988, 2011, 2037, 2048). Mez, *Renaissance d. Islams*, p. 84 confounds Ṣā'id with Ḥasan b. Makhlad, who was al-Mu'tamid's vizier, but was appointed in 264 (Ṭabarī 3, p. 1926 last line) and dismissed in 265, for which year Ṭabarī 3, p. 1931 reports the nomination of Ismā'īl b. Bulbul (cf. also Amedroz in *JRAS*, 1908, p. 451). In 272, on the day after Ṣā'id's disgrace, Ismā'īl was nominated Kātib of al-Muwaffaq, but without military command, as Ṭabarī, p. 2109-2110 states expressly. Fakhrī does not mention Ṣā'id in the list of the caliph's viziers, because he was, as we have seen, only the prime minister of his brother. Zambaur, *Manuel... de Chronologie... de l'Islam*, p. 7, is right in following Fakhrī here, but I cannot see why he makes Ḥasan b. Makhlad die in 263, —one year before he assumed office.

[3] Quoted by I. Goldziher, in his article on titles in dual form, *Wiener Zeitschrift für die Kunde des Morgenlandes*, 13 (1899), p. 325.

[4] The British Museum (*Catalogue of Oriental Coins* I, no. 366) also possesses a coin struck under al-Mu'tamid A. 278, with the honorific surname Dhu 'l-Sayfayn, "the man with the two swords", of which Lane-Poole says that it does not occur on any other coin yet published. As Ṭabarī, 3, p. 2040 reports, this title was given to a Turkish commander in A. 269, the same year in which Ṣā'id was surnamed Dhu 'l-wizāratayn and most probably not without connection with this event. The title Dhu 'l-Sayfayn appears also in al-Khwārezm's list quoted by Goldziher in his article mentioned above.

It was, however, only in later times and in the states of Muslim rulers other than caliphs that the military command was permanently combined with the vizierate.[1]

Concerning the century following al-Ma'mūn's death it will suffice to point out that, with the exception of the insignificant Ismāʿīl b. Bulbul,[2] no vizier was in office for ten years, while vizierates of one year or of even a few months were nothing unusual. In a constitutional state the frequent change of the prime minister belongs to the very nature of representative government, while in an autocratic state the shortness of a minister's service betrays the limited nature of his powers. With the rise of the Buwayhids in 334/946,[3] the Abbasid vizierate came to an end. It was not revived till a century later, when it shared its insignificance with that of the contemporary caliphate.

Meanwhile, however, other Muslim rulers like the Buwayhids, Fātimids, and Sāmānids had adopted viziers. The office rose to the highest importance when barbaric conquerors of Turkish and Mongol origin ruled over large Muslim populations, of which they understood neither the language, nor the complicated social and economic order. Under those circumstances the delegation of the highest civil authority to a competent official chosen from the conqueror's cultivated subjects became imperative. The most outstanding example of a vizier of this later type is the famous Niẓām al-Mulk (born 1018, murdered 1092). For thirty years he led the administration of the Seljuk empire, the largest state on Muslim soil at that time. In response to a request of Malik Shāh, the Seljuk Sulṭān, Niẓām al-Mulk in the last year of his administration and life wrote a book on government, the famous *Siyāsat Nāma*. It is very interesting to find what Niẓām al-Mulk has to say about government by delegation. He most urgently advises his monarch to put no trust in any of his servants, not excluding the vizier. The officials should be controlled by spies of all sorts, while the Sulṭān, like the first

[1] Cf. Mez, *Die Renaissance des Islams*, p. 80.

[2] As we have seen, the actual prime minister during the greater part of his administration was Ṣāʿid, the kātib of the caliph's brother.

[3] Or even some years earlier, with the nomination in 324/936 of the Amīr al-Umarā' Ibn-Rā'iq, who held both the highest military and civil authority in the caliph's state. With regard to this event, says Harry Bowen in his book (mentioned above, p. 168), p. 356: "With the year 324 (935-6) vanished the system of government that had come into being with the Abbasid dynasty. Its titles and some of its forms indeed remained; but its reality was dissolved. The glory of the vizierate had passed away." Cf. also ib., p. 392.

caliphs, should fix days for public audiences where he should receive complaints and make decisions in person.[1] Niẓām al-Mulk's verdict against government by deputy is the more deserving of notice since he himself, approximately at the same time, expressed the belief that he was prime minister by heavenly providence, in the same way as Malik Shāh was Sulṭān.[2] Thus we see that even this true Iranian and powerful minister was in theory far from recognizing the *wizārat al-tafwīḍ*, the vizierate with unrestricted powers, defined half a century earlier by the lawyer and courtier Māwardī[3] as compatible with the welfare of a Muslim state.

The main results of our inquiry may be summarized as follows:

1. The vizierate was not borrowed by the Muslims as a fixed and well-defined institution from the Sassanians or anyone else. On the contrary, its beginnings under the special historical conditions prevailing at the end of the Umayyad rule and its gradual development during the reign of the first eight Abbasid caliphs can be traced in the sources step by step.

2. This being so, there is no need to look for a Persian derivation of the word *wazīr*, which, in any case, competent scholars have so far failed to produce. On the other hand, the use of the Arabic word *wazīr* in the sense of helper and assistant can be traced from pre-Islamic times down to the last years of the Umayyad period, when it was given the specific meaning of the title of a government officer.

3. This took place when Abū Salama was made representative of the common Abbasid cause, before a caliph was enthroned. A constitutional abnormality like that called for a special title, which was found in the form of "the Helper (wazīr) of the House of Muhammad."

4. After the accession of Abu 'l-ʿAbbās, the first Abbasid caliph, there was no place for an office like that held by Abū Salama, and thus he was soon removed. Although a prime minister with extensive

[1] Cf. Nöldeke, *ZDMG* 46, pp. 763-4.

[2] "He who gave thee the crown, placed on my head the Turban" (E. G. Browne, *A Literary History of Persia*, II, p. 185). One should not forget that Malik Shāh was only seventeen or eighteen years of age when he succeeded his father on the throne, while it was Niẓām al-Mulk who saved the empire for him during the troubles ensuing upon his accession. For his services, the vizier received the title Atābek, 'Father-Lord', which reminds us of the way in which Hārūn al-Rashīd addressed Yaḥyā the Barmecide, see above. There is, of course, no direct connection between these two titles.

[3] Both in his general book on statecraft and in the *Risāla* quoted above, which is especially devoted to the vizierate.

powers acted under the last Umayyad, the Abbasids did not follow this model immediately, but tried to govern through family rule controlled by the strong personal authority of the caliph, which was most conspicuously demonstrated by the second Abbasid al-Manṣūr.

5. It is highly doubtful whether any of the ministers of the first two Abbasid caliphs bore the title of vizier. It seems that the first man who was so addressed officially after Abū Salama was Ya'qūb b. Dā'ūd, the second prime minister of al-Mahdī, the third caliph.

6. It was, however, al-Manṣūr himself who laid the foundations of the future vizierate by putting his young son and heir under the supervision of an experienced man of affairs, who became the prime minister of his ward after the latter's accession. This practice was followed by al-Manṣūr's successors, and, as the five caliphs succeeding him were young men or mere lads on assuming authority, this had the greatest influence on the development of a vizierate with wide powers.

7. The model for this practice is to be found in Arabic custom, according to which the slave is charged with the education of the son and the protection of the orphan of his lord, whereas the bonds between the slave or freedman and his lord—often strengthened by "milk-relationship"—are regarded as the truest safeguards for the well-being of the latter.

8. This origin of the vizierate from personal service explains more than anything else why its powers were never properly defined, but were continually expanded or restricted according to the inclinations of the caliph, and also why it could be altogether suspended at the very moment when it had reached exceptional competence, as was the case during the caliphate of al-Ma'mūn and possibly also of Hārūn.

9. The viziers of the period under consideration were exclusively freedmen emerging from the civil administration, and as a rule held only civil authority. With few exceptions, this state of affairs remained until the discontinuation of the Abbasid vizierate in 324/936, but, probably owing to the example of Yaḥyā the Barmecide and Faḍl b. Sahl, who both held the rank of an Amīr (without, however, excelling in military deeds), the viziers got precedence over all other officials including those of highest military rank.

10. The office of the vizier reached its fullest importance at a time when Turkish and Mongol conquerors were forced by their ignorance of the language and civilization of their subjects to entrust the

administration of their territories to better qualified persons. But even the greatest of all viziers of this type, Niẓām al-Mulk, declared government by deputy to be incompatible with the duties of a Muslim ruler. The familiar conception of the caliph drinking wine while his vizier is doing his work, if taken to be the rule, is not in conformity with the facts of history.

In conclusion we may remark that our denial of the Sassanian origin of the vizierate does not mean that we exclude the possibility of Iranian influence on some of its aspects. But such influence must be studied and demonstrated with the same regard to detail as we have tried to apply in the present paper in discussing the internal development of the office.

APPENDIX

ON THE ORIGIN OF THE TERM VIZIER

In his review of Dominique Sourdel's magnum opus *Le Vizirat 'Abbāside*, H. A. R. Gibb, after surveying and appraising the book, concludes with the following remark: "As regards the word *wazīr* itself, Mr. Sourdel again confines himself to the philological and literary evidence for its Arabic derivation, to the exclusion of a Persian origin. The argument is entirely convincing, yet it remains a question how such a strange term (strange in an Arab environment) as "burden-bearer" came to be used in the sense of "confidant" or "spokesman". The question may be presently insoluble, but the possibility of some outside source for the concept is not a priori to be excluded."[1]

Professor Gibb's remark is to the point. We have to prove, how, under specific historical circumstances, the general and almost poetical word "burden-bearer", "helper", became a technical term, meaning "representative". In the following lines, we shall try to fill the gap and to provide the missing link.

In his study "The Origin of the Vizierate and its True Character" (above, Ch. IX), the present writer has shown that the word *wazīr* was widely used in Umayyad times, and in particular in Khorāsān, in the meaning of "assistant", "aid". Additional material to the same effect has been adduced by Sourdel in his masterly book. Furthermore, the writer argued, Abū Salama, the champion of the Abbasid cause, had to adopt a title with a general meaning in order to be able to receive the oath of allegiance for a still non-existent caliph. The trouble is that we know very little about Abū Salama[2] and therefore cannot say what caused him to choose this term in preference to others.

The truth is, however, that Abū Salama was not the first to bear this title. It was created by a man about whom we know very much and whose historical career explains why he did so. This man was Al-Mukhtār.

To be exact, Abū Salama did not call himself *wazīr*, but more

[1] The *Middle East Journal* 14 (1960), p. 344.
[2] Cf. D. Sourdel, *Le vizirat* I, p. 65-70.

elaborately: *wazīr āl muḥammad*, "the Helper of the House of M." It was this title which was first adopted by Al-Mukhtār. When he decided openly to start the Shiʿite revolt, the step was officially announced by his spokesman Abū ʿUthmān al-Nahdī with the words: *wazīr āl muḥammad qad kharaj*, "The Helper of the House of M. has begun the revolution."[1] In the letter, genuine or spurious, of Muḥammad ibn al-Ḥanafiyya, the Mahdī, to Ibrahīm al-Ashtar, the military commander of the Shiʿa, al-Mukhtār is described as *naṣīḥī wawazīrī wathiqatī wa'amīnī*, and Ibrahīm is promised high reward, *in naṣartanī wasāʿadta wazīrī*.[2]

The idea of helping the house of the Prophet was the shibboleth of the Shiʿa. When the *Tawwābūn*, "the Penitents"—as they called themselves, according to the Koranic story of the repentant Children of Israel—assembled to initiate the first Shiʿite revolt after Ḥusain's death, they confessed: "Our prophet's grandson asked us to help him, but we did not help him."[3] Al-Mukhtār is described in our sources as a man without any convictions and driven solely by an insatiable lust for power and glory. Once, al-Madā'inī tells us, he rode through the market with al-Mughīra b. Shuʿba, a man without scruples like himself. Looking at the crowd, the old fox said: "I know a catchword with which a dexterous man could rally to him all these people, and in particular the non-Arabs." "What is it, uncle," asked al-Mukhtār. "Helping the family of the Prophet and revenging their blood." These words made a deep impression on al-Mukhtār.[4] After having tried in vain to become viceroy of Iraq in the service of Ibn Zubayr, he put himself at the head of the Shiʿite revolt.

In all his public announcements, al-Mukhtār called himself *wazīr* or helper of his messiah Muḥammad ibn al-Ḥanafiyya.[5] He also used other words of a similar or of the same meaning, but he was constant in the use of *wazīr*, and, as we have seen, *wazīr āl muḥammad* was the title under which he appeared at the head of the revolting Shiʿites. His preference for this word is easily explained. In addition to its simple meaning of helper it had a religious connotation: "We gave Moses the Book and appointed together with him Aaron, as

1 Balādhurī, *Ansāb al-Ashrāf* 5 (Jerusalem 1936), p. 225, line 15, and the parallel sources indicated there in the Annotations.

2 *Ibid.* p. 222, line 20, and 223, line 1.

3 *Ibid.* p. 205, lines 7-8. The verb used here is *nṣr*.

4 *Ibid.* 223, ll. 17-21. No parallel source.

5 *Ibid.* 207, line 14; 218, line 11; 222, line 3.

his *wazīr*" (Sura 25:35). Thus al-Mukhtār stood in a relationship to his Mahdī similar to that of ʿAlī to the Prophet.[1] Our sources, and in particular al-Balādhurī, have preserved many of al-Mukhtār's rhymed prophetical pronouncements, and there can be no doubt that he wanted to pass as a man with supernatural gifts. The title *wazīr āl muḥammad* gave him a share in the spiritual gifts of the House of the Prophet.

As is well known, Abū Hāshim, the son of Muḥammad ibn al-Ḥanafiyya, bequeathed his claims on the caliphate to the grandson of ʿAbdallah b. ʿAbbās, the Prophet's cousin. Thus, al-Mukhtār's heritage passed on to the Abbasid movement. This explains why the title *wazīr āl muḥammad* reappeared in Islamic history, when a situation similar to that in which al-Mukhtār found himself required similar solutions. There is no need to look for any outside, non-Arab source for the term *wazīr*.

[1] ʿAlī is called by al-Mukhtār *al-waṣiyy*. *Ibid.* 218, line 11.

CHAPTER TEN

ATTITUDES TOWARDS GOVERNMENT IN ISLAM AND JUDAISM

The formulation of our problem demands some comment. A happier choice might have been "Attitudes towards the State". But the concept of state is alien to the political glossary of both Islam and Judaism. It is a loan word, a translation from the Greek *polis* or *politeia,* and was naturalized in Arabic and Hebrew only after Greek philosophy had gained a foothold in Islam and consequently in medieval Judaism. The concepts that will be dealt with, those that are native to Hebrew and Arabic, are e.g.: kingship (*malkhūt*), rule (*serārā*), communal leadership (*rabbānūt*), the authorities (*rāshūt*), and equivalent Arabic terms, especially *sulṭān*. In early Islam, which is the period under consideration, *sulṭān* does not signify the person of the ruler, and this is especially true in religious literature. Rather, it stands for what we generally refer to as "the authorities". The corresponding Greek terms, familiar from the New Testament, are *exousia* and *archontes*.

By "Judaism" we refer to the flowering period of classical Judaism, from the first to the fifth century A.D. Later authorities, such as Maimonides (1135-1204), are also consulted whenever they express, in our opinion, the essence of classical Jewish tradition. "Islam" here means Islam full-grown, namely the period stretching from the second through the fifth centuries A.H. or, from Abū Yūsuf, the counselor of Hārūn al-Rashīd and one of the earliest jurisconsults whose writings we possess, up to Ghazālī, the fifth century's "Renovator of Islam". Again, some of the later authorities are consulted, for example, the sixteenth century mystic Shaʿrānī, the last great encyclopedist and religious genius of Islam who in typical fashion knots together the many strands which weave their way along the protracted religious history of Islam.

A comparative study, in which the characteristic attitudes of the two religions throw light on each other, has a good deal of merit in spite of certain inherent difficulties. The Judaism of that period was self-contained both in the ethnic sense and through its rejection of alien influences. It appears that it was more unified and had become more crystalized than classical Islam. The community of Islam was in constant flux racially and it was receptive to the most divergent alien teachings. We may therefore assume at the outset that whenever Islam and Judaism share common ideas about authority, they would be formulated more consistently and with greater emphasis in Judaism than in Islam. On the other hand, early Islam was not subject to exile and foreign rule, which was the lot of Judaism and which fashioned the character of the latter in many respects. Therefore a comparison with Islam might help us to distinguish the essential from the accidental in Judaism. In order that this comparative study be not one-sided, views about the state in the Greco-Roman world on the one hand, and of the church fathers on the other, will be taken into account.

We should however point out a fact which at first glance contradicts what has just been said about the difference between Islam, which was possessed of political authority, and Judaism, which was not. Jewish religious writings manifest a more active interest in public life and in the problem of authority than the corresponding Islamic writings. Certainly it is not due to mere chance that neither the ninety seven books of Bukhārī—the most sacred collection of Islamic oral tradition—nor the forty books of Ghazālī's Iḥyā' 'ulūm al-dīn ("the Revivification of the sciences of religion")—Islam's *Summa Theologica*—contain a single book devoted to the problem of government. In Maimonides, on the other hand, the laws of kingship occupy a special and honored place in his great code—they form the last of its fourteen books.

This contrast is partially due to a circumstance which certainly is not accidental. The last of the Five Books of Moses discusses royal institutions and establishes several positive as well as negative precepts concerning them. Moreover, the Bible touches on the problem of kingship again and again. Consequently, no complete systematic account of the religion of Israel could ignore this subject. The Koran, on the other hand, says nothing whatsoever about the political regime and the religious duties pertaining to it. In keeping with this, it is hardly surprising that a well-known twentieth century Muslim Scholar, 'Alī 'Abd al-Rāziq, states in his book *Islam and the Principles of Government* (Cairo, 1925) that the Caliphate is not an obligatory Islamic institution and that Islam as a religion had no theory with regard to the most preferable form of state and communal organization. At the time of its appearance, the book aroused violent opposition and its author was disavowed both by his former colleagues in the al-Azhar university of Cairo and his superiors of the Muslim Supreme Court of Egypt. His book was termed "hyper-modern" in a Dutch Ph.D. thesis devoted to it. Meanwhile, however, wide Muslim circles have come to similar conclusions. A sober analysis of the problem by a member of the Central Institute of Islamic Research in Karachi, founded recently by the government of Pakistan, states that the caliphate was not based on any injunction contained in the holy book of Islam or any oral instruction given by the Prophet.[1] Thus we have to concede that the position of the state within the religious system of Islam differed widely from that of Judaism.

This divergency had its roots not only in the holy scriptures of the two religions. The dissimilarity between Maimonides, who concludes his code with the laws of kingship, and Ghazālī, in whose magnum opus this subject does not have even one chapter devoted to it and is dealt with only in passing[2], is partly to be explained by the varying attitudes of Judaism and Islam to messianism.

The idea of a king having the gifts of a prophet, who by his heavenly inspired wisdom and justice brings eternal peace to a world groaning under oppression and strife, was ingrained in Judaism since the days of Isaiah. The hope for his appearance was a mainstay of Jewish faith. Therefore, the doctrine of kingdom in general was an essential part of Jewish theology.

Islam, too, awaits the coming of the Messiah, the *mahdī*, who is expected to "fill the world with justice—just as today it is filled with evil". Still, this belief has no foothold in the Koran and is not an important principle of orthodox (Sunni) Islam. The situation was different in Shi'ism. Therefore every Shiʿi system of theology treats the doctrine of the Imām, the ecclesiastical as well as temporal ruler, as a basic article of faith.

In addition to the difference in the scriptural background and the divergent attitudes towards messianism, there were certain histori-

[1] Manzooruddin Ahmed, "The Classical Muslim State", *Islamic Studies, Journal of the Central Institute of Islamic Research*, Karachi 1, No. 3 (1962), pp. 83-104.

[2] See below. The Risāla al-Qudsiyya of Ghazālī does, it is true, end with a short note on the Imāmate (see *Iḥyā'*, book 1, pp. 93-103), but the problem is discussed there as a part of the controversy with the Shīʿa.

Cf. also Dr. M. ʿAbd al-Muʿizz Naṣr, "Ghazālī's Political Philosophy" (in Arabic), *Abū Ḥamīd al-Ghazālī*, Cairo 1962, pp. 451-476.

cal circumstances which shaped the contrast that we have pointed out between rabbinic and Islamic literature, and made talmudic Judaism more attentive to the problems of public life. The Jewish communities were small, and dispersed, but cared for the poor, the sick and the old, as well as for the education of impecunious children; they had to raise funds for the upkeep of the houses of worship and the emoluments of the community officials; and to some extent they also fulfilled governmental functions such as the administration of justice, local police, and the collection of taxes.

These multiple services required a considerable amount of communal organization. Thus the individual members found themselves continually confronted with the problems of leadership and following, while the amorphous mass of Muslims, who were ruled by autocratic caliphs or sultans, had little opportunity to develop interest in the conduct of the state.

Moreover, classical rabbinic literature developed at a time when the Greco-Roman polities and corporations were still largely in operation, while by the advent of Islam next to nothing had been left of them. Thus the difference in time and environment was also of considerable impact.

Taking note of these reservations we may now re-examine the theories of Judaism and Islam about the origin of authority, as well as the attitude of religion towards the state. We must not expect to find systematic expositions about these matters in Jewish and Islamic religious literature, in the Talmud and the Ḥadīth, similar in strictness of formulation to the writings of the Roman jurists. What we do find are generalized precepts and ethical aphorisms more comparable to the rhetoric of a Seneca than to the definitions of an Ulpianus.

The three monotheistic religions unite in believing in the divine origin of government. The most outspoken expression of this view, which has parallels in the Old Testament, is found in the famous passage of Paul's epistle to the Romans (Ch. 13), which the church fathers and their followers never ceased to cite. These are his words (Revised Standard Version):

"Let every person be subject to the governing authorities, for there is no authority except from God, and those that exist have been instituted by God. Therefore he who resists the authorities resists what God has appointed, and those who resist will incur judgment. For rulers are not a terror to good conduct, but to bad.

Would you have no fear of him who is in authority? Then do what is good and you will receive his approval, for he is God's servant for your good... Therefore one must be subject, not only to avoid God's wrath, but for the sake of conscience."

Further on in this chapter Paul elaborates and specifically states that by "government" he means not only "the" government, i.e., Roman rule, but every form of authority.

Carlisle[1] justly rejects the view that this passage, as well as similar pronouncements (I Peter 13:14; Titus 1:3), allude to and oppose Jewish national aspirations. Moore,[2] however, is perhaps too extreme when he says that Paul's view expresses faithfully the position of Jewish scholars, though they undoubtedly have much in common. Since authority is one of God's attributes, every existing authority must ultimately be due to Him. With reference to I Chronicles 29:11 "To you, oh God, belong all government and superiority", a Babylonian rabbi made the following statement: "Even the supervisor of water allocation for irrigation"—the lowest authority with whom every farmer used to come into contact—"is appointed by Heaven".[3] Therefore, everyone holding a position of authority must be obeyed. "Even the smallest of the small, once he is appointed to a public post, is to be regarded as equal to the greatest of the great."[4] The basic concept that earthly kingdom is but a reflection of heavenly rule[5] finds legal expression in the obligation to pronounce a blessing on seeing a king, even a non-Jewish one: "Blessed be He who gives of his glory to his creatures".[6]

There is then a sacred halo over the head of any bearer of authority. Rabbi Yūdān said: "Showing impudence toward a king is like showing impudence toward God".[7] And, "When the commoners obey the mighty, the mighty decide before God, and He carries out their decisions".[8] That is to say, God is but an agent of the powers that be.

Nevertheless, Judaism never ceased to emphasize, just as the Roman jurists did, that ultimately supreme authority is held by the aggregate which empowers it, by the people. This is explicitly stated

[1] *Mediaeval Political Theory in the First Centuries of the Christian Era*, I, Cambridge, Harvard University Press 1927-30, pp. 91-92.

[2] G. F. Moore, *Judaism*, vol. II, pp. 113 sq.

[3] Baba Bathra 91b.

[4] Rosh Ha-Shana 25b.

[5] Berakhoth 58a.

[6] *Ibid.*

[7] Bereshith Rabba, chapter 94, ed. Theodor-Albeck, p. 1183.

[8] Devarim Rabba, chapter 1.

in the fifth Book of Moses as well as in the Prophets. "And *you* will say: *I* wish to appoint a king (to rule) over myself", "*you* shall appoint a king (to rule) over yourself", "*you* shall not appoint over *your*self etc.".[1] The Jerusalem Talmud enlarges on this: "It is *not* written: I, God will appoint, but *you* shall appoint, it is you who put a king over yourself".[2]

Many stories in the Bible, like Jotham's parable (Judges 9:7-10), the election of king Saul (I Samuel 11:15), the covenant with the elders by which David became ruler of Judea (II Samuel 5:1-3) and the repudiation of the house of David by the Ten Tribes (I Kings 12:1-17) underline the idea that the ruler receives his office from the ruled. Even more significant is the fact that throughout Biblical legislation, the highest juridical authority rests with the *ʿēdā*, the organized community, while the king has no place in it altogether, at least in the Five Books of Moses.

However, Biblical precedence alone could not have accounted for the rabbinical emphasis on the people as the origin of authority. As alluded to above, it was the very intensive community life of the Jews in talmudic times which did not permit full acceptance of the idea of absolute obedience due to the authorities, as expounded by Paul: "You all are standing this day before the Lord your God, your chiefs, your tribal lords, your elders, and officers." On this Biblical verse the rabbis comment as follows: "Although I did appoint chiefs and elders for you, you are all equal in my sight, for," the verse continues, "you are all the men of Israel".[3]

In this spirit a law (theoretical, of course) was formulated that no king may be installed except through election by the supreme court consisting of seventy one members.[4] The same attitude gave rise to the practical ruling "No community official is appointed without ascertaining the will of the community".[5] And, in general: "No public business is transacted without prior assurance of the public's consent".[6]

[1] Deuteronomy 17:14-15.

[2] Sanhedrin, chapter 2, end, fol. 20 d. Most significantly this chapter contains a number of reports about friction between the nāsī, or patriarch, the head of the Jewish community in Palestine, and the religious scholars, cf. below.

[3] Tanḥuma Niṣṣavim, ed. S. Buber, p. 49. The quotation is from Deuteronomy 29:9.

[4] Tosefta Sanhedrin 3:4, ed. Zuckermandel, Jerusalem 1937 (reprint) p. 418.

[5] Berakhoth 55a.

[6] Tosefta Sanhedrin 2:13.

This notion of "public opinion" and of acceptance by the majority is not common in Islam.[1] It is alien even to the revolutionary sect of the Khārijites, for whom the right of opposition to established authority is basic. This "right of opposition", however, is derived for the Khārijites from the rationale that a corrupt ruler, ipso facto, cannot be God's annointed.

The *bay'a* (the clasping of the hands of the ruler to signify acceptance of his authority) cannot be considered an "election" under any circumstances. It is an expression of mutual obligation, and comes to recognize a ruler whose authority has been gained by appointment, inheritance, usurpation, or any other means. The bay'a bears a certain similarity to the ancient Israelite covenant on the one hand and to the ceremony surrounding a royal accession in the Teutonic states on the other. The Teutonic ceremony, too, did not define the origin of authority. But, in Europe, participation, however limited, in royal accession, as well as the tradition of an independent judiciary opened the way for the rise of modern constitutional government. In contradistinction, two generations after the death of Muhammad the bay'a had lost most of its practical significance, and the cadi, the judge, was but an official dependent upon the ruler's whim. Abū Yūsuf, who preceded the first canonical collection of ḥadīth by many years, is aware of only one source of authority: God's choice by which the caliph becomes a vice-regent of God on earth. This concept was expressed by dropping the word "rasūl" (messenger) from the formula *Khalīfat rasūl-allāh* (the deputy of God's messenger), which thus made the caliph a representative of God himself. It is instructive that already Abū Yūsuf, as well as a number of most prominent compilers of ḥadīth collections rationalize the religious obligation of absolute obedience to the existing powers by citing the following saying attributed to Muhammad (reported on the authority of the well-known rebel Abū Dḥarr): "Yield to and obey even a flat-nosed, shrunken-headed Abyssinian slave once

[1] A reference to this idea is seemingly found in Ghazālī, Ihyā' I, p. 102. Having described the necessary qualifications of a ruler (wisdom, religiosity and origin from the Prophet's tribe Quraysh), he continues: "If these qualities are found in several persons, the ruler is he whom the majority recognizes. Whoever opposes the majority, is a sinner." This statement, however, is not an instruction concerning the election of a caliph, but a warning not to oppose a ruler who has won general recognition. This religious injunction of obeying the ruling monarch and being careful not to break the staff of Islam, i.e. its unity, is common and old. See below.

he is appointed".[1] Goldziher believes that this saying is of Khārijite origin and mirrors the Khārijite opposition to dynastic claims.[2] And yet this very saying is used by Abū Yūsuf as a prime argument (contained in a volume dedicated to the caliph) in defense of blind submission to authority. For it means, according to Hārūn al-Rashīd's cadi, that actual possession of power is the necessary and sufficient argument for the exercise of authority, irrespective of the ruler's personal qualifications.

Three centuries later Ghazālī makes use of this very tradition in support of the legitimacy of the military usurpers who had gained authority throughout the world of Islam.[3] The sixteenth century mystic Sha'rānī goes even further. In his view every person in authority, not just the caliph who is of the house of the Prophet, is in a sense sacred, one can almost say, magically so. And this is the same Sha'rānī whom we shall know later on as a consistent holder of the traditional negative attitude towards authority. "When going to see a ruler", he says, "one should be of pure body and soul, for rulers—for that matter anyone to whom God has granted authority to look after his creatures—are gates leading to the presence of God. A request from a ruler is a request from God."[4] One must humble oneself in the presence of the man in authority, for God resides in him. One may kiss the ruler's hands and feet just as one may honor a scholar who does not practice what he preaches.[5] The prayer of a ruler is heard as long as it is made for the sake of others, notwithstanding his not being righteous. The great Sha'rānī claims to have verified this last statement, when in 1538, after having continuously beseeched God on some matter in vain, he was immediately granted his request when the Turkish pasha in Cairo prayed for him.[6] A deposed ruler, however, should not be honored. What counts is the post, not the man.[7]

[1] Abū Yūsuf, *Kitāb al-Kharāj* 1346, p. 10. For the Ḥadīth collections cf. A. J. Wensinck, *Concordance... de la tradition musulmane*, Leiden I (1936), p. 327, with quotations from Muslim, Ibn Māja, Tirmidhī and Aḥmad B. Ḥanbal. Cf. also next note.

[2] I. Goldziher, *Vorlesungen über den Islam*, Heidelberg 1910, p. 205.

[3] *Iḥyā'*, vol. II, p. 124.

[4] Al-Sha'rānī, *Al-baḥr al-mawrūd*, p. 118.

[5] *Ibid.* pp. 205-9.

[6] Exactly the same notion in the Jerusalem Talmud, Ta'anit 1:4, p. 64 b: "When a man is appointed as a communal leader, his prayer is accepted (i.e. God grants the requests expressed in his prayers)".

[7] Al-Sha'rānī, *ibid.* p. 203, and pp. 155-6, where al-Shāfi'ī is given as authority.

We can see, then, that while the views of Judaism and Islam on the origin of authority have much in common, they differ in no small measure with regard to this subject. They are, however, unanimous in their attitude towards those in authority, and in their objection to participation in government, a unanimity which is indeed surprising and deserving of closer study. The views of ancient Islam on the subject should be studied first, since they were unencumbered by the sufferings of exile and pagan domination. Still in Islam, perhaps more than in Judaism, authority—in spite of its divine origin—is regarded as the very root and seat of evil, the contact with which should be avoided at all cost. ʿOmar II, who was a caliph himself, is reputed to have said "Do not spend your time in the company of a prince, even if you are guiding him the right way, for the sin of spending time with him is greater than any good you could effect".[1]

Practice conformed to this view. The greatest Muslim scholars, such as Abū Ḥanīfa, Sufyān al-Thawrī and others preferred exile, prison and public whipping to government service. And that was in the golden age of the Abbasids.[2] Abū Yūsuf, whose memorandum on public law is a very human document and betrays an exemplary attitude of a God-fearing scholar to his ruler, was not recognized as a faithful traditionist, *maʿa ṣuḥbatihi 'l-sulṭān*, because of his association with the government.[3] The negative attitude toward authority is also encountered in the biographies of other scholars and is comparable to the Rabbis' view that some members of the Sanhedrin avoided Mordecai after he assumed authority and joined the court of the Persian king.[4]

This problem of a religious scholar being a member of a ruler's entourage, *ṣuḥbat al-sulṭān*, is often dealt with in legal and moral texts. Abu 'l-Layth al-Samarqandī, one of the most esteemed expounders of Islamic ethics during the fourth (the Christian tenth) century, paid particular attention to this problem. Quoting Anas, Muhammad's personal servant, al-Samarqandī says that scholars

[1] *Ibid.* p. 250. One is reminded of the Talmudic aperçu: "'Do not approach her (i.e. the harlot's) door'—Proverbs 5:8—the government is meant." ʿAvoda Zara 17a.

[2] Cf. H. F. Amedroz in JRAS 1910, p. 775, A. Mez, *Die Renaissance des Islams*, Heidelberg 1922, pp. 209-10. Some of these stories are probably spurious, but others are not.

[3] This is the great Ṭabarī's verdict of him, quoted in Abū Yūsuf's biography in Ibn Khallikān's Wafayāt.

[4] Megilla 16 b.

"are the depositaries of the prophets; yet when they draw near to the rulers and take part in the dealings of this world they betray the prophets. One should beware of such scholars and avoid them".[1] And in the name of Ibn Masʿūd, another member of Muhammad's entourage, he says: "A religious man who goes to see a ruler loses his religion. For the things by which he pleases the ruler anger God."[2] Al-Samarqandī is quite moderate in his views on business profits and the accumulation of capital, but vehemently forbids dealings with the government. Very similar opinions were held by the Jewish theologian Saadya Gaon, who preceded Abu 'l-Layth by one generation. While the enjoyment (to a certain extent, of course) of food and drink, sex, money, and children was permissible, "one should never desire authority at all. Only if authority is thrust upon a person, should he accept it, and then only in order to fulfill the law and make it possible to guide men aright".[3]

Ghazālī treats this problem in extenso and wrestles with it on many occasions. The chapter devoted to it in the *Iḥyā'* is called "Association with the evil rulers", but it becomes clear from the discussion that nearly all of the rulers of his time fit that description, and that every utilization of authority was suspect from the religious point of view.[4] He quotes Muhammad in the name of the anarchist Abū Dharr, mentioned above, "Whenever a man acceeds to authority, he drifts away from God".[5] He concludes by saying that it is a religious obligation to avoid the authorities and summarizes, "*falā yarāhum wa-lā yarawnah*". "The scholar should neither see, nor be seen by them."[6] This saying was sufficiently well-known to be finally attributed to the Abbasid caliph al-Ma'mūn: "Happy is the man who has a large home, a beautiful wife, sufficient means—and neither knows us nor is known by us".[7] When a religious scholar meets a corrupt ruler in public, he should honor him, so as not to

[1] Abu 'l-Layth al-Samarqandī, *Tanbīh al-Ghāfilīn*, p. 178.
[2] *Ibid.*
[3] Saadya, *Emunot* etc., chapter 10.
[4] *Iḥyā'* II, p. 122.
[5] *Ibid.* p. 129, fifth line from bottom.
[6] *Ibid.* p. 128, sixth line from bottom.
[7] Ghuzūlī, *Maṭāliʿ al-budūr* I, p. 12, quoted by G. E. von Grunebaum, *Medieval Islam*, Chicago 1946, p. 250, note 67. The saying seems to be a reminiscence of two talmudical aphorisms: a) "Three things make a man happy (literally: broaden his heart): a beautiful home, a pretty wife—pay attention to the sequence—and fine clothes," Berakhot 57 b; b) A schoolmaster is described as a happy man because "the messenger (*firistāqa*, Aramaicized Persian) of the king never passes his door", Kethubboth 62a.

incite to rebellion, which Islam strictly forbids. On the other hand, when meeting the ruler in private, the scholar must not even rise before him—in order to show him the superiority of religion.[1] Ghazālī deals with a number of legal problems arising from the oppressive character of government both in the *Iḥyā'* and elsewhere.

The similarity of the problems ventilated by him in this respect with those discussed in the Talmud is astounding and extends to small details. Thus, both sources pose the following problem: Is it permissible to cross a bridge seeing that it has been built by the government out of stolen goods and with forced labor?[2] For that matter, Ghazālī claims that any material benefits derived from the rulers and their functionaries are religiously forbidden, for all the money which they possess is either stolen or is suspect of being so. Needless to say, receiving gifts from the mighty was regarded as a religious opprobrium. Qushayrī, in the introduction to his Epistle on Sūfism, written in 1045, believes that the reason for the decline of the Sūfi movement is grounded in the fact that individual Sūfis regularly accepted gifts from government officials. Sha'rānī, who was mentioned above as a staunch defender of the sacred character of the ruler, testifies to the fact that he never passed under the shadow of a prince's palace, since this would mean enjoyment of protection from the glaring sun by a building erected through unjust means.[3] He does penance whenever he gets together with a ruler for purposes not religious and tells of scholars who, when invited by a prince to a banquet, would hide a piece of bread under their cloak which they would munch on during the festive meal so as not to partake of the prince's dinner.[4]

Naturally, such behavior was exacting and sometimes even dangerous. In time there arose a whole gamut of sayings and stories attempting to prove that the great and saintly of Islam actually did accept gifts from those in authority.[5] Already Ghazālī was familiar with this type of literature, but he and others were able to disprove the conclusions from whatever true or manufactured stories there were.

The prohibition against accepting a government position also

[1] *Iḥyā'* II, p. 128, l. 10.

[2] *Ibid.* p. 134, l. 1. Baba Qamma 103b. The rabbis discussing that problem lived in the fourth century A.D.

[3] *Laṭā'if al-Minan wal-Akhlāq* I p. 5, l. 8 from bottom.

[4] *Ibid.* II. p. 11.

[5] Zakī Mubārak, *Al-taṣawwuf al-islāmī*, Cairo 1938, II. pp. 188-9.

was not practicable. Some authors were not so strict and permitted government service in case of financial hardship. They insisted, to be sure, that the office holder remain honest.[1] Yet it was generally regarded as inconsistent with piety to *seek* government service.[2] Therefore we read stories about righteous rulers who only consented to their appointment after being forced to do so, having refused at the outset.[3] This motif of refused dignity is not restricted to Islam. The Bible, beginning with Moses, provides ample evidence for its diffusion. In China, seeming rejection of office was required by etiquette.[4] In Islam, however, this was not merely a polite custom, it was a matter of conscience. That Medinese cadi whom the caliph al-Mahdī forced to consent to government service by public whipping certainly did not consider his whipping as a humiliation but rather as a rite of purification from the sin of associating himself with the rulers.[5]

It is true that the doctors of Islam sometimes attempted to make use of civil authority in order to crush opinions they considered pernicious.[6] Such actions reflect the old Persian saying that government and religion are brothers. This maxim, which Arabic literature reports many times as part of the Persian king Ardashir's testament to his son Shābūr, is ascribed to Muhammad by a spurious ḥadīth. It is, however, most characteristic that the Muslim scholars themselves declared this tradition as invented, and it is indeed not found in any of the canonical collections.[7] According to Islam, government and religion are not brothers, but opponents.

Turning now to Hebrew literature on the subject, we exclude all references to Roman, Persian or other non-Jewish governments and

[1] Cf. R. A. Nicholson, JRAS 1912, pp. 511-8. H. S. Nyberg, *Kleine Schriften des Ibn ʿArabi*, Leiden 1919, p. 103 ff.

[2] Cf. Ibn Saʿd, *Ṭabaqāt* VIII, part 2, p. 141, l. 1. Abū Nuʿaym al-Iṣfahānī, *Tadhkirat al-awliyā* VIII, p. 80, l. 9.

[3] E.g. Mujīr al-Dīn, *Al-Uns al-Jalīl* I, p. 217.

[4] A. J. Wensinck. "The Refused Dignity", *A Volume of Oriental Studies Presented to E. G. Browne*, Cambridge 1922, pp. 491-499. Wensinck shows that pious monks refused to become bishops in the same way as Muslim religious scholars objected to their appointment as cadis. See also Martin Buber, *Das Königtum Gottes*, p. 187.

[5] Cf. the sources quoted above p. 205, Note 2.

[6] See about this trend e.g. I. Goldziher in *Wiener Zeitschrift für die Kunde des Morgenlandes* 15 (1901), p. 36, Note 4. Schreiner, ZDMG 52 (1898) pp. 537-9. 62 (1908), pp. 9-14.

[7] I. Goldziher, *Revue d'histoire des religions* 43 (1901), p. 7, Note 2; ZDMG 62 (1908), p. 2, Note 1.

confine ourselves to the opinions voiced with regard to leadership within the Jewish community. By doing so, our comparison with Islam will be more direct and unimpaired by the element of foreign domination, which was absent from the early centuries of the development of Islam. Just the same, the similarity between the concepts of the two religions is amazing. Despite all the praise for "those faithfully attending to the needs of the community", not seeking communal leadership was thought of as far more virtuous. "Love labor and hate office", i.e. try to make a livelihood in any profession except public service, is the advice given in the Sayings of the Fathers at the time of King Herod.[1] Two hundred years later we read: "Office buries its holder", exemplified by references to Biblical passages, where a prophet—the prototype of the rabbinical scholar—outlived four kings (Isaiah 1:1, Jeremiah 1:1-3).[2] Nothing is so indicative of the generally accepted views as the story about Rabbi Ammī, who, on his deathbed, regretted his not having taken part in communal life. His disciples and friends found that this was precisely his greatest title of honor: "Above all your other virtues you have avoided acting as a judge and have never permitted yourself to seek public office."[3] A sentiment similar to that expressed by Abū Dharr, cf. above p. 206, is contained in the poignant saying: "Woe to public office! It strips its holder of the fear of God."[4] This is exactly what Maimonides—himself being "Head of the Jews" under the Ayyubids—wrote in one of his epistles: "Most religious men lose fear of God, when they gain authority."[5] He was referring to the officials of the "Prince of the Diaspora", or secular head of the Jewish community in Iraq and other lands of the eastern caliphate, who, unlike himself, received remunerations for their services. "Earning one silver coin as an employee in tailoring, carpentry or weaving is preferable to the emoluments granted by the Prince of the Diaspora."[6]

In keeping with this teaching and with the Muslim one as well, Rabbi Elazar refused any gifts from the Nāsī—the Palestinian counterpart of the Iraqian Prince of the Diaspora—and rejected

[1] Pirqe Avoth 1:10.
[2] Pesaḥim 87b.
[3] Tanḥuma, Mishpaṭim 2.
[4] Midrash ha-Gadol, ed. S. Schechter, p. 412.
[5] *Mose ben Maimon, Epistulae*, ed. D. H. Baneth, Jerusalem 1946, p. 63.
[6] *Ibid.* 68. The crafts mentioned were rated lowly at that time. In addition, working as an employee was regarded as a degradation, cf. below, p. 277.

every invitation to dine at the Nāsī's house.[1] Perhaps the sharpest expression of the pessimistic Jewish view of authority is the following opinion of a most prominent talmudic teacher about King Saul's dynasty: "Why did the Saulian dynasty come to an early end? Because it was not stained by misrule." For "no one is accepted as a public leader except one carrying a bag of impure reptiles on his shoulders", i.e. a leader succeeds only if prepared to disregard the rules of ethics.[2]

What was, in the last instance, the reason for this negative attitude towards government and public leadership in general, found in so many statements of the most authoritative expounders of Islam and Judaism? Naturally, there were many accidental circumstances in the long history of the two religions which favored this cleavage. Confining ourselves to Islam, we may argue first that the spirit of freedom and even anarchy prevailing among the pre-Islamic Arab tribes was revived in Islam on religious grounds in the form of opposition to the established government. This argument is supported by the undeniable fact that the strongest religious opposition party in early Islam, the Khārijites, was composed mostly of genuine Arab tribesmen. Similar trends are discernible in the history of ancient Israel.

Moreover, chance had it that only few rulers arose in classical Islam who could be regarded as champions of religion. According to the Islamic theory only the first four caliphs were *rāshidūn*, treading the right path. What followed was *mulk ʿaqīm*, "barren rule", i.e. power deprived of religious values. To be sure, this statement is too sweeping. For already the third of the four "righteous caliphs", although being a well-meaning old man, allowed his rule to degenerate to shameless nepotism with the result that he was murdered in the name of Islam. On the other hand, there were quite a number of rulers after the first four "righteous caliphs" who took Islam seriously, both among the Umayyads, who immediately followed the righteous caliphs, and the Abbasids, who replaced the former. Still, with the exception of ʿOmar II, who ruled only about three and a half years, none of the Umayyads could be credited with special fervor in the cause of religion. With the Abbasids the situation became even worse. For although their rule was based on

[1] Hullin 53b.

[2] Yoma 22b. Samuel, one of the founders of the Jewish academies in Babylonia-Iraq is credited with this remarkable saying.

the claim of being the Prophet's cousins and true successors, most of them displayed a mode of behavior which was the opposite of sanctity, while the senseless luxury of the court was made possible only through ruthless oppression of the common people.

During the crucial formative period of Islamic spirituality, the rule of the Umayyads, there was another accidental factor which contributed to the alienation of religion from the state. Islamic religious lore, law and thought developed mainly in Iraq. Iraq, however, the most populous and most Arab of the newly conquered countries, found itself in an almost uninterrupted state of revolt against the Umayyad government, which had its seat in Damascus and relied for its preservation on the Syrian tribal contingents. Thus the antagonism between the rulers and the men of religion became accentuated by regional tensions and animosities.

Finally, less than a hundred years of Abbasid rule had passed, when the caliphs and their governors began to employ foreign barbarian mercenaries as their guards and troops, and very soon the latter became the actual lords of the empire. Thus in Islam, at a very early stage of its history, a situation was created which was similar to that of Judaism during its most fertile period: government meant domination by foreigners, who were, or were regarded as, inferiors.

However, it was not only negative factors which contributed to the estrangement of the Islamic religious scholars from the state. It was the very strength and authoritative position of this group which made its adamant attitude towards the authorities possible. The very nature of Islam, as well as of Judaism, presupposes the existence of a free community of religious scholars. It stands to reason that there was some historical connection between the two, i.e. that Islamic religious scholarship came into being partly through the example of and in contact with the Jewish.[1] However, it was specific historical circumstances which made the class of Muslim fuqahā', or religious scholars in the widest sense of the word, so numerous and so independent. The early followers of Muhammad and their descendants were, during the first three or four generations, in receipt of regular payments by the Islamic government. This handy and steady income enabled many to live a life of ease and others to take part in the new economic ventures made imperative

[1] For details cf. S. D. Goitein, *Jews and Arabs*, New York 1964, p. 46 ff., "The Jewish Tradition in Islam."

and possible by the upheaval caused by the Muslim conquests. Many used the leisure and riches thus acquired to lead a dissipated life or for the enjoyment of music, poetry and belles-lettres. There were, however, others who occupied themselves with the practical and theoretical problems posed by religion. Thus, during the first three centuries of Islam a large community of economically independent scholarly people developed, whose main concern was the correct interpretation and strict observance of Islam. As a rule, these people did not need the government. Therefore, they could easily keep aloof from it, whenever their conscience recommended to them such a course of action.[1]

In later centuries, when the ʿulamāʾ, or Muslim religious scholars, used to gain their livelihood mostly as employees of the government (as judges, secretaries or professors), the situation changed fundamentally. The push for promotion inevitably lead to subservience to the rulers. The wordliness of their colleagues caused much anguish to the best of the later exponents of Islam, such as Ghazālī and Ibn Taymiyya, and determined to a large extent the religious reforms proposed by them.[2]

The negative and positive factors discussed above go a long way in explaining the critical attitude towards the rulers and the authorities in general found in Islamic religious literature. It seems, however, that before and above all these there was some basic element in Islam, as well as in Judaism, which made such an attitude almost inevitable. Religion, historically speaking, preceded the state. Muhammad acted as a prophet a long time before he organized the Muslim community of Medina, and there too, he derived his authority as head of the new state exclusively from his office. Moses was the teacher of Israel and transmitted to it a religious law, and only by doing so, he became "king in Jeshurun".[3] The heavenly revealed law, which, in both religions, was authoritatively expounded by the religious scholars, was placed above the law of the state, or more exactly, the state had no law of its own at all. Both religions, Islam from its outset, and Judaism, as it developed in the last centuries of the second Temple, stressed the futility and transitoriness of life in this world. Thus, by their very nature, the political

[1] The development of this class is sketched below, 217 ff.

[2] Cf. W. Montgomery Watt, *Islamic Philosophy and Theology*, Edinburgh 1962, pp. 159-60.

[3] Cf. Deuteronomy 33:4-5.

institutions regulating this life had only limited and relative value. At best, they were instrumental in assisting the individual in his preparation for the world to come.

This basic attitude towards the state is poignantly expressed in an Islamic criticism of a most famous Greek saying, quoted by a Muslim writer, not in the name of its author, Plato, but attributed to another Greek philosopher, Diogenes. Al-Tawḥīdī (died 1009), in a delightful book that pretends to render learned conversations held in the presence of a vizier interested in literature and science, lets the latter make the following remark: "Diogenes was once asked: When will the world prosper? Said he: When the kings will be philosophers and philosophers will be kings. Said the vizier: This saying must be spurious. For philosophy may be acquired only by one who rejects this world and turns his heart towards the world to come, but how can a king reject this world?" This passage beautifully illustrates the contrast between the Greek polis, where the quintessence of wisdom was the perfect conduct of state, and another civilization, in which all mundane occupations, and in particular public service, were regarded only as impediments to one's own perfection.[1]

[1] Al-Tawḥīdī, *Al-imtāʿ wal-muʾānasa* II, p. 32. Seeing that already ancient heads of Plato's Academy, such as Polemon and Erkesilaos, kept away from public life entirely (Diogenes Laertius, Book IV, para. 19 and 40), it is likely that a similar criticism of the Platonic aphorism is found somewhere in later Greek philosophical writings, which paved the way for the transcendental mood which finally captivated Islam. Abū Bakr al-Rāzī, the Persian philosopher, takes pains in showing that he associated with the princes only in his capacity of physician and counselor, not as general or minister, which would have robbed him of his title of philosopher, cf. Abū Bakr al-Rāzī, *Opera Philosophica*, ed. Paul Kraus, 1939, p. 109, l. 19.

PART THREE

ISLAMIC SOCIAL HISTORY

CHAPTER ELEVEN

THE RISE OF THE MIDDLE-EASTERN BOURGEOISIE IN EARLY ISLAMIC TIMES

"Nous ne connaissons pas l'histoire sociale de l'Islam. La connaîtrons-nous jamais?" asks Fernand Braudel.[1] It is in the very nature of scientific progress that when such a question is asked, the answers are already in the air. The new, sociological, trend in Islamic studies was underlined by the late Professor J. H. Kramers of Leiden in his lecture "La Sociologie de l'Islam" at the Twenty-second International Congress of Orientalists at Istanbul in September, 1951, and again, with special emphasis on the economic factors, by Professor Cl. Cahen, then of Strasbourg, at the Congress held in Cambridge in August, 1954.[2] A major confrontation with this problem occurred in September, 1961, when twenty Islamists from seven different countries convened in Brussels and devoted four days of deliberations and discussions exclusively to the social aspects of Islam.[3]

As a matter of fact, the subjects covered by the term sociology have occupied the minds of Arabists for over a century. In the wake of François Guizot, H. T. Buckle and Jacob Burckhardt, Alfred von Kremer wrote his brilliant *Culturgeschichte des Orients unter den Chalifen*,[4] and although he filled the gaps in our knowledge with more elegance than accuracy, this and other books of his cannot be overlooked by the sociologist. These were echoed in the *History of Muslim Civilization* by the able Christian Arab, Jirjī Zaydan.[5] The works of the great masters of Islamic studies, I. Goldziher, J. Wellhausen, Ch. Snouck Hurgronje, C. H. Becker and C. A. Nallino, are mines of information for the student of sociology.

[1] *La Méditerranée et le monde méditerranéen a l'époque de Philippe II* (Paris, 1949), p. 637. Quoted by R. Brunschvig, "Perspectives", *Studia Islamica*, I (Paris, 1953), p. 5.

[2] J. H. Kramers, in *Proceedings of the Twenty-Second Congress of Orientalists* (Istanbul, 1953), pp. 85-95, and *Acta Orientalia*, XXI (Copenhagen, 1953), p. 243-53. Cl. Cahen, "L'histoire économique et sociale du monde musulman médiéval", *Studia Islamica*, III (Paris, 1955), pp. 93-115.

[3] *Colloque sur la sociologie musulmane, Actes, Centre pour l'Étude du monde musulman contemporain*, Brussels (1962).

[4] Vienna, 1875-77.

[5] Cairo, 1902-6; in Arabic.

The series of books on *The Dawn, The Morning* and *The Noon of Islam* by the late Egyptian scholar, Aḥmad Amin, which appeared in the thirties and the forties of this century, are also sociological in concept and execution.

Although—as these few outstanding examples show—the sociological aspects have not been neglected by the historians of Islam, the task presently at hand is one of greater specialization and integration. The abundant literary and historical sources have to be scrutinized in close connection with the results of Muslim archaeology, epigraphy, numismatics and papyrology—to which also non-Muslim material has to be added—and the whole must be integrated into one coherent picture of the society studied. The late E. Lévi-Provençal's monumental *Histoire de l'Espagne Musulmane*[1] and the work of other French Arabists, in particular the late Jean Sauvaget, are models of such treatment. On the other hand, special phenomena of great historical importance which are sufficiently well documented, should be singled out and brought into full relief by detailed and, where possible, exhaustive research.

A subject worthy of such special study is the middle class of early Islam. This class developed slowly during the first hundred and fifty years of the Muslim era, emerged into the full light of history at the end of the second century, became socially "admitted" during the third and asserted itself as a most powerful socio-economic factor during the fourth. However, it never became an organized body and, as a class, never obtained political power, although many of its members occupied first and second echelon in the state. The turn from the tenth to the eleventh century (the Muslim fourth and fifth), which witnessed the apogee of the Middle Eastern bourgeoisie, also marks the complete ascendancy of castes of slave soldiers, mostly of Turkish extraction, which dominated the history of that part of the world for the following eight hundred years. At the same time, the monetary and mercantile economy of the Middle East gave way to an economy in which feudalistic trends became dominant. Before all this happened, however, Islam as a religion and civilization had fully taken shape, and it was largely members of the bourgeoisie who had developed Muslim religious law, the backbone and very essence of Islam,[2] as well as the kindred disciplines of the Traditions

[1] Paris, 1950 sq.

[2] Cf. Joseph Schacht, *An Introduction to Islamic Law*, Oxford 1964, p. 1 ff.

of the Prophet, the reading and the exegesis of the Koran and theology.

We are able to study these processes in detail, since the Muslims have left us vast collections of biographies of their scholars and men of letters. It is no exaggeration to say that, for the time prior to the Crusades, we possess no fewer than ten thousand biographies of Muslims, many of which contain details not only about their literary activities and connections, but also concerning their occupations and economic position. Some time will be required before this vast material can be critically sifted. However, even a cursory perusal of it brings out two basic facts: first, how extremely specialized the economy of the Middle East was in those days, and, secondly, that in early Islamic times, it was predominantly merchants who were engaged in the development of the religious sciences of Islam.

No wonder, then, that the full-fledged religion of Islam, as it appears to us through the writings of the third and fourth centuries of the Muslim era, is pervaded by the spirit and ideas of the rising merchant class. The proud conviction of being economically independent[1] of the governing cliques, a feeling of prosperity and success, a sober and business-like attitude towards this world and the world to come, lent their colors to the new religion. Islam possessed a Law and a Dogma which vindicated the absolute omnipotence of God—and of His representatives, the men of religion—over the mighty of this earth that contained safeguards for the protection of the life, freedom, property and honor of the Muslim citizen and in which man's inner security was achieved through the teaching of trust in the All-merciful, which offset the fears of the Last Judgment.

Naturally, a civilization which had amalgamated so many different peoples and spiritual climates could not be made of one piece. As G. Levi Della Vida has pointed out in his brilliant sketch "Dominant Ideas in the Formation of Islamic Culture",[2] it was the characteristic—and, according to him, the failure—of Muslim civilization that it never fully integrated its conflicting elements. Economic independence and prosperity were one way to attain spiritual freedom and inner security. There was another way:

[1] It is significant that the word *istiqlāl* which, in our times, has gained so much vogue as a political catchword, was used in early Islamic literature especially in the sense of economic independence and affluence, see e.g. Mas'ūdī, *Murūj*, vol. VIII, p. 118, l. 8; Al-Shābushtī, *The Book of the Monasteries*, ed. Gurgis 'Awāḍ (Baghdad, 1951), p. 81, l. 15.

[2] *The Crozier Quarterly*, 21 (July 1944), p. 215.

renouncing the world and living the life of an ascetic who had nothing to fear, precisely because he had nothing to lose. The various trends of Muslim ascetism amalgamated during the third century of Islam into the movement known as Sufism. Whether Sufism, as a way of life, actually originated in a class lower than the bourgeoisie, is a question to be discussed separately.[1] In any case, although the ideal of renouncing the world was always a strong undercurrent in Islam, its representative opinion during the period considered here postured a favorable attitude towards earning and amassing capital and, with some qualifications, even towards certain aspects of luxury. During that time the merchant class attained a social position and correspondingly, self-esteem, which it secured far later in Europe. In the following, this religious and social self-assertion of the Muslim bourgeoisie will be studied in outline.

II

It is very instructive to read a document of early English capitalism, such as Richard Steele's[2] *The Tradesman's Calling*, in conjunction with a similar book, written by a prominent representative of the new Muslim bourgeois class about a hundred and fifty years after the death of the Arab Prophet. The book is called *On Earning*[3]

[1] Attention is drawn to the fact that the prominent leaders of Sufism in the third Muslim century bore names indicating a lower class origin: Sarī al-Saqaṭī (dealer in old clothes or secondhand goods; died 867), Abū Ḥamza al-Ṣadafī (workman processing mother-of-pearl; died 882), Abū Sa'īd al-Kharrāz (cobbler; died 890), Ḥamdūn al-Qassār (fuller, or Qaṣṣāb, butcher; died 884), Abū Ja'far, the master of Junayd, al-Ḥaddād (blacksmith; died 910). Cf. about most of these men A. Mez, *Die Renaissance des Islams* (Heidelberg, 1922), pp. 270-1 and the Arabic translation by Abū Rīda (Cairo, 1941), II, p. 17.

The accepted Sufic view that earnings by manual labor were preferable to business is pointed in the same direction, cf. Abū Ṭālib al-Makkī, *Qūt al-Qulūb* (Cairo, 1932), III, p. 22, l. 23. To be sure, Sufism as a whole was an extremely ramified movement, having, among others, as patron-saint the Buddha-like Ibrahīm Adham, who exchanged the cloak of the beggar for the princely purple.

[2] This Richard Steele (1629-1692) was a nonconformist divine and is of course not to be confused with his namesake and younger contemporary, the famous essayist. *The Tradesman's Calling* appeared first in 1684. Copious quotations from it in R.H. Tawney, *Religion and the Rise of Capitalism* (Pelican Books, 1940), pp. 216-20.

[3] In Arabic: *Kitāb al-Kasb*. The original of the book is lost, but much of it is included in an abridgment—and refutation—made by the author's pupil Ibn Samā'a (died 847) under the title *Al-iktisāb fi'l-rizq al-mustaṭāb*, "On

and was written by Muḥammad Shaybānī (died 804), the co-founder of the most widely diffused Muslim School of Law, the Ḥanafites. Shaybānī was a Mawla, a member of the sedentary subject population, whose father—or grandfather—had adopted Islam and been transferred—or emigrated—from Syria to Iraq.

Shaybānī's problem was very similar to that which Richard Steele had to tackle. He had to prove that the vigorous striving of the new Muslim trading people for a decent living was not only not opposed by Islam, but was actually regarded by it as a religious duty. He, like Richard Steele, had to overcome deep-seated religious prejudices against making money, convictions made popular by mendicant ascetics who might be compared to the begging friars and monks, against whom Steele wrote so eloquently. As is well-known from other quarters, Muslim ascetism of that time was tinged by Christian influence.

It is remarkable that economic ethics should have formed the subject of a special treatise as early as the second half of the second century of the Muslim era. Shaybānī was not the only author who wrote a book *On Earning*. Kātib Celebi,[1] the seventeenth century Turkish bibliographer of Arabic literature, knew of other books bearing the same title, written by two authors who lived in the third century of Islam: Aḥmad ibn Ḥarb Nīsābūrī[2] (died 848) and his pupil Aḥmad ibn Yaḥyā Ḥulwānī[3] (died 909). Both professed ascetism and both came from northeastern Iran, then, with the possible exception of Iraq, the most important business center of the Muslim world. Chapters on economic ethics were included in religious books, as we shall see later on. However, the most common form of expressing views on the subject—and indeed on any subject—was, according to the atomistic and aphoristic character of the Muslim mind, that of sayings and maxims, attributed to the Prophet

Lawful Livelihood" (Cairo, 1938). The title of Shaybānī's work is preserved in the great bibliography of Arabic literature *Kashf al-Ẓunūn* (Maʿārif, 1943), II, p. 1452, and in Ibn Samāʿa's abridgment, p. 27, l. 14-5. Shaybānī's work begins on p. 14, l. 15 of the Cairene edition of the latter (to be quoted in the following as Ibn Samāʿa).

The authorship of Shaybānī should not be doubted, since his pupil hardly would have mistaken a spurious treatise as his master's work. For the purpose of this study it does not make much difference whether this essay was written around 800 or 830.

[1] Kashf al-Ẓunūn, quoted in the previous note, *ibid.*

[2] Cf. his biography in Al-Khaṭīb al-Baghdādī, *Taʾrīkh Baghdād* (Cairo, 1931), IV, pp. 118-9.

[3] *Ibid.*, V, pp. 212-3.

or to one of his Companions, the so-called Ḥadīths or "Traditions". Some of the Traditions on economic ethics are included in the canonical collections of Ḥadīths published in the third century of the Muslim era. Many more are scattered throughout the general literature of that and the following centuries. A very great number are included in later compilations, particularly in Suyūṭī's Kanz al-'Ummāl (Hyderabad, 1894-5), in the chapter "On Commerce", which perhaps deserves a full translation into a western language.[1] Shaybānī's book *On Earning* quotes many such sayings and is indeed the oldest extant source for most of the Traditions on economic ethics contained in it. Thus, the book is representative of its time not only because of the personality of its author, but also because of the sources used by him.

Shaybānī opens his book with the blunt statement, later refuted by his pupil Ibn Samā'a[2]: "Seeking one's livelihood is a duty incumbent on every Muslim, as is the seeking of knowledge". This statement is corroborated first by a number of sayings (certainly apocryphal) attributed to the Prophet and secondly by an oft-quoted sentence put into the mouth of the Caliph 'Omar I, under whom the great Muslim conquests were made: "I prefer dying on my camel's saddle, while travelling on business, to being killed in the Holy War: has not Allah himself mentioned those that travel on business before those that fight 'on the Path of God' (cf. Koran, ch. 73, verse 20)?" Shaybānī then goes on to show that, beginning with Adam, all the prophets gained their livelihood by following some profession. Adam was a farmer, Noah a carpenter, Abraham a cloth merchant[3] and, since the Arabs regarded themselves as his

[1] A selection from this chapter is to be found in H. Ritter, "Ein Arabisches Handbuch der Handelswissenschaft", *Islam*, (Berlin, 1916), pp. 28-31. A modern Turkish scholar compiled a collection of 47 Ḥadīths encouraging a positive attitude towards earning, cf. Ahmed Nazmi, *The Attitude of Islam towards Wealth* (Istanbul, 1921-3; in Turkish). Quotations from this book in W. Björkman, "Kapitalentstehung und-anlage im Islam", *Mitteilungen des Seminars für Orientalische Sprachen, Westasiatische Studien*, 32, (Berlin, 1929), p. 81-2.

[2] Ibn Samā'a, pp. 25 sq.

[3] This seems to be a Muslim invention. Abraham's garments play some role in Jewish legend, cf. Louis Ginzberg, *The Legends of the Jews* (Philadelphia, 1909-46), I, p. 332 and V, p. 259; however, his role as patron of the cloth merchants in Islamic folklore has nothing to do with this, but is a result of the extraordinary importance of the textile business in early Islam, cf. Mez, *Renaissance*, p. 453, and the quotations from the Kanz in Ritter (see above), p. 29, e.g. "Nine tenths of all profit in this world is made in textiles". "If there

descendants (through Ishmael), the Prophet recommended that they become cloth merchants like their forefather. David, it is true, first lived on his revenue as king, but he soon was instructed by a heavenly apparition that living by some trade was religiously preferable to receiving a salary from the government and he became an armourer (cf. Koran 34:10-11).

Here Shaybānī strikes a note which became commonplace in later Muslim literature: namely, that the profession of the honest merchant, or indeed any trade, pleases God more than Government service.[1] Indeed, even as early as the close of the second century after Muhammad's death, Shaybānī was not alone in this opinion. Thus Ibn Sa'd (died 845) quotes in his Ṭabaqāt[2] a saying attributed to a hero of the battle of Qādisiyya, in which the Arabs crushed the army of the Sassanid king: "I prefer earning one dirham by commerce to receiving ten as my soldier's pay". We are, of course, in no position to check the authenticity of such a saying. In the first century of Islam, the *'aṭā'*, or soldier's pay, formed the basic income of any Arab who emigrated from Arabia to the camp towns founded all over the new Muslim empire. It is a historic fact that even in that early period some people had scruples about the ways of collecting the revenue from which the *'aṭā'* was paid. In any case, this and similar sayings which praised business and preferred income from it to a salary received from the Government, must have been in vogue for some time before they were included, around the year 200 of the Muslim era, in the collections of biographies or religious law and lore.

Shaybānī is on firmer ground when he refers to the fact that all the early champions of Islam had been businessmen or possessed other sources of regular income.[3] Thus Abu Bekr, the first caliph, was a cloth merchant, 'Othmān, the third caliph, a very well-to-do importer of cereals, etc. He is equally correct when he quotes a number of passages from the holy book of Islam, in which *ma'āsh*,

was trade in Paradise, I would become a cloth merchant there". To be sure, Abū Ḥanīfa, the founder of the Ḥanafite School of Law, was engaged in the same trade.

[1] Above p. 208.

[2] Ibn Sa'd, *Ṭabaqāt*, ed. E. Sachau *et al.*, Leiden 1904-40, VI, p. 68, l. 17. It is reported of the same man that he refused to accept an appointment to a Government post, *ibid*, pp. 66-7, and that he was in receipt of a salary while serving in one, *ibid*, p. 65, l. 20. The famous Sha'bī is credited with a particularly severe condemnation of the *'aṭā'*, cf. Ibn Sa'd, VI, p. 175, l. 17.

[3] Ibn Samā'a, pp. 21-22.

earning one's living, or outrightly *tijāra*, commerce, are mentioned either as the normal occupations of the true-believers or are even lauded as such.[1]

More interesting for us, however, are those passages of Shaybānī's work in which he justifies his opinions theoretically. Of course, the ultimate aim of man's life is to serve God. But in order to be able to serve God one needs a sound body, clothes, etc., and these can be lawfully acquired only by work.[2] Trust in God is a prerequisite of the true believer, but this means only that one should work as hard as one can and "bargain with God",[3] i.e. leave it to him to send his blessings. Once, Shaybānī reports, the caliph ʿOmar saw a group of pious men sitting with downcast heads. These, he was told, were the *Mutawakkilūn*, people trusting in God and therefore refraining from professing any trade. "No", said the caliph, making a pun, "these are the *Muta'akkilūn*" (those who eat up other people's money). "You had better lift up your heads and earn your own livelihood".[4]

A most important part of Shaybānī's book consists of sections in which he deals with the question whether a Muslim should work only in order to keep body and soul together or whether the acquisition of luxuries was lawful. In view of the most extravagant luxury in which many of the Muslims indulged, even those of the first generation, this was a question that occupied the minds of everyone. Shaybānī's answer is affirmative. As to precious clothing —the most common object of indulgence of the time—Shaybānī quotes a saying attributed to the Prophet: "When Allah gives riches to a man, he wants them to be seen on him". This is a dictum ascribed to the Prophet, which in a slightly different and even more characteristic form is found both in the canonical collections of Traditions[5] and in Ibn Saʿd's Biographies,[6] where various heroes of classical Islam quote it in order to justify their wearing silk and brocade

[1] Shaybānī refers to such passages of the Koran as 2:275/276: "Allah has made buying and selling lawful" or 2:282 (legal details about business), or 62:10: "When the Friday prayer is over, disperse in the country and seek Allah's bounty (i.e. engage in business)" or 2:198/194: "There is no harm in seeking Allah's bounty (during the holy pilgrimage)".

[2] Ibn Samāʿa, p. 16.

[3] *Ibid*, p. 37.

[4] *Ibid*, p. 21.

[5] "Allah wishes to see the favors he bestows on a man apparent on him". Abū Dā'ūd, Chapter "Libās", para. 14. Tirmidhī, Chapter "Adab", para. 54.

[6] Ibn Saʿd, *Ṭabaqāt*, IV, part II, p. 29, l. 10.

or similar luxurious materials. This problem of luxury in personal appearance was so central during the first two centuries of Islam that we read in literally hundreds of places in the old biographies about the costly attire—or simple, as the case may be—of the ancient Muslims, their way of perfuming or dyeing their hair, their wearing golden—or iron—rings and jewellery, etc. The general impression left by the perusal of the relevant literature is that many of the early Muslim religious men indulged in luxurious dress to a far greater degree than the religious law, which became fixed later on, deemed permissible.

Similarly, it was asked whether a man who was already married to one or several wives, did not transgress the lawful limit of pleasure in this world by acquiring one or more beautiful slavegirls (who served, according to Muslim law, also as concubines). During the years of conquest setting in with the Prophet's death, an unlimited supply of this commodity was available and it is only natural that some pious people had scruples about the wide use made of it. Not so our jurist. Shaybānī[1] points out that both the Prophet and his son-in-law, later the caliph ʿAlī, kept concubines of foreign extraction in addition to their numerous wives; thus there could be no harm in any Muslim following their example. From what I know of the pietist literature of the first five centuries of Islam, keeping beautiful slave-girls met with less objection than did any other form of luxury. This attitude was certainly one of the reasons for the enormous expansion of the slave-trade in the early centuries of Islam.

Contrariwise, extravagant expenditure on buildings was so widely resented that Muslim religious literature censured even excessive spending of money on mosques.[2] This censure was incorporated in the canonical collections of Traditions of the Prophet. However, it would be completely erroneous to attribute the trend to the distaste of the Bedouin for town life. The Arabs who emigrated to the camp-towns were great builders; in many places in Ibn Saʿd's Biographies we find details about the building of houses and palaces by the early Muslims. Dislike of wasteful building was inherent in the *sedentary* population even before Islam; excessive expenditure on synagogues was censured in the Talmud in the same vein as that in which Islam later discussed mosques. The real reason for this attitude was the great suffering inflicted on the middle and lower

[1] Ibn Samāʿa, p. 79.

[2] Cf. EI[1], s.v. Masdjid (by J. Pedersen), chapter D, section 1 at the end.

classes both by forced labor and by the senseless squandering of public funds on costly buildings. The books of the early Muslim historians, such as Balādhurī, Ṭabarī or Mas'ūdī, are full of stories about the enormous sums wasted in this way. When, in 744, the Umayyad caliph Yazid III ascended the throne, he promised, in his first public speech, not "to lay one brick upon the other". To such a degree had the building activities of his predecessor been hateful to his subjects.[1] The Abbasids were even more reckless in squandering the money of their subjects on buildings of little practical value. Thus the caliph Mutawakkil (847-861) erected for himself nineteen different palaces, all of which are known by name and some also by sight, spending on them, according to a well-informed contemporary, the enormous sum of 247 million dirhams (silver coins) and 100 million dinars (gold pieces).[2]

In these circumstances, it is natural that Muslim religious literature which echoes the views of the middle class, who had to bear the cost of such extravagancies, was unfavorably inclined toward expenses on buildings. It is, however, characteristic of the trend represented by Shaybānī, that he has no scruples with regard to the beautifying of mosques or even of private houses,[3] and the well-to-do Muslim bourgeois of his epoch took pride in his house, just as a successful modern businessman would do today.

If luxury was regarded in early Islam as permissible and, to some extent, even laudable, there was another question of economic ethics which was extremely disturbing to religious minds: was it permissible to hoard riches? Was this not in outright conflict with Allah's command, an injunction to trust in God, repeated so often in the Holy Koran? Of the rich literature on the subject I would like to quote one author who has treated the theme more extensively than anyone preceding him and who was himself a most characteristic representative of early Islam: the mystic Abū Ṭālib al-Makkī (died 996),[4] who, as is well known, was one of the main sources of

[1] Ṭabarī, *Annales* (Leiden, 1879-98), II, p. 1834, ll. 14-6.

[2] Shābushtī, *The Book of the Monasteries* (Bagdad, 1951), p. 120 and 230-5, according to the imperial postmaster and intelligence officer Ibn Khordādbeh.

[3] Ibn Samā'a, p. 79. Similarly the economic-minded theologians of this early period ruled—against the opinion becoming law later—that even the building of new churches should be tolerated, because it contributed towards the general prosperity of the country: cf. Kindī, *The Governors and Judges of Egypt* (Leiden, 1912), p. 131 sq., quoted by Mez, *Renaissance*, p. 39.

[4] In his great religious compendium *Qūt al-Qulūb* (Cairo, 1932), III, 1-56, especially pp. 28-9.

inspiration for Ghazālī (died 1111), the greatest theologian of medieval Islam.[1] Abū Ṭālib was a prominent member of the Salimiyya movement, which professed, in addition to certain theological dogmas, the ideal of Zuhd or renunciation of this world. However, these pietists were very well-to-do people, and one has the impression that the great traveller Maqdisī (Moqaddasi), who describes them as such,[2] sees some connection between their piety and their material success. Likewise, Abū Ṭālib, after weighing the pros and cons of living the life of a beggar, who "manifests" his trust in God by renouncing the world, and that of a successful businessman, who "conceals" it, yields the palm to the latter.[3] The amassing of capital (*Iddikhār* in Arabic) is not in conflict with the trust in God, if it is done "for Him and in Him", with the intention to serve God and to induce His favor.

Serving God with one's money means of course in the first place spending it on charity, for religious foundations or purposes, for works of public utility, etc.[4]. However, the modern idea that good service rendered to one's fellow-men in business or trade is in itself meritorious was by no means foreign to the religious literature of early Islam. "The best man is he who is the most useful to other people", says a dictum attributed to Muhammad.[5] This idea is expounded in more detail in an interesting passage contained in the treatise "How to Behave Oneself towards One's Fellow-Men" by the famous mystic Sulamī (941-1021). "When you leave your house for the bazaar", says Sulamī, "do so with the intention of satisfying the wants of a Muslim; if, in addition, you make a profit, regard this as a favor granted to you by God and a blessing bestowed on your customer for your sake."[6] Meticulous honesty, and even consideration and delicacy were required in business relations, which, as we

[1] Ghazālī's most detailed and highly instructive exposition of the attitude of Islam towards economic life falls outside the scope of this article. It is summarized by H. Ritter, op. cit. (see p. 222), pp. 31-44 and by Heffening, EI[1] s.v. Tidjāra, chapter c, where further literature is given.

[2] *Descriptio Imperii Moslemici* (Leiden, 1906), p. 126, ll. 7-10.

[3] As far as I can see, this remarkable idea was first expressed by the renowned second century mystic Abū Ayyūb al-Sakhtiyānī ("The Leather Merchant"), see Ibn Sa'd, *Ṭabaqāt*, VII, part II, p. 16, l. 9.

[4] To be sure, "Charity begins at home" is commonplace in early Muslim literature; "The best dinar is that spent on one's own family", Ibn Samā'a, p. 62, and the sources quoted there. Also *Qūt al-Qulūb*, III, p. 6, l.23.

[5] *Ibid.*, p. 38 and parallels given there by the editor.

[6] *Kitāb Ādāb al-Ṣuḥba*, ed. M. J. Kister, Israel Oriental Society (Jerusalem, 1954), p. 54 sq.

have seen, were surrounded by a kind of halo of service to God and men.[1] Oaths, concealing of defects, praising what one sells or blaming what one buys and interfering with other people's transactions should be strictly avoided. One should never press a debtor who is in dire straits; one should stick to one's own obligations, but if a customer wants to cancel a contract, etc., one should not insist on his keeping it. One should measure or weigh generously for others, but level for oneself. Clearly the people whom Sulamī addressed were themselves business people, and there was certainly some soulsearching among them as to whether such a worldly-profession as that of a merchant was not, religiously speaking, *'ayb*, a shame. "When you see your fellow-Sufis sitting in their shops, believe they do so because they have small children or poor parents to look after; when you sit in your shop, consider that whatever you give up of this world, you will win". One need not be greedy, for losses or gains are ordained by God. Thus, as a profit is a gift from Heaven, one should take particular care not to spoil it by illicit practices. Still, as the Arabic pun had it: *Al-tujjār fujjār*, "Merchants are scoundrels", it is difficult to do business without coming into conflict with the exigencies of strict ethics. Therefore, Sulamī advises the merchant to atone for possible slips by accompanying each transaction with a gift of alms for the poor.[2]

This survey of representative opinions on the subject from the second to the fourth century of the Muslim era has shown that early Islam as a whole took a positive, or at least lenient, view of economic activities, luxury and the amassing of capital and saw in the profession of a trade a service to one's fellow men not devoid of religious value. The attitude of the majority of Muslims is perhaps best expressed in the saying attributed by Shaybānī and others to the Prophet Muhammad: "Poverty is almost like apostasy".[3] This

[1] A century later, this idea receives its exact, legalistic, formulation by Ghazālī. He defines the calling of a business man as a *farḍ kifāya*, a religious obligation incumbent on those who are able to fulfil it in case there are not enough other persons able to do so. An obligation of this type is e.g. service in the army in the Holy War. As the world cannot exist without commerce, a man, by engaging in it—and indeed in any other indispensable profession—fulfils a religious duty, cf. H. Ritter, op.cit. (p. 222), p. 41.

[2] Both the pun and the advice are attributed to the Prophet, cf. the literature adduced by Kister, p. 54, section II, notes 146 and 147. In Ibn Sa'd, *Ṭabaqāt*, VI, 167, l. 9, the pun is ascribed to the caliph 'Alī.

[3] Ibn Samā'a, p. 28 and parallels quoted by the editor. Apostasy is a crime for which the penalty is death.

implies that the true servant of God should be affluent or at least economically independent. The booths of the money-changers in the great mosque of the camp-town Kufa[1] possibly illustrate the fact that there was no necessary conflict between business and religion in Islam.

It is true, the Sufis were fully aware of the contrast.[2] The phrase *yalḥaq al-sūq*, "let him take up business", denotes in their language nothing less than giving up the Sufi way of life. Still, the world-renouncers and world-affirmers did not necessarily constitute two hostile camps. The peaceful co-existence of the two attitudes is tellingly exemplified in the story of the pious Abū Barza al-Aslamī who never rode a horse or wore silk, while his brother was the champion of extravagance. Far from being critical of each other, each of them used to say of his brother: "In our whole tribe, there is no better man than he".[3] The vast literature of the Traditions of the Prophet, which was assembled in canonical and semi-canonical collections during the third and fourth centuries of Islam, is a living testimony to this state of affairs. For, as we have seen, it contains, along with sayings extolling poverty, many others urging man to strive vigorously for a prosperous living. However, the conciliatory attitude of such prominent Sufis and ascetics as those quoted in the previous pages indicates that the scene was dominated by the rising bourgeois class, with the result that its economic activities were religiously evaluated in a positive way not unlike that described by R. H. Tawney in connection with the English bourgeoisie class of the seventeenth century.

III

In an intensely religious society, such as early Islam, a rising class has first to justify itself from the *religious* point of view. How this was done by the new Muslim bourgeoisie was shown in the previous

[1] Balādhurī, *Futūḥ al-Buldān* (Cairo, 1932), p. 283-4.

[2] Cf. e.g. the concluding chapter of Qushayrī's exposition of Sufism, where *ḥirfa*, "profession", *al-sa'y fi'l-'amal*, "working for one's livelihood", and *ma'lūm*, "capital" are the very things which a Sufi novice has to give up (Cairo, 1912, pp. 184-5). To be sure, Qushayrī lived in the fifth century of the Muslim era.

[3] Ibn Sa'd, *Ṭabaqāt*, IV, part II, p. 35, ll. 5-16. The idea that riding on horses was an indication of human pride and of luxury is of course as old as Biblical times (cf. Hosea, chapter 14, v.3). However, it is remarkable that it should be attributed to an Arab at the time of the Conquest.

chapter. Turning now to the question of how this class obtained the *social* position which it occupied by the end of the third century of Islam, we have of course to bear in mind that the Meccans, the rulers of the new Muslim state, had themselves originally been the sons of a merchant city.[1] That merchants should change into generals and governors, is not a unique phenomenon. It has its parallels in twentieth century Arabia[2] and in the history of the Phoenicians, the Greeks and the Italian cities of the Middle Ages. The question is, whether the new ideal of the warrior-saint, which no doubt was predominant during the first century of Islam, fundamentally changed the attitude towards the merchant profession. A. Mez, Die Renaissance des Islams, p. 442, asserts that the Arabs, like other martial peoples, looked with contempt on business and that the world of the Umayyads had no understanding of the merchant profession, which is hardly mentioned in their records. However, this statement, although repeated by various authors, cannot be maintained. The books on the general history of the fourth century of Islam (when the merchant class, according to Mez himself, was the real bearer of Muslim civilization) were not different in this respect from our sources for the first century; as their interest centered around religion and rulers,[3] they normally had little opportunity to make mention of business.

The position of the merchant in the heroic early years of Islam needs more detailed study. There can be little doubt that the majority of the new Muslim aristocracy preferred to obtain a post (*ʿamal*) in the government or in the army, or to amass riches as relatives of such people or through drawing a pension (*ʿaṭāʾ*) from the state.

[1] Cf. H. Lammens, *La Mecque à la veille de l'hégire* (Beyrouth, 1924) and numerous other publications on the subject by the same author, enumerated in EI[1], s.v. Mekka (by Lammens), chapters 1 and 2 (rich in documentation, but to be used with reservation). Cf. now A. Abel, "L'incidence de l'activité commerciale de la Mekke (sic!) sur son développement urbain", in *Dalla Tribu allo Stato*, Ac. Naz. dei Lincei, Rome 1962, pp. 124-136.

[2] See the description by H.St.J.B. Philby, *Arabian Highlands* (Ithaca, 1952), pp. 229-30, of the career of Ibrahim Nashmī, who "was by profession a merchant... and a leading light of the... caravaning traders on the routes to Transjordan and Syria... He first came into prominence as a military leader during the siege of Madina by the Wahhabis in 1925". After the submission of that town, he first became governor of its environment and later on of a similarly exposed province, Najrān, which had been snatched away from Yemen by King Ibn Sa'ud.

[3] The greatest compilation of ancient Arabic historiography, the "Annals" of Ṭabarī (died 923), is called "The Book of Prophets and Kings".

However, others remained who continued the profession of their forefathers, and still enjoyed the highest social standing. A characteristic representative of that type was Saʿīd ibn Musayyab, a noble Qurayshite (i.e. belonging to the "tribe", which had formerly inhabited the town of Mecca), who lived in Medina and pursued as his hobby the collection of the juridical decisions of the first five caliphs, as well as of traditions of historical content.[1] As a prominent Qurayshite, he was on the payroll of the Muslim state, but he was also a busy merchant[2] who preferred dealing in textiles to other branches of business.[3] There is not the slightest indication in the very detailed biographies of Ibn Musayyab, that his profession was detrimental to his relations with other members of the Muslim aristocracy. He was styled "The Lawyer of the People of Medina and the Doyen of the Quraysh" and various caliphs sought his company. Moreover, the records reveal that even governors of provinces did by no means shun business. Thus we are told, for example, how Abū Hurayra, the famous "Companion" of the Prophet, accumulated wealth from commerce during his governorship of Eastern Arabia, in addition to his income from his *ʿaṭāʾ*, from his part in the spoils of war, and from horse-breeding.[4] When, in 721, a new governor was appointed for Khorāsān in Eastern Iran, one of the richest provinces of the Empire, he received explicit instructions from his superior not to engage in business since that would be unfair to his subjects.[5]

The surest indication of the Islamic attitude is to be found in religious law. From its very inception this law occupied itself with the Muslim merchant and protected his interests. Far from leaving

[1] About him see Ibn Saʿd, *Ṭabaqāt*, V. pp. 92 sq. Balādhurī, *Ansāb*, V ed. S. D. Goitein, Jerusalem 1936, index, passim. His biography is found also in all of the later compilations about the prominent men of the first Muslim century.

[2] Ibn Saʿd, *ibid.*, p. 97. Once, it is reported, a sum of 30 000 dirhams had accumulated in the public treasury from his pay, which he refused to cash in because he disapproved of the conduct of Government, *ibid.*, 95, l. 13. Had he not been an independent business man, he could not have allowed himself such a luxury.

[3] *Ibid.*, p. 99, l. 12. Normally the merchants of that time, although specializing in one branch, handled other commodities as well.

[4] *Ibid.*, pp. 59-60, especially p. 60, l. 15. The report itself may be unhistorical. What counts, is the assumption that a man who is on the Government's payroll of pensions and, in addition, a governor, should engage in business.

[5] Balādhurī, *Ansāb*, VII (prepared by F. Gabrieli, printed only in part), p. 22, l. 4.

business to the despised non-Muslims—as the Ottoman Turks did in their great imperial times—the Arabs, in the oldest lawbooks extant,[1] reserved special rights for their own merchants. While, on passing any customs station, the subject of a foreign state had to pay 10% of the value of the merchandise transported by him, and a non-Muslim subject of the Arab state 5%, a Muslim merchant had to give only 2½%. This clearly indicates that the ruling class intended to keep its ascendancy over the vast subject population not only by taxing it heavily, but also by furthering Muslim trade to the detriment of non-Muslim business. The provision, ascribed to ʿOmar I, that no consignment of a merchant should be searched,[2] also shows that the caliph's own people were the merchants meant by the law.

Thus it is evident that the sedentary Arab even of the first century of Islam had no social prejudices against business, although it was natural that the honored and often far more lucrative posts in the administration and army (which were then still largely identical) attracted the more enterprising brains. On the other hand, contempt and even hatred of the merchant profession was felt in two sections of the population, which, to be sure, were very conspicuous at that time: the Arab Bedouins, who had retained most of their traditional notions, although now living largely a sedentary life, and the old Persian aristocracy, which had not changed its social outlook much after adopting Islam. Life in the Bazaar, with its continuous habits of swearing and giving witness and its general talkativeness, was in flagrant contrast to the Bedouins' conceptions of honor and dignity.[3] In addition, the Bedouins loathed the merchants and

[1] Abū Yūsuf, *Kitāb al-Kharāj* (Cairo, 1927-8), p. 147, French translation by E. Fagnan (Paris, 1921), p. 205. Abū Yūsuf, *ibid.*, pp. 158-64. Shāfiʿī, *Kitāb al-Umm* (Bulaq, 1908-9), VII, p. 228. Cf. A. Grohmann, *Arabic Papyri in the Egyptian Library* (Cairo, 1934-8), II, pp. 9-10 and the literature quoted there. According to Abū Yūsuf, pp. 161-2, the custom duties were introduced when merchants from Manbij in Northern Syria, who lived in Byzantine territory asked ʿOmar I for permission to trade with the Muslims. ʿOmar II (717-20) is credited with having made minor alterations in the customs rules. These incidents may be based on historical facts.

[2] Abū Yūsuf, *ibid.*, p. 161. This was, of course, a pious wish, as the complaints about ruthless searchings at the customs stations show, cf., e.g. Moqaddasi, *Descriptio Imperii Moslemici* (Leiden, 1906), p. 133, l. 16.

[3] Two characteristic incidents from the end of the first Muslim century: When a man of the Tamīm tribe wanted to give witness in court, he was reminded by a bystander that only common people and merchants did so, but not a nobleman ("Sharīf"). Balādhurī, *Ansāb*, Ms. ʿAshir Ef., 597/8ʿ

moneylenders, who exploited their frequent needs for a loan or a respite. The Ḥamāsa of Buḥturi, a most representative collection of classical Arabic poetry, contains three chapters devoted to verses in which the Bedouin poets boast how they evaded fulfilling their obligations towards the detested merchants, whether Persians or Arabs.[1] These poems, most of which belong to the first Muslim century, are certainly authentic and convey a vivid impression of those social tensions. It may be remarked in passing that E. Garcia Gomez sees in the famous episode at the beginning of El Cid, where the hero boasts of not paying his debts to the Jews of Burgos, a survival of a literary genre, originally developed by the ancient Arab Bedouin poets.[2]

In some respects, the mountains of Iran were conducive to the development of concepts similar to those formed in the Arabian desert. Although the Persian merchants in early Islamic times had the reputation of being particularly efficient,[3] the Persian aristocracy indulged in the prejudice that business was incompatible with the standing of a nobleman. Most characteristically, it was a merchant who reminded Yaḥyā the Barmecide (died 805), Hārūn al-Rashīd's great vizier, when, in his early days of poverty he intended to engage in business, that, as a "Sharīf", he could not possibly do so.[4] Unlike the Indian caste system, where the merchants took third place after the priests and warriors, in the Iranian classification of society the bourgeoisie was conspicuous by its absence.[5] Since the new class of the secular bureaucracy of the Muslim state, which

Istanbul, fol. 1002 a (I owe this quotation to Mr. M. J. Kister, who is preparing, an edition of the volume of the Ansāb dealing with the Tamīm tribe). When the noble Yemenite, Yazid ibn Muhallab was asked by the caliph ʿOmar II to corroborate by oath his statements about his income during a governorship, he preferred severe imprisonment to the shame caused by Arabs saying of him that he swore for money's sake. Most characteristically, his son had no such scruples: Balādhurī, *Ansāb*, VII, p. 37 and parallels.

See also Mez, *Renaissance*, p. 442.

[1] Buḥturī (Cairo, 1929), pp. 413-32, chapters 171-3. Cf. C. A. Nallino, *La littérature arabe*, trad. française par Ch. Pellat (Paris, 1950), pp. 144-6.

[2] Verses 78-212. See E. Garcia Gomez, "Esos Judios de Burgos", *Al-Andalus* (Madrid-Granada, 1951), pp. 224-7.

[3] Mez, *Renaissance*, 448-9. Moqaddasi, *Descriptio*, p. 33, l. 6; p. 294, l. 10. Jāḥiẓ, *Tria Opuscula* (Leiden, 1903), p. 84.

[4] Jahshiyārī, *Wuzarā* (Cairo, 1938), p. 186, l. 4-5. Quoted also by A. A. Dūrī, *The Economic Life of Mesopotamia in the Tenth Century* (Baghdad, 1948, in Arabic), p. 112.

[5] Cf. G. E. von Grunebaum, *Medieval Islam* (Chicago, 1946), p. 203; R. Ghirshman, *Iran* (Pelican Books, 1954), pp. 309-10.

came into great prominence during the second century of Islam, was largely composed of members of the ancient Persian aristocracy,[1] these Kuttāb or "Scribes" showed great contempt for the merchant profession—an attitude which found literary expression in pamphlets devoted to the subject.[2]

In addition to the impact of traditional notions, it is natural that in a century of war and conquest the merchants as a class remained in the shadows. Only in a few cases are they mentioned as participating in military exploits, and these are exceptions which confirm the rule. When, on the 26th of August 683, a Syrian army sent by the caliph Yazid I attacked the inhabitants of the Holy City of Medina,[3] the latter forced the "Perfumers", a kind of merchants' guild originating in Dārīn on the East coast of Arabia, to march with them against the Syrians. The perfumers, 400 in number, tried to excuse themselves by arguing that they were only merchants. However, they had to join the Medinese forces and formed a special corps. Their military duties were carried out in quite an ingenious fashion; they fixed their standard in the ground and fastened it with stones, while absenting themselves quickly. The Syrians took the flying flag as an indication of a position held and through this mistake almost lost the battle; the caliph was so enraged about this, that he retaliated by imposing a fine of 400,000 dirhams on Dārīn, the perfumers' town of origin.[4]

That a single merchant should be employed in a ruse destined to overcome an enemy, is, of course, of no great importance. However, it is instructive to read the story about the Tyrian used by the caliph Muʿāwiya (661-80) for such a purpose; this is told beautifully and with many characteristic details by Masʿūdī, Murūj, VIII, pp. 75-87. The caliph wanted to get hold of a Byzantine Patrikios or high commander, who had insulted a noble Muslim prisoner by slapping his face. For years the Tyrian went to and from Constantinople with his ship full of precious merchandise of all descriptions, until he found out that the commander concerned was infatuated

[1] Already ʿUbaydallah ibn Ziyād, the Umayyad viceroy of Iraq, preferred Dihqans—members of the Persian gentry—to Arabs for his administration, Balādhurī, *Ansāb*, IV, ed. M. Schloessinger, 109, ll. 16-21. Similarly his successor Ḥajjāj, *ibid.*, 123, 15-18.

[2] See below, p. 241 and note 5. Jāḥiẓ' *Praise of the Merchants* (see p. 241) is a refutation of a pamphlet against the merchants.

[3] About this event see J. Wellhausen, *Das arabische Reich* (Berlin, 1902), p. 98.

[4] Balādhurī, *Ansāb*, IV, p. 43.

with Susanjird, pillow cases made of Persian embroidery. The next year, our Tyrian returned to Constantinople with his ship loaded with the most exquisite Susanjird and while the Patrikios was engaged in admiring those wonders of workmanship, he set sail—until Muʿāwiya's foe was safely brought to the Syrian coast. As the narrator himself alludes, the remarkable thing about the story was that the Tyrian, who had excelled in naval warfare before, played the role of overseas trader so well.

Of a different nature is the case of ʿAbdallah the Iṣfahānī, a Persian, who put at the disposal of the Governor of Iraq his 400 slaves or Mamlūks[1] and himself commanded the right wing in the battle which brought the Shiʿite revolt of Mukhtār to an end (A.D. 687). He obviously belonged to the colony of Iṣfahānī merchants living in Basra.[2] When, a few years earlier, in a time of great anarchy, the famous Muhallab was entrusted by the nobles of Basra with the task of fighting the terrible menace of the Khawārij bands, he found that the treasury of the town contained only 200 000 dirhams, a sum not sufficient for the equipment of his 12 000 choice troops. He sent word to the merchants, explained to them how much business had been damaged by the Khawārij and asked them to join him and to grant him a loan. After some bartering the merchants agreed. Muhallab was victorious, collected the taxes in the districts recovered and repaid the merchants. Immediately everyone joined him "in expectation of spoils and business".[3]

These instances belong to the later part of the first century of Islam. In the second century things began to change. The main concern of the state was no longer expansion, but, rather, keeping control over the many disrupting internal elements. Both sides, the authorities and their opposition, had to finance their forces and make propaganda for themselves. For both purposes, the business people, who possessed the means and were experts in advertising, became indispensible. They were already conspicuous in the movement which overthrew the Umayyads (750 A.D.). The leader of the Abbasid propaganda, who bore the proud title "The Vizier of the House of Muhammad"—the first man in Muslim history to bear

[1] It seems that this is the first authentic occurrence in Muslim literature of the term "Mamlūks" denoting a corps of slave soldiers.

[2] Balādhurī, *Futūḥ* (Cairo, 1932), p. 359, esp. ll. 16-7; cf. Baladhurī, *Ansāb*, V, p. 263, l. 16. Or was this Iṣfahānī perhaps a professional condottiere?

[3] *Kāmil* of Mubarrad with Marsafī's commentary (Cairo, 1937-30), VIII, pp. 11-13. I have to thank Mr. Kister for this reference.

the title Vizier—was none other than Abū Salama, the vinegar merchant; his assistant, Ibrahīm ibn Salama, was rewarded for his propaganda services with al-Khawarnaq, the most ostentatious castle of early Islamic times.[1] In a memorandum written a few years after the rise of the Abbasids, Ibn al-Muqaffaʿ, the Persian aristocrat who did so much for Arab literature, expressed his dismay at finding the new caliph's entourage composed of people of low rank, including—*horribile dictu*—even some who had once done work with their own hands.[2]

Still, during the first century of Abbasid rule, Ibn al-Muqaffaʿ's class, the descendants of the old Persian gentry, were most prominent in the administration of the State. At the beginning of the third century of Islam, however, the merchant class succeeded in penetrating into the highest spheres. It was the time when a witty poet could address a vizier saying:

"Money and intelligence enable a man to stand in the courts of the Princes; as you see, I possess neither."[3]

Faḍl ibn Sahl, the greatest vizier of the caliph Ma'mūn (813-33), had a Persian corn merchant as his most honored table companion.[4] When Ma'mūn, at the end of his reign, launched an inquisition against certain theological views, we find among the notables with whom the caliph argued personally, men bearing epithets like "the manufacturer of bottles" or "the date merchant".[5] That these were not mere family names—which also would be significant—is proved by the caliph's angry remark about the date merchant that his intelligence was as base as his business.[6]

Under Ma'mūn's successor, Muʿtaṣim (833-42), representatives

[1] Cf. above p. 172. About Ibrahīm ibn Salama see Balādhurī, *Futūḥ* (1932), p. 286.

[2] See above p. 161.

[3] Ibn Ṭabāṭabā, *Al-Fakhrī* (Cairo, 1938), p. 198.

[4] Jahshiyārī, *Wuzarā* (Cairo, 1938), pp. 229-31; 319-320. That the vizier let his guests wait for dinner until his friend arrived, or that he arranged with the corn merchants of Baghdad a partnership which brought him the great sum of 50,000 dinars, possibly is not very significant. However, that the vizier inquires after the merchant's wife and daughters is mentioned as an indication of utmost intimacy.

[5] Ṭabarī, *Annales*, III, p. 1121, ll. 7-10.

[6] *Ibid.*, p. 1128, l. 9. The wording shows clearly that it is not business in general which is regarded as base, but that particular trade. However the caliph's remark that his theological opponents believe in "the religion of the Dinar and the Dirham", *ibid.*, p. 1129, l. 6, does not necessarily refer to the merchants' profession.

of the merchants' class became the highest executives of the State. The first vizier appointed by him was a "Mr. Miller", Ibn ʿAmmār al-Ṭaḥḥān, an extremely wealthy business man from lower Iraq.[1] His most famous vizier, and indeed one of the most remarkable personalities of his time, was Zayyāt, "the Oil Merchant" (family-name), whose father had been purveyor to the Abbasid court.[2] Once, when Zayyat, who continued the profession of his father, appeared at court in black dress and girded with a sword, he was stopped by the caliph's first secretary with the remark: "You are only a merchant, why do you appear in court dress?" But it was not long before Zayyat became vizier and kātib, secretary, and it was he, who built Samarra, the most gorgeous capital erected in Islamic times.[3] Another of the highest dignitaries of State under Muʿtaṣim was a "Mr. Tailor", Jaʿfar al-Khayyāṭ, who was connected with the army.[4]

For the next two hundred years, many members of the business class occupied prominent positions in the Middle Eastern states. The material on the subject is abundant, but has not yet been sufficiently collected and studied. A few examples may illustrate the situation.

Ibn Jaṣṣāṣ,[5] a very great business man, was the envoy of the Ṭulunid ruler of Egypt to his nominal overlord, the caliph of Bagdad, in 892, and arranged the marriage of the former's daughter to the latter. He settled in Bagdad, but when he gave asylum to Ibn al-Muʿtazz, the princely poet, who had sat on the throne of the caliphs for one day, he was liquidated by the latter's successful rival.[6] The proceeds from this liquidation had the value of 5,500 000 dinars—a sum comparative to the treasures left by the caliphs at their death.[7] The high degree of dependence of the rulers of Iraq

[1] Al-Fakhrī (Cairo, 1938), p. 207. Before Ṭaḥḥan, a former private secretary of Muʿtaṣim continued to serve him for some time as vizier.

[2] Not in oil, but in tents, parasols and similar utensils, *ibid.*, p. 1182.

[3] *Ibid.*, p. 1184. "All that Muʿtaṣim built in Samarra, on both sides of the Tigris river, was executed by Zayyāt".

[4] *Ibid.*, p. 1195, 1254, etc.

[5] The family name means Plasterer. However, Ibn Jaṣṣāṣ made his riches in the jewellery business.

[6] At least, this is the reason given by his contemporary and compatriot Masʿūdī, *Murūj*, VIII, p. 283. To be sure, Ibn al-Muʿtazz was killed in 908, while Ibn Jaṣṣāṣ' liquidation occurred in 914-5. About his riches see Masʿūdī, *ibid.*, pp. 117-20.

[7] E.g. al-Mutawakkil, the sumptuous, left (in 861) 4 million dirhams (Masʿūdī, *ibid.*, VII, p. 276); al-Muktafī (died 908) 8 million dinars and 25

during the tenth century upon the bankers and merchants is evident from many pages of Ibn Miskawayh's "Eclipse of the Abbasid Caliphate."[1] As far as the Jewish merchants are concerned, the material has been thoroughly discussed by W. J. Fischel in his *Jews in the Economic and Political Life of Mediaeval Islam* (London, 1937). Owing to the rich Jewish literature on religious law and through the treasures of the Cairo Geniza, we are at present better informed about the economic activities of the Jews of that time. The historical sources, however, mention many more non-Jewish bankers, Christians as well as Muslims (cf. only the names mentioned by Fischel himself ibid., p. 5 and p. 29, note 1), and the Geniza papers clearly indicate that the great merchants of the eleventh and twelfth centuries were mostly Muslims.[2] The Jewish capitalists of that time were representative of their class, not of their religio-national group.[3]

In Egypt, during much of the tenth century, an Iraqi Persian family, the Mādharā'iyyūn, held all but supreme power.[4] The

million dirhams (*ibid.*, p. 225); al-Mu'taḍid (died 902): 9 million dinars and 40 million dirhams (*ibid.*, VIII, p. 114).

[1] Edited and translated by H. F. Amedroz and D. S. Margoliouth (London, 1920-1). Cf. A. A. Dūrī, *The Economic Life of Medieval Mesopotamia in the Tenth Century*, pp. 158-179.

[2] The Cairo Geniza documents of the eleventh century mention various cases of Jews borrowing money on interest from Muslims. However thus far not a single opposite case has come to the knowledge of this writer. The whole question of the denominational factor in medieval commerce is discussed in the present writer's *A Mediterranean Society*, Chapter III, where reference is made also to Prof. A. K. S. Lambton's short paper "The Merchant in Medieval Islam" in *A Locusts' Leg* (London 1962), pp. 121-130.

[3] One should avoid drawing an analogy between the Jews in the thoroughly feudal societies of medieval Western Europe or sixteenth century Poland and their coreligionists inside the highly mercantile civilization of the Middle East during the first four centuries of Islam. Thus—unlike the situation in Poland—no coins with Hebrew inscriptions are known from early Islamic times. The statement to the contrary by Charles Pellat, *Le milieu basrien et la formation de Jāḥiz* (Paris, 1953), p. 238, is a lapsus in an otherwise admirable book.

[4] They form the subject of a thorough monograph by H. Gottschalk, *Die Mādarāijjūn* (Berlin und Leipzig, 1931). C. H. Becker, *Islamstudien* (Leipzig, 1924), I, p. 216, calls them the leading capitalists of the third (Muslim) century. It may be that these capitalists came from a family of "scribes". However, as the sources do not mention that their first representative came to Egypt as the secretary of a governor, I suppose—contrary to Gottschalk, *ibid.*, p. 29—that he went there on business. The close connection of this family with the Muslim science of Ḥadīth (*ibid.*, pp. 35-6) also seems to indicate that the family came from the merchants' class and not from the secular bureaucracy.

Fatimid empire, which centered around Egypt, from 969, was organized by a Jewish businessman of outstanding capacity, Ibn Killis, who, in his later days, adopted Islam and became the first vizier of the new state. He too came from Iraq, but, before becoming connected with the Fatimids, held in Ramle (then the capital of Palestine) the office of Representative of the Merchants, an office, which has some affinity with, and may have been the model for, that of the Consuls in the Italian merchants' colonies.[1] Similarly, a generation later, a merchant (and a Jew), Abū Sa'd Tustari, whose family had come from Southern Persia via Baghdad to Egypt, was for some time the most powerful man in the Fatimid state.[2] No wonder that a tenth century writer, pointing to the fact that a bill of exchange was accepted with greater readiness than an allocation of income from taxes, came to the conclusion that

"Merchants are more powerful than viziers".[3]

As the bourgeoisie rose, it had to adapt itself to the ways of life and cultural ideals of the ruling class, otherwise it would not have been "admitted" by it. A few examples may illustrate this development. Balādhurī reports that a particularly "aristocratic" estate in southern Transjordan which had belonged to the Umayyads even before Islam, and which, after its confiscation in 750, was handed down in the Abbasid family, finally passed into the hands of oil-sellers in Kufa.[4] A Baghdad ice- (or actually: snow) merchant, after having sold a Ṭāhirid prince three pounds of ice for 10 000 dirhams each—the prince's favorite slave-girl was seriously ill and it was a day of burning heat—immediately used a pound for himself, in order to show that he could allow himself the same luxuries as the members of the ruling clique.[5] In his General History, Ṭabarī finds it worthwhile to record that the caliph al-Mahdī (775-85) was the first to use Tabaristan upholstery.[6] In the third quarter of the ninth century, a visitor to Baghdad still notes that at the caliph's court one sits on Tabaristans.[7] However, in the many marriage

[1] Cf. pp. 345 ff. About Ibn Killis see W. J. Fischel, *ibid.*, pp. 45-68.

[2] *Ibid.*, p. 78–87.

[3] *Eclipse of the Abbasid Caliphate*, III, pp. 138-9.

[4] *Futūḥ* (Cairo, 1932), p. 135. A similar instance (the Khawarnaq castle) is mentioned above, p. 236.

[5] Ibn al-Jawzī, *Muntazam* (Hyderabad, 1938-40), VI, pp. 118-9.

[6] *Annales* III, p. 356. Quoted by R. B. Serjeant, "Islamic Textiles", *Ars Islamica* (Ann Arbor, 1946), XI, p. 98.

[7] Cf. the sources quoted by Ch. Pellat, "Jāḥiẓ à Baghdad et à Samarra", *Rivista degli Studi Orientali* 37 (Roma, 1952), p. 55, note 3.

contracts, which have found their way into the Cairo Geniza from the 10th century onward, any well-to-do Jewish bride had Tabaristans in her trousseau. So common was this item that in the deed of betrothal of an India merchant's daughter, dated Monday, 11th November 1146, it is stated that she was given "a real Tabari—from Tabaristan"; this detail was mentioned, because there were imitations on the market, since no middle class bride consented to be married without the luxury that once had been reserved for the caliph's court.[1] Equally common in the marriage contracts was the Persian Susanjird embroidery, which, as we have seen, p. 235, was sought after so eagerly by a Byzantine grandee.

A similar development can be observed in the realm of the spirit. While in the first centuries of Islam, the merchants had been mainly concerned with the religious sciences, and a pamphlet directed against them could describe them as devoid of secular education,[2] we read in a third century source even of a Jewish merchant who was a great maecenas of Arabic men of letters and himself a sort of poet.[3] That an Iraqi merchant who was shipwrecked near Aden, should work his way up in that town by his poetical talent, is reported to us as something not very extraordinary, while from the same town and the same time a number of poems (in Hebrew) written by a North African Indian trader have actually been preserved in the Cairo Geniza.[4]

Subsequent to the rise of the merchant class, its doings began to attract the attention of the public and the litterateurs, which formerly had been exclusively focused on the ruling clique and its entourage. When, at the table of the caliph al-Muʿtaṣim, the famous gluttons were mustered, with regard to the Umayyad period, caliphs and viceroys were mentioned, but of contemporaries—a date merchant, a dealer in corn, the proprietor of a bath and a butcher (or manager of a slaughter-house).[5] The passion of a silk merchant from Kufa for a slave-girl formed the subject of an Arabic love story,[6] while the bourgeoisie of Basra was depicted in Jāḥiẓ'

[1] Bodleiana, Oxford, ms. heb. d. 66, fol. 47-8. (Many other marriage contracts contain a similar statement).

[2] Quoted in full in Tawḥīdī, *Imtāʿ wa-Mu'ānasa* (Cairo, 1944), III, p. 61-2.

[3] Ch. Pellat, *Milieu basrien*, p. 230.

[4] Cf. S. D. Goitein, "Two Eyewitness Reports, etc.", *BSOAS* (London, 1954), XVI/2, p. 249, note 1.

[5] J. Sauvaget, *Historiens Arabes* (Paris, 1946), p. 43 (Masʿūdī).

[6] C. Brockelmann, *Geschichte der arabischen Literatur*, Supplement (Leiden, 1937), I, p. 248.

writings.[1] Special mention must be made, of course, of the 22. Maqāma of Hamadhānī, that immortal satire on the successful businessman, who is exceedingly proud of his house and all his other possessions and convinced that all he owns is really first class.[2]

The "bourgeois revolution" of the Middle East during the early centuries of Islam had many repercussions on world history.[3] To mention just one: through it the Jews, who up to that time had been engaged mainly in agriculture and other manual occupations, were converted into a predominantly commercial people.[4]

This all too rapid survey may be fittingly concluded with a reference to two literary documents of high interest, one a panegyric of the merchant profession by the famous Basrian litterateur Jāḥiẓ and the other a Handbook on Trade composed, of course, by a member of that class itself. In his "Praise of the Merchants and Blame of the Courtiers", Jāḥiẓ extols the independence and safety of the merchant—who is "a king in his own court"—as opposed to the humiliating and precarious life of a courtier.[5] Dimashqī's Handbook, which certainly deserves a full translation into English, contains an almost scientific exposition of a theory of economics, of the nature of the business profession and the various commodities handled in the author's time. The most impressive aspect of the book of this Middle Eastern Pegolotti is the pride taken in his profession. For him, making money is a noble calling: "If there was nothing to say about wealth but that it is one of God's attributes, this would be a sufficient honor and distinction".[6]

[1] Pellat, *Milieu basrien*, p. 247.

[2] Cf. *The Maqamat by... Hamadhani*, translated from the Arabic by W. J. Prendergast (London, 1917). This translation has not been seen by the present writer.

[3] Cf. R. Lopez, "Les influences orientales et l'éveil économique de l'occident", *Cahiers d'Histoire Mondiale*, 1, 3 (Paris, 1954), pp. 594-622.

[4] See S. D. Goitein, *Jews and Arabs, their Contacts through the Ages*, New York, 1964, ch. VI, "The Economic Transformation... of the Jewish People in Islamic Times", pp. 89-124.

[5] *Rasā'il* (Cairo, 1906), pp. 155-8. Only the beginning of this highly interesting treatise has been found thus far.

[6] H. Ritter, "Handbuch" (see p. 222), p. 47.

CHAPTER TWELVE

THE MENTALITY OF THE MIDDLE CLASS IN MEDIEVAL ISLAM

It has often been emphasized that the existence, the absence or else the new formation of a middle class is of decisive significance for the economic rise and constitutional development of modern Middle Eastern societies. As late as 1960, an Iraqi expert stated in a scientific journal that there was no middle class worth speaking of in Iraq.[1] What was the situation in the High Middle Ages, during the creative period of genuine Islam?

In a well known essay entitled "The Types of Ideal Personalities in Islamic Culture" Hans Heinrich Schaeder found only three types as representative of the civilization in question: the autocratic ruler, who was praised as God's shadow on earth and as the very incarnation of justice, although he very rarely, if ever, lived up to this ideal; the beggar for God's sake, who by renouncing this world tried to free himself from the yoke of autocratic rule, but often degraded his religious status by misusing it; and, finally, the literati, "die Literaten", the heirs of the ancient scribes of Babylonia and Egypt, who knew how to write and how to moralize about everything, but did not take anything very seriously and thus contributed their part to the insincerity of king and beggar alike.[2]

Schaeder's analysis, although thought provoking, is both one-sided and incomplete. It is too pessimistic, in so far as it takes excesses and decadence for the very essence. Moreover, it is too sweeping in its definition of the literati. We have to distinguish carefully between two different types of men of letters in Islam: the *kuttāb*, the scribes or government officials, who were the main cultivators of that cheap encyclopedic knowledge which is rightly denounced by Schaeder, and members of the independent middle

[1] Mohamed Alwan in *Middle East Journal*, 14 (1960), p. 479. Cf. Morroe Berger, "The Middle Class in the Arab World", in *The Middle East in Transition*, by Walter Z. Laqueur, New York 1958, pp. 61-71, and, in the same volume, the remarks of Charles Issawi, p. 40, and of A. F. Mills, p. 13.

[2] Hans Heinrich Schaeder, "*Die typischen Persönlichkeitsideale in der islamischen Kultur*", first published in 1929 and reprinted in *Der Mensch in Orient und Occident*, München 1960, pp. 272-306.

class, who, as a rule, were not connected with the government and were also learned, though in religious studies and not in general Adab. Following a hint by Adam Mez, who stated in his *Die Renaissance des Islams* that in the tenth century the merchants had become the bearers of Islamic civilization,[1] subsequent research revealed that this role was indeed far older and had become conspicuous already by the end of the eighth century. This, of course, is the period in which Islamic thought and practice were condensed into dogma and law. Thus, the very character of Islamic religion was deeply influenced by the spirituality of the class which was more than any other active in its formulation. If so, a study devoted to the mentality of the middle class in medieval Islam needs no justification. It is essential for the understanding of Islam itself.[2]

In the preceding paragraphs, the middle class was identified implicitly with that of the merchants. This, to be sure, is a generalization. Industry and commerce were not rigidly separated from each other in those days; people producing a commodity often also traded in it as well as in similar products, while even mere artisans sometimes attained economic prosperity and social prestige, which qualified them to belong to the middle class.[3] But in general, the limitation of the term middle class to the world of business and finance is valid. There was also a very important technical aspect involved. The art of writing was acquired by prospective merchants just as by future scholars, but not by artisans, who had no need for it.

This statement requires some explanation. Every boy who went to a Koran or Bible school had to do exercises which consisted of the writing of the letters of the alphabet as they appeared in books. This was a means to learn reading, and many leaves with such exercises have been preserved in the Cairo Geniza (see below). However, once the children had mastered reading, the art of writing was not pursued further in the regular elementary school. Therefore we find in the Geniza hundreds of signatures on documents, not in the cursive script, which was used in day to day writing, but in the monumental ductus common in books. These signatures often have rather shaky and awkward forms. They were written by artisans and shopkeepers of low standing, who had not gone beyond the

[1] A. Mez, *Die Renaissance des Islams*, Heidelberg 1922, p. 442.
[2] Cf. above pp. 217-241.
[3] See below Chapter XIII.

elementary stage of schooling.[1] For the same reason there is a responsum, or *fatwa*, by Maimonides about persons signing documents which they were unable to read. Documents were mostly written in the cursive script, which these people had not learned. Only at a higher stage of schooling was the art of writing taught systematically, including, in addition to calligraphy, the composition of letters and legal deeds.

Four types of students attended such courses: future government officials, physicians, scholars and merchants. The officials and the doctors (who often served as court or army physicians), as well as the judges in the capital cities, in other words the people connected with the government, formed a separate group, as is clearly evident from the Geniza records. They could be described as upper, or upper middle class. The rank and file of the middle class consisted of merchants and religious scholars, such as judges of lower rank, preachers and cantors. It should be noted that religious scholars often engaged in business or even in a craft, while merchants acted regularly as judges and as socio-religious leaders in other fields. In short, the art of writing—not of reading, which was diffused far more widely—was the distinctive mark of the middle class and of government circles.

In our study of the mentality of this class we shall confine ourselves to the High Middle Ages, approximately the years 1000-1250, in Muslim terms 400-650 A.H., in other words, the period of the Fatimids and Ayyubids. This period differed much from the 250 years preceding and following it. The Muslims themselves were well aware of the continuous changes in society. Al-Tawḥīdī, who lived around 1000, deals with the subject at length and summarizes it as follows: "With each century people acquire new habits and a mentality which they had not possessed before."[2] A hundred years later, as is well known, al-Ghazālī expressed the belief that the Muslim year 500 initiated a new period and that he himself was destined to be the renewer of Islam. Such beliefs, it seems, were not confined to the circles of the elite. In a detailed will of a Jewish merchant, made at that time, he leaves all his possessions to his only daughter, but stipulates that she should not marry before the

[1] To be sure, there were also some scholarly persons who used to sign in book script. This was an act of piety, and was done in order not to shame their less educated co-signers. However, the scholarly hand is immediately recognizable by its regularity and elegance.

[2] Al-Tawḥīdī, *Al-Imtāʿ wal-Muʾānasa*, III, p. 3.

end of the Arab year 500, for this year marked "the termination of this era".[1] Again, one hundred and twenty years later, at the end of our period, a man from Alexandria writes in a letter: "First we had prophets, then sages, finally Geonim (these were the heads of the Jewish academies in Jerusalem and in Bagdad, who used to issue authoritative rulings in religious and in legal matters). Now, this too has come to an end."[2] One is reminded of the great Muslim mystic Ibn al-ʿArabī, who lived at the same time and regarded himself as *khātam al-awliyā*, the seal and the last of the true saints.[3]

We have chosen the High Middle Ages for both methodological and practical reasons. The two and a half centuries preceding it saw the formation of the Muslim middle class, and the period following its decline. During the Fatimid and Ayyubid periods, and in particular during the former, the middle class appears to us as fully developed with solidly established patterns of life and fixed scales of values. Therefore, it easily lends itself to systematic exposition and also serves as a good point of departure for the study of the earlier and of the later stages.

The practical reason for our choice is the fact that the source material which we are going to use comes mostly from this period. There is no dearth of general source material for the knowledge of the class which forms the topic of this paper. Since it was the exponent of Muslim religion, to some extent, the whole of Muslim religious literature written in the period under discussion can be adduced for its study. Naturally, there are some branches of literature which are particularly useful: the biographies of scholars, accounts of travel and works devoted specifically to social and economic questions. However, all these books have one disadvantage: they are books. One is never sure where theory ends and life begins. People who write books are suspect of being a particular species of humanity. Therefore, in order to study the mentality of a class, it is extremely advantageous to have access to direct testimonies given at random and unwittingly, such as are contained in letters and documents of various descriptions. Now, the survey provided by Adolf Grohmann in his book *From the World of Arabic Papyri* shows that the known collections of Arabic fragments on paper (not: papyrus)

[1] University Library Cambridge, Taylor-Schechter Collection 13 J 14, fol. 4.

[2] David Kaufmann Collection, Budapest, IX.

[3] Cf. Arthur J. Arberry, *Sufism*, London 1950, p. 101.

amount to about 33,000, and these, as far as we know, come mostly from our period.[1] Whether these fragments on paper touch on administrative matters or contain correspondence mainly from villages, as the published papyri mostly do, or whether they reflect the urban middle class, we do not yet know, since these papers have not yet been studied sufficiently.

Thus, for the time being, we must utilize a similar source, the records from the Cairo Geniza, documents written in Hebrew characters, but mostly in the Arabic language, many of which have come down to us from this period.[2] Most of these were written by middle class people and thus form a broad basis for our research.

From the Islamic point of view it is of course disadvantageous that this material was written by Jews. However, having devoted most of my time during the last ten years to the study of these papers, I have come to the conclusion that specific Jewish aspects do not form its most characteristic element. I am even inclined to believe that, to a large extent, the Geniza records reflect Mediterranean society in general. When one reads legal documents on the same topic in Arabic, Aramaic, Hebrew and Byzantine Greek, one realizes how similar they are not only in legal conceptions, but even in their very wording. The same applies to business letters and even to private correspondence, as far as we have material for comparison. Specifically Jewish are matters of religious ritual, family law and community life.[3] However, even with regard to Jewish community life, which seems so specific and reminiscent of the world of Greco-Roman corporations rather than of Islamic society, one may doubt whether it really differed so much from its environment. What do we actually know about the life of the Islamic middle class during the eleventh and twelfth centuries? Claude Cahen's recent studies on urban "autonomism" in medieval Islam have opened our eyes and made us wonder whether we have not to qualify some generally accepted views about Islamic society in the High Middle Ages.

As to the evaluation of the Geniza records as a source for our study, we should first bear in mind that they are mostly in Arabic, i.e. in the standard Arabic then in use in each country, in Egypt,

[1] Adolf Grohmann, *From the World of Arabic Papyri*, Cairo 1952, pp. 2-3.
[2] Cf. below Chapter XIV.
[3] Cf. S. D. Goitein, "The Local Jewish Community in the Light of the Cairo Geniza Records", *The Journal of Jewish Studies* 12 (1961), pp. 133-158.

Tunisia, Spain, Yemen, etc. This is, of course, very essential for the problems we are dealing with here. Secondly, as we know now from Geniza documents coming from Fustat, Cairo, Alexandria, al-Maḥalla and other places in Egypt, from Kairouan, Jerusalem, Damascus and Aleppo, Jewish houses often bordered on those of Muslims or Christians or both. There was no ghetto, but, on the contrary, much opportunity for daily intercourse. Neither was there an occupational ghetto. I have counted so far about 360 occupations of Jews, of which about 240 entailed manual work. There was constant cooperation between the various religious groups to the point of partnerships in business and even in workshops. In order to assess correctly the admissibility of the Geniza records for general sociological research, we have to free ourselves entirely from the familiar notions about European Jews in the later Middle Ages and those about Oriental Jews as we know them today, or rather, as we knew them yesterday.

In short, I estimate that the Geniza documents represent in the first place the class, the period and the country from which they come, while only a limited section of their contents is peculiar to the religio-national group in which they originated. This is, of course, merely a working hypothesis. For the time being, our sole concern is to present the facts as exactly and fully as possible. Subsequent research in the related fields of Islamic and European history will corroborate or qualify the validity of the assumptions just mentioned. In other words, our approach is descriptive. It is *sociographic*, not sociological.

The first point we have to clarify in order to understand the people speaking to us in the Geniza is their relationship to God. When the medieval mystics declared that God was the only reality in existence, they expressed by this overstatement a feeling which was general. God was the most powerful reality in every man's life; therefore, even people of a strong practical bent took him constantly into account and continuously attempted to be on good terms with him. When we read in every third line of Ibn Jubayr's travel account that God is praised or thanked or invoked, we are inclined to take this as the manner of speaking of a religious scholar embarked on the Holy Pilgrimage. However, we find the same in all Geniza letters of people high and low, simple and sophisticated. No person is mentioned without a complimentary phrase, containing the name of God, attached to his name. No consignment sent or traveller on his way is referred to without a phrase such as "May God ordain its, or his, safe arrival". No arrival is announced without a Hebrew or Arabic quotation expressing gratitude towards the Creator. One would not simply say: "I bought this or that", but: "I let God choose for me the best and then bought" *istakhart allāh washtarayt*, or: "God gave me the right idea or inspiration", *alhamanī*. Even in a formal contract one would state: "We let our Creator choose for us and concluded this partnership etc."[1] The many cases of misfortunes reported in letters are invariably described as decreed or even caused directly by God, and contrite submission to God's decrees is always expressed or recommended. When a man escaped from great danger, as happened to a citizen of Sfax during the civil war in Tunisia (1062-1063), when he was chained and handed over to the hangman for execution five times, but was saved each time at the last moment, he would emphasize that this was not due to his own merits and good deeds, but solely to God's mercy. The only allowance he made for his own part in the matter was the remark: *wabārakanī bi'afwih*, "He blessed me with his forgiving"; meaning that his escape from danger was an indication that God had pardoned his sins.[2]

I believe that it would not be correct to say about the people represented in the Geniza records what the prophet Jeremiah said about the ancient Judeans: "Near are You to their mouths, but far from their hearts" (12:2). God was really in their hearts. This is proved by their absolute belief in the efficacy of prayer. In countless letters people ask their relatives and friends, especially the older ones and in particular the women, to pray for them (or vice versa, are assured by the writers that they constantly do so). For example, a novice in the India trade, who for the first time in his life embarked on a stormy ocean so different from the quiet sea near his native Tripoli, Libya, implores by name each and every member of his family and of his rather large circle of acquaintances to save him through their prayers.[3] There was nothing particularly mystical about such requests or assurances. It was a practical way of ensuring one's safety or success. When the Muslim and Jewish theologians of the Middle Ages stated that all man's actions were created by God,

[1] Taylor-Schechter Collection, 16.170, Fustat 1095 A.D.

[2] Dropsie College, Philadelphia, Geniza ms. 389, line 11.

[3] Taylor-Schechter Collection, 12.392, to be published as No. 173 in S. D. Goitein, *Records from the Cairo Geniza on the India Trade during the Middle Ages*.

they did not play with words, they only formulated what every one felt. Naturally, if it is God who decides everything for us, we try to influence him, indirectly by our behavior and directly through prayer and other works of piety.

One wonders what the Geniza has to reveal about Satan, God's antipode. In his classic *Medieval Panorama*, G. G. Coulton has the following to say about the subject: "In most minds Satan bulked as large as God; in some, even larger". This may have been true with regard to the dark, humid North. In the bright sun of the Mediterranean and the sober minds of a busy middle class, Satan evaporated entirely. His name does not appear in the letters of the Cairo Geniza. Even where a man accuses himself of having acted foolishly, it is God and not Satan who is credited with having induced him to act in such a way.

Similarly, there are only a few references to Fate or to the stars. A request for help is introduced by the remark: "I have struggled with Fate, until I was subdued". Or, a man apologizing to a high dignitary about a disrespectful utterance against him, would charge *al-falak*, the heavenly spheres, for his misbehavior. But remarks like these are extremely rare. We read about astrologers, both male and female, generally poor persons, who were in receipt of alms from the communal chest. Clearly, they served only the lower strata of the society. In our records, not a single reference to the services of an astrologer could so far be traced, with the exception of one or two horoscopes, written in the hand of a well known scholarly scribe. On the other hand, at the courts of the sultans, astrologers were much in demand. However, just as we find in a Geniza letter that alchemy was an occupation befitting persons belonging to the entourage of kings, but not ordinary people,[1] so astrology was confined as a pseudo-science to the service of the great and as a superstitious practice to poor people in despair. The middle class, it seems, had little use for it.

Thus the mentality of the writers of the Geniza records was dominated by an undiluted, sober monotheism with a strong ethical coloring. When a man's *dīn*, or religion, is invoked, as is indeed done very frequently, what is meant is simply his conscience, his morality. The form *diyāna*, which is also used in that connotation, seems to comprise, in addition, the minute observance of the ritual.

[1] Taylor-Schechter Collection, Loan 17, published by S. Assaf, *Responsa Geonica*, Jerusalem 1942, p. 115.

However, as the contexts indicate, people assumed that a person meticulous in his duties towards God could also be trusted in his dealings with his fellow men.

Religiosity in the meaning of ecstatic pietism was confined to small circles of persons designated as *ʿĀbid* in Arabic, or *Ḥāsīd* in Hebrew, the former having a more technical connotation than the latter. There were also women, described as *ʿĀbida*. With regard to such a person we could read the following in a letter of introduction: "The bearer of this letter, the religious and devout Mr. So and So, who has been Godfearing from his youth (a Biblical phrase), is a disciple of our lord, the Nāgīd. My tongue cannot express the praise of a person like him, who has pushed the world of existence from his heart and seeks only the Creator".[1] This type of person was an exception. The middle class as a whole had little inclination for ecstatic religion—it should be emphasized again—during the period under study.

There is, however, one strain of spirituality discernible in the records of the Cairo Geniza, which distinguishes the middle class reflected in it most favorably from its modern counterpart: the reverence of its members for scholarship, their will to learn and to pursue formal study during the whole of their lifetimes. The synagogue—and the same applies with some qualification to the mosque—was a house of learning not only for scholars, but for the community at large. Even in smaller localities the Sabbaths and holidays were devoted to study. The nights of the week were used for the same purpose, and in particular the nights preceding Monday and Thursday, the "holy weekdays" in both Judaism and Islam. No one could qualify as a communal leader or even merely as a man of standing without a certain degree of scholarly knowledge and perseverance in the study of religious literature.

Together with *dīn*, religion, a man's *muruwwa*, or "virtue", was often appealed to in Geniza letters. *Muruwwa* at that time largely meant generosity, liberal spending, but had still retained its more general connotation of gentlemanly behavior, e.g. towards a needy debtor or a young and unruly wife. *Muruwwa*, in short, is the characteristic of a man who does more than his duty.

[1] The Nāgīd, or Head of the Egyptian Jews, Abraham, the son of Maimonides, is referred to. His chef d'oeuvre is called *Kifāyat al-ʿābidīn*, The Complete Guide for the Devout. The quotation is from Taylor-Schechter, 12.289, translated in S. D. Goitein, *Readings in Mediterranean Social History*.

Equally frequent are appeals to a man's *faḍl*, or nobility of character, often invoked or praised together with his *sharaf*, or nobility of descent or social standing. On the other hand, *ʿirḍ*, honor, reputation, never seems to be invoked, but only attacked or defended. It is not always clear to us what was regarded as detrimental to one's honor. Thus a man, probably a schoolmaster, writes a very excited letter to his superior in Cairo, emphasizing repeatedly that he had to come to the capital in order to clear his honor after it had been alleged that he had gathered young men or boys and danced with them *zuhdī*, dances accompanied by mystical poems.[1]

Most significant are the numerous observations about a man's character, *akhlāq*, nature, *ṭabʿ*, mentality, *ʿaql*, or frame of mind, *qālab*. These people had a sharp eye for the individuality and the specific qualities of a person, a fact reflected also in the enormous amount of nicknames occurring in the Geniza records. I am inclined to see in this trait an Arab heritage. In pre-Islamic poetry I have counted no less than eighty synonyms for the notions "character" and "character trait".[2]

Turning now to the more material aspects of life, it is perhaps not out of place to quote an ancient Arabic proverb which, I believe, was coined in the second century of Islam. It says: "Muslims enjoy sex above all, Christians—money, Majūsīs (Persians)—status, and Jews—food". The implication is, of course, that sex is the highest and food the lowest of human enjoyments.[3]

As to food, it is characteristic of a highly developed bourgeoisie that food is extremely variegated and its preparation devolved from the shoulders of the housewife to specialized industries. In those days they had no canned or frozen food, but a very practicable equivalent: all dishes, hot or cold, were prepared by specialists in the bazaars. All a smart housewife had to do was to tell her husband in the morning what to bring home for dinner in the evening.

Thus food was variegated and refined, but its quality did not form a topic of polite conversation. So far, I have not found a single

[1] British Museum Or 5542, f. 13.

[2] This was done with the aid of the Concordance of Pre-Islamic and Umayyad Poetry, prepared by the Institute of Asian and African Studies of the Hebrew University, Jerusalem. At present, the Concordance comprises over one million index cards.

[3] Quoted by Ibn Mujāwir, ed. O. Löfgren, p. 36, l. 16: *inna lil-muslim farjahu, lil-naṣrānī mālahu, lil-majūsī jāhahu walil-yahūdī baṭnahu*. At the time when this saying was coined, the majority of the Jews under Islam belonged to the lower classes.

reference to good or bad food in the Geniza letters, even where one would expect such a detail, e.g. when a man describes a journey, or praises the hospitality of his host. To be gluttonous or to have a belly was regarded as a disgrace. In short, the Geniza people definitely were not food-oriented.

As to wealth, these people were mostly business men and, naturally eager to make money. However, the whole of the Geniza letters is pervaded by a strangely detached attitude towards material gains. These people did not get unduly excited either by large profits or by heavy losses. This was due partly to *Adab*, or "good form", which played such an enormous role in this society, but it must have also been a philosophy of life. Perhaps they felt that if they served Mammon too much, God the Almighty would not approve and would retaliate.

Sexual involvements and romance were not entirely absent, but we have next to no record about them. As a curiosity, I may mention an affair between a Christian doctor and a Jewish girl, reported by Muslims, while the Jews believed that she was a Muslim woman. We possess some remarkable letters from husbands to their wives, which do not differ very much from what an intelligent middle class man of our day would write under similar circumstances. In one of these letters, *al-maḥabba l-ahliyya*, marital love, is invoked. On the other hand, we have no letters worth speaking of from wives to their husbands, but quite a number from sisters to their brothers. In general it seems that tender feelings between persons of different sexes were in those days more common, or perhaps more freely expressed, between brothers and sisters than between husbands and wives.

Before concluding, I wish to draw attention to three minor, but still very characteristic traits of the Mediterranean middle class discernible in the Geniza records. First, one is impressed by the lucidity and even eloquence to be found in many a Geniza letter. One breathes the air of a cultural region which produced Demosthenes and Cicero, *balāgha* and *badī'* (Arabic rhetoric and stylistics). Most of the writers of Geniza letters are ordinary people, but they express what they have to say clearly and forcefully.

Moreover, they are, as a rule, extremely polite. It is astounding how many polished and pleasant phrases are at the disposal of the average writer. Many of these, most probably, were learned in school together with Arabic and Hebrew calligraphy. However, there is more to it than mere phraseology. Real refinement is to be observed in many of these letters. Clearly, as has happened often in human history, a style of life developed by a higher class was emulated and absorbed by the lower ranks.

Thirdly, a word about the attachment of the Geniza people to their homelands and hometowns. "Homesickness", says H. A. R. Gibb in his Introduction to his English selections from Ibn Battūta, "was hardly to be expected in a society so cosmopolitan as that of medieval Islam".[1] Indeed, the extent of travel and migration reflected in the Geniza records is astonishing. However, no less remarkable is the frequency of expressions of longing for one's homeland and the wish to return to it, as well as the fervor with which compatriots stuck together when they were abroad. This feeling is called *al-baladiyya,* obviously an abbreviation of *al-maḥabba al-baladiyya,* the love of one's countrymen. One speaks also of *ḥukm al-baladiyya,* the obligation to help a needy countryman. It stands to reason that this love of one's home country was a natural antidote against the excessive mobility of the age.

I should like to conclude this all too brief survey with a short discussion of status and social prestige, subjects which loom larger in our records than any other human concern. In the Arabic proverb quoted above, status is regarded as coveted in particular by Persians. The word generally used in this connection is indeed Persian: *jāh,* literally place, position, rank. A maxim, quoted in a Geniza letter, states: *al-insān bijāhih,* "man's life depends on his social position". Losing face was regarded as the worst of all disasters. Above everything else, a high and impregnable social position was craved. It is no exaggeration to say that four fifths of all the good wishes found in the Geniza letters—they form an almost interminable list—are connected with the addressee's *jāh,* his lofty rank, his redoubtable position, the humiliation and crushing of his enemies, his great reputation and the fame of his good deeds.

Here, as in the case of fine manners, discussed previously, the patterns of court life had been assimilated by the middle class. However, as is again proved abundantly by the testimony of the Geniza records, there was something very real behind that grand phraseology: a man could subsist only when he occupied a strong position or at least had connections with a person of high rank. The internal

[1] H. A. R. Gibb, Ibn Battuta, *Travels in Asia and Africa,* New York 1929, p. 9.

security, administration and judiciary of the states in those days were weak. Even if a man had a very good case, his rights could rarely be secured without a letter of recommendation or the personal intervention of an influential dignitary or notable. Thus, social position was a means for survival.

In addition, however, we are able to observe in the Geniza records the most eager competition for the honors to be obtained inside the local denominational community. There, as a rule, no vital interests were involved, and the primary drive was solely the satisfaction of man's social instincts, honor for honor's sake. The notorious avidity of the Muslim middle class for high-sounding titles, attested to for the centuries under discussion, points in the same direction. So we see that the members of this class, and in particular its more prominent representatives were extremely eager to obtain power and honor. We wonder, therefore, why the Middle Eastern bourgeoisie of the Middle Ages as a whole did not strive to gain political power and to take over the state. Why did the well-to-do bourgeoisie in all Islamic countries leave the leadership of the state in the hands of barbarian soldiers? The answer to this crucial question lies in the character of this class, as defined in our study. It was the standardbearer of Muslim religion, and the attitude of Muslim religion towards the state was thoroughly negative. The religious Muslim did not oppose the state, but tried to have as little to do with it as possible. The Muslim middle class did not conquer the state, because it did not strive to obtain this goal. However, its failure to achieve political power was its undoing. The continued misrule of barbarian soldiers, coupled with the decline of international trade in the Mediterranean, accounts for the poor condition of the middle class in the Middle East on the threshold of modern times. This verdict of history should not induce us to minimize the great role played by this class in the past. More than the three types chosen by Schaeder as the representatives of medieval Islam, it is the broad mass of the middle class which is to be regarded as the main bearer of medieval civilization around the southern and eastern shores of the Mediterranean.

CHAPTER THIRTEEN

THE WORKING PEOPLE OF THE MEDITERRANEAN AREA DURING THE HIGH MIDDLE AGES

Scope and Method

This study is based mainly on the documents of the so-called Cairo Geniza, which is, as we have seen, a huge treasure of contracts, court records, letters and accounts, from the tenth through the thirteenth centuries, originally preserved in a synagogue of Fusṭāṭ, or Old Cairo.[1] Most of the persons mentioned in these documents were Jews. Therefore the general title given to this essay requires some explanation. As we shall presently see, there was no professional ghetto in those times and places, just as there was no physical ghetto, no forced concentration of Christians or Jews in separate quarters. To be sure, each socio-religious group favored certain occupations to a degree, as is the case even today, e.g. amongst certain minorities in the United States. However, there were no watertight compartments in this respect. Consequently, with some reservations to be made presently, the Geniza documents, as far as they deal with the artisans, are indicative of their period and region rather than of anything specifically Jewish.

Similarly, since these documents were found in Egypt, one might assume that they solely reflect conditions prevailing in that country. However, here again it would be methodologically wrong to regard our sources as referring exclusively to the country in which they were discovered. The mobility of people in those days was astounding. We find in the Geniza records craftsmen from Spain, Morocco, Byzantium, Palestine, Lebanon, Syria, Iraq, Iran and even from Tiflis, today Tbilisi, Georgia. As we shall see, the internationality of the arts and crafts is also proven by many other indications. Only where we are able to show positively that a certain branch of industry was typically Egyptian are we allowed to evaluate a Geniza document as a testimony to specific local conditions.

The Arabic handbooks on market supervision, our most important

[1] See above p. 246 and, in particular, below Chapter XIV.

Muslim source on the working people of the period under discussion, as well as other literary sources bearing on the subject naturally have also been used for this study—but only as a corrective and check on the Geniza material presented in the following pages. At this early stage of research into the social history of Islam, the safest approach seems to be that each scholar working in the field should try to give as exhaustive an account as possible of the sources to which he has access, leaving the attempt of a wider synthesis, based on a series of similar studies, to a later period.

Division of Labor and Specialization

The technical aspects of medieval industry in the Mediterranean basin will not be treated here, since they have been discussed in detail in a recent publication of the present writer.[1] There are, however, some technical factors which require special consideration, since they were of greatest significance for the social life of the working people.

Most impressive in this respect is the high degree of specialization and division of labor apparent in the Geniza records. Thus far, about two hundred and sixty five different arts and crafts have been encountered in them.[2] This number must be regarded as very high, since the craftsmen, unlike the merchants, had little need for business correspondence and even less opportunity for making contracts in writing or for appearing in courts. Still, it can easily be proven that the total of two hundred and sixty five manual occupations counted thus far in the Geniza papers, impressive as it is, constitutes only a fraction of those actually in existence. Out of the twenty four crafts which gave names to bazaars in Maqrīzī's description of Cairo, eleven have not been found as yet in the Geniza, although there is no doubt that they were in existence at that time.[3] In his study of the "corporations" of artisans in Damascus during the twelfth century, Nikita Elisséeff enumerates fifty one localities, each named after a special branch of industry. Of these, fifteen are not repre-

[1] "The Main Industries of the Mediterranean Area as Reflected in the Records of the Cairo Geniza", *JESHO* 4 (1961), pp. 168-197.

[2] The article mentioned in the previous Note, p. 168, makes mention of two hundred and ten manual professions. However, since the writing of that study the present writer has had opportunity to scrutinize hundreds of unpublished Geniza records. Hence the difference.

[3] Maqrīzī, *Khiṭaṭ*, Būlāq 1270/1853, II, pp. 94-106.

sented in the records forming the basis of the present study. A similar discrepancy is to be observed with regard to the handbooks of market supervision contemporary with the Geniza records.[1]

The idea behind this far-reaching division of labor seems to have been that each finished product required a specialist to manufacture it. Shoemaking appears to us as a fairly specialized craft. In the Geniza records we find that it was subdivided among a number of expert craftsmen. One document mentions three types of shoemakers together, and there were at least two others, corresponding to the various kinds of footwear in vogue at that time. In addition, there were many types of leatherworkers, besides the saddlers, e.g. the manufacturers of leather bottles, who had a bazaar of their own in Old Cairo. Naturally, in the absence of synthetic fabrics, bottles and bags of all descriptions made of leather were in those days of far greater importance than they are at present. Similarly, each household possessed at least one pleasantly decorated hide, which used to be spread beneath the low movable table on which one dined. The preparation of hides for this particular purpose was a craft in itself.

In an area in which timber was scarce and where very little wooden furniture was used, the carpenters' profession seems to have had a rather limited scope. Still, in the period under discussion, it comprised at least five different crafts: the carpenters proper, who mostly did the woodwork in buildings, the sawyers, who appear in building accounts regularly before the carpenters (the timber was sawn to the dimensions required on the site of the building), the chestmakers and turners—both had bazaars called after them in Old Cairo, and the makers of wooden door locks, who were of particular importance, since "the safety of property and the guarding of women" depended upon them.

A dyer would confine himself to a certain material and certain coloring stuffs, such as dyeing wool with various shades of purple or coloring silk with turquoise blue or crimson. There were specialists for knives, ladles and spoons, tongs, hooks (such as those used in a butcher's shop), razors, needles and the like. Each of these professions was called by a specific name. Additional details in the sources

[1] N. Elisséeff, "*Corporations de Damas sous Nūr al-Dīn*," *Arabica* 3 (1956), pp. 61-79. There are some slight differences in the terms used in the Geniza and the literary sources referred to.

make it possible to ascertain that the persons concerned were indeed craftsmen and not merely traders in the articles referred to.[1]

As may be expected, many specialities are found in the Geniza records which have no counterpart in our economy today. Sawdust was used, instead of sand, to dry the ink on a freshly written page and has been actually found between the leaves of medieval Arabic manuscripts. Therefore, when we encounter the family name "Sawduster", we are justified in assuming that a man could make a livelihood by collecting, handling and selling this material. In many a marriage contract the little stick with which the kohl, or collyrium ("eye make-up") was applied to the eyes, appears as a separate item of the bride's trousseau, because it was often made of a precious material, such as crystal, gold or silver. Consequently, it is not surprising that the manufacture of kohl sticks formed a profession in itself. Examples of similar cases could easily be cited.

This far-reaching specialization must have affected the life of the craftsmen concerned in many ways. In some occupations, it reduced the skill and technical knowledge required to a minimum, comparable to that of a modern factory laborer working on an assembly line. In others, it gave opportunity for reaching highest perfection. We still admire the exquisite workmanship displayed in pieces of metal-work and pottery, textiles and woodwork which have survived from those days. In view of the great discrepancy in both the value of the material and the refinement of technique involved in the various occupations, the craftsmen of this period can, by no means, be regarded as forming a unified social class. We shall come to similar conclusions when scrutinizing the economic aspects of those professions.

Confinement of Each Craft to a Separate Place—How Common

Reference has been made, previously, to the topographical concentration of various professions. The Geniza records contain a considerable number of such details. They mention, e.g. a Lane of the Leatherbottle-makers, a Lane of the "Almonders" (makers of sweet meats containing almonds), a street of the Turners, also a Gate of the Turners (a gate of the ancient Byzantine fortress

[1] For these and the following details cf. the article mentioned on p. 256. Maker of hides: *naṭṭāʿ* in UL Cambridge Or 1080 J 79 (N229). Maker of tongs: *zanājilī*. This profession had a street to itself, TS K 6, f. 118b.

of Old Cairo which was called after that street) a Bazaar of the Woolworkers, and a Square of the Perfumers. Mostly, however, concentrations of craftsmen would be referred to without describing them as lanes, streets, bazaars etc. Thus one would say "we met on the Coppersmiths", "I was staying in The Lentilcooks", "This street leads to the Chestmakers and the Sellers of Sesban" (a local herb still commonly used), "on the corner of the Furriers and the Little Bazaar of the Tanners" (this detail refers to Aleppo, Syria), and the like.

Such references are found mainly in legal deeds describing houses which changed their proprietors by sale, gift or inheritance. Not infrequently it is possible to coordinate the data given in a document with those provided by literary sources. Still it is doubtful whether all this material together could enable us to sketch the economic geography of Old Cairo, at least as it had developed by the twelfth century. For it seems that at that time no coercion was exercised with regard to the location of a craft. According to a deed of partnership, dated 1125, glass was manufactured in a store which was situated in the bazaar of the coppersmiths and which had formerly served as a shop for the sale of copper vessels. Linseed oil, olives and lemon juice were sold in a store at the Gate of the Turners as shown by another contract of partnership, dated 1104. Authorized money assayers had their seat in the street of the alchemists according to two depositions made in court, one in December 1081 and the other approximately at the same time. A physician had his office in a shop "at the end of the Waxmakers" (1143), and a textile merchant kept a store in the street of the *qushāshiyyin*, sellers of various kinds of straw (1148).

In a contract dated October 1194, a pious foundation leases a ground floor of one of its houses on condition that the tenant should not manufacture there rosewater, or litharge (an oxide of lead, frequently mentioned in the Geniza), or arsenic, or any other product requiring the use of fire. Thus it was assumed that the same premises could be used for such widely differing occupations as the processing of lead or arsenic and the making of perfumes. In a query submitted to Abraham Maimonides, the Nagid, or Head of the Jewish community of Egypt, the complainant asserts that his neighbor had converted a house in a residential area into a dyeing workshop and that the smoke from the latter's fireplace spoiled all wool and linen spread out by him (around 1220). Had fixed police rules existed with regard to the location of the different crafts, the Nagid would not have decided the question according to Jewish law. Similarly, when we find a twelfth century Spanish handbook of market police strongly emphasizing that each craft should be concentrated in a separate place assigned to it, we may safely assume that the reality was palpably different.[1]

The topographical concentration of the crafts goes back to remote antiquity, and had, then as later, technical as well as administrative purposes: it facilitated for the authorities the task of supervising the workmen concerned.[2] It is, however, characteristic of the free economy of the eleventh and twelfth centuries that government control in this, as in many other respects, was comparatively loose.

Denominational Preferences for Certain Crafts—but no Occupational Ghettoes

Liberty in the choice of one's profession was another aspect of that free economy just referred to. With a few insignificant exceptions, such as the prevention of the sale of wine or pork to Muslims, no restrictions were put on Christians and Jews with regard to their economic activities. The instructions to Muslims not to work for members of the minority religions in occupations of a servile character, found in the Spanish handbook mentioned above, prove only that such relationships were commonplace. The very fact that the Geniza makes mention of at least two hundred and sixty manual occupations pursued by Jews shows that not only Muslim law, but also the social structure of that period, in particular the absence of rigidly organized guilds (see below), was conducive to occupational freedom.[3]

On the other hand, the Geniza clearly shows that the different socio-religious groups had definite preferences for certain occupations. In other words, there were some branches of industry in which

[1] The Geniza manuscripts and the Abraham Maimonides Responsa referred to here are discussed in *A Mediterranean Society*, chapter II, section 2. For the Spanish handbook of market supervision cf. E. Lévi-Provençal, *Séville Musulmane au début du XII Siècle*, Paris 1947, p. 95. Arabic text in *Journal Asiatique* 224 (1934), p. 233, ll. 9-10, and *Documents arabes... sur la vie... en Occident musulman...* I, Cairo, 1955.

[2] Cf. Bruno Meissner, *Babylonien und Assyrien*, I, Heidelberg 1920, p. 231.

[3] Cf. Antoine Fattal, *Le statut légal des non-Musulmans en pays d'Islam*, Beyrouth 1958, pp. 144-160. E. Lévi-Provençal, *Séville musulmane* (cf. Note 1), p. 108, para. 153.

the Jews were seemingly dominant—or, to define the situation more cautiously: there were certain crafts and arts which were particularly popular within the Jewish community.

As for textiles, the most important branch of industry during the Middle Ages, the Jews specialized in all aspects of silk work, from the unravelling of the cocoons to weaving and dyeing. This was an extremely ramified and highly specialized industry and we find Jews engaged in it in all countries of the Mediterranean, including Christian Byzantium. Correspondingly, the silk trade, both in the raw material and in finished products, was one of the main objects of Jewish commercial activity. On the other hand, flax, although no less important than silk in both local and international Jewish trade, did not attract Jews very much, as far as the higher stages of its manufacture were concerned. Jews were occupied in the processing of flax, from its harvest to its readying for export; however, the weaving of linen, at least its more artistic aspects, seem to have been mainly the domain of the local Christians.

Dyeing, together with other processes of endowing a material with a specific appearance, such as iridescence, gloss, and glitter, was a veritable Jewish specialty, as may be concluded from literally hundreds of references in the Geniza. Muslim sources mention even professional secrets in this field, known to Jews alone. It tallies with this that dyeing stuffs were high up on the list of commodities traded by Jews in the countries of both the Indian Ocean and the Mediterranean. Similarly, the preparation of drugs and the processing of medical herbs was to a considerable extent a Jewish profession and again both the local and the international commerce in these commodities loom very large in the Geniza papers.

Metalwork of all descriptions is represented in the Geniza, gold and silversmithery and work in the caliphal mint being by far the most important. Another Jewish specialty was the manufacture of glass and glass vessels.

How is this occupational group specialization to be explained? In general, one has of course to bear in mind that normally a son followed the profession of his father. The socio-religious group is to be regarded as composed of a number of extended families each specializing in a profession handed down from one generation to another. In addition, however, the particular circumstances under which each group took to certain occupations have to be studied, although many problems in this respect may elude solution forever.

Thus silk might have become popular with Jews, because it was already at home in Palestine, or because of the early contacts of the Jewish merchants with China. Glass also was an ancient Palestinian product. It seems, however, that the main reason for the specializations mentioned above is to be sought in the fact that the Jews, as a widely dispersed people, often consisting of newcomers in a country, were, from the socio-economic point of view, a weak group. As such, they had either to be satisfied with hard work, not very eagerly sought after by others, or had to move into areas of economic activity not yet occupied, or only partially occupied by the local populations. The manufacture of glass or of coins (melting metals!) or dyeing required continuous work over a fire, which could not have been very pleasant in a hot climate under the primitive working conditions of those days.[1] The industry of silk could be taken up by Jews, because it was comparatively new and not monopolized by long standing traditions, such as the ancient industries of linen, wool and cotton. Finally, Jews were welcome as gold-and silversmiths, as well as workers in the royal mints, because it was more convenient to confide precious metals to them than to members of more powerful groups, who, in case of fraud or theft, were backed by their clans and their connections.[2]

Despised Professions

Should we assume that the occupations in which a minority group was prominent were despised and avoided by the majority? The sources of our information do not justify such an assumption. In his painstaking Ph.D. thesis[3] on the professions and the economic background of the religious scholars in Islam during the first four hundred and seventy years of its existence, Mr. Hayyim J. Cohen enumerates fifty five Muslim gold-and silversmiths and workers in the mint, twenty two manufacturers of glass and glass vessels and one hundred and thirty one silk workers and merchants. The

[1] This explanation was first suggested to the present writer by Dr. Richard Ettinghausen, the Head Curator of Near Eastern Art in the Freer Gallery, Washington, when we discussed the prominence of the glass industry in the Geniza records.

[2] The source material for this subsection is to be found in the article quoted on p. 256.

[3] Submitted to the senate of the Hebrew University, Jerusalem, in January 1963. The results of this important study will soon be published in a European language.

perfumers with four hundred forty three representatives constitute, next to the drapers, the most numerous (semi-) manual profession both in the Muslim and in the Jewish middle class. Even dyeing is represented by twenty three scholars called by the name of that profession.

Islamic law knows of despicable professions, which disqualify their members from marrying a girl of a good family or even from being admitted as a witness in court. Most of these occupations, such as those of cupper, bathhouse attendant, cleaner of sewers and cesspools or street cleaner never appear in the Geniza, although they must have been mentioned in the many lists of the poor supported by the Jewish community, if it had comprised such persons. Of the weavers, who also belong to this category (as mentioned already in the Talmud), a Muslim legal source remarks that in Alexandria they were regarded as respectable people. This was certainly true in the Geniza times.[1]

One of the base professions, that of the tanner, is described in some Muslim sources as exercised mainly by Jews.[2] This could not have been the case during the period represented in the Geniza. In all of the types of writing found in it—lists, accounts, legal documents, business or private correspondence—tanners are extremely rare and the same applies to the family name Tanner. Scores of Jewish merchants and scholars from Tunisia are known to us by name, but thus far, none with the family name Tanner has been found by me in the Geniza. However, a prominent Muslim author of that country (13th century) was called thus. Mr. Cohen's list (cf. page 262) enumerates eight early Muslim scholars bearing that name.

In later, more fanatical times, the minority groups were pushed or forced into the base professions. Thus we hear that in Muslim countries so widely distant from each other as Morocco, Yemen and Bukhara, Jews were compelled to serve as cleaners of cesspools. However, the period and area reflected in the Geniza records was one of remarkable socio-economic freedom and mobility. As we tried

[1] The subject of despised professions in Islam has been discussed with particular attention to its treatment in Islamic legal sources by R. Brunschvig, "Métiers vils en Islam," *Studia Islamica* XVI (1962), pp. 4-60. Cf. also Farhat J. Ziadeh, "Equality (kafā'a) in the Muslim Law of Marriage," *American Journal of Comparative Law* 6 (1957), pp. 503-17.

[2] Cf. S. W. Baron, *A Social and Religious History of the Jews*, IV, pp. 116/7, where also non-Muslim sources are reviewed.

to show, the natural forces active wherever groups of different strength live side by side inevitably led to certain specializations, but these forces were not oppressive to the degree of economic discrimination sanctioned by the law or enforced by administrative measures.

The Internationality of the Arts and Crafts

The socio-economic freedom characteristic of the High Middle Ages in the Mediterranean region manifests itself also in the frequency and enormous range of the transfer of industries from one country to another. To be sure, this fascinating process goes back to pre-historic times and is revealed to us with great clarity by archaeological and historical evidence from the ancient Near East. Egyptian craftsmen found their way to Babylonia and to the land of the Hittites. The Assyrians transferred by force all the skilled laborers of a conquered city to their own country, and the Babylonians, as we remember from the Bible (2 Kings 24:14), followed their example.[1] The Persians did the same in such a systematic way that some of the most important Iranian industries of the Middle Ages owed their origin to the transplantation of colonies of Armenians, Greeks and others. The process reached gigantic dimensions in Islam, which first by enslavement and forced labor, and later—mainly in the period considered here—through free intercourse, mixed the peoples from the outskirts of China to the borders of France and molded them together into a world of constant exchange of products, men and techniques. This situation is well illustrated in the records of the Cairo Geniza.

There is no need to point to the continuous flow of goods between the Middle East and Europe during the eleventh and twelfth centuries.[2] As to the mobility of craftsmen, it has already been said that in those days one could find in Egypt workmen coming from all countries between Spain in the West and Georgia and Iran in the East. The Geniza makes mention of silk dyers, goldsmiths, furriers, tailors, cobblers and copyists (of Hebrew books) from Rūm, i.e. Byzantium or the Christian countries in general; of Syro-Palestinian

[1] Cf. B. Meissner (see p. 260), pp. 229-230.

[2] This vast subject is treated in Chapter III of the present writer's *Mediterranean Society* and his book on the India trade, cf. the Bibliographical Note below.

glassmakers, silkweavers and dyers coming to Egypt in such masses that their competition was felt by the local artisans; of a silversmith from Ceuta, Morocco, and of two other Maghribī silversmiths emigrating via Egypt and Aden to far away Ceylon; of a shoemaker and a manufacturer of *zurunbāq* (a Spanish material) from Spain; of a blacksmith from Bagdad; of a maker of silver spoons from Iran and a dyer from Tiflis. In a few cases it is stated that the persons concerned left their respective countries because of persecutions or other dire circumstances. In others, this may be concluded from the fact that they appear in the lists of receivers of alms. There can be however, little doubt that their presence cannot have been without influence on local workmanship, particularly in case of keen competition.[1]

In this connection it is highly significant that the names of goods which were derived from the localities of their original production became designations of the products themselves. Dabīqī, a linen named after an Egyptian town, was manufactured in Kāzirūn, a city in Persia. Formerly, a Muslim geographer tells us, Egyptian flax or linen was imported by sea to Shīnīz, the port of Kāzirūn, but in his time (last third of the tenth century), the fine fabric was manufactured from locally grown flax. Tavvaz, another Persian town near the coast and therefore originally exposed to the import of linen from Egypt, also excelled in the production of linen material to such a degree that it gave the name to one variety used a long time after it had been actually manufactured in Kāzirūn.[2] Now, the Geniza letters show us that, from the beginning of the eleventh century, there lived in Egypt Jews bearing family names derived from these three Persian towns, namely Kāzirūnī, Shīnīzī and Tavvazī. Whether the ancestors of these families actually came to Egypt from Persia (which is probable), or sold or produced in Cairo the fabrics called after these towns, we do not yet know. It is quite possible that these names suggest the three alternatives together, i.e. that the families concerned emigrated from Persia to Egypt and were among those who introduced there the manufacture of the fabrics for which their home towns had been famous.

[1] The Geniza material for this and the following paragraphs is included in Chapter I (2) of *Mediterranean Society*. For the migration of artisans and craftsmen cf. R. Ettinghausen, "Interaction and Integration in Islamic Art", *Unity and Variety in Muslim Civilization*, ed. G. E. von Grunebaum, Chicago 1955, pp. 110-113.

[2] See A. Mez, *Die Renaissance des Islams*, Heidelberg 1922, p. 434.

Another, and very prominent, Jewish family from Persia, the Tustaris, also bore a name referring to both a town and a material called after it. From the correspondence preserved it is evident that the original Tustaris dealt in choice textiles, but did not limit themselves to the variety whose name they bore. In one letter, they send, among many other materials, a Rāzī (i.e. a robe made in, or called after, Rayy, a city in northern Persia) from Cairo to Kairouan, then the capital of Tunisia.[1] In three cases we find Tustari cloth imported to Egypt from the West, by persons bearing the name Andalusi (which, however, does not necessarily mean that it was produced in Spain. It could have been made in Sicily or Tunisia as well. A family called Andalusi appears as long established in eleventh century Kairouan).

It is characteristic that concerning a precious material, frequently mentioned in literary sources, the Sūsī, it is not evident from them whether the designation refers to Sūs (the ancient Susa) in southern Persia, or to Sūsa in Tunisia. However, in the Geniza letters from the eleventh century they undoubtedly refer to the latter. For we read in them repeatedly about merchants exporting Egyptian flax to Sūsa, Tunisia, and importing from there at the same time the fine linen made from it. Cairo itself had a Sūsī bazaar. Whether this material was not only sold there, but also manufactured, we do not know.[2] However, a Geniza record, dated 1098, mentions *sūsī rūsī*, Sūsi linen produced in Russia, which was confided to a merchant setting out for India and eventually secured an exceptionally high price. Thus we see that a fabric, actually manufactured in its town of origin, at the same time was imitated in a country far away.[3]

The most common example of such a situation is to be found in the Tabari, i.e. upholstery originally made in Tabaristan on the southern shores of the Caspian sea, and imitated elsewhere. In a number of marriage contracts from the Geniza, the bride receives "a Tabaristan Tabari", i.e. a genuine one. In most of them, however, this qualification is omitted, and in one she gets instead a *ṭabarī ramlī*, i.e. a Tabari made in Ramle (name of a town in Palestine and also in Egypt). Cf. also above, p. 240.

[1] TS 12.133, line 28.

[2] Cf. R. B. Serjeant, "Islamic Textiles", *Ars Islamica* XV-XVI (1951), pp. 47-48.

[3] Cf. the present writer's paper "From the Mediterranean to India" *Speculum* 29 (1954), p. 192, Note 20.

We wish to conclude this survey of migrating industries with a case which becomes particularly illustrative through the coinciding testimonies of a Geniza record and a literary source. A Muslim geographer remarks that in Qalʿat Ḥammād, then the capital of Algeria, "they made excellent felt, called Ṭālaqān" (after a town in northern Iran). In a Geniza letter a Ṭālaqān felt is exported from Tripoli, Libya, to Egypt, which means either that this originally Persian industry was imitated also in Tripoli, or that we have here a case of re-exportation. Both the literary and the documentary sources refer to the eleventh century.

No Guilds

A final indication of the freedom of movement and individualistic spirit of enterprise characteristic of the world of the Mediterranean craftsmen during the eleventh and twelfth centuries is the absence of rigidly organized professional corporations.

Of late, it has become fashionable to talk about Muslim guilds. While such organizations, connected with the mystical brotherhoods of Islam, are attested to for the late Middle Ages, it has yet to be shown that they were in existence during the eleventh and twelfth centuries. While reading the relevant article about the subject (Ṣinf) in the Encyclopaedia of Islam, one realizes that it does not provide a single real proof of their activities prior to the thirteenth century. The assertion made there that the manufacture of drugs and the processing of precious metals was reserved in Muslim states exclusively to Christian and Jewish "guilds" will appear strange to the readers of this paper who have taken notice of the great number of Muslim perfumers and gold- and silversmiths active even before the year 470 of the Muslim era.

The term "guild" designates a medieval union of craftsmen or traders which supervised the work of its members in order to uphold standards, and, for the same reason, laid down certain rules and made arrangements for the education of apprentices and their initiation into the union. The guild protected its members against competition and, in Christian as well as in Islamic countries, was closely connected with religion.

Scrutinizing the records of the Cairo Geniza or the Muslim handbooks of market supervision contemporary with them, one looks in vain for an Arabic equivalent of the term "guild". There was no such word, because there was no such institution. The supervision of the quality of the artisans' work was in the hands of the state police, which availed itself of the services of trustworthy and expert assistants. In the case of professions which either required highly specialized knowledge such as that of the physicians, or were particularly exposed to fraud or other transgressions of the law, the appointment of "a reliable, trustworthy man from their own profession" is recommended in order to secure proper service. The whole tenor of the books on market supervision, as well as the very recommendation just mentioned, prove that the artisans were not organized in corporations of their own which fulfilled the task of upholding professional standards. It is noteworthy that the most detailed work on market supervision from this period recommends the appointment of special supervisors or heads for only a very small fraction of the many professions treated.[1] In the Geniza, too, the *ʿarīf*, as such a chief was called, appears only very rarely and then, unfortunately, without an indication of the group headed by him. A Geniza document mentioning a contribution by the *ʿarīf al-naqqādīn*, or chief of the money assayers, is from the thirteenth century.[2]

Regarding apprenticeship and admission to a profession, no formalities and no rigid rules are to be discovered in our sources. Parents were expected to have their sons learn a craft and to pay for their instruction. "How could you have let the boy leave the capital before he has learned a craft", writes a daughter from the countryside to her mother in Old Cairo concerning a younger brother. In a marriage contract with a divorcee, written in a town in the Nile Delta in 1110, the bridegroom undertakes to feed and to clothe the son of his future wife and to have him learn a craft. In a settlement between a husband and his wife, made in Old Cairo in 1244, the mother promises to pay the board and poll tax of their elder boy

[1] The *Maʿālim al-Qurba*, ed. Reuben Levy, Cambridge 1938, English summary p. 57 (physicians), pp. 89-92 (potters, needle-makers, henna sellers, oil merchants and sieve makers). The Spanish police guide mentioned above (p. 260), p. 119, para. 187, while speaking about the cattle market, expresses the pious wish that each profession should have a "prud'homme", *amīn*, watching over it. The wellknown study by Bernard Lewis, "The Islamic Guilds" in *Economic History Review* 8 (1937), pp. 20-37, deals mainly with the Akhī of Anatolia and does not contain material concerning the period studied here. For the Akhī cf. the article about them under this name in EI[2] (by F. Taeschner).

[2] Cf. *Mediterranean Society*, Chapter II (2), Notes 13-15.

for two years, as well as for his training in the art of silversmithery. Wherever feasible, a son followed the profession of his father or his uncles and learned by working with them from his early youth. It will be shown, however, that this practice was by no means all comprising.[1]

Had there existed rigid grades of initiation into a profession, as was the case in the European guilds, the police handbooks referred to could not have failed to treat such an important subject. Their silence proves that there was no fixed system in this matter at all. To be sure the profession of a physician, which also was regarded as a *ṣināʿa*, or craft, could not be exercised independently, as a rule, except after the receipt of an official diploma.[2] The Spanish police handbook mentioned above says that the *ṣibyān*, which should not be simply translated as "young men", but as "employees", "apprentices", should be held to say their prayers regularly. This injunction is illustrated by a Geniza letter in which an apprentice complains that he was kept so busy that he had no time even for prayer.[3]

The protection of the local industries from competition by newcomers and outsiders is richly documented by the Geniza records, but nowhere do we hear about a professional corporation fulfilling this task. It was the Jewish local community, the central Jewish authorities, the police, or influential notables who were active in these matters. On the one hand, we find that the largest single group of receivers of alms in the Geniza lists were foreigners, many of them being craftsmen. This seems to indicate that newcomers must have incurred difficulties in finding work. On the other hand, there is a complaint by a group of artisans against a local community, which, under the penalty of excommunication, did not permit them to exercise their profession. All this shows that there were no hard and fast rules in these matters comparable to those developed in the guilds of the later Middle Ages.[4]

The associations of artisans and traders in imperial Rome, or

[1] The Geniza sources in S. D. Goitein, *Jewish Education in Muslim Countries*, Jerusalem 1962 (in Hebrew), pp. 121-3.

[2] For details cf. the present writer's paper "The Medical Professian in the Light of the Cairo Geniza Documents", *Hebrew Union College Annual 34 (1963)*, pp. 177-194. See also the next note.

[3] Séville (see p. 260), p. 119, para. 186. TS NS J 9, lines 13-14. This Geniza letter refers to an oculist who had not yet received his doctor's diploma.

[4] For documentation cf. *Mediterranean Society*, ch. II (2), Notes 16-17.

at least part of them, bore a religious character and were often connected with the local cult of the town from which the founders of an association had originated. Similarly, the Christian guilds of the late Middle Ages had their patron saints and special rites. The fourteenth century was the heyday of Muslim corporations, especially in Anatolia (present day Turkey), which adopted the doctrines and ceremonies of Muslim mystic brotherhoods. One looks in vain for similar combinations of artisanship and religious cult in the period and the countries discussed in this paper. When we find mosques frequently called after the names of professions, we learn from the sources reporting these facts that the reference is *topographical*, designating the mosque as situated in a street or bazaar bearing the name of that profession. In the same way our sources would speak of the canal (or pipe) of the sievemakers, the needlemakers, the butchers etc., simply indicating its location.[1]

On the other hand we learn from a responsum given by Maimonides (around 1190) that Muslim and Jewish silversmiths and glass makers concluded partnerships, sharing even their implements in common. The Muslim received the gains made on Saturday, the Jew those of Friday, which—by the way—seems to indicate that at least some Muslim craftsmen must have adopted the custom of taking a day off, although Islam, unlike its sister religions, does not know of an obligatory day of rest.[2]

Our findings thus far suggest that the organization of the arts and crafts during the High Middle Ages, at least on the southern, western, and eastern shores of the Mediterranean, must have been markedly different from that of late antiquity or of later medieval times. The largely negative evidence presented in the preceding pages is fully substantiated by detailed positive information culled from the Geniza records.

Free Partnerships—The Normal Form of Industrial Cooperation

Professional corporations, as we have seen, did not form the base of labor organization in the period and the area discussed in this paper. The employment of wage earners, to be treated later on, was of limited scope. Slave labor was of no importance, as far as the

[1] Cf. Ibn Šaddād, *Topographie Historique* (*Al-Aʿlāq Al-Ḫaṭīra*), ed. Sami Dahan, Damascus 1963, pp. 18-27, nos. 9, 23, 32, 47, 48, 75, 88, 107.

[2] Moses b. Maimon, *Responsa*, ed. J. Blau, Jerusalem 1960, p. 360.

arts and crafts were concerned.[1] Rather, contracts of partnerships, concluded on terms similar to those found in commercial associations, constituted the main form of industrial cooperation.

The nature and scope of those partnerships have been studied by the present writer in the second chapter, section two, of his *Mediterranean Society*, with the aid of twenty six documents. Twenty two of these have been preserved in the Cairo Geniza and four are referred to in queries written in Arabic and submitted to Moses Maimonides (died 1204) and to his son and successor Abraham (died 1237). In date, the contracts range between 1016 and 1240, in the sums invested between four and six hundred dinars[2], and in the duration of the partnerships between six and a half months to almost a lifetime. The industries involved were the manufacture of glass, dyeing, gold- and silversmithery and work in the mint, metal work, silk treatment, weaving, tailoring, tanning, breadbaking, pharmaceutics, and two or three cases of sugar factories.

The mercantile character of these industrial contracts is evidenced by their great variety. Most of them differ from each other. Thus, it was not custom and tradition, but the specific economic circumstances of the partnerships concluded which prescribed the conditions agreed upon.

In case the partners contributed capital, work and implements in equal shares, the situation was comparatively simple. They would divide also profit or loss according to their contribution and take out from the "partnership purse" certain sums for their lunch or supper.[3] When partnerships of three or five lasted for years, they assumed the character of companies. In a query submitted to Maimonides we read about a company of partners in a silk workshop in al-Maḥalla, an important town in lower Egypt, who opened a branch near the workshop of another such company in Old Cairo. The latter, fearing the competition, agreed to admit one of the silkworkers from al-

[1] Cf. the present writer's "Slaves and Slavegirls in the Cairo Geniza Records", *Arabica* 9 (1960), pp. 1-10.

[2] Because of the enormous difference in living standards between our own times and the eleventh and twelfth centuries it is extremly difficult to appraise the purchasing power of a gold piece of this period. Several sources indicate that a lower class family could live modestly on two dinars per month. The standard price for a simple *thawb*, the normal attire of a man or woman, which often lasted for a lifetime, was one dinar. For the same price one could buy three hundred pounds of bread. Thus the tentative equation of the actual value of a dinar with that of fifty dollars today is perhaps admissible.

[3] About one and a half silver pieces, cf. below p. 276.

Maḥalla into their company, while one of their own members would move to the provincial town and join the partners there. This was agreed upon, but the capitals of the two companies were not merged.[1]

Similarly when we read in letters about dealings with "the silk-workers" in Alexandria, "the pattern-painters" in Qayrawān, or "our coreligionists, the glass makers", we may assume that the references are to such companies, and not to families specializing in those professions. For in the three cases mentioned, the Arabic plural is used, while clans, like those of "the sieve makers", "the indigo dyers", "the scarfmakers" etc. are invariably referred to in the singular feminine. Additional material will probably enlighten us with regard to this detail.[2]

It is strange that one industry which by its very nature lends itself to the formation of companies, the private (as opposed to the government) overland mail service, was organized on a strictly individual basis, as must be concluded from the many references to the subject in the Geniza records. Ships, too, were, as a rule, the property of individuals. We learn that one out of fifty boats mentioned in the Geniza records was owned in partnership.[3]

Occasionally, all the capital invested in a partnership was borrowed from others. However, the normal way for an artisan with little or no cash was to associate with a fellow worker in the same profession who was able to contribute the necessary funds or materials. In a contract, dated 1217, two glass workers undertook to work together, one providing red (Beyrouth) and local Egyptian glass to the value of one hundred ninety nine dinars, while the other invested only six dinars together with a small quantity of material, costing approximately another ten gold pieces. In another such contract, dated 1134, one glass maker had no capital at all and even received a personal loan of ten dinars from his partner, who also contributed raw material valued at twenty dinars. The capitalist partner would work two days a week and the other—four days. Otherwise everything was divided equally: expenditure on fuel, on a journeyman

[1] Maimonides, *Responsa*, pp. 177-8, "A company of partners in a silk workshop", *jamāʿat sharika* (another ms.: *shurakā'*) *fi qāʿat ḥarir*. The word *qāʿa* designates the ground floor of a house, which was often rented out for a workshop, cf. above p. 259. The two companies are referred to later in the letter as *al-qāʿatayn*.

[2] Cf. *Mediterranean Society*, Chapter II, section 2, Note 12, and section I, Note 13. "Pattern-painter" is a tentative translation of *lawwān*.

[3] Cf. *ibid.*, Chapter IV, sections 3 and 7. See below, p. 307.

and on small items taken out from the partnership, and finally the profit was to be divided at the termination of the contract. This particular partnership was foreseen for six and a half months only, presumably the period during which the debtor was able to earn the sum borrowed for himself personally.[1]

In general, it is somewhat surprising to find quite a number of such partnerships concluded for a comparatively short time, such as one year. This was natural for mercantile partnerships, for it was common practice to set out in spring with the first convoy of ships sailing to do business abroad during the summer and to sell the goods imported at home in the course of the following winter. However the full benefits of an industrial partnership could be earned only during a more prolonged period of cooperation. It stands to reason that, generally, the short time contracts were intended for periods of trial and were renewed, after satisfactory results had been obtained.

Finally, and this is highly characteristic of the age and area considered here, the commenda, the popular form of commercial cooperation, was transferred also to industry. In a commenda, one or more capitalists who provide the money associate with one or more agents who do the work.[2] The same form of partnership was applied to the arts and crafts. In some cases we find the conditions imposed by the capitalist on the craftsman surprisingly generous, in others rather harsh. Again we meet that "freedom of contract", that absence of rigid traditionalism which is indicative of a competitive and individualistic society.

No Strict Separation Between Industry and Commerce

Some contracts of partnership state expressly that they were made for the manufacture *and sale* of the commodity concerned or even that in the common workshop also goods other than those made by the partners would be sold, as when a tailoring workshop offered textiles for sale. In case no further details are provided, we are often at a loss to know whether the name of an occupation derived from a product refers to its manufacture, or its sale, or to both. Thus a

[1] New York, Jewish Theol. Sem. Geniza Misc. 27. Oxford Bodleian Library, ms. Heb. a 3 (Catal. 2873), f. 8. Both translated in *Readings*.

[2] Cf. of late A. L. Udovitch, "At the Origins of the Western Commenda," *Speculum* 37 (1962), pp. 198-207, where further literature.

jabbān, or "cheeseman", could be a manufacturer of cheese or a trader in this commodity. In most cases he would sell his own products, while the sale of cheese imported from Sicily or Crete to Egypt would normally be handled by merchants, of whom we positively know that they did not occupy themselves with cheese making.

These rather complicated relationships could be roughly summarized as follows. Professional merchants would never engage in a craft requiring manual work, except, of course, when, by some force majeur, they lost their capital, as when a clothier writes that, while he was out of business, he earned his livelihood as a tailor. Contrariwise, artisans normally sold also the products manufactured by them, although the commercial aspects of the trades differed widely. Thus, in a contract of partnership with a weaver the latter is confined to "selling on the market", i.e. he is not permitted to use his workshop as a store for the sale of his fabrics, but is held to let them be sold by a market crier or an agent. Finally, there were craftsmen who worked as wage earners either because of lack of capital or standing or because this was required by the very nature of their profession, such as those of masons and carpenters working in the building industry.

Laborers and Craftsmen in the Service of Others. The Wages

An equivalent to the modern labor class, i.e. a large section of the population employed in the service of industrialists, is absent from the Arabic sources and the Geniza records related to the eleventh and twelfth centuries, just as we could not find in them guilds, the form of industrial organization of the later Middle Ages. With the possible exception of paper mills and sugar factories, production was confined to individual workshops run by small or extended families or by partnerships often formed only for short periods. Paper mills, as may be mentioned in passing, had a history of their own. This was an entirely new industry, introduced into Islamic (and later Christian) countries after the capture of Chinese craftsmen in 751 A.D. and, from the beginning, was operated in large workshops owned by caliphs and governors. When the bourgeoisie took possession of this industry, it continued the form of its organization as it originally had been developed. At least this is the impression gained from a Geniza record where an enormous quantity of paper coming from Damascus bears the trademark of one factory, while wholesale merchants in textiles would regularly carry products from many workshops, obviously handpicked in the bazaars.[1]

Sugar factories, or rather some of them, also must have resembled modern industrial plants, as may be concluded from two interconnected facts: we sometimes find their owners being capitalists, not workmen—even in case of those operated in partnership—and the sums invested are far too large for small workshops. In addition, the sugar distilleries, as we know from the books of the Muslim antiquarians, were real landmarks in the topography of Old Cairo. The production of sugar, we remember, like that of paper, was a new industry which, originally brought from India to southern Persia, expanded in early Islamic times still further westwards. The novelty of the industry made for capitalistic forms of organization unlike the long established crafts which stuck to their traditional ways.[2]

On the other hand, the government workshops, such as the mints or the houses for the manufacture of robes and other pieces of clothing embroidered with the name of the ruler, should not be regarded as industrial plants. For according to all we know thus far, the persons employed there were not laborers receiving fixed wages, but rather independent craftsmen who worked at piece rate. This applies of course only to the period under discussion.

Laborers, i.e. workers not operating a shop of their own, are represented in the Geniza records by three types: persons called "boy", or "young man" (*ṣabī, ghulām*), others designated as "hireling, employee" or simply "workman" (*ajīr, ṣāniʿ*), and finally those described as unskilled laborers (*raqqāṣ*, literally "runner", "errand boy" and similar expressions).[3]

The terms mentioned first designate basically a state of apprenticeship, but are used in the Geniza records in a general way for employees connected with an employer in a personal relationship of long standing. Such a "boy" could be described as "sheikh", elder, i.e. he would be addressed like any other respectable citizen. The two terms were applied also to slaves and freedmen. Only the names and other circumstances mentioned in connection with such

[1] Cf. *Mediterranean Society*, Ch. II (2), Notes 2-4.
[2] Cf. EI[1] s.v. Sukkar, and *Medit. Soc.* Index s.v. Sugar—industry and trade.
[3] As far as is not otherwise indicated, the documentation for the Geniza material used in this section is provided in *Mediterranean Society*, Ch. II, section 3.

persons would indicate that they were free born men. This nomenclature was applied equally in commerce and in industry and we would find a "master" (*mu'allim*, the word is used also in commerce) referring to the "education" (*tarbiya*) given by him to his former employee in more than one Geniza letter.

One or more laborers would be employed in the workshop of a craftsman. They are mentioned, for example, as contributing to a public appeal together with their master. It is, however, noteworthy that the letters and legal deeds of the Cairo Geniza refer to them very sparingly. More frequently mention is made of the "runners" and other unskilled laborers, especially those employed in the building trades.

As to wages and working conditions, we have to bear in mind that normally no contracts were made in writing for hiring a laborer. In some cases, however, especially when a longer period was envisaged and special circumstances accompanied the hire, a document was drawn up. By mere chance, fragments of both the draft and the final copy of such a contract of employment written in 1057 in Old Cairo have been preserved. Two glassmakers, partners in a workshop, hired another glassmaker, described as a laborer, to work on the melting furnace for the duration of one year. He received five silver pieces (dirhams) and lunch worth one dirham on any day he worked. During the period of the contract he could not work for others. A fine of five gold pieces was to be paid by him to the chest of two specified synagogues in Old Cairo in case he violated any of these stipulations.[1]

More information about the subject can be gleaned from the statements on the expenditure of the Jewish community in Old Cairo, over a hundred of which have been preserved. In a number of these, ranging in date between 1040 and 1199, we find details about the wages paid to masons, carpenters, "boys" and unskilled laborers engaged in the building trades and to overseers controlling them. In a statement from 1199, the mason receives five dirhams and lunch equivalent to the value of 1¼ dirhams, i.e. almost the same emoluments as those obtained by the glassmaker in the contract of 1057.

[1] The purchasing power of the dirham, as well as its relationship to the dinar (see p. 271) changed slightly from year to year and even from one city to another in the same year. Nevertheless we see the courts, in records dated between 1052 and 1169, awarding half a dirham per day as alimony for minors. The average ratio between silver and gold pieces during the eleventh and twelfth centuries was 1:36.

Throughout, the skilled craftsman receives a remuneration of 4-6 dirhams, as well as lunch, while the "boys" and laborers earn between $1\frac{1}{2}$ and $2\frac{3}{4}$ dirhams, but never—lunch. Even when a mason undertook repairs on a building lasting almost a month, and was not paid daily, but received a gross sum, the accounts listed lunch for him every day, but not for his assistants, who were paid on a daily basis. The "white collar worker" who supervised the operation and kept the accounts was paid least of all: he received two dirhams a day or even less.

Using the data about the cost of living known to us from the Geniza in other sources we arrive at the conclusion that an independent craftsman obtained a fair margin above the average of two dinars per month (cf. pp. 271 and 276) needed by a lower class family. The others averaged incomes falling far below this minimum.

Two Classes of Workers: Those With Means and The Proletarians. The Social Position of the Craftsmen

The preceding discussion of both the technical and economic aspects of Mediterranean arts and crafts of the eleventh and twelfth centuries leads to the conclusion that the craftsmen did not form a unified and egalitarian "working class", opposed to a class of commercial and financial capitalists. Rather, the dividing line is to be sought between the masters of the higher crafts, who normally worked with their own capital or formed free and often short-term partnerships, and others with little or no means, mostly the pursuers of lower professions, the hired laborers and paupers in general.

The artisans of good standing, as we have seen, normally sold their own products and often also were partly traders and, we may add, even capitalists. Thus when we find a goldsmith also doing some business in flax, we have to remember that, in Egypt at that time, this commodity played the role of stocks and securities in our own society.[1] The fact that a person was engaged in manual work did not in itself assign him to a special class. If his family was financially independent and if he had received, as was usual in such families, a proper education, he was "an elder", a respectable citizen.

Employment, on the other hand, as any form of dependence, whether in industry or in commerce, was regarded as humiliating. "I eat bread in the service of others; every minute of the day I gulp

[1] TS 16.148. Translated in *Readings*.

the cup of death because of my degradation and that of my children"—writes a merchant who had suffered shipwreck and was compelled to enter the service of another firm.[1] This negative attitude towards employment did not, of course, apply to the transitory period during which a person learned a craft or a trade as "the boy", or servant, of another. We read above about such a "boy" who was addressed as an "elder". However, after that period no one would agree to the status of a "hireling" except when forced to do so by dire financial circumstances. The present writer has already encountered in the Geniza three cases in which an employee was indebted to his employer and worked under him in order to pay off his debt.

We do find in the Geniza references to tensions between social classes. The rule of the "elders", the respectable citizens, was challenged by the *ṣibyān*, "the boys", or "the young men", as exemplified in letters from Alexandria by dyers, cobblers and oyster gatherers and in one letter from Old Cairo by potters. The members of these professions were singled out by the writers as examples of lower class people, not as representatives of the artisans in general. Particularly the Jewish oystermen from Alexandria must have had a bad reputation. In one letter they were charged with such offensive behavior as drinking beer in the Crusaders' taverns of Acre.[2]

The assertion that, in the period and area under consideration, manual professions as such did not confine their members to a self contained and closely knit class is demonstrated by the spectacle of social rise richly attested to by the Geniza. Merchants of high priced goods and shipowners bear the names of craftsmen, such as combmaker, spinner, potter or saddler. The phenomenon also appears amongst families whose pedigrees are included in the commemorative lists preserved. Such drastic occupational changes were possible because the Mediterranean society of the eleventh and twelfth centuries, not unlike our own, enjoyed a high degree of mobility and freedom of movement, which was in marked contrast to both the preceding and the following periods.

[1] TS 10 J 12, f. 20 (N 144), margin.

[2] Cf. the present writer's "The Local Jewish Community in the Light of the Cairo Geniza Documents," *Journal of Jewish Studies* 12 (1961), pp. 133-158.

CHAPTER FOURTEEN

THE DOCUMENTS OF THE CAIRO GENIZA AS A SOURCE FOR ISLAMIC SOCIAL HISTORY

Geniza (pronounce Gheneeza) denotes the store-room of a synagogue or any other place in which papers covered with Hebrew letters were discarded. For according to Jewish belief, which has its parallels in Muslim and Coptic customs, no paper on which the name of God is found should be destroyed. So far, only the Genizas of a synagogue in Fusṭāṭ (Old Cairo) and of the nearby cemetery of al-Basātīn have been found. These two are called, by a common designation, "The Cairo Geniza". There is, however, little doubt that the many flourishing Jewish communities which, during the Middle Ages, were spread all over Egypt, from Qūṣ and the Fayyūm down to practically all the provincial towns of the delta, have also left us Genizas. Future excavators and buyers of antiquities should pay attention to this possibility.

The treasures of the Cairo Geniza, under circumstances which have often been described,[1] were dispersed to many libraries all over the world. This occurred mainly during the last decade of the nineteenth century, beginning in 1890, when a considerable amount of valuable Geniza papers was acquired by the Bodleian Library, Oxford,[2] and culminating in 1897, when Solomon Schechter transferred the whole of the then still extant treasures of the Geniza chamber to the University Library Cambridge, England.[3] A very important collection is found at the Jewish Theological Seminary in New York, originally brought from Egypt in 1896 by E. N. Adler of London.[4] A smaller, but still extensive and valuable fund of

[1] See Paul E. Kahle, *The Cairo Geniza* (Oxford 1959), chapter 1. N. Golb "Sixty Years of Genizah Research," Judaism, VI (1957), pp. 3-5.

[2] Cf. A. Neubauer and A. E. Cowley, *Catalogue of the Hebrew Manuscripts in the Bodleian Library*, II (Oxford 1906), pp. xii-xvi.

[3] No printed catalogue exists of the enormous treasures of the Taylor-Schechter Collection of the University Library, Cambridge. However, hand lists covering important sections were prepared by the meritorious keeper of manuscripts E. J. Worman (died 1909) and are available to visitors engaged in research.

[4] Cf. *Catalogue of Hebrew Manuscripts in the Collection of E. N. Adler*, Cambridge 1921.

Geniza papers whose beginnings go back to 1891, is owned by the library of Dropsie College, Philadelphia,[1] while the Freer Gallery of Washington possesses about fifty, mostly very well preserved documents, which were acquired by Mr. Charles L. Freer in Egypt in 1908. Nothing is known about the provenance of these papers,[2] but it stands to reason that they came from the cemetery al-Basātīn, where Mr. B. Chapira of Paris, at the beginning of this century, excavated Geniza papers in considerable quantities.[3] A small collection belonging to the University Museum of the University of Pennsylvania as well as the Gaster Collection in the British Museum, London, have been described by the present writer.[4] All in all, nineteen libraries are known to possess Geniza documents, and there may still be some papers in private hands.

The amount of material brought to light from the Cairo Geniza is very considerable. The late Solomon Schechter estimated that he alone had brought to the University Library in Cambridge over a hundred thousand leaves, which certainly is an under estimate.[5] Of these, according to H. Hirschfeld[6] about 12,000 are in Arabic, though mostly in Hebrew characters. It is useful to compare with this the numbers given by A. Grohmann, *From the World of Arabic Papyri*, Cairo 1952, pp. 2-3. Grohmann estimates that in all collections known to him there exist about 16,000 papyri and 33,000 pieces of paper written in Arabic characters, making a total of some 50,000.

A large number of papers written in Arabic characters have also been preserved in the Geniza, e.g. contracts, petitions to authorities, and even letters exchanged between Jews. The use of Arabic characters must have been very common among Jews; for there

[1] Cf. B. Halper, *Descriptive Catalogue of Genizah Fragments in Philadelphia* (Philadelphia 1924).

[2] See Richard Gottheil and William H. Worrell, *Fragments from the Cairo Genizah in the Freer Collection* (New York 1927), p.v.

[3] B. Chapira, *REJ* 82 (1926), 317.

[4] "The Geniza Collection of the University Museum of the University of Pennsylvania," *JQR*, 49 (1958), 35-52. "Geniza Papers of a Documentary Character in the Gaster Collection of the British Museum", *JQR* 51 (1960), pp. 34-46.

[5] According to J. D. Pearson, *Oriental Manuscript Collections in the Libraries of Great Britain and Ireland*, London 1954, pp. 26-7, the so-called Taylor-Schechter Collection of the University Library, Cambridge, contains about 27,700 items. But most of these are literary texts composed of several, and sometimes of very many, leaves, In addition. starting in 1955, thousands of fragments which had not been registered before were identified and received pressmarks. This is the New Series of the Taylor-Schechter Collection (TS NS).

[1] "The Arabic Portion of the Cairo Genizah," *JQR* 15 and 16 (1902-4).

have been found in sizeable quantities transcripts of the Hebrew text of the Bible into Arabic script, often, curiously enough, equipped with the Hebrew vowel signs.[1] In many communications written in Hebrew characters, the address or additional notes are given in Arabic.

Purely Muslim material has also found its way into the Geniza. The University Library, Cambridge, has sorted these manuscripts out and keeps them in separate boxes.[2] Recently, Dr. Samuel M. Stern of Oxford has dicovered interesting Muslim items among the Geniza papers, such as the oldest Arabic zajal, a poem composed of stanzas, a letter by the famous Muslim mystic Junayd, the existence, but not the text of which had been known, and about twenty pieces from the chancellery of the Fatimid caliphs. Obviously, the Jewish secretaries working there had put them aside and partly used them for writing Hebrew texts on their backs. Even illustrated pages of Muslim manuscripts have been found.

Generally speaking, everything coming from the Geniza has some bearing on the medieval civilization of the Middle East. For almost all this material was written in that part of the world, and mostly by people whose mother tongue was Arabic. However, it is the non-literary, documentary Geniza papers which are of direct import for the social history of Islam. The present writer has worked through all the known collections of Geniza material, and is now in a position to form some idea about the extent and the character of the material preserved.

At the present state of research it is not yet possible to determine the exact number of Geniza papers of *documentary* character. To begin with, there exist perhaps a quarter of a million leaves covered with texts of *literary* content, whilst on the reverse side of such leaves, or hidden away between them there may be writings containing interesting historical information. Secondly, many thousands of fragments are so tiny that, although being of documentary character, they could hardly be listed as significant sources of social history. Confining ourselves to more or less self-contained units, we arrive at a total of approximately ten thousand items ranging from fragments of three or four lines, carrying in themselves a full

[1] The reason for this strange combination is that Arabic has only three vowel signs, while Hebrew has ten.

[2] Closer scrutiny of these boxes revealed that they contain also a considerable amount of material which is not Islamic.

message, to letters comprising a hundred to one hundred and fifty or more lines.

The vast majority of these papers is composed in Arabic. It is by no means easy to define when a man would prefer to use the Hebrew language and when the Arabic. It seems that most letters concerning communal or religious affairs were written in Hebrew, whilst most private and all business letters are in Arabic. Legal deeds, except marriage contracts and writs of divorce, are also mostly in Arabic.

As to the places of origin of these documents, very many were written outside Egypt, the country where they were found. The order of frequency of these countries of provenance seems to be the following: 1. North Africa, including Sicily and Spain; 2. Palestine and Syria; 3. Iraq, no private or commercial correspondence, but mostly letters and legal opinions, emanating from the Babylonian Jewish Academies; 4. Yemen and India; 5. Byzantium. Very little material has been preserved from Western Christian Europe.

Comparatively few documents have survived from the tenth century. There are not very many from the period of the later Middle Ages, say between 1250 and 1500. If we disregard the more modern papers, which are numerous (and certainly deserve special study), the Geniza documents are therefore a source mainly for Fatimid and Ayyūbid times. Our study is solely concerned with this, the "classical" Geniza, to the exclusion of documents coming from the sixteenth through the nineteenth centuries.

As to form and content, more than one half of the material preserved consists of public, private or business correspondence. On the whole, these letters are markedly different from those published in the various collections of Arabic papyri. They are, as a rule, more extensive and elaborate and far more expressive of sentiments and thoughts. This difference certainly does not reflect the fact that they were composed by Jews, while the Arabic papyri were mostly written by non-Jews. It is the difference of time that counts: the average Geniza letter is 250 years later than a letter written on papyrus. I have little doubt that as soon as more Arabic letters written on paper are published, they will prove to be more or less of the same character as those found in the Geniza.

There may still be another reason why most of the letters preserved in the Geniza are different in character from those published so far in the collections of Arabic papyri. The latter come mainly from officials or from people of provincial towns or villages. The

Geniza, too, has preserved a considerable amount of letters from the Rīf, the Egyptian countryside. Most of its material, however, comes from the urban, metropolitan population of the Mediterranean and Middle Eastern countries, and therefore from a social milieu different from that of the papyri.

The second largest group are deeds and contracts, some of public character, such as letters of appointment, resolutions of public bodies, circulars or decrees of Jewish authorities, but most contain private transactions, such as the selling or renting of houses or other immovable property, the granting or the payment of loans, the formation or dissolution of partnerships, wills and donations, manumission or sale of domestic servants (who often also acted as responsible business agents) and, of course, contracts of marriage and writs of divorce. A marriage contract is often accompanied by a *taqwīm*, an evaluation of the various items brought in by the bride. These lists constitute a rich source for the knowledge of the material civilization of the time.

All in all it appears that in Fatimid times civil cases were still largely brought before Jewish courts, although actions or deeds made before a cadi are often referred to. Frequently, and for reasons which still need clarification, the same transaction was made simultaneously before a Muslim and a Jewish court, or one part of it was brought before a public tribunal and a complementary action before a Jewish court. This interplay of Jewish and Muslim law revealed by the Geniza papers is a fascinating subject of research.

Another characteristic group of Geniza documents are pages from the record books of the rabbinical courts. These minutes of the proceedings of the courts have always struck me by the vividness and lucidity with which they reproduce the depositions of the parties and witnesses. I understood the reasons for this fact when I collected letters of installation of synagogue beadles, who acted also as attendants to the Courts.[1] There it is made incumbent on the attendant to take down verbatim all that is said in the form recapitulated by the presiding judge. The court itself normally had among its three or more members one scholar who usually was a professional scribe and who, as we can see from rough copies preserved, also took notes of the proceedings, as they were going on.

[1] A similar deed of the appointment of the farrāsh of a mosque in 967 is preserved in the Egyptian Library, cf. A. Grohmann, *Arabic Papyri from the Egyptian Library* II, 103-106.

Thus we hear in these minutes people talking as they did in Old Cairo eight or nine hundred years ago.

Finally, the Geniza contains commercial or private accounts, inventories of libraries and estates, *taṣqīʿ*, i.e. lists of revenue, in particular from rented houses belonging to pious foundations, lists of donators or taxpayers, or of the receivers of bread, clothing or cash provided by public charity, medical prescriptions, calendars, amulets, charms, etc.

Mention has been made already of the legal opinions or responsa, written in reply to questions submitted to religious authorities. Thousands of such responsa have been preserved, but only a fraction of them can be regarded as documentary, i.e. dealing with actual issues of significance for social history.

It goes without saying that such vast and variegated material is apt to enhance considerably our knowledge of the medieval civilization of the Middle East. As a matter of fact, use of Geniza material has already been made by students of Muslim History, e.g. by Dr. Rāshid Barāwī in his thesis about the Economic History of Egypt under the Fatimids.[1] Dr. Barāwī had at his disposal only Jacob Mann's book *The Jews in Egypt and in Palestine under the Fatimid Caliphs*, which is based almost exclusively on Hebrew Geniza papers and which, as its subtitle indicates, was intended to be a contribution to the history of the Jews in the countries referred to, not to that of the general civilization of the time.[2] Even so, Dr. Barāwī was able to glean some interesting data from Jacob Mann's book. However, once the Arabic documents of the Cairo Geniza will have been studied in full, whole sections of Islamic social and economic history will be illustrated by first hand and significant information. This will enable us to revise and enrich the impressions gained from literary sources. Chapters 12-13 and 15-18 of this book, which are based on a preliminary, albeit rather extended, study may serve as examples of the gains which can be expected from a scrutiny of the Arabic portion of the Cairo Geniza.

It should not be denied that this study is confronted with a number of considerable difficulties. To be sure, the fact that most of the Arabic material is written in Hebrew characters should not deter the Islamist. The knowledge of an alphabet consisting of twenty two letters may be acquired in a matter of hours. After this initial step

[1] In Arabic, Cairo 1948.
[2] Oxford 1920 and 1922.

is taken, the student will be baffled by a new obstacle: some Hebrew letters represent two or more Arabic letters because the Hebrew alphabet is six letters shorter than the Arabic. Thus the Hebrew *g* stands for Arabic *j* and *gh*, *k* for *k* and *kh*, *ṣ* for *ṣ* and *ḍ* and often for *ẓ*. This inconvenience, however, is infinitely smaller than that experienced in the reading of Arabic papyri or other medieval documents, where one single sign may denote such different sounds as *b*, *n*, *t*, *th* and *y*.

As may be expected, each country and each period cultivated a particular type of script. A student who reads easily the beautiful and clear hand of the clerks of the business houses of Aden, South Arabia, will hardly be able to decipher even a single line of the equally beautiful, but entirely different script of the intellectuals of Spain who lived at the same time. After having mastered the very intricate handwriting of the Mediterranean merchants of the eleventh century, one is disappointed in finding that it is necessary to start anew in order to learn the script of their colleagues of one hundred and fifty years later. Moreover, most writers have whims and idiosyncrasies of their own. Some, as many of us do today, would indulge in uncommon and fanciful renderings of letters. Others would use different forms for one and the same letter or, vice versa: practically the same sign for different letters. Particularly irritating is the writing of two letters as one and, even more so, the writing of one as two. However all these are hardships with which any student of handwritten documents has to put up. As a whole, the Hebrew paleography of the Arabic portion of the Cairo Geniza presents less difficulties than the Arabic writings. The former may even serve occasionally as an aid for the deciphering of the latter.[1]

A few words concerning the highly interesting Arabic language of the Geniza records can be found at the end of this article. Since these records were mostly written in the living idiom of the period

[1] Thus, the sounds *ḥ*, *j* and *kh* are represented in Arabic mostly by one and the same sign, while in Hebrew script they are expressed by three different characters. Many Geniza letters are addressed to *ṣayyidī wa-mawlā'ī wa-jalīlī*, which means "my illustrious lord and master". The third word, as found in an Arabic letter has been read by the most competent papyrologist of our time *wakhalīlī*, "my friend", which is p eographically possible, but unlikely in the face of the parallel found in so many Arabic letters written in Hebrew script, which use exactly the same phraseology. Cf. A. Grohmann, *Arabic Papyri in the Egyptian Library* (abridged in the following as *APEL*) V, p. 24, no. 291.

and not in the standardized literary language, their interpretation often is puzzling. As the present writer has learned from Professor D. H. Baneth, the founder of the scientific study of the Arabic Geniza, it is not the rare and uncommon words and forms which present pitfalls. They take care of themselves. By their very strangeness they induce the student to stop and to look for parallels or sources which could assist him in finding their meaning. Real trouble is caused by the familiar forms and phrases which are used in medieval Arabic in ways which differ from the regular usage of the literary language. One comparatively simple example may suffice as an illustration: *karīma*, "the dear one", denotes in modern literary Arabic the *daughter*, but in the Geniza writings invariably the *sister*. Naturally, the present writer read many letters before he became aware of this discrepancy. Once this was recognized, he had to work his way back through the material covered, in order to make sure that in the whole of the classical Geniza the word was used exclusively in the latter sense.[1] The change in the meaning of phrases is even more elusive.

As the survey above has shown, the Geniza contains much material of a highly technical character, such as business letters and accounts, records of the sessions of a court, or the detailed lists of jewelry, clothing, bedding, copper and other household goods forming the marriage portion of a bride. Naturally, many of these terms are not to be found in any dictionary and are not in use any more in the present day Arabic vernaculars, which otherwise are very useful for the understanding of the language of the Geniza papers. Fortunately most of the technical terms recur in several documents and in varying combinations so that it is possible to define their meaning approximately and often even exactly. Just as one gains control over the script, after having collected and deciphered a sufficient number of Geniza papers coming from the same country, period and social layer, so one is able to cope with the language on the basis of a systematic study of as many documents as possible belonging to one and the same type.

Unfortunately, in his endeavor to study documents of a similar character coming from the same place and time the student is

[1] The usage is attested from the eleventh through the fifteenth centuries, the latest testimony being a document dated 1451 A.D. in which the *karīma* of a person is described as his sister by both father and mother (ms. University Library, Cambridge, TS 8 J 25, f. 5).

handicapped by the very nature of the Geniza. We positively know that the medieval Jewish courts and business firms kept their records for years.[1] However the Geniza was not an archive, an orderly collection of carefully preserved records, but rather the opposite, a kind of waste paper basket, where books and documents were disposed of after they had lost all value for their proprietors. Often the papers had been torn or damaged by water or other disintegrating agents before being discarded. Moreover, the Geniza room was in constant use for about nine hundred years. People would search it for an old prayer book, a legal formulary or simply a piece of paper. Thus the whole content was continuously turned upside down and whatever coherent material was deposited in it was dissolved and separated in the course of the centuries. This process of dissolution was enhanced by the way in which the Geniza treasures were dispersed among many libraries all over the world. Therefore, the fragments of one single letter may be found today in libraries in three different countries.[2]

In view of these difficulties, any serious work on the Geniza requires long range planning and protracted preparation. However having overcome the initial labors of deciphering and collection one will find this study most fascinating and rewarding. The main fields for which information may be gathered from this source will be surveyed in the following pages.

Political and military history is only sparsely represented in the

[1] This fact is proved both by direct and indirect evidence from the Geniza. A woman who had lost her marriage contract would apply to a rabbinical court for a copy years after her wedding and we read that a transcript was made from the copy kept in the courts. Many court records are docketed as belonging to the dossier of a case and some such dossiers could actually be pieced together. A merchant would be asked to look up his account-books from previous years, and of one merchant and scholar, Nahray b. Nissim, a native of Qayrawān, Tunisia, who lived in Egypt between 1048 and 1095, about two hundred letters addressed to him have been preserved—certainly only a small fraction of his original archives. These letters, together with other Geniza material related to Nahray b. Nissim, have been treated by Mr. M. Michael in a Ph. D. thesis submitted to the Hebrew University, Jerusalem, in April 1965.

[2] Such is the case of a letter which states that in 1161, the Exilarch Daniel ben Hisdai of Bagdad installed Nethan'el, the Head of the Cairine Jewish Academy, who served as head of the Jewish community of the Fatimid empire. The letter was reconstituted by S. Assaf from one fragment in the Jewish Theological Seminary of New York, another in the University Library, Cambridge, and a third in the Antonin Collection in Leningrad. Cf. J. Mann, *Texts and Studies* I, (1931), 230-5. The collection of papers concerning the trade to India contains quite a number of documents composed of fragments found in different collections.

Geniza. The letters often contain short references to major events—which mostly meant tribulation or even disaster for the subject population— such as the expansion of the Almoravids and Almohades in North Africa or the incessant maritime warfare and piracy in the Mediterranean. Northern France and northern Italy, for all intents and purposes lay outside the view of the Geniza people. These Arabic speaking Jews regularly travelled on Genoese or Pisan ships and "Rūm" ships travelling from North Africa to Sicily or along the Sicilian coast. The latter seemed to have been Italian rather than Byzantine. Marseilles was frequented by these Jews, but with few exceptions no mention is made either of visits to North Italian ports, or of events of general impact on the mainland of Europe. There are many references and allusions to Muslim dignitaries and other personalities all over the Muslim world, from Spain to Syria and from Sicily to Yemen. However, these references to personalities are, as a rule, as short as those to events. The value of both consists in the fact that they illustrate their topic from an angle naturally absent in our historical sources, namely from the viewpoint of the non-Muslims.

In some cases, more detailed descriptions of events of general significance are found in the Geniza papers. Thus, the persecution of Christians and Jews under the Fatimid caliph al-Ḥākim appears now in a very different light from that derived from the literary sources. As late as January 1012, al-Ḥākim is praised in a Hebrew "Scroll" as a Messiah-like prince of justice, who protects the non-Muslims against unfounded accusations. The sudden outburst against Christians and Jews appears now to have started as a popular outbreak against the "liberal" rule of the Fatimids rather than as a personal whim of a caliph. Many details about this event and its aftermath have been found in the Geniza, as the reader may learn from Jacob Mann's aforementioned book. Likewise, the predominant role of the Jewish Tustarī brothers at the Fatimid court, who came to a cruel end in 1048, is illustrated by many Geniza fragments published or discussed by Mann in the book referred to, as well as in his later publication *Texts and Studies in Jewish History and Literature*. Two extensive letters referring to the conquest of Jerusalem by the Crusaders in 1099, published by the present writer, will be welcomed by the medievalists, as they come from a time and a place from which only very few letters have survived.[1]

[1] *Journal of Jewish Studies* 3 (1952), pp. 162-177.

There exists a plethora of Geniza letters coming from or referring to Palestine in the time of the Crusades.[1] Two eyewitness reports of an attack on Aden by the ruler of Kish (Qais) in the Persian Gulf in 1135 are useful, as they allow us to compare the technique of the Arab historiographers of the time with factual reports.[2] An interesting letter from Aden dated 1202, published by D. H. Baneth in the J. N. Epstein Memorial Volume, Jerusalem 1950, echoes vividly the tribulations which befell Yemen, when its ruler, Saladin's nephew al-Malik al-Muʿizz, was murdered and replaced by his infant brother, while the Atabek Sunqur actually ruled the country. A letter from Mosul, written in December 1236, vividly describes the slaughter wrought by the "Tatars" in the environs of that city especially round al-ʿImrāniyya, a place of pilgrimage for Muslims and Jews.[3]

These examples, which stretch over three centuries and come from four different countries, are apt to illustrate the type of information to be gathered from the Cairo Geniza in respect of the general course of history. The Geniza is particularly rich with regard to the administration of the Muslim states, especially—but not exclusively—as far as the non-Muslim population was affected. There are many references to the jāliya or jizya, the poll tax imposed on the non-Muslims. It must have constituted a heavy burden, for we frequently read about imprisonment in connection with this imposition. The indigent and the invalids, contrary to the provisions of ancient Muslim law, had to pay the poll-tax. As had been the case in Byzantine times and in the period of the Arabic papyri,[4] the tax had to be paid in one's place of origin, and everyone had to carry with him a barā'a certifying that he had fulfilled his duty. Thus a Palestinian schoolmaster, teaching in a little town in Egypt, had to go to Cairo every year to pay his poll tax to the *Jāliyat al-Shām*, the office for Palestino-Syrians. This was an interruption of his work which (with the possible exception of his pupils) caused much irritation to the community. A notable from Ascalon recommending to one of his Cairine friends a scholar from Damascus

[1] Published in Hebrew with English summaries in articles quoted as Goitein, No. 23, 28, 32 and 52 in A *Tentative Bibliography of Geniza Documents* by S. Shaked, Paris-le Haye 1964.

[2] *BSOAS* 16 (1954), pp. 247-257.

[3] Cf. *Studi... G. Levi Della Vida* I (Roma 1956), p. 398 ff.

[4] Cf. A. Grohmann, *APEL* (see p. 285) III, 137-8, and *Die Arabischen Papyri aus der Giessener Universitätsbibliothek*, Giessen 1960, pp. 19-28.

travelling to Egypt, assures him that the traveller carried with him a fully certified barā'a of his poll-tax, so that his hosts might be sure that they would incur no trouble. The foreigners caused much annoyance with their jāliya. Thus a young man, serving as *muqaddam*, or head of the Jewish community in a little town in Egypt, writes to his father, a judge of the rabbinical court of Cairo, that he would prefer to study instead of wasting his life chanting the prayers for the villagers and having to look after the foreigners all the time.[1]

The care of foreigners was only one of the many functions of the local muqaddam in which the central government was interested. Normally, all the social services, such as provision for the poor, the widows and orphans, the sick and the invalids, for education and of course all religious needs, including burial, were left to the initiative of the community. This explains, why even in small places the elected muqaddam had to receive authorization from the Sultan.[2]

How far the life of the Jewish communities in general, and especially in the larger towns, with their honorary and paid officers, their ecumenical and local leaders, and their democratic institutions, was characteristic of the period in general or rather was a belated survival from Hellenistic and Roman times, remains still to be investigated.[3]

It would be wrong to assume that the Muslim government did not take interest in the inner life of the non-Muslim communities. The Academy of Jerusalem, the highest Jewish religious authority in the Fatimid state, received a substantial grant towards its maintenance from the Fatimid caliphs, which gave the latter, of course, some influence on the election of the Head of the Academy. A similar grant was given to a Jewish house of learning in the Egyptian capital.[4] Even purely religious matters were brought before the Muslim

[1] Cf. the present writer's paper "Evidence on the Muslim Poll Tax from Non-Muslim Sources", *JESHO* 6 (1963), p. 278 ff.

[2] This detail may be gathered, as well as many other interesting aspects of life in the smaller Egyptian communities, from a number of documents published by D. H. Baneth in the *Alexander Marx Jubilee Volume, Hebrew Section*, New York, 1950, 75-93.

[3] Cf. the present writer's "The Jewish Local Community in the Light of the Cairo Geniza Records", *Journal of Jewish Studies* (1963), pp. 133-158.

[4] Cf. "Congregation versus Community", in *JQR* 44 (1954), pp. 291-304; "Petitions to Fatimid Caliphs", *ibid.*, 45, 30-38, and Jacob Mann, *The Jews in Egypt etc.* I, p. 38.

government, as when the opponents to the pietist reforms of Abraham, the son of Maimonides, decried them as a *bid'a*, a forbidden innovation, in a petition to al-Malik al-'Ādil, Saladin's brother and successor to the throne of Egypt.[1]

Reference has already been made to the many documents, in which we see Muslim and Jewish law in operation at one and the same time. Future research into this matter will have to consider also the Byzantine local law of pre-Islamic Egypt, which seems to contain many rulings and records of formularies similar to those found in the Geniza. In some cases, particularly with regard to immovable property, direct influence of Muslim juridical practice is evident, e.g. in the calculation of the shares in the proprietorship of a house on the basis of twenty four parts.[2] In a thirteenth century lawsuit (Bilbeis 1232), one party contended that it was customary for transactions on houses to be brought also before a Muslim court. "Partnerships according to Muslim law", i.e. between one or more investors and one or more managers, often were brought before rabbinical courts.

The very nature of commerce between different places requires statements in writing. Therefore it is natural that the Geniza has much to contribute to economic history. Over three hundred documents connected with the India trade of the eleventh and twelfth centuries have been collected and studied by the present writer, cf. below Ch. XVII. The items referring to this great chapter of economic history are, however, only a small fraction of the business documents preserved. The prices of houses and rents and of merchandise of all descriptions, its transfer from one country to another, the technique of business, its scope and ethos, the cost of living, the organization of industrial undertakings, such as the manufacture of glass or sugar—all this and many other topics are illustrated by the Geniza. A petition to a Fatimid caliph in favor of a Karaite weaver employed in a state workshop in Damascus brings home the importance attached to the artisan in Muslim civilization. It is astonishing how much the Geniza has to tell us about the life of the working people, although craftsmen and laborers had little opportunity for making statements in writing.[3]

[1] *Homenaje a Millas-Vallicrosa*, Barcelona 1954, 707-720. Cf. "The Muslim Government—as seen by its Non-Muslim Subjects", *J. of the Pakistan Historical Society*, 12 (1964), pp. 1-12.

[2] Cf. e.g. *APEL* (see p. 285).

[3] Cf. above Ch. XIII.

Another subject on which the Geniza is particularly rich in material is family life. A marriage deed in that time was not a formulary, but a real contract. It is usually very informative with regard to the economic and social position of the two parties. In addition to the numerous marriage contracts, there are many rulings and records of courts and, last but not least, countless letters deal mainly or exclusively with family matters.

Even a cursory perusal of the material at hand shows that the actual position of women was far more favorable than might have been gathered from the books of lawyers and other literary sources. Jewish society—as befitting a middle class— was almost entirely monogamous. In the hundreds of relevant documents studied by me, I have found only one single case of bigamy so far, and that in a provincial town (Bilbeis), in the lowest stratum of society and in quite special circumstances: for, as the nuptial agreement stipulates that the second wife should take care of her future husband's daughter, clearly the first wife was insane or ill or otherwise incapable of looking after her child.[1] Normally a marriage contract—including the case just mentioned— contains the condition that the future husband is not allowed to take an additional wife or a concubine. In the Arabic papyri, the wife sometimes receives the right to "dismiss" the second wife, if she does not please her.[2] I wonder, however, whether the still unpublished Muslim marriage contracts, which are contemporary with the Geniza papers, do not contain the same "usual condition"—as it is called—, namely that the husband undertakes not to marry a second wife at all.[3] In the Geniza contracts, the wife often receives the right to choose the domicile of the family, and the husband is not allowed to travel except "with her consent or on her command". Naturally, there exist also contracts where the husband fixes the domicile and

[1] There are also one or two cases of the so-called levirate marriage, by which a man, even when already married, is forced by law to take the widow of his brother who died childless, in the event he is unable to prove his incapacity of contracting a second marriage. The very fact that levirate marriages were so rare shows how strongly the society represented in the Geniza objected to bigamy.

[2] Cf. *APEL* (see p. 285) I, p. 72, lines 12-14; p. 87, line 8.

[3] It should be noted, however, that neither a Muslim marriage contract dated 1207 (cf. A. Dietrich, "Eine Arabische Eheurkunde," *Documenta Islamica Inedita*, Berlin 1952, pp. 121-154), nor four others, dated 1278, 1290, 1334 and 1342 respectively, published by Dr. Su'ād Māhir, Cairo, contain such a condition.

reserves for himself the right to take his wife with him on any travel he may undertake. To be sure, all such details were discussed in Jewish legal literature (the "Talmud") already in Roman times, but the Geniza shows how they worked in practice—often to the advantage of the female partner.

According to Jewish (Talmudic) law, a wife cannot dispose of her own property as long as her husband is alive. In the Geniza papers we see that women often freely dispose of their property and that a husband, upon going on travel, sometimes grants to his wife the right to dispose even of his own property. In this development the influence of Muslim law was perhaps less substantial than the social concepts of the bourgeoisie class to which a considerable part of the Jewish community belonged.

Women frequently appear as senders of letters, but these were mostly written by professional scribes or by other men, and in some cases it is possible to identify the handwriting of the men who wrote letters sent by women. Likewise, the very tenor of most letters sent to women seems to point to the fact that they were destined to be read to them. There existed, however, literate women, and in the rare cases in which letters destined for the eyes, and not the ears, of a wife, have been found, one is struck by the tenderness and the note of complete equality expressed in them. Normally, letters sent by a mother to her son or by a brother to his sister are more personal than letters exchanged between husband and wife.

Illness looms very large in both private and business correspondence. I wonder whether this phenomenon prevails to the same extent in the Greek papyri. It is not unusual to find the complaint that business could not be done because everyone was confined to bed, or that after treatment the state of the patient had considerably worsened. As today, people sought to be treated by a famous specialist. A detailed description of the state of the sick person would be sent to the great doctor—who often would be also a person of high social status—through the mediation of some notable, and the doctor would send his prescription back through the same channel. It is characteristic of this bookish civilization that the physician would let his patient know according to which book of which famous author he treated him.[1]

As pointed out above, the great majority of the Geniza fragments

[1] Cf. "The Medical Profession in the Light of the Cairo Geniza Documents", *Hebrew Union College Annual* 34 (1963), pp. 177-194.

consists of literary texts. These, together with the many inventories of books preserved, convey a vivid picture of the spiritual life of the time. They show that the educated Jews read not only books of Jewish content, but also had a lively interest in secular subjects, especially philosophy and science. However, the literary Geniza texts are outside the scope of this study.

Needless to say, the Cairo Geniza is also a particularly rich source for the history of the Arabic language and of the changes affecting its morphology, syntax, vocabulary and style. Many types of Arabic are found in these documents, from the elaborate creations in purely classical Arabic, of the Spanish Jewish men of letters, to plain prose bearing the imprint of the Maghribī, Egyptian, Palestinian, or Yemenite dialects. Very rarely, however, does the language become actually colloquial or "vulgar". It is a semi-literary style bearing local color rather than an undisciplined idiom. Strangely enough, some Egyptian vulgarisms which occur already in the Arabic papyri, have not yet been found in the Geniza.[1]

In conclusion I should like to say that the highest reward of the arduous task of deciphering and interpreting Geniza papers is the intimate insight they give us into the soul and thought patterns of the members of a highly refined medieval civilization. Not only private letters, but business letters also, generally make good reading. These merchants were very human, extremely polite and also took a philosophical view about gains and losses. Many of them were scholars and public figures, and some even poets.

God's presence was felt strongly and sincerely, while bigotry and fanaticism were next to being absent. Religious scholarship was the main subject of learning of the educated middle class, but the secular erudition of the physicians and the refined ways of life of the courts were influential as well. There is also considerable material in the Geniza illustrating folk ways and the life of the man in the street.

[1] See Joshua Blau, *A Grammar of Medieval Judaeo-Arabic*, Jerusalem 1961, (cf. the present writer's review in *ZDMG* 113, 1964, pp. 379-381) and the same author's *The Emergence and Linguistic Background of Judaeo-Arabic: A Study of the Origins of Middle Arabic*, Oxford 1965.

APPENDIX

THE PRESENT STATE OF RESEARCH ON THE CAIRO GENIZA DOCUMENTS

A survey of the contents of the Cairo Geniza documents somewhat more detailed than the one provided in the preceding article is contained in the present writer's "The Documents of the Cairo Geniza as a Source for Mediterranean Social History," *JAOS* 80(1960), pp. 91-100. *A Tentative Bibliography of Geniza Documents, prepared by S. Shaked under the direction of D. H. Baneth and S. D. Goitein* has just come out. This bibliography consists of two parts: a list of all the published Geniza records with details about their publication and discussion, and a list of books and articles containing such publications or discussions, arranged in alphabetical order by author. The first section enumerates also the Geniza items included in M. Michael's reconstruction of the archives of Nahray b. Nissim, cf. above p. 287, as well as those to be published by S. D. Goitein in his book on the India trade, see below, Ch. XVII. Since the publications on the Geniza are dispersed all over the world in a way not unsimilar to the Geniza fragments themselves, Mr. Shaked's bibliography is an absolutely indispensable tool of research.

Besides the book on the India trade referred to above, the present writer is preparing for publication a comprehensive study on the society of the Mediterranean countries, as far as it is reflected in the Cairo Geniza documents. This study will be accompanied by a volume to be called *Readings in Mediterranean Social History*, containing translations in English of selected Geniza records. Both works are nearing completion. The same applies to the publication of a collection of particularly well preserved Geniza documents (the series 18J of the Taylor-Schechter fund of the University Library, Cambridge) prepared by Professor N. Golb of the University of Chicago.

CHAPTER FIFTEEN

THE UNITY OF THE MEDITERRANEAN WORLD IN THE "MIDDLE" MIDDLE AGES

An Arabist reading Jérome Carcopino's classic *Daily Life in Rome* is overwhelmed by the many striking parallels, often pointed out by the author himself between the life described in that book and the life we know from Mediterranean Muslim towns which have preserved their medieval character. Carcopino gives us a picture of imperial Rome, the capital of the pagan world, about 900 years before Islamic civilization reached its apogee, and still there is much in common between the two.

This continuity of the Mediterranean heritage has been brought into full relief by the recent studies of Professor Claude Cahen on the development of the Islamic and Western towns. Until then, it was generally believed that the European town was somehow a continuation of the Graeco-Roman polis, whilst in Islam a town in the sense of a self-contained, organized community never existed. On the whole, the latter assumption is correct, but in the West, too, there was little of autonomous city life in later Roman times, whilst in early Islam various organizations enjoying local autonomy, such as the *Aḥdāth*, "the young men", a kind of local militia, were active and recognized by the authorities.[1] The final differentiation between East and West came about during the twelfth century, when new and specific historical forces were at work in Europe and when power was completely taken over by barbarian soldier slaves in almost all of the Muslim states.

However, during the "middle" Middle Ages, around 1050, the unity of the Mediterranean world was still a fact. This is all the more remarkable, since the European shore of the Mediterranean, including Spain, as well as the African and Asian sides, were split up into many separate politicial units, often at war with one another. However, despite the many frontiers and the frequent wars, people

[1] Cf. Claude Cahen, "Mouvements populaires et autonomisme urbain dans l'Asie musulmane du Moyen Age", *Arabica, Revue d'Études Arabes*, tomes V et VI, 1958-1959. Tome VI, p. 260 quotes Geniza documents showing that around 1050, the Aḥdāth were a fixed institution even in a comparatively small town such as Jerusalem.

and goods, books and ideas travelled freely from one end of the Mediterranean to the other. As far as the Islamic side is concerned, we can deduce this fact from literary sources, such as the biographies of scholars, or, in particular, from some of the excellent books of travel which were written around that time. Even more impressive is the documentary evidence to be derived from the letters and deeds preserved in the Cairo Geniza. For here we have records of life as it really was, especially of the middle and lower strata of society, uncensored by literary selection and presentation.[1]

To be sure, the writers of the letters and deeds found in the Cairo Geniza were mostly Jews. However, at least eighty per cent of the documents preserved were written not in Hebrew, but in Arabic, the lingua franca of the time; Muslims and Christians are frequently mentioned in them, and one does not get the impression from them that the Jews at that time moved about more than the members of other communities. In any case, the enormous degree of freedom of communication enjoyed by the people mirrored in the Cairo Geniza would not have been possible had it not been favored by the legal position and the general political climate in the states concerned.

The first and most eloquent testimony of this freedom of movement is the silence about its curtailment in the thousands of preserved fragmentary or complete business and family letters. A person would refer to his travel to Palermo, Genoa, Marseilles, or any place in Spain, North Africa, Egypt, or the Syrian coast, or even to places in Byzantine Greece, such as Salonika or Thebes; or he would write a letter in Arabic from Seleucia, today Selefke, in Asia Minor to Cairo, mentioning his journey through Jaffa, Rhodes, Chios, and Constantinople, without ever alluding to any difficulties incurred because of political boundaries. Merchants would commute freely every summer between Fatimid, Shiʿite, Egypt and Zirid, Sunni, Tunisia even at the time of great tension between the two countries, or would travel on the direct route between Alexandria and Seville or Almeria in Spain. To be sure, everyone had to carry a barāʾa, which is not a passport, but a certificate to the effect that he had paid his taxes. Without such a barāʾa, one could not travel at all, even inside Egypt. We frequently read in the Geniza papers that persons carried these certificates or forgot them at home,[2] or we

[1] Cf. above Ch. XIV.
[2] "Please search in the pocket of my dove-colored robe", writes a merchant

read about persons taken off a Nile barge, while travelling from one village to another without carrying a *wuṣūl al-jāliya*, or receipt for the poll tax paid. When the Spanish Hebrew poet Judah ha-Levi on his pilgrimage to the Holy Land made a rather prolonged stop in Cairo, his friend and agent in Alexandria had to make arrangements with the authorities for his poll tax certificate. This we know from a highly interesting letter addressed to him from Alexandria, where, at that time, his poems were collected and published.

However, these measures of precaution taken by the fiscal authorities cannot be called an infringement of the freedom of movement. Only in later times, under Saladin's rule, e.g. in a letter sent from Alexandria to Aden, a man expresses his apprehension that the *nāẓir*, or superintendent, of the port would not let him travel because he regarded him as suspicious for the mere reason that he had arrived on a Frankish boat. However, as is well-known, the famous Spanish Muslim geographer, Ibn Jubayr, travelled as late as 1183 from Acre to Sicily, and from there to Spain on Christian ships; and in the Geniza it is absolutely commonplace for Jews from Muslim countries to travel on boats belonging to citizens of non-Muslim states, such as Normans, Byzantines, Genoese, or Pisans. A man could write from Spain to his wife in Cairo: "I intend to come on the Gaetani, i.e. the ship belonging to the merchant from Gaeta" (in Italy), just as we would say today: "This summer, I shall be travelling on a Dutch boat."

In practice, freedom of movement was very much disturbed by piracy and warfare, and there are many references to both in the Geniza papers. More astonishing are the casual remarks of these people about travel to distant countries and long journeys. Just a few examples: First, a hasty note, sent by a merchant from Alexandria to Cairo; he wrote it on Friday afternoon, i.e. on the Eve of Sabbath, remarking, "I have already taken my bath"—meaning, of course, that no business was normally done at such a time. What do we read in this note? "I have just arrived from Almeria, Spain. Your business friend in Fez, Morocco, sent me a bar of gold—certainly from the Sudan—to buy with it Spanish silk for you. I, however, thought this was not a good idea, and am forwarding you the gold, as it is. On the other hand, a friend of your business friend there

after his arrival in Cairo from Alexandria, "you will find my barā'a there; please send it immediately, for I have already deposited a bail bond for it".

delivered such and such a quantity of ambergris[1] to me, which I forward herewith, and asks you to send back five flasks of musk equivalent to its price; please sell the ambergris on the arrival of this letter and buy the musk, for I have to send it off immediately."

Or we read in a letter of recommendation by Solomon b. Judah, the Gaon, or Head of the Jewish Academy in Jerusalem until his death in 1051: "The bearer of this letter is a Jew from Khorasan, highly recommended to me by my friends in Seville; he is now proceeding to Cairo; please look after him." We do not know how this Jew from Northeastern Iran came to Spain. It is likely that he came back to Jerusalem on the Northern route, via Sicily and Tyre or Acre. The Gaon, who was the spiritual head of Western Jewry, had, owing to the institution of the pilgrimage to Jerusalem, close, personal connections with peoples from all over the Mediterranean world. Still, the short, business-like way in which the widely travelled Khorasani is introduced here shows how small the world had already become at that time.

Another impressive illustration of the unity of the Mediterranean world in the "middle" Middle Ages is the frequency of intermarriage between persons from different countries. We have a great deal of material about this question in the Geniza. Not only did the families leading in business, scholarship, and communal life (say, in Spain, Tunisia, and Egypt) intermarry, but the slaves, doing business for their masters in different countries, also contracted such unions. There seems to have been some system in the matter. In a document from Tyre on the Lebanese coast, a girl gives power of attorney to a gentleman to select a husband for her in Cairo and to arrange a marriage contract with him in her name. This was not confined to Muslim countries. We have a letter, written in beautiful Hebrew, by a lady from Egypt whose brothers still lived there. She had been married in Europe and her daughter already bore a Greek name, spelled Zoi.

Perhaps the most significant aspect of the age revealed by the Cairo Geniza is the fact that political boundaries did not interfere with the unity and autonomy of religious or ethnic groups. Regular contributions were made by the Jewish communities all over the Fatimid empire for the benefit of the two great Jewish academies

[1] Ambergris is a waxy substance, secreted by whales. It was and still is used in the manufacture of perfume. The reference above is to the yellowish variety coming from the Atlantic ocean. Cf. also below p. 339.

in Abbasid Bagdad. Likewise, yearly collections were held in the communities of the Sunni West, in Spain and North Africa, for the academy in Jerusalem, which was under the rule of a Shiʿite dynasty. Similarly, donations were sent to Bagdad and Jerusalem from Christian countries, e.g. from Lucca in Northern Italy, from Narbonne and Montpellier in France, or Mainz, Germany. All these communities submitted their questions concerning matters of faith, rite, or civil law to those seats of learning, and countless replies have been preserved. These replies, which in character as well as in form are similar to the *fatwas*, or legal opinions of Muslim religious scholars, were heeded even in distant countries in a way comparable to the authority of decisions of the Supreme Court in the United States.

Moreover, unbelievable as it may appear, documentary evidence shows that the official head of the Jewish community in Fatimid Egypt, who was confirmed in his office by the Fatimid caliph, was installed by the Jewish exilarch who had his seat in Bagdad.[1] Likewise, Jewish judges and other dignitaries, whether in Egypt, or somewhere in Tunisia or Morocco, were approved by the heads of the academies in Jerusalem or Bagdad. Similar relationships must have existed between the other Christian communities and that of Zirid Tunisia, which was of considerable size.

How is all this to be explained? Of course, the machinery of the state was still relatively loose in those days, i.e. the technique of making life unbearable was not yet as perfected as it is in our own time. In addition to this, there were three positive factors, all interconnected; one legal, one socio-economic, and one historical, which worked in favor of the freedom of movement and the unity of the Mediterranean world: (a) The conception that law was personal and not territorial, i.e. an individual was judged according to the law of his community, or even his sect, rather than that of the territory in which he happened to be; (b) the consequences of the bourgeois revolution of the eight and ninth centuries, which still dominated the "middle" Middle Ages[2] (a mercantile civilization was alive around the Mediterranean with merchants as its most conspicuous bearers; and business makes for free movement); (c) finally—as alluded to at the beginning of this paper—all these countries had a great and long-standing tradition in common. The fact that most

[1] Cf. above p. 287, note 2.
[2] Cf. above Ch. XI.

of them had once been united within the confines of the Roman empire is perhaps of secondary importance. It is the cultural tradition, which begins with the ancient civilizations of Iraq, and even of Iran—for all these countries belong to the Mediterranean world—which counts. The unity of the Mediterranean world was disrupted only when the Islamic countries were taken over by intruders from the outside, mostly from Central Asia and the Caucasus, who had no share in that tradition.

SEAFARING AND OVERLAND MAIL IN THE MEDITERRANEAN BASIN

The unity of the Mediterranean world during the "middle" Middle Ages was achieved through the great extent of seafaring carried on in that "tideless midland sea". The records of the Cairo Geniza contain abundant material about the subject. So far, sixteen types of ships and details of over one hundred and ten individual boats, as well as thirty-six kinds of containers for the transportation of goods and about one hundred and fifty classes of commodities carried by ships have been noted. The ownership and management of ships, the seasons of sailing, numbers of passengers, routes taken, duration of passages, reports about the movements of ships, jettisoning, shipwrecking, piracy and ransoming, and many other related subjects are illustrated by the Geniza records. To be sure, the numbers given above refer solely to the Mediterranean basin. The equally rich Geniza material about the Indian ocean is of a very different character and must be treated separately.

In the following pages, some aspects of medieval sea, river and overland traffic are discussed in order to exemplify the type of information to be gathered from the Geniza records and the problems posed by it.

1. Whenever feasible, people travelled by water and not on land. To quote an extreme case: Around 1140, an Italian Jew, on business in Tripoli, Libya, wanted to travel to Gabes in nearby Tunisia. He was advised by his friends to board a large ship, which was sailing to Seville, Spain and which, with a good wind, would make the passage in eight days, without touching land. Then he was to transfer to another large boat to al-Mahdiyya, the main seaport of Tunisia, and to try to reach his destination from there. This is, of course, quite an exceptional route, but conditions at that time cannot have been too insecure, for in the end the man actually travelled

by land. In general, I estimate the ratio between references to overland travel and references to seafaring in the Geniza, wherever such an alternative existed, as being 1:50.

This statement has to be qualified by two considerations:

(a) A disproportionally large number of Geniza papers comes from the second half of the eleventh century, when overland communications might have been disrupted owing to the invasion of North Africa by the bedouin hordes of the Banū Hilāl and Sulaym. In fact, Geniza references to caravan traffic are more frequent in the first half of that century than in any subsequent period. Still, even at that time, I should estimate the ratio between travel on land and seafaring as 1:20.

(b) Most of the Geniza letters were written by Jews, and Jews did not travel on Saturdays and holidays. A Jew travelling in a caravan, which was en route for more than six days, either stayed behind or hurried ahead of the caravan to celebrate his Sabbath—both cases are mentioned in our records. This, of course, required a special escort and was both expensive and dangerous. If the traveller was rich and particularly influential, he could induce the whole caravan to make a stop on the Sabbath, which is also attested to in a Geniza paper. It may be mentioned in passing that these conditions remained unchanged down to the nineteenth century. The renowned Orientalist Professor A. S. Yahuda (who died in New Haven, Connecticut, in 1951) recounts in his collected essays that his grandfather, when emigrating from Bagdad to Jerusalem in 1852, stipulated that the caravan with which he was travelling, should rest each Saturday, which cost him a huge sum of money. It was due to these circumstances that consignments were confided by Jews to Muslim business friends or pilgrims bound to Mecca, or that we find remarks like the following in letters: "If there be a caravan and if trustworthy Muslims travel in it, kindly send the goods with them." However, such remarks are not very common. As a rule, people travelled by sea, wherever such an alternative existed, even for such a short distance, as Acre—Ramle (viz. Jaffa), Palestine, or Tyre—Tripoli, Lebanon.

Although conditions varied widely, sometimes even during one and the same year, it seems—although this is by no means sure—that discomfort, expenses, and lack of security were greater in travel on land than by sea. Still, there might have been other reasons for this discrepancy between the two methods of transport.

2. Caravan traffic and seafaring were closely coordinated. In winter, when the sea was closed, up to three caravans passed from Sijilmāsa, the great desert port of Morocco—which meanwhile has disappeared—through Kairouan, Tripoli and Barqa to Egypt. In summer, too, caravan traffic had to fill a gap in seafaring. The ships normally sailed in convoys leaving in the spring and setting sail for the return journey at the Feast of the Cross, the ʿĪd aṣ-Ṣalīb, which is celebrated on September 26 or 27. Other convoys departed in the Coptic month of Baoone, which begins on June 7. In between, at the end of May, the summer caravans set out, which needed two to three months for the distance between Egypt and Tunisia, as business was done at the intermediary stations. In one letter, referring to Kairouan, it is stated that the fair connected with the arrival of the caravan lasted twenty days. These long distance caravans were called *mawsim*, the same word which, in the Indian Ocean, designated the seasonal winds, and which, in the form *monsoon*, has entered the English language in the latter meaning. These mawsims and their relationship to seafaring need further clarification.

3. Another most important complement to seafaring, the privately managed overland mail, is almost entirely neglected in the accounts of the Muslim geographers and historians. Passengers and goods went by sea, mail was largely sent by land. In literary sources we hear much about the *barīd*, the mail service maintained by the Muslim governments, just as was the case in medieval China and in the Byzantine empire. However, this service was reserved for the exclusive use of the government and its officials and functioned largely as a means of supervision of the local administration. In the Geniza papers, however, we hear much about another, commercially run, private postal service, which was of utmost importance for the population at large. It was operated by couriers, called *fayj* ("runner")—a Persian word—all over North Africa, and *kutubī* ("bearer of letters") in Western Asia. In one characteristic aspect, this private service followed the practice of the government post. Whilst this last institution maintained numerous relay stations, where the riding animals were changed, one and the same messenger carried the dispatches confided to him from the starting point to the final destination. The same was done by the private couriers. One and the same man would transmit the mail from Kairouan all the way to Cairo, or even from Almeria, Spain, through the whole of North

Africa, to Alexandria. This service was comparatively inexpensive. A letter sent from Almeria to Alexandria cost only one and a half silver dirhams, four letters having been dispatched to the same address, while an urgent, special-delivery letter from Jerusalem to Ramle cost half a dirham. Almost invariably, in letters sent to another country by overland mail, reference is made to goods and business friends going at the same time by boat.[1]

4. In the Middle Ages, owing to the comparatively small size of vessels, no strict distinction was made between seagoing craft and rivercraft. It is therefore not surprising that we occasionally find in the Geniza boats coming from the sea and continuing their way on inland waters or vice versa. Thus we read, e.g., about the ships of a rich Muslim judge from Tyre, Lebanon, which went, via Damietta and the eastern arm of the Nile, to Old Cairo and from there, via the western arm of the Nile and Alexandria, to Tunisia. However, the overwhelming testimony of the Geniza records proves that, as a rule, passengers and consignments left the seagoing vessels in the Mediterranean ports and continued their way inland by other means of transport; mainly on the Nile. The reason for this might have been that owing to the continual changes which took place in the configuration of the bottom of the Nile, navigation on it was dangerous—we read indeed about many shipwrecks on the Nile—and therefore special skill was required, which the ordinary Mediterranean sailor did not possess. A number of special types of craft were used on the Nile: the *ʿushāri*, the river boat; the *jarm*, the barge; the *sumayriyya*, a type imported from Iraq[2]; and a longish, swift boat, called *khīṭī*, for which, under the form *khīṭiyya*, I have found several references for Iraq in earlier Islamic times, but none for Egypt and for the time under discussion, the eleventh and twelfth centuries.

5. As for navigation on the high sea, ships usually sailed in convoys, which in times of danger were accompanied by warships. We read indeed that often the merchantmen were ready to sail and waited only for the men-of-war to join them. Normally, a larger ship was accompanied by a smaller vessel, belonging to the same proprietor or to one of his relatives or friends. Obviously, under certain conditions of rough seas, a smaller craft had more chances

[1] Cf. EI² s.v. *Fuyūdj* and the literature indicated there.

[2] Full literature about this craft in S. M. Stern, "Three Petitions of the Fatimid Period", *Oriens* 15 (1962), p. 175-6.

of survival than a larger one, especially when the latter had lost its sails and rudder, which is reported to have happened. In one case, we read in a Hebrew letter that the "maidservant" boat—as it was called—picked up the survivors from the main ship. Thus far, no references have been found in the Geniza records to lifeboats carried on board, and I am inclined to believe that they were not in use at that time.

6. Of the special types of seagoing craft mentioned in the Geniza records, the most common was a large sailing ship called *qunbār*. This word has not been found as yet in an Arabic dictionary or in Muslim literature. However, the Byzantine Emperor, Leon the Wise (886-912), says in his book on the art of war that the Greek equivalent of *qunbār*, *kombarion*, was borrowed from the Saracens, and his son, the Emperor Constantine VII, describes it as a particularly large ship. The Venetians, too, used this type of vessel in the tenth century, calling it a *gombaria*. However, while the Greeks and Italians refer to the *qunbār* as a man-of-war, the Geniza—to be sure, a century later—knows it only as a ship used for the transport of heavy cargo and passengers.

7. In addition to sailing ships, light galleys, *ghurāb*, propelled solely, or mainly, by oars, were used for travel and transport. The galley had both tactical and nautical advantages over the sailing ship: as it could be turned with ease, it had better prospects of escape from attacks by the ubiquitous pirates, and it was, of course, less exposed to the caprices of the wind. Still, the galley as merchantman is comparatively rare in our records. Seafaring, even along the coasts, appears to have been entirely dependent on the winds. To give just one example: A letter from Alexandria complains that during thirty-three days, with the exception of one large Spanish boat, no ship had arrived, for the winds were neither east nor west winds. In addition, only twenty-three days were left until the ʿĪd al-Ṣalīb, the term for the return journey, so that practically no time was left for business. I wonder whether the economic ascendancy of the Italians over the Arabs was not due partly to the fact that the former built large-sized, oar-propelled galleys for mercantile shipping.

8. Another common type of Mediterranean bottom was the *khinzīra* (not *khinzīr*, which means pig and was used in Syria also as the name of a fish). The word designated in the language of the period a hub or nave of a wheel, which is a rather strange name for a

type of vessel. With this, however, the nickname of a ship, *duwwāma* ("spinning top"), might perhaps be compared. The khinzīra is attested to for Sicily, Tunisia, Tripoli, and Egypt, and a Tunisian khinzīra is once mentioned as sailing on the Nile. Under the form *jansira* it appears in the treaty of October 19, 1181 between the two Italian cities of Pisa and Lucca.

The word *shakhṭūr(a)* has been used until the present day for a coastal craft and is also rather common in the Geniza records. Once, around 1130, we read that such a boat made the journey from Alexandria to Almeria, Spain, in sixty-five days, but went still faster than two Spanish sailing boats, which were about to set sail when it left the harbor of Alexandria. Shakhṭūrs are mentioned in particular on the route between Tunisia, Tripoli and Egypt.

Hajm, normally designating a large drinking bowl, was the name of a type of ship en route between Sicily and Egypt—a name appropriate for a ship with a round hull. Another type, used on the same route, was called *qarrāba*, meaning box, chest. Perhaps it was similar to the East Roman *dromon*, which "was a blunt ship with angular, rather than smoothly flowing lines".[1]

For one type of ship, spelled *sh-ʾ-k-h*, the present writer is unable to provide even the correct pronunciation. It could be *shāka* or *shākha* (and, of course, also *shākka*, etc.), for the Hebrew letter *k* stands for both Arabic *k* and *kh*.[2]

As Spanish Hebrew poets of that period, when describing sea voyages, refer to both sails and oars—although their ships were dependent mainly on the winds—it might be assumed that some of the unidentified types of boats appearing in our records were, like the Italian *tarida*, a cross between a sailing ship and a galley.

9. On various occasions, the Geniza records speak of warships and naval war. Here, too, I would like to single out a detail, for which a parallel from literary sources would be appreciated, namely, the tactical combination of one heavy warship, called *usṭūl*, operating together with light galleys, called *qaṭāʿī*, literally "pieces". The word *usṭūl*, which is, of course, the Greek *stolos* ("fleet"), but designates in the Arabic of that period one heavy warship, as well as *qaṭāʿī*, in the sense just described, are known from other sources.

[1] Cf. Lionel Casson, *The Ancient Mariners*, New York 1959, p. 243, and the photograph of the model made by R. H. Dolley of the British Museum, *ibid.*, opposite p. 219.

[2] Cf. above p. 285.

However, I have not read about their maneuvering together in Arabic sources outside of the Geniza, which mentions this more than once.[1] The term *qaṭāʿī*, or rather *aqṭāʿ*, was used also for boats employed on the arduous trip from Cairo upstream to Qūṣ in Upper Egypt, from where they returned after a stay of only two days. Likewise, the word *ghurāb*, which we have met already as designating the galley used as a merchantman, was applied also to men-of-war. On the other hand, *shīnī*, which, according to Ibn Mammāti, *Qawānīn al-Dawānīn*, p. 240, is a synonym of *ghurāb*, is reserved in the Geniza exclusively for warships, and *aṣḥāb al-shawānī* is a general term for pirates.

10. Finally, the greatest puzzle of Mediterranean shipping, as reflected in the Geniza papers, is its organization. While most of the international trade was based on a widely ramified system of partnerships, destined to minimize the risk of overseas undertakings, a ship was normally owned by one single proprietor. There is nothing in the Geniza comparable to the provisions for joint ownership of boats, so prominent in medieval European sea-contracts, nor to the *loca* or shares in a boat, which dominated Genoese shipping at the end of the twelfth and the beginning of the thirteenth centuries. The situation was rather similar to that prevailing in Genoa at the end of the thirteenth century, when the accumulation of great wealth and power in the hands of the leading families made it possible to dispense with the system of shares. Still, the contrast between the methods generally in use in overseas trade and those regarding the ownership of ships calls for comment.

There is an additional problem in connection with the proprietorship of seagoing vessels—the almost complete absence of local Christians. No reference is made here, of course, to the ships of European Christians, those of Marseilles, Genoa, Pisa, Gaeta, and Norman Sicily, which appear in the Geniza papers of the twelfth century. Of local Christians who bear Arabic names, so far, only two have been found who are explicitly mentioned as ship-owners, and one or two other names of ship-owners, such as al-Iskandar, might have been borne by Christians. It seems that 400 years of naval warfare between Islam and Byzantium had an adverse influence on local Christian shipping.

[1] I learn from a communication by Dr. Lionel Casson that the tactical combination of heavy vessels supported by lighter ones was a common practice in the Hellenistic and Roman fleets.

CHAPTER SIXTEEN

MEDIEVAL TUNISIA
THE HUB OF THE MEDITERRANEAN

A Geniza Study

The country known today as Tunisia is named after the city of Tunis, which became its capital in the second half of the twelfth century. Its previous name was Ifrīqiya, an Arabicized form of Africa, the name of the ancient Roman province occupying approximately the same territory. Frontiers are made by men. Nowhere was this saying truer than with regard to the country in question. The extent of the territory held by the rulers of Ifrīqiya changed incessantly and often included parts or even the whole of present day Algeria and Libya and sometimes even Morocco, or contrarywise, was confined to some sections of the coastal strip of Tunisia proper. Because of this constant fluidity of frontiers, these parts of the Muslim world were mostly known by the general designation al-Maghrib, the West, and its inhabitants as Maghribis, or Westerners.

At a time when traffic moved slowly, the geographical position of Tunisia proved to be exceptionally favorable. It lies halfway between Morocco and Egypt and thus was the very center of the caravan traffic between western North Africa and the countries south of the Sahara on the one hand and Egypt and its eastern and southern neighbors on the other hand. Sicily, the bridge to Europe, could be reached even in small boats, and Tunisia's central position in the Mediterranean made it the natural entrepôt for Eastern and Western goods, as long as it had not yet become habitual for ships to make the long voyage from Spain or France to Egypt or Syria directly.

Everyone knows that Carthage, which is situated in the vicinity of present day Tunis, was the mistress of the middle and western Mediterranean in antiquity, before it was vanquished by Rome. Rebuilt by the Roman emperor Augustus, it regained much of its former splendor and economic power, and became again the capital of an independent state when the Vandals occupied the country in the thirties of the fifth century. In a famous war, Africa was recaptured by the heir of Rome, Byzantium, around 533 A.D., but was lost to the Arabs by the end of the seventh century.

The Arab conquerors had no use for Carthage as a capital, since it was exposed to the raids of the still powerful Byzantine navy. Instead, they built their capital at the safe distance of a two days march from the coast, calling it Kairouan, a name derived from the same Persian word as the English *caravan.* However, in the course of time, the new inhabitants of the country took to the sea, and, during the ninth century, the whole of Sicily and much of southern Italy were conquered by the warriors of Islam. This new turn in the fortunes of Tunisia was followed by the transfer of the capital from the interior of the country to its coast. Meanwhile, another great change had taken place. A Muslim sect, the Ismāʿīlīs, coming from the East, had succeeded in winning over the Kitāma, one of the Berber peoples on which the military strength of Tunisia was based, and, in 909 A.D., al-Mahdī of the dynasty of the Fatimids, which represented one branch of the Ismāʿīlīs, was recognized as ruler of the country. He founded a new capital, a seaport and fortress on the coast east of Kairouan and called it after himself al-Mahdiyya. From their base in Tunisia, the Fatimids expanded over the whole of the Maghrib, including Morocco, and in 969 succeeded in taking Egypt and shortly afterwards parts of Syria. The days of ancient Carthage had reverted or were even surpassed: before the Fatimids moved to Egypt, Tunisia had become again the center of a Mediterranean empire.

How is this ascendancy of Tunisia during the ninth and tenth centuries A.D. to be explained? Generalizations are hazardous in a region in which civil war was endemic even in periods of glorious expansion and where the political constellation changed every few years. It seems evident, however, that the country owed its efflorescence largely to an exceptionally favorable economic constellation. In the whole of Western Europe, particularly in Spain, France and Italy, the darkness and misery of the early Middle Ages had given way to a bright and vigorous economic revival. The products of the East were much in demand. On the other hand, big ships, carrying regularly five hundred passengers together with their goods, and sailing straight from Spain to the Levant, as we find them in the Geniza documents with regard to the eleventh century, were not yet common.[1] Thus it fell to Tunisia and Sicily (and soon also to the

[1] Details in the present writer's forthcoming book *A Mediterranean Society,* Chapter IV.

maritime cities of Italy) to act as distribution centers. Some capable rulers and administrators certainly had their share in bringing about the flowering of the Maghribi empire of the Fatimids. But it was the merchants who formed its economic backbone.

The importance of the Tunisian merchants impressed itself on the present writer with each additional step made in the study of the Judaeo-Arabic documents of the Cairo Geniza.[1] To be sure, no documents from the ninth century and only a few from the tenth have survived. However, during the period between 1000 and 1150, Tunisian merchants appear in the Geniza papers as predominant in the Mediterranean as well as in the India trades. Yet the same source proves that Tunisia itself lost its supremacy during the early decades of the eleventh century, and its enterprising merchants were looking for other countries in which to invest their capital, skill and experience. What was the cause of this eclipse? The transfer of the center of the Fatimid empire to Egypt certainly was a great loss to the country, but the viceroys left by them in al-Mahdiyya vied with their overlords in Cairo in luxury and extravagant undertakings, and no disasters of particularly large dimensions are reported from Tunisia with regard to the first half of the eleventh century. We must therefore assume that factors other than political upheavals, warfare or catastrophes wrought by nature were at work in this process. It was the change in the technique of seafaring alluded to above, coupled with the attainment of maritime supremacy by Christian Europe which robbed Tunisia of the unique position which it had occupied during the ninth and the tenth centuries. International traffic and trade began to bypass the former entrepôt, a change which led automatically to its decline.

On top of this economic eclipse, Tunisia was afflicted with a disaster which, more than three hundred years later, was still remembered with a shudder by the greatest of its sons, the historian Ibn Khaldūn. In the fifties of the eleventh century, when the viceroy of Tunisia broke with the Fatimid caliph, the latter, or rather his vizier, who had been personally offended by the Tunisian ruler, sent against him the Bedouin hordes of the tribes of Hilāl and Sulaym, which previously had emigrated from the Ḥijāz, or north-western Arabia, to Egypt. These tribes devastated and later occupied the open country, sacked and all but destroyed Kairouan and other leading cities, and, being themselves constantly at loggerheads

[1] See above Chapter XIV.

with each other, threw the country into a permanent state of anarchy and confusion. Only al-Mahdiyya and some of the coastal towns remained more or less intact, but, having lost their hinterland, were exposed to attacks by the Italians and subsequently by the formidable Normans. Sicily, which received only feeble support from Tunisia, was gradually occupied by the Normans, and, in 1148, al-Mahdiyya itself, together with the whole coastal zone, fell into the hands of the Christian kings of Sicily. This event was regarded by the writers of the Geniza letters as a great visitation. It was, however, overshadowed, twelve years later, by the conquest of the country by the fanatical Muslim sect of the Almohads, who put to the sword Christians and Jews, as well as Muslims who did not accept their tenets. This final catastrophe is no longer covered by reports from the Geniza, as far as Tunisia is concerned (a detailed report about the Almohads in Morocco and Algeria exists). From that time on, a curtain of silence is drawn over that country, which before had been so often referred to in the Geniza records.

Thus we see that the period between 1000 and 1160 was for Tunisia one of economic decline, followed by catastrophes of unusual magnitude. Yet it is a testimony to the vitality of a great tradition that throughout this period and during the very times of troubles, Tunisia's commerce remained alive, albeit often interrupted by states of war. This, as the Geniza shows, was true not only of the relations with the Muslim countries of the Mediterranean, from Spain in the West to Syria in the East, but in no small degree also of the trade with the Christians, and, in particular, with the Italian city states such as Pisa, Amalfi and Salerno. At the same time, a large exodus of the merchant class must have taken place, in which whole families were transplanted from Tunisia to Sicily and to Egypt and even further afield. It is this great population movement which is to a large extent responsible for the preponderance of Tunisians in the Cairo Geniza.

It took the present writer some time, before he became aware of the unique position of medieval Tunisia. After most of the Geniza material related to the eleventh and the early twelfth centuries had been assembled and scrutinized, it became evident that, in many cases, persons bearing the family names Andalusī, Fāsī, Tāhertī, Siqillī, Iṭrābulsī, etc. did not come from Spain, Morocco, Algeria, Sicily, or Libya, respectively, but had their base in Kairouan and its sister city, al-Mahdiyya.[1] Likewise, of many prominent merchants active in Egypt, not only in Old Cairo (Fusṭāṭ) and Alexandria or the great textile centers of Buṣīr and Tinnīs, but also in many smaller places where flax and indigo, the staple export crops, were grown, it could be established that they were Tunisians who were there on business or had settled in Egypt quite recently, their families often remaining in Tunisia for the time being. That eleventh century Jewish Jerusalem also was largely Maghribī could be concluded from the Geniza texts already published.[2]

This preeminence of the Tunisians in the Geniza papers may have been due in part to some specific circumstance. Most of the "Cairo Geniza" was found in a room for discarded writings attached to the synagogue of the Palestinians in Old Cairo, i.e., people who came originally from Palestine, or at least prayed according to the rite of that country, and were under the jurisdiction of the Palestinian Gaon, or spiritual head of the Jews of that country. Like the churches and other synagogues throughout the Fatimid empire, this synagogue was demolished during the persecution of the religious minorities under the caliph al-Ḥākim. This happened around 1012, but before al-Ḥākim died in 1021, permission for the reconstruction of the destroyed buildings was given. The Palestinians in Old Cairo had great difficulty in rebuilding their place of worship, since the synagogues in Palestine itself, which also was under Fatimid rule, had been destroyed as well. In their distress, they tried to attract the Tunisian merchants who frequented the capital of Egypt—and succeeded. This is born out by the copy of a letter from the main officer of the synagogue to the Gaon of Jerusalem, urging him to confer honorific titles on the Maghribīs, in order to entice them into becoming members of the synagogue of the Palestinians,[3] and is further confirmed by a letter of an Alexandrian visiting Old Cairo, in which he states that the synagogue of the Palestinians was desolate at the time of his visit, because all the Maghribis had gone home

[1] The same can be shown concerning a number of persons with family names derived from towns in Tunisia itself, such as Sfaqsī, Qābisī, Majjānī, Jerbī, etc.

[2] Cf. Dr. H. Z. Hirschberg's "The Relations Between the North African Jewries and Palestine", *Eretz-Israel* V (Mazar Jubilee Volume, Jerusalem 1958), pp. 213-219 (in Hebrew).

[3] Ms. TS 13 J 26, f. 24. All manuscripts bearing the mark TS are preserved in the University Library, Cambridge. Honorific titles were as avidly sought after by the members of the bourgeoisie as by the emirs of Tunisia.

TS 13 J 27, f. 14 is a fragment of a letter by the same officer of the syna-

that particular year.[1] Thus the abundance of material about Tunisia and Tunisians in the Cairo Geniza might have had its reason partly in the fact that, early in the eleventh century, the Geniza synagogue had attracted many members from that country.

On the other hand, of course, the authorities of the synagogue of the Palestinians would not have cared to attract the Tunisians, had they not been prosperous and arriving in considerable numbers. Moreover, as is proven by many Geniza documents, the Kairouanese Jews were in far closer contact with the Jewish academies of Bagdad than with that of Jerusalem and, as the first source quoted p. 312, n. 3 indicates, had joined the Iraqian synagogue in Old Cairo prior to being attracted to the Palestinian. Thus the prominence of Tunisians in the Geniza papers of the eleventh and the first half of the twelfth centuries cannot have been caused mainly by the specific circumstance mentioned above, but must be regarded as a testimony to the general importance of their home country for the Mediterranean trade in that period.

THE TYPES OF SOURCES: I. "RESPONSA"

What is the nature of the Tunisian material found in the Cairo Geniza and how extensive is it?

In this paper, we deal exclusively with *documents,* i.e., legal deeds, accounts, letters, and similar writings, but not with literary creations of Tunisian Jews, many of which have been found in the Geniza. However, mention must be made of one type of material which borders on both kinds of writings: the *responsa,* the *answers* of the heads of the Jewish academies in Bagdad to learned questions addressed to them by Jewish scholars from Kairouan and other cities of Tunisia. These Jewish *responsa* are an equivalent of the Muslim *fatāwā* and, like these, form an important source not only for the knowledge of the development of religious rite, law, and thought, but, to a certain extent, also for social and economic history. In this field, too, Tunisia, has provided far more material than any other country.

gogue of the Palestinians to the same religious authority in Jerusalem (the Gaon Solomon b. Judah) and also speaks about the Maghribīs. However, the fragmentary state of the ms. does not allow any conclusions to be drawn from it besides the fact that Maghribīs figured in the correspondence between these two men.

[1] Ms. TS Box 25, No. 106.

2. LEGAL DEEDS

Of legal deeds, which otherwise constitute about one half of the documentary Geniza, naturally only little could have reached Old Cairo from Tunisia. There are some deeds from Kairouan, dated 977/8, 1032, 1050,[1] and 1055,[2] two from Zawīlat al-Mahdiyya, dated 1047, and 1063 respectively,[3] and a few others which can be placed in the same period. The Kairouan deed from 1055 can compete in size, beauty of script, and excellence of formulation with the very best we have in the Geniza; and in the whole of the Geniza, I have not found anything comparable to ms. Hebr. b3, f. 32 of the Bodleian Library, Oxford, which comes from Zawīlat al-Mahdiyya. This is a fragment of a deed of sale of a bathhouse with a *furnāq*,[4] or heating room, which, by the way, bordered on Muslim property.[5] The deed is written in huge, thick Hebrew letters and must have been enormous in size when complete.

3. ACCOUNTS

Similarly, the accounts coming from Tunisia or Tunisians are among the largest, the most orderly, and partly also the most calli-

[1] The first, TS 12. 468, published by J. Mann, *Texts and Studies* I (Cincinnati 1931), pp. 361-3, the second, TS 8 Ja 2, f. 1, by H. Hirschfeld in *JQR* 16 (1903-4) p. 576, the third, Bodleian ms. Heb. a 2, f. 23, by S. Assaf in *Tarbiz* 9 (1938), p. 215. The rough copy of another Kairouanese document, which must precede the year 1044, Bodleian ms. Heb. c 28, f. 41, is printed *ibid.*, p. 214. The first and fourth of these documents are in Hebrew, the second and the third in Arabic.

The last document deals with a house in Kairouan "at the Bāb Abu 'l-Rabīʿ, "which it describes in detail. However, it was not written in K., as its editor believed, but in Old Cairo. This can now be proved by another document, dated 1040, which deals with the same house and also was made out in Old Cairo (Cambridge Or 1080 J 7). By the way, that house once had been the domicile of the famous scholar Hananel, see p. 317.

The copy of a document drawn up in Zawīlat al-Mahdiyya 1074 is included in a court record from Alexandria, dated 1075 (TS 28.6).

[2] This one, which is in Hebrew, was pieced together by me from the fragments TS 12.634 and 24.18.

[3] Ms. TS 13 J 9, f. 5, and TS 20.187.

[4] From Latin *fornax*. Other parts of the bathhouse mentioned are *bayt al-wasaṭ*, the middle room, *bayt al-ḥawḍ*, the pool, and *al-bīr*, the well. The document is in Arabic.

[5] The fact that the Jews and Muslims in Kairouan lived in close proximity can also be deduced from the fourth document listed in Note 1; for there, too, one side of a Jewish habitation borders on a Muslim house.

graphic of all those found in the Geniza. Some are written on vellum and were obviously copied from letters sent out and were kept in properly bound account books.[1] A very old example is ms. T-S Box K3, no. 36 (Cambridge), which deals with consignments of henna and indigo going by ship from Tripoli to the town of Tunis and from there to Palermo, and huge quantities of robes (*kisā*), hides, and sanitary napkins (linge de propreté pour les femmes) dispatched to Tripoli with the caravan of one Abū Shujāʿ al-Lawātī. Of particular value are three large accounts from the years 1024, 1044-46 and 1046-1048, as they are very detailed and come from the same Kairouanese firm. Naturally, most of these valuable documents have been severely damaged in the course of the nine hundred years which have elapsed since they were written down. However, in the exceptional case, when we have a copy entirely intact, we have to concede that no book could have been written on whiter vellum and in characters more monumental than such an eleventh century account.

From published material, the reader may form an idea about the appearance of such an account by consulting R. Gottheil and W. H. Worrell, *Fragments from the Cairo Genizah in the Freer Collection*, New York 1927, pp. 164 ff., where a facsimile is provided. This is an account for a shipment of purple cloth sent from Old Cairo via Alexandria to the Tunisian seaport of Sfax, containing no less than fifty eight items of expenditure on transport and customs. The sender, although resident in Egypt, is known from other papers as al-Mahdawi, a man whose native city was al-Mahdiyya.[2]

4. LETTERS

While the number of accounts preserved is comparatively small, a great many letters emanating from Tunisia, and even some sent there, have survived. To be sure, it is by no means simple to establish the provenance of a letter and its destination. For only in one out of three letters has the destination, and only in one out of four, has the place of the writer been indicated or preserved. As the letters were usually carried by business friends or by couriers personally

[1] The holes for the threads of the binding are still clearly visible.

[2] Both the transcript and the translation are completely faulty. However, the editors are not to be blamed, for, as the present writer has always emphasized, only after the collection of much material of the same type is the satisfactory publication of a Geniza document possible.

known to both parties, the senders often felt that they could safely dispense with these details. Utmost care has to be taken in determining the place of writing and the destination, if they are not expressly stated in the originals. Even a letter containing a detailed list of prices from Kairouan proved, after close examination and identification of all the persons mentioned in it, to have originated in Alexandria.

In addition to the letters dispatched to and from Tunisia, we must, of course, consider the far greater number of letters written by Tunisians active in Sicily, Egypt, Palestine and Syria.[1] To be sure, Tunisia is also referred to in the correspondence of persons who undoubtedly did not originate in that country. Thus I have collected ten letters by one Isaac ha-Levi Nīsābūrī, whose very name and, in particular, whose faulty Arabic style and spelling prove that he was of Iranian origin. Still, his papers contain valuable information about the trade between Egypt and Tunisia.

However, even if we confine ourselves to letters written by Tunisians, the number of manuscripts encompassed is very considerable. If we disregard many fragmentary pieces, we have at present approximately seventy letters coming from, or addressed to, Tunisia and about four times as many written by Tunisians outside their country. Together with the accounts and the documents discussed above, we arrive at a total of about four hundred Geniza papers connected with eleventh century Tunisia. Many of these are fairly lengthy, the like of which is mostly found only in the business letters from the countries of the Indian Ocean. The longest Geniza letter preserved, containing about four thousand words, was sent to Old Cairo by a Tunisian from Sfax, who was settling in Mazara, Sicily.[2]

THE PEOPLE REPRESENTED IN THE DOCUMENTS DISCUSSED

Naturally, most of the people represented in the papers under discussion were Jews and most of them belonged to the business

[1] We hear in the Geniza frequent mention of Spanish goods reexported from Tunisia. But so far, I have come across only one document from Spain referring to the trade between the two countries (TS 12.570, dated Denia, January 10, 1083, and dealing with a consignment of cinnabar).

[2] Ms. Dropsie College, Philadelphia, Geniza 389 and 414. These documents have been studied by the present writer and have been copied either by him or by Mr. Murad Michael, who is preparing a dissertation on the papers of Nahray b. Nissīm, a merchant, scholar and public leader from Kairouan, who settled in Egypt around 1045, where he was active until 1095.

class. A closer study reveals that many were connected with each other by family or business ties or both. Thus about thirty-five Tunisian families emerge from these documents, of which about ten were particularly prominent. These families in turn were interconnected and formed groups between which, it seems, at certain times some rivalry prevailed. Finally, close, and sometimes very cordial,relations existed between these Tunisian families and some of the leading Jewish families in other countries. Thus the famous Tustarīs of Cairo, i.e., the two uncles and the father of Abū Sa'd al-Tustarī, who in the forties of the eleventh century became the most powerful man of the Fatimid empire, entertained friendly relations with both the Tāhertīs and Majjānīs, two rival clans in Kairouan, cf. above pp. 311-312. Their main representative in that city was Judah b. Joseph, a prominent scholar and member of a family which provided Kairouan with at least four generations of Jewish judges and which was also influential at the court. Judah b. Joseph's son-in-law emigrated to Egypt, where he was, for a time, the Tustarīs representative in Alexandria.

It is noteworthy to remark that the three most prominent Jewish personalities of Kairouan during the first half of the eleventh century have left few traces in the documentary—as opposed to the literary—section of the Cairo Geniza. These were the Nagid (pronounced Nagheed), or official head of the Jewish community, Abū Isḥāq Ibrahīm b. 'Aṭā, who also served as court physician to Bādis, the viceroy of Tunisia (died 1016), and in particular, the latter's son and successor, Mu'izz;[1] R. Hananel, one of the greatest medieval Jewish scholars; and R. Nissīm b. Jacob, also a famous scholar and author.[2] The reason for this must either have been that these men did not engage in business, or that those who did, directed their business to countries other than Egypt. As is well known, Nissīm's

[1] Cf. about him the present writer's "New Sources Concerning the Nagids of Qayrawan", *Zion* 27 (1962), pp. 11-23, and "The Qayrawan United Appeal and The Emergence of the Nagid Abraham ben 'Aṭā", *ibid.*, pp. 156-165 (in Hebrew with English summaries). Another important letter about him, written in August 1015, and another sent by him are published in *Tarbiz* 34 (1964/5), p. 162. See also H. R. Idris in *Annales de l'Institut d'Études Orientales* 13 (1955), pp. 55/6, where an anecdote about him from a Muslim source is quoted.

[2] The distinguished Tunisian scholar H. H. Abdul Wahab devoted a paper to him in *al-Nadwa*, Tunis 1953. A letter from Kairouan by this Nissīm b. Jacob, written in the Arabic language, was published together with a facsimile by J. Mann in *Texts and Studies* I, pp. 142-5. Mann's transcript needs corrections in some places.

daughter was married to the son of Samuel, the Nagid of Granada, Spain.

THE SIGNIFICANCE OF THE GENIZA DOCUMENTS FOR TUNISIAN HISTORY

Despite their origin in one specific religious community, the Geniza documents under discussion have a bearing on Tunisian history in general. They deal with such topics as imports and exports, prices, industry and shipping, as well as the overall situation in the country, thus throwing interesting side-lights on its economic and social life. The political history is illustrated to a lesser degree, and for two reasons. The letters are dated, if at all, according to day and month, but, as a rule, not by the year. Therefore, the exact date of a letter can usually be fixed only if it refers to an event, the date of which is known to us from a literary source. Thus we read in an important letter about Sharaf al-Dawla's (i.e., Muʿizz b. Bādis) expedition against Tripoli in 1022/3,[1] in another, equally interesting, letter about the death of the great Muslim condottiere Ibn Thumna, in 1062, in a third about a raid by the latter on Girgenti,[2] in a fourth about Sultan Tamīm's victory over the rebellious Qā'id of Sfax in 1063/4, and there are, of course, many most eloquent testimonies to the destruction of Kairouan and the inland towns by the Bedouin invaders, around 1057 and the sufferings of al-Mahdiyya and the coastal cities at the hands of the Italians around 1087. Still, the absence of exact dates is embarrassing. Secondly, the value of allusions to political events is often impaired by the use of cryptic language and reference to messages to be delivered orally; the writers of those letters were cautious businessmen who did not want to get into trouble, in the event that their letters fell into the hands of people for whom they were not destined.

Still, the Geniza papers provide food for thought even for the historian interested in the political history of Tunisia. I have in mind, in particular, those passages in the letters from Kairouan which deplore the general decline of the Muslim West during the first decades of the eleventh century, long before the invasion of the

[1] Cf. Ibn Athīr, *Chronicon*, Vol. 9, pp. 230-1.

[2] The Geniza paper speaks about a raid, or *ghazā*, not the conquest of Girgenti. Thus we are here in the fifties of the eleventh century. The raiders took the textiles, but left a hundred skins with oil—certainly because these were too heavy for them, from a ship sailing from al-Mahdiyya via Mazara in Sicily to Alexandria.

"Ḥijāzian" bedouin hordes, as they are called in the Geniza. At the beginning of the century, an angry Kairouani writes to his business correspondent in Cairo: "The little we have here in the West is worth as much as your plenty over there".[1] In a letter written around 1040, another citizen of Kairouan congratulates the addressee on his marriage into a Jewish family in Egypt and his intention to settle in that country, for "the whole West is not worth a thing any more" and in a letter dated August 9, 1048, Kairouan is described as "weak", i.e. poor, "as soon as goods arrive in larger quantities they cannot be sold".[2] Somewhat earlier, Joseph Berechia, one of the leading men of the Jewish community of North Africa at that time, asks a business friend in Cairo whether he could not help him leave the country.[3]

TUNISIAN MUSLIMS IN THE GENIZA DOCUMENTS

In addition, it is perhaps not superfluous to remark that we find quite a number of Tunisian Muslims mentioned in the Geniza papers of that time. Whatever Mālikī or Ismāʿīlī law may say, there were Muslims who contracted standing partnerships with their Jewish countrymen. The greatest business houses seem to have been Muslim, and banking seems to have been in Muslim, rather than Jewish, hands. We read that one such magnate owed the merchants the enormous sum of 4000 gold dinars and when he was unable to fulfill his commitments, the Government ruled that he pay the foreign merchants, while the local people were to be patient until after the ships had sailed. Money and goods were entrusted to Muslim business friends travelling by caravan or ship, while most (if not all) of the many skippers mentioned were Muslims. We find in the Geniza letters warm words and recommendations for Muslim merchants, and Jews would visit their Muslim business friends at home and congratulate them on their holidays.

ECONOMIC LIFE AND EXPORTS FROM TUNISIA

The most important contribution to be expected from the Geniza

[1] David Kaufmann Coll., Budapest, ms. Geniza 13, verso, l. 22.

[2] Bodleian ms. Heb. a 2, f. 17. Catalogue Neubauer-Cowley no. 2805, no. 17. TS 20.69, lines 13-14.

[3] Cf. S. Assaf, *J. N. Epstein Jubilee Volume*, Jerusalem, 1950, p. 185.

papers described above is, of course, the information about the economic life of the country.

The great days for business were the *mawsims*, the fairs connected with the arrival of ships during the summer and of caravans all the year round, but in particular in winter. According to one paper, such a *mawsim* lasted twenty days. Many merchants travelled abroad during summer and "wintered" in Kairouan selling at leisure and slowly laying in stores for their forthcoming trips. While the general principle of Mediterranean medieval trade, viz., selling goods abroad and bringing home goods (but no cash), was also followed in Tunisia, we see, in addition to this, an unceasing stream of gold and silver flowing east; it could be said indeed that the precious metals were one of the main export commodities of the country. Only in absolutely exceptional cases do we hear of cash going west, and then it is old silver money out of currency; and once we hear that the silver sent was melted down in Kairouan.

The list of other goods exported is remarkable both in variety and length. The first items were local fabrics of all descriptions, in particular, the famous sūsī, so called, of course, after the great industrial center of Sūsa.[1] These textiles were partly made of linen, largely imported from Egypt, or of locally grown cotton or of a combination of both. When they were made of silk or brocade or other particularly precious material, this was expressly indicated.

Connected with the textile trade was the commerce in carpets of all descriptions.[2] A particularly valuable and desired article was the *killa*, or canopy, consisting of two parts, e.g., the green variety fabricated in Gabes.

The second largest item of export was silk of all varieties and types of finishing. We seem to have more information about this subject than about any other. As we hear of Spanish and Sicilian—and even more specifically, Syracusan—silk, this was, perhaps, largely a case of re-export.

The same may hold true for the third largest type of goods exported: metals. Copper, lead, tin, and mercury figure regularly in the lists of goods sent from Tunisia, together with some minor by-products of metallurgy. However, iron, which looms so large in the

[1] Cf. above p. 266.

[2] Most of the terms for carpets discussed by G. Wiet in his article "Tapis Egyptiens", *Arabica* 6 (Paris 1959), pp. 1-24, appear in the papers under discussion.

Indian trade, occurs very rarely in the papers under discussion. Whether the Jews had no access to iron in the Mediterranean at that time, or whether the iron trade was limited in general, is a matter for experts to decide.

Of agricultural products, oil and its by-product, soap, took first place. Wax (but not honey) was a very great item of export, as were also the dyeing plant saffron and tar. Shelled almonds were of considerable importance. Salted tuna fish was perhaps sent to Egypt more as a present than as a commercial item.

I have not yet formed a definite opinion about the consignments of wheat mentioned in the Geniza papers as going from Tunisia to Egypt. The quantities involved mostly seem too small for mercantile purposes. Perhaps the wheat was ordered late in spring when it had already become apparent that the Nile was low and that prices would be high in Egypt. Or did the taste of bread made from Tunisian wheat differ from that made from Egyptian, and the Tunisians abroad did not want to forgo their usual diet?

Livestock must have been most abundant in Tunisia at that time. Hides, *naṭʿ*, were one of the staple exports, and are rarely absent from any larger consignment going east. On the other hand, wool played a negligible role in overseas trade—as far as our sources go.

Needless to say, coral beads, both strung and unstrung, were among the standard items of export, as they had been already in Roman times. The prices for this commodity were naturally low in comparison with the quantities involved.

Finally—and this is most characteristic—books, both in Hebrew and in Arabic—were an important item of export to the East. Kairouan was a great center of learning and active in the production of books, and booksellers were as eager to acquire the libraries of famous scholars at that time as they are today. Thus a cousin of the aforementioned Nahray, who was an ardent dealer in books, writes to him from Alexandria: "I have heard that so and so, the son of the sister of the Dayyān (the Jewish judge of Kairouan) has died. He possessed the choicest codices and books from the libraries of our masters, Nissīm, Hananel, and Berechia; please take notice of this."[1] In another letter to the same person, a scholarly merchant from al-Mahdiyya explains that life in Tunisia had become un-

[1] TS 10 J 20, f. 18, verso, ll. 4-6 (No. 36 of Mr. Michael's collection of the papers of Nahray b. Nissīm). For the names mentioned here cf. above pp. 317 and 314.

bearable. One of the things which still kept him there was the prospect of acquiring some rare books from the libraries of the great scholars who had lived in that country.[1]

IMPORTS

There is no point in trying to enumerate the many items of import to Tunisia during the eleventh century. This would be tantamount to a list of commodities needed by any civilized Mediterranean society of that age. There were, of course, the Oriental spices and perfumes, the most important being pepper, cinnamon, clove, ginger, myrabolan, musk and camphor; the dyeing plants, and above all indigo and brazilwood (*baqqam*); the varnishes, and in particular lacquer, a most important article; the interminable list of medical plants and drugs, coming from almost every part of the ancient world and often bearing curious names; some chemicals, headed by sal ammoniac, a staple good; materials for jewelry, such as pearls, precious stones, lapis lazuli, various kinds of beads, as well as cowrie shells. Of foodstuffs, sugar and rose marmalade were of some importance.

There was, however, one staple good which outweighed all the others both in quantity and value; Egyptian flax, of which about seventeen varieties appear in the Geniza papers. Flax was so much the normal freight going to Tunisia that one often wrote in a letter: I am sending you so and so many *ʿidl*, or bales,[2] without specifying what was in them, because it was understood to be flax.[3] From this flax, the famous sūsiyyāt and other Tunisian fabrics were produced, which, in turn, went eastwards.

In addition to this raw material, a great variety of finished textiles was imported into Tunisia. The rich Kairouanis seem to have had extravagant tastes for costly and gorgeously colored fabrics, those of Iranian provenance in particular. The textiles referred to were *aʿlāq*, single pieces of special value, rather than articles sold in large numbers, although these, too, were found among the textiles imported.

[1] TS NS J 271.

[2] An *ʿidl* nominally contained 500 pounds, packing included. The net weight used to be around 490 pounds, but often also much less.

[3] Of course, in the bill of lading, *tadhkira* or simply *ruqʿa*, which was sent separately (some have survived), the exact weight and value of each bale and often also the variety of linen concerned would be indicated.

PRICES AND MONEY

Business intelligence was as important in the middle ages as it is in our own times. Therefore, we find much information about prices—not only those actually obtained or desired, but "market prices", sometimes long lists of them. For Kairouan we have even the particular case of two such lists written by the same person to the same address and separated from each other by only four days, so that slight fluctuations can be observed and—through the accompanying letter—be explained.

This vast subject cannot even be touched upon here. However, two basic facts emerge from the hundreds of details: the prices for the commodities of import and export show an amazing stability on an international scale for almost a century. Fluctuations caused by changes in supply and demand (often explained in the letters), circumstances of war or intensified piracy, the non-arrival of ships that were expected or the arrival of unexpected ships must, of course, be taken into consideration. On the other hand, the two main staple crops of the country, wheat and oil, exhibit the most incredible ups and downs even in subsequent years—a fact only partly discernible in the literary sources.

The relative stability of prices implies the existence and relative stability of the currency. Money in the Geniza papers is another bewildering and most diffuse subject. However, the more material we have about both the Indian and the Mediterranean trade, the clearer certain basic trends become. Standard money is *jawāz al-sharq*, Fatimid gold dinars coined in the East. The value of silver money sent from Tunisia varies according to the mint, age, and the state of the coins concerned. There were three entirely different types of dirhams; one, whose exchange rate with the dinar was 1:12-16; another, and this was the normal, 1:36 (with many variations, from 1:33, 3 to 50); and thirdly, a whole group, differentiated according to the names of the minters or other designations, varying from 1:125-260, with 200 as the average, and with one exceptional and sudden devaluation to 1:1600.[1] Sicilian quarter dinars

[1] In the Bodleian ms. Heb. b 13, f. 49 (Catalogue Neubauer-Cowley 2834, No. 30), a letter written around 1060, we read, l. 28: "Then I went down to Sūsa (from al-Mahdiyya) to see the family and to sell the consignment brought with me (of course, flax from Egypt). When I left, the rate of exchange was below 200. It became, while my dirhams remained there in cash,

or *ṭaris*[1] were extremely frequent, and as early as ca. 1063 pepper was traded in al-Mahdiyya only for Sicilian and Pisan coinage.[2]

SHIPPING

As far as the transport of goods is concerned, there was a marked difference between the first and the second half of the eleventh century. While caravans are frequently referred to in the earlier period, in the second, traffic, to a large extent, seems to have been confined to the sea. The bedouin conquest of North Africa seems to have made traffic by land almost impracticable.

The Geniza abounds in information about sea traffic. Tunisia had more than its fair share in this economic activity. We frequently read about *markab al-sulṭān*, the ship of the sultan, and it is evident that in this period the reference is to the ruler of Tunisia. For at one time—perhaps owing to a state of war—when no ships except the Sultan's boat was making the voyage to Egypt, Judah b. Joseph, the Jewish notable of Kairouan mentioned before, obtained the special privilege of sending goods belonging to himself and to three Jewish business friends in it.[3] It also seems that ships bearing names such as *al-maymūn*, "the auspicious", and *al-mubārak*, "the blessed", were government ships. Boats belonging to the "Illustrious Lady", *al-sayyida al-jalīla*, are also referred to; perhaps this was Umm al-ʿUluww, the sister of the Sultan Muʿizz. She received one million dinars as her dowry and had to invest her capital somehow. Thus apparently, she bought ships, as did other royal ladies down

1600. Thus one dinar was reduced to the value of one qirāṭ." (The writer says, with some exaggeration, that the value of his (silver) money was reduced to 1/24; a dinar has twenty four qīrāṭs).

[1] Without wishing to advance a new theory about the much debated origin of this term, the present writer would like to draw attention to the fact that the Geniza papers speak about "fresh" dinars, in Arabic ṭarī, e.g., in the letter quoted in the following note (with regard to dinars of the Fatimid caliph al-ʿAzīz (976-996). Thus it may be that this usage has something to do with the name of the Norman quarter dinar.

[2] TS 16. 163.

[3] He was, however, advised to pack the goods not as usual in bales (*ʿidl*, see above, p. 322), but in *barqalōs* (a package of nominally 200 pounds), certainly in order to make the ship more manageable in the case of an enemy attack.

The word *barqalō*, which is extremely common, most probably is derived from *barca*, barque, just as modern Italian *barcata*, ship's load, but sounds more like a misunderstood *barcaiuolo*, boatman.

to Marie Antoinette.[1] A *markab al-qā'id*, a ship belonging to a general or governor is also frequently referred to.

Finally, mention should be made of Jabbāra b. Mukhtār, emir of Barqa, who was under the suzerainty of Tunisia.[2] He looms large in the Geniza papers as a redoubtable pirate, a carrier of goods and as a protector of ships against other pirates—three roles which went well together in those times.

Private shipping was also largely in Tunisian hands. The proof for this, however, has to be deferred until the Geniza material on seafaring in the Mediterranean has been fully investigated. The ships were normally called after their proprietors or captains, or had fanciful names, such as *mi'ḍād*, butcher's knife (so called perhaps because of its quick cutting of the waves), *'abūr*, sirius (the brightest star in the sky), *'arūs*, bride, etc. Very rarely does the skipper's name refer to a port, such as the frequently mentioned *markab al-binzertī*, the ship of the man from Bizerta. The Westerners, i.e., the Tunisians, were so renowned as good sailors, that all poor Maghribis found in Cairo were pressed indiscriminately into the service of the Egyptian navy.[3]

THE PERSONALITY OF TUNISIA

The Tunisian Jews, whose correspondence was discussed in the previous pages, formed a prosperous society, because Tunisia in the tenth and the first half of the eleventh century provided a congenial environment for them. It was a country where, as in the Talmudic saying, "the scholars were the kings". The leading economic and social position of the Jewish scholars in their own community was parallelled by similar phenomena in the Muslim society of that country. We have had opportunity to refer to prominent Jewish scholars and community leaders of the eleventh century. From the preceding century it is sufficient to mention Isaac Israeli, one of the most conspicuous medical writers of the middle ages, and his disciple

[1] Cf. E. Fagnan, *Al-Bayano 'l-Mogrib I*, Alger 1901, pp. 406-7. The actual amount of the dowry was probably only a fraction of this figure. The sayyida bestowed robes of honor and other favors on one of the Tāhertīs, most probably one of her agents. Professor H. R. Idris, who kindly read the manuscript of this paper, suggests that the title "Illustrious Lady" may refer to the aunt of Sultan Mu'izz Umm Mallāl.

[2] Fagnan, *op. cit.*, p. 432 (referring to 1051/2; however, Barqa was given by al-Ḥākim already to Mu'izz' father, in 1012/3, see *ibid.* ,p. 385).

[3] Maqrīzī, *Khiṭaṭ*, Bulāq 1270/1853, I. p. 368.

Dunash b. Tamim. The scholarly atmosphere of Tunisia can be seen not only in the *responsa*, but in personal and business letters as well. A good example is a letter sent by a merchant and scholar in or shortly before 1062, from al-Mahdiyya to Old Cairo, congratulating his younger brother on the birth of his first-born son and then going on to discuss business and public affairs. Despite the many subjects touched upon, emphasis is clearly laid on the fact that the addressee, although engaged in big business, had not neglected his study of the Bible, the Mishna, and the Talmud. These he studied under the direction of a "master" (*Rāv*) who was a native of Tunisia, and whose very coming to Egypt had led to a revival of Jewish studies in that country. That *Rāv* followed the methods of the great Tunisian scholar already mentioned, Nissīm b. Jacob, who was still alive at the time that letter was written. The newborn child was presented by the whole family with a Bible codex—an extremely precious gift—which had been lost during the pillage of Kairouan, but had been ransomed from the raiders. A considerable part of the codex was missing. It was to be restored—of course, in Tunisia—before being sent off to Egypt.[1]

Another characteristic trait of Tunisia at that time was the love of music, called *li'b*, literally, play, in the vernacular of the country. As is well-known, the ruler of Tunisia, Mu'izz b. Bādis, was himself a great musician, and as a famous Tunisian of the fourteenth century has remarked, the population of a country normally has the same inclinations as its rulers. According to the letter just mentioned, the news of the birth of the baby in Fusṭāṭ was celebrated with much *li'b* by the family in al-Mahdiyya, and it is certainly not by chance that the famous *responsa* against instrumental music by the Gaon Hay of Bagdad (died 1038) were addressed one to the scholars of Kairouan and the other to those of Gabes, Tunisia.

We have already referred to the extravagance in clothing—to which perfuming is also to be added—indulged in, even by prominent scholars. There are indications that this indulgence was curbed, either by Government policy or arbitrarily by powerful officials who coveted the exquisite garments for themselves.

There are interesting peculiarities in the form of letters coming from Tunisia, which to explain here would lead us too far afield. Naturally, the local language and popular wisdom have also found

[1] TS 16. 179. Translated into English in the present writer's *Readings in Mediterranean Social History*.

their echo in the Geniza papers. Expressions such as *aṣbaḥ*, "prettier", or *rākhī*, "inexpensive", are typically Tunisian, and there are many other instances of the local vernacular, especially in spelling and grammatical usage. As almost all the writers of these letters were widely travelled, we cannot know with certainty which of the proverbial sayings used by them were particular to their countries of origin, even if we do not find them in other Geniza letters. In one case, a proverb is quoted as used in Tunisia; the writer of the letter summarized above, p. 326, makes the following remark: "How could I worry about twenty dinars, after what I have lost in Kairouan. Here, they say in the way of a proverb: If all that's left of your food is a crumb, throw it into the sea."[1]

Finally, Tunisians are often recognizable by their names. There are family names which clearly indicate Berber or ancient African origin, such as Yijū, Sighmār, or Masnūt,[2] while personal names like Labrāṭ, Līmāṭ, or Dunash (mostly written *dnsh*) seem to belong to the same category. There are the countless names ending in *ūn*, such as ʿAbdūn, ʿAllūn, ʿAzrūn, Barhūn, Faḍlūn, Farḥūn, Farjūn, Gannūn, Ḥakmūn, Ḥayyūn, Karmūn, Khalfūn, Naṣrūn, Rabʿūn, Saʿdūn, Sahlūn, Samḥūn, Saydūn, Sḥaqūn, Shaʿbūn, Shaʿyūn, Ṣalḥūn, Tībūn, Zaydūn. Similarly, there are a number of very common names having the form *faʿʿūl*, such as ʿAbbūd, Ḥassūn, Khallūf and ʿAllūsh.[3] Finally, there are names, both in Arabic and in Hebrew, which are common in the West, but so rare in the East (before it was flooded with Tunisians from ca. 1050 on), that one must assume that their bearers were of Maghribi extraction; thus we find the name Maymūn seven times in a very ancient document from the town of Tunis,[4] among forty names preserved, and Raḥamīm (Hebrew for "mercy") three times, names which were next to

[1] *Idhā lam yabqa min zādak illa kaʿba, iṭraḥhā fi 'l-baḥr.*

[2] Professor L. Galland of the École des Langues Orientales Vivantes, in his letter to me, dated May 20, 1958, kindly drew my attention to J. B. Chabot, *Recueil des Inscriptions Libyques* (Paris 1940), p. XIX, where names with *MSN* recur twenty times, with two cases of *MSNT* and one, particularly significant, of *MSNBT* (No. 330). Thus we have Libyan origin of the name of at least one Jewish family, which is attested to both by various Geniza documents and in literary sources, Samuel b. Nissīm Masnūt being the author of a well-known commentary on Job and of other works; cf. S. Buber in *Harkavy Jubilee Volume* (St. Petersburg 1908), p. 391, and *Qiryat Sepher* 38 (1963), p. 287.

[3] Meaning "lamb" in the local vernacular (see M. Beaussier, *Dict. Arabe-Français*, Alger 1958, s.v.).

[4] TS 16. 177.

unknown in Egypt at that time. In the West—but not in Egypt—the girls sometimes bore the names of Biblical heroines, which also testifies to the more scholarly atmosphere of Tunisia.

GENIZAS IN TUNISIA?

I should like to conclude this sketch with an appeal to archaeologists active in the countries of ancient Ifrīqiya. Seeing that the Jews of Tunisia were accustomed to deposit even their accounts and their business letters in the Geniza of Old Cairo, one wonders whether they have not done the same at home. There may be places in Tunisia, Algiers and Libya with climatic conditions similar to those of Cairo, i.e., favorable to the conservation of paper. Perhaps, one day, a Geniza may be discovered in North Africa even richer than the Cairo Geniza with regard to the subject dealt with here.

CHAPTER SEVENTEEN

LETTERS AND DOCUMENTS ON THE INDIA TRADE IN MEDIEVAL TIMES

Until a few years ago, no letters or documents illustrating the medieval trade with India had been known to exist on either the Arabian or the eastern shores of the Indian Ocean. Yet the India trade was the backbone of international economy in the Middle Ages in general and inside the Islamic world in particular. More than anything else it stimulated interterritorial traffic, furthered the rise of a flourishing merchant class and created close and fruitful links between the countries of Islam and the Far East on the one hand and Europe on the other. In later medieval times, it was the search for the direct sea route to India which led to the discovery of America and other hitherto unknown parts of the globe and thus inaugurated the age of the unification of all mankind.

The archives of the cities and kingdoms of Italy, France and Spain have preserved records concerning their trade with the countries of the southern and eastern shores of the Mediterranean, especially from the twelfth century onwards. This was to a large extent a transit trade, a re-export of Oriental goods, originally brought from the countries of the Indian Ocean to Egypt, Palestine, Lebanon and Syria. However, no such archives have existed, or have been saved in the countries of Islam.[1] Yet it is difficult, if not impossible, to draw a detailed picture of such a complicated socio-economic phenomenon as a great international trade without the help of letters and documents illustrating how this trade actually worked. Fortunately, it has been possible to assemble during the last ten years or so a collection of records, written mostly in the Arabic language, albeit nearly exclusively with Hebrew characters, which provide much of the desired information. These Judaeo-Arabic documents are mostly of the eleventh and twelfth centuries. They had been originally preserved in the so-called Cairo Geniza and are dispersed at present in many libraries of Europe and

[1] Cf. J. Sauvaget-Cl. Cahen, *Introduction to the History of the Muslim East*, Univ. of Calif. Press 1965, p. 16.

the United States.[1] A first report about the Geniza papers as related to the India trade was provided in *Speculum*, the Journal of the American Mediaeval Academy, in April 1954.[2] Meanwhile, many new finds have been made and the whole material was subjected to a systematic re-examination. In the following pages, a preliminary report about the main results of this scrutiny will be provided.

In order to forestall misunderstandings, I should like to remark at the outset that the share of the Jewish merchants in the India trade seems to have been comparatively modest. Their papers are treated here for the simple reason that thus far they are the only ones which have survived.

The present writer's occupation with this valuable material came about quite fortuitously. Being interested in the interplay of Muslim and Jewish law, as it was evident in many records of the rabbinical courts found in the Geniza, I began collecting such records. One day, while browsing through an ancient stock of Geniza papers preserved in the University Library, Cambridge, England, I came upon the minutes of a court session dealing with a business trip to India, made by a merchant from Tripoli, Libya, called Joseph Lebdi. Examining other Geniza collections preserved in the same library, and while commuting between Oxford and Cambridge, I was able to piece together the whole dossier of this case, comprising the records of eleven sessions held between November 9, 1097 and August 18, 1098. Four other documents connected with this lawsuit were also found. This was a startling discovery. For up to that time, only very few and disconnected Geniza fragments dealing with the India trade had been published (including one treated by the present writer). If such precious material about as fascinating a subject as the India trade during the eleventh century had escaped the attention of the scholars up to that time, one was entitled to assume that the Geniza contained much more information about it not yet registered. Subsequent visits to the libraries concerned proved that this assumption was more than justified. Slowly, the disjointed fragments became meaningful and the personalities of the more important merchants and communal leaders took shape. In the article of 1954, referred to above,

[1] Cf. above Chapter XIV.

[2] "From the Mediterranean to India: Documents on the Trade to India, South Arabia and East Africa from the Eleventh and Twelfth Centuries", *Speculum* 29 (1954), pp. 181-197.

the present writer was able to report about one hundred and thirty Geniza papers dealing with the India trade. At the time of the writing of these lines (July 1965), the number of relevant items has risen to three hundred and thirty. However, no substantial increase is expected, except of course in case some new Geniza collections should be discovered.

This search for Geniza records needs some elucidation. As has been explained elsewhere, the Geniza is not an archive, but the opposite of it, a kind of wastepaper basket, into which discarded writings were thrown often after they had been torn apart and in which all its contents were mixed up topsy turvy.[1] Thus one leaf of the minutes of a court session dealing with the case alluded to above was found in Cambridge and the second in Oxford. Of a letter sent from Aden, South Arabia, to India, three fragments have been preserved in three different collections, and there are at least ten other cases of documents pieced together from fragments preserved in two or three separate collections of manuscripts.

As a rule, there is no connection whatsoever between one Geniza fragment preserved in a library and the other following it in the same series. Under these circumstances, there is no other way for the student but to try to scrutinize the whole of the existing Geniza documents (there are about ten thousand of them), a task made difficult not only by their very number, but also by the poor state of preservation of many of them and the additional difficulties of palaeography, language and subject matter. The existing catalogues of Geniza collections are of no help, since they are not detailed enough to indicate whether a fragment refers to the India trade or not. Thus, the best of all printed catalogues, that of the Bodleian Library, Oxford, gives one instance of a letter from India, while in fact over thirty documents in that collection deal with our subject.

There are, however, some mitigating circumstances. A considerable part of the material preserved represents the remnants of archives of families or individual merchants. Once the pieces which originally had emanated from one and the same source have been reunited, many puzzles find their solution and coherent stories can be reconstructed. Similarly, in each period certain personalities and issues were predominant, a circumstance which also enables us to coordinate the *disjecta membra* of the Geniza. Finally, the letters, contracts and court records are mostly written in a clear and factual

[1] Cf. above p. 287.

fashion, so that even small fragments often contain a complete and intelligible piece of information.

The term India trade is taken here in the widest sense of the word, comprising commercial activities and travel stretching from the ports of the Red Sea in the West to the shores of Sumatra, Indonesia, in the East. As may be remarked in passing, not a single Geniza letter referring to direct contacts with China has been discovered thus far. A number of items, not related to the area of the Indian Ocean, as defined above, but connected with prominent India traders, has also been included. For when we find a merchant one year out in India, and the following year in Spain and Morocco selling Oriental products, it stands to reason that his activities in the farthest West were closely connected with those in the countries of the Indian Ocean. In addition, some documents throwing light on the personality and the cultural level of the merchants concerned were also taken into consideration. About eighty of the three hundred and thirty items referred to above have only an indirect bearing on the subject.

On the other hand, hundreds of Geniza papers not included in the collection described here are of importance for the history of the India trade. These are letters dealing with the commerce between the countries of the Mediterranean basin, mainly during the eleventh century, in which regular mention is made of the products of the Orient alongside of those of the countries directly concerned. For reasons of expediency these Mediterranean papers are dealt with separately.

Most of the Geniza papers related to the India trade are letters. Many were sent from Aden or another town in Southern Arabia, from a Red Sea port, or from India to the capital of Egypt, or vice versa. Others—the most interesting ones—went from Aden to India or vice versa, or even from one place in India to another. Still others were exchanged between Arabia and ports of the Red Sea. It is astonishing that all these letters have found their way into the Cairo Geniza. Many of them must have remained in India (whose climate and termites are not very merciful to paper) for a considerable number of years and then were exposed to travel by sea via Arabia to a Red Sea port and from there to a march through a terrible desert, until a town on the Nile was reached. The journey on the Nile, which also required several weeks, was by no means safe from danger. Despite all this discomfort, the merchants kept their records for so long a time in order to protect their rights. Neither Muslim nor Jewish law of that period knew forfeiture by the statute of limitations and, as an Arab proverb has it, "the bankrupt rummages the business papers of his father" (in order to find a forgotten claim against a debtor).

Due to the precariousness of communications, letters were usually sent in duplicates or triplicates in two or three different ships, and many statements referring to this custom are found in the Geniza papers. The present writer has repeatedly found fragments of two and even of three copies of one and the same letter. This proves, of course, that in the cases concerned, all the copies had arrived safely and were carried by the receiver all the way from India to the capital of Egypt. Copies of the same letter are often written in different hands, which shows that a larger firm employed two or more clerks. The original, written by the head of the firm, would also be sent along.

A few family letters sent e.g. from Aden to Sicily, or from Dahlak on the southern tip of the Red Sea to Tripoli, Libya, or from Alexandria to India, have been found in the Geniza, but not a single business letter going from a place south-east of Egypt to a Mediterranean country west of Egypt, or vice versa. This can hardly have been due to mere chance. Rather, it indicates that Old Cairo served as terminus both for the Mediterranean and the Indian trade. Although, as we shall presently see, most of the India travellers came from the Western countries of the Mediterranean, it was impracticable to do business between India, or even Arabia or East Africa, and Sicily, Tunisia or Spain directly. The fluctuation of prices on the bourses of Old Cairo was so great and the time required for travel from the western Mediterranean to the countries of the Indian Ocean so long that it was of no avail to place orders from one of those distant parts to the other. One sold and bought in Old Cairo. Even from Alexandria one would normally order Oriental goods from the capital of Egypt, not from any point beyond it.

Business letters invariably open with polite and often very dignified phrases which occupy between four to sixteen lines, depending on the circumstances, five to eight lines being the average. From the wording of the introduction one can immediately recognize the respective social position of the two correspondents, as well as the state of business between them. Unfortunately, the recipients had the habit of cutting off this preamble, which was not needed for reference, and used the free space on the back as scrap paper. Since that space regularly also contained the address, this habit is, from our point of view, rather disappointing. One may ask how the recipients themselves remembered the names of the senders; for letters, as a rule, were not signed, but bore the sender's name on the left side of the address. The answer is that the identity of the sender was recognized by his handwriting or that of his clerk.

The first part of the main body of a letter acknowledges the arrival of the goods, letters or messengers sent by the addressee or announces their loss through shipwreck or attack by pirates. The letter then describes the actions taken with respect to the addressee's orders. In the second part, the writer would deal with his own shipments. Personal or communal affairs would also be referred to, as a rule briefly, but sometimes at great length.[1] Near the end, the presents accompanying the goods ordered would be enumerated, a section usually opening with the phrase; "I am enclosing also items of no value or significance whatsoever". In the Mediterranean correspondence, one out of fifty letters would contain such a section. In letters going between Aden and the Malabar coast it is commonplace. Thus one is induced to assume that the regular attachment of presents to commercial shipments was a custom taken over from the Indian merchants.

Practically every letter concluded with greetings to the recipient's household (including his Indian business agent, who was legally his slave) and his friends. For us, these greetings are of great importance, for the names mentioned in them often enable us to identify the addressee and in some instances also the writer, in case the address has not been preserved.

Items of private correspondence of the India merchants have also found their way into the Geniza. Novices in those foreign parts would describe the terrors of the Indian Ocean, which was so different from the quiet waters of the Mediterranean, and the ships which were held together by ropes instead of nails, or complain about their loneliness and miserable home-sickness. The merchants would send home presents and goods for the use and maintenance of their families or more distant relatives, as well as donations for religious scholars or institutions. Announcements of such shipments as well as thanks for their receipt, often very elaborate, have been preserved. The presents were of the greatest possible variety, rank-

[1] As in the letters published in "Two Eyewitness Reports on an Expedition of the King of Kish (Qais) against Aden", *BSOAS* 16/2 (1954), pp. 248-257.

ing from Oriental spices and costly textiles to Chinese porcelain or an Indian slave girl of six, whom the merchant's wife back home would bring up to become her personal attendant.

As far as we are able to ascertain, merchants normally did not take their wives while travelling to the countries of the Indian ocean. Since it was customary to remain in the East for several seasons, long years of separation ensued, and sometimes tensions resulted which are reflected in the Geniza letters. Travel, no doubt, had also a romantic aspect. The beauty and sweetness of the women of Yemen is praised in both the Hebrew and the Arabic literature of the period. In one instance, a traveller from Spain married a Yemenite girl; the representative of the Jewish merchants of Old Cairo most prominent in the Geniza papers was married to a lady from Aden. It should be remarked that not only the wives, but also the parents, sons or brothers of the India travellers displayed great distress over the long absence of their beloved. All in all, the family letters are a valuable source of information for the social aspects of overseas commerce.

The second largest group of Geniza papers referring to the India trade is composed of documents of legal character. Invariably, a merchant embarking on so long a journey did business not only for himself, but also for others, or acted at one and the same time as an agent for one or, usually, several investors. In such a case, a deed of *commenda*, or "partnership according to Muslim law", as it was called in Jewish legal parlance, would be drawn up. When the traveller came home, or even when he returned only from India to Aden, he would make a statement about his dealings in the interest of his partners and deposit it with the local rabbinical or Muslim court. The partners, on their part, would write out a release showing that the transaction had been concluded to their complete satisfaction. Naturally, things did not always go smoothly. The resulting disputes would be aired before the rabbinical court, which had largely the character of a merchants' court, since most of its members were experienced business men. Custom, reason and expedience, rather than any written law, formed the basis of their decisions. Since shipwreck was a recurrent feature of seafaring on the Indian Ocean, statements about men perished and goods lost, or goods retrieved by divers, were made before the nearest court and forwarded to the parties concerned. The estates of merchants whom death overtook on their travels would be carefully listed, in order to preserve them for their heirs back home—to be sure, as far as they could be saved from the rapacity of the Sultans in whose territories the death occurred. Discord about communal leadership (which was not unrelated to business, the safety and efficiency of which depended largely upon the local representative of the merchants) is also reflected in legal documents. Even poems extolling the merits of these leaders are not without historical value.

In addition to letters and legal documents, the Geniza has preserved a variety of smaller items related to the India trade. Memos accompanying shipments specify the goods sent, their quantity and often also their price and also contain sometimes instructions on how to dispose of them. We have some accounts of a brass factory in India, specifying the materials used and the wages paid. Unfortunately, items of this type are comparatively rare, presumably because there existed no religious scruples about their destruction, since they did not contain the name of God.

As to subject matter and personalities mentioned, the Geniza records on the India trade collected thus far refer to the following topics:

1. The Lebdi lawsuit of 1097/8, alluded to above p. 330. A detailed description of Joseph Lebdi's travel to India, his commercial activities and experiences, as well as some additional information about him and the other persons involved in the lawsuit, have been provided in the *Speculum* article referred to above.[1] This family of India traders can be traced in the Geniza through two and a half centuries.

2. The family of Maḍmūn ben[2] Ḥasan ben Bundār, a shipowner and representative of merchants in Aden. His father was representative of the merchants in Aden at the time of Joseph Lebdi's trip and is mentioned as such also in other Geniza papers from the second half of the eleventh century. Maḍmūn himself was active during the first half of the twelfth century (he died in 1151) and was succeeded by his eldest son. Another Maḍmūn (ben David), presumably his great-grandson, held the same position in Aden around 1220.

3. Abraham ben Yijū[3] of al-Mahdiyya, Tunisia, resident in India

[1] Pp. 191-195.

[2] Arabic and Hebrew for "son". The pronunciation of this little word was subject to changes not recognizable in the script of the Geniza records.

[3] The family name Benichou, written today in Arabic and Hebrew *bnyshw* (as it is occasionally spelled also in the Geniza), is common today among all

during the years 1132 through 1149. The letters addressed to and sent by him during this period constitute the most important part of the India papers preserved. Ben Yijū possessed also a brass factory in India, about which we hear much. After his return to Aden, he spent several years in Yemen. However, after his only son died there, he went back to Old Cairo in order to marry off his only daughter to a member of his family, which had emigrated from Tunisia to Sicily during the years of his absence. Three nephews followed the invitation of the old India trader and travelled from Mazara, Sicily, to Old Cairo. The rich heiress' marriage contract with her eldest cousin is preserved in the Public Library of Leningrad.

4. Ḥalfōn ben Nethanel Dimyāṭī (family name derived from Damietta, the Mediterranean port on the right arm of the Nile) of Old Cairo. In a letter from Spain he was called "the man who is the center of all the leading personalities of his time"—a designation well deserved in view of his extended travels, his wide cultural interests and his high social position. We are able to follow his commercial and other activities in Egypt, India, Yemen, Morocco and Spain from approximately 1125 through 1146.

5. Other important India merchants:

(a) Abū Zikrī Kohen Sijilmāsī, from Sijilmāsa (once a great caravan city in Morocco), a representative of merchants in Old Cairo who made prolonged journeys to India and also entertained close relations with his home country Morocco. Dated documents: 1132 through 1148.

(b) ʿArūs ben Joseph from al-Mahdiyya, Tunisia, possessor of a purple-dye workshop in Old Cairo and active both in the Mediterranean and the Indian trade, but more prominent in the former. First quarter of the twelfth century.

(c) and (d) Two Adenese merchants and public figures, cousins of Maḍmūn I, referred to above, No. 2 and closely connected with Nos. 3, 4, and 5a.

(e) A dozen other merchants, often referred to, but only slightly represented by letters sent or received by them.

6. Legal matters, such as contracts of partnerships or releases, court records, memos etc. emanating from persons other than Nos. 1-5.

the Jews of North Africa, cf. M. Eisenbeth, *Les Juifs de l'Afrique du Nord*, Alger 1936, p. 98. In view of this, the name of the India merchant is certainly to be pronounced Yijū. Note 17 in *Speculum* 29, p. 191, is to be corrected accordingly.

7. Merchants and travellers other than those described above in Nos. 1-5. Several hundred of them are mentioned, and for many of them the approximate time and place can be fixed. Some Muslims, known from literary sources, such as Bilāl ben Jarīr, the actual ruler of southern Yemen in the 1140's, or Rāmisht, the great ship-owner, who was buried in Mecca in April 1140, are copiously mentioned. A Christian Indian and a number of Hindu merchants are also referred to, some of them repeatedly.

Trying now to point out which categories of information are provided by the material just described, we would like to remind the reader that in view of its specific character utmost circumspection is recommended in its perusal. Most of the records come from a comparatively short period, approximately 1080-1160 A.D., with a mere sprinkling of documents from the years 1160-1240. What was true for these years must not have been necessarily applicable to the early eleventh or the late thirteenth centuries. Most of the hundreds of merchants mentioned came from a comparatively closely knit group. This has the advantage that we are able to study at least one segment of the India trade very intimately. However, generalizations on the basis of this material should be made only with great caution. Even within this limited group, chance or the whims of men played an important role with regard to the information which has come down to us. For example, no less than sixty-two orders of payment signed by a single merchant (No. 5a. cf. p. 337) have been preserved.[1] However, of all the hundreds of other persons who have left us their writings, taken together, less than five orders of payment have been found. This proves, of course, that normally such material was not deposited in the Geniza. Only the aforementioned merchant and one or two others had religious qualms about its destruction.[2]

[1] These sixty-two orders are contained in five numbers of my collection of Geniza papers related to the India trade (Nos. 137-139, 229, 300).

[2] The orders of payment of money are all dated and closely resemble the formulas used by us: "Kindly pay to bearer (without name) such and such a sum of (in *words*) dinars only". In addition, often, but not always, the number is written in Coptic *numerals* at the head of the order. A tiny piece of paper, the size of half of a modern check was sufficient for an order of one hundred dinars (worth about $ 5000). Most of the orders bear on the right upper corner the letter *b*, an abbreviation of the Aramaic formula *In Your name, oh Merciful* (which corresponds to and may have been the model for the Muslim formula *In the name of God, the compassionate and merciful*). In addition, the Hebrew word for *Truth* often was written on the head of an order of payment. Since Truth was one of the epithets of God,

Naturally, the Geniza records contain particularly rich information about the goods exchanged between the countries of the Indian Ocean and the Mediterranean, their prices in the different cities in which they were traded, their modes of transport, customs duties and other expenses connected with them, and details about their relative importance. A provisional list comprises seventy seven commodities going West and one hundred and three exported to the East.[1] Those coming from or through India and other countries of the Indian Ocean may be classified as follows:

A.	Spices, aromatics, dyeing and varnishing plants and medical herbs	36 items
B.	Iron and steel (a chief commodity)	6 varieties
C.	Brass and bronze vessels	12 items
D.	Indian silk and other textiles, made mainly of cotton	8 items (only!)
E.	Pearls, beads, cowrie shells and ambergris	4 items
F.	Shoes and other leatherwork	2 items
G.	Chinese porcelain, Yemenite stone pots and African ivory	3 items
H.	Tropical fruits, such as coconuts	5 items
I.	Timber	1 item
	Total	77 items

This list requires some explication. Group A outranks by far all the others not only in number, but also in the frequency of occurrence and in value. It may be, however, that this prominence was partly due to the fact that the professions of perfumer, druggist, apothecary

some merchants might have had scruples with regard to the destruction of papers on which such orders were written. As may be remarked in passing, the Hebrew word for Truth was regarded in this connection as an acrostic or abbreviation of Psalm 85:12 "Truth springs out from the earth" in the meaning: any misuse of the order will be discovered in due course.

The orders to drugstores, groceries, wine merchants etc. for the delivery of commodities to bearers are never dated.

[1] This table was drawn up upon the assembling of about one hundred and fifty Geniza papers related to the India trade. Although the number of such records has meanwhile doubled, no substantial change in the relation of the various groups could be observed, although the actual number in most of the groups will have to be increased. The fact that one hundred and fifty papers provided approximately the same picture as three hundred and thirty is encouraging. It seems to prove that the Geniza is indicative of the actual situation, at least as far as the group mainly represented in it is concerned.

and dyer were extremely popular among the Jews in the countries of Islam. Thus the denomination of the traders might have had something to do with the character of their trade.

Different types of iron and steel loom large in the Geniza records, but only as raw materials. Indian swords, so famous in Arabic literature, are never mentioned. Whether the Middle East Muslims preferred to manufacture their own weapons, or whether the Jews, for one reason or another, refrained from trading in this commodity, needs further elucidation.

The details about the fabrication of copper vessels are very remarkable and certainly deserve the attention of the specialists. Southwestern India was famous both for its copper mines and its bronze and brass industry. The Geniza shows us (a) that large quantities of copper, lead and other ingredients of that industry were imported to India from the countries of the West; and (b) that old or broken vessels and implements of all descriptions were sent from Aden to India and worked there into new utensils according to order, i.e. according to specifications provided. This seems to indicate (a) that the demands of the bronze and brass industry of southwest India were far larger than the local copper ores were able to satisfy; and (b) that the Indian industry was so highly esteemed that the Adenese merchants took the trouble and the risk to order vessels from India rather than from Yemenite coppersmiths, although these too must have had a long tradition behind them.

As to textiles, Indian muslin, called in some letters *lānis* and in others *lālis*,[1] as well as clothes made of it occur frequently, but mostly as presents sent by the India traders to their wives or business friends or to religious dignitaries. On the other hand, Indian cotton fabrics were traded in considerable quantities, but still were only of secondary importance. Since textiles took up much cargo space, only precious textiles were, as a rule, considered worth while to ship; but the Jewish traders represented in the Geniza catered mostly to middle class customers.

Similarly, Chinese porcelain and such rarities as Yemenite stone pots appear in lists of presents (or household goods ordered), but not as objects of regular commerce.

Timber must have been one of the great exports of India, but

[1] Cf. R. B. Serjeant, "Material for a History of Islamic Textiles up to the Mongol Conquest", *Ars Islamica* 15-16 (1951), p. 81 and Notes 21 and 22 (his sources have only *lānis*).

the shipbuilders of Arabia most probably carried the timber needed by them on their own dhows, while the building industry in the Egyptian cities must have made use of importers other than those represented in the Geniza. In any event, Indian timber is almost absent from our records.

In the whole of the "classical" Geniza, i.e. the documents coming from the tenth through the thirteenth centuries, there is not a single reference to slave trade by Jews, either in the Mediterranean and African or Indian waters. Naturally, slaves are frequently referred to, especially as domestic help and as business agents, and we read about the acquisition and sale of such persons, but nowhere are Jews the merchants handling this business. According to literary sources, Jews traded in slaves during the ninth century, and the sixteenth century Geniza records prove that, in the time of the great Ottoman conquests, they became again active in this line, but for reasons which cannot be discussed here, they did not participate in the slave trade during the period which forms the subject of this paper. Consequently, the Geniza papers do not contain any information about this important part of the Indian and African trade.[1]

As eastbound, i.e. sent from the ports of the Red Sea or from Aden, the following categories of goods have been noted in the Geniza papers:

A.	Textiles and clothing	36 items
B.	Vessels and ornaments of silver, brass, glass and other materials	23 items
C.	Household goods, such as carpets, mats, tables, frying pans etc.	7 items
D.	Chemicals, medicaments, soap, paper, books	19 items
E.	Metals and other ingredients for the copper industry	7 items
F.	Coral (a staple article of great importance)	1 item
G.	Food-stuffs, such as cheese, sugar, raisins and olive oil, linseed oil for lamps, etc.	10 items
	Total	103 items

This list, which, after an exhaustive study of the Geniza material, will be certainly enlarged by many items, is impressive, but mis-

[1] See the present writer's "Slaves and Slavegirls in the Cairo Geniza Records," *Arabica* 9 (1962), pp. 1-20.

leading. If one compares it with the list of westbound goods given above, one may jump to the conclusion that India and the Orient mostly sent agricultural products and raw materials, while the Middle East exported mostly industrial products and consumer goods. Thus one might be led to assume that the situation bore a certain similarity to the relations of Europe with her spheres of colonial expansion in modern times.[1]

This, however, was not the case. The industrial and consumer goods sent to India were of the greatest variety, but their value, as a rule, amounted to comparatively small sums. They were used by the Middle Eastern merchants and their families, not by the local population. Only in exceptional cases, as in that of Joseph Lebdi's India trip,[2] most of the Oriental goods were purchased with the price obtained for Middle Eastern products. Mostly, gold and silver, in particular Egyptian gold pieces, the dollars of that period, accompanied orders for Indian goods, or raw materials for the Indian bronze industry were sent as an equivalent.

Three accounts, included in letters sent from Aden to India, may serve as an illustration. As accounts go, they are composed of many details, but are simplified here in order to put into relief the main facts. All reckonings are made in Mālikī, i.e. local Yemenite dinars. At that time, 2.35 Mālikī dinars had the value of one Egyptian gold piece.

India book[3] No. 26.

A. Sent from India to Aden:

Pepper	worth	402 Mālikī dinars
Less customs etc.		87
	Balance	315
Iron		247
Less customs etc.		27
	Balance	220
	Total Assets	535

[1] This was indeed assumed by the present writer at an earlier stage of his research into the subject, cf. *Studia Islamica* 3 (1955), p. 83.

[2] Cf. above, p. 336.

[3] I.e. the collection of Geniza records related to the India trade, assembled by the present writer.

B. Sent from Aden to India:

Copper	423
Plus packing etc.	16
Lead	$29^7/_{12}$
Household goods	$16^3/_4$
20 Egyptian dinars	47
Cash (i.e. Mālikī d.)	7
Total liabilities	$535^1/_3$

An order for Indian goods is accompanied in another letter (No. 28) by a list of the following shipments:

Copper	worth	102 Mālikī dinars
Soap		5
100 Egyptian goldpieces		235
200 dinars of Zabīd[1]		200
$21^3/_4$ dinars of Dhu 'l-Jibla[1]		$21^3/_4$

Another letter (No. 30) enumerates the following shipments to India:

Yemenite sweetmeats made of walnuts	$2^3/_4$ Mālikī dinars	
Wheat	3	
Doura (sorghum, a widely eaten grain)	$1^1/_6$	
Several pieces of Egyptian clothing	9	
Glass vessels, Egyptian and Yemenite	$1^1/_2$	
(Total consumer goods	$17^5/_{12}$)	
2 silver ingots weighing 605 dirhams worth		124
100 Egyptian gold pieces		(not preserved)
Cash, owed to the recipient		300

Whenever possible, the merchants preferred sending goods instead of gold. In a certain period (1137-1140), silk, coming perhaps from as far west as Spain, sold well on the Malabar coast of India, and the Adenese letters (e.g. Nos. 51, 56, 60) make mention of this commodity as "means of payment" "in the place of gold". However, the very use of this phrase shows that it was customary to pay for the products of the Orient in cash. Thus, the question raised by R. S. Lopez, how the Middle East made good its apparently un-

[1] Towns in Yemen. Dhu 'l-Jibla was at that time the capital.

favorable balance of gold in its trade with India, is still valid.[1] The material alluded to in the preceding lines seems to indicate that there is no clear-cut answer to this question. It is to be hoped that a full publication and translation of the India records from the Cairo Geniza will enable the historians of economics to study these aspects of medieval economy in detail.

Turning from the goods to those who handled them, one is struck by the predominance of merchants from North Africa in the India trade. This could be concluded already from the details given above, pp. 336/7, concerning the persons whose papers form the main stock of the Geniza records discussed in this article. However, the same holds true concerning the hundreds of other persons mentioned in them. The coastal towns of the Red Sea, Arabia and India were flooded with people coming not only from the larger cities of the Muslim West, such as Barqa and Tripoli, Libya, Kairouan and al-Mahdiyya, Tunisia, Tlemcen, Algiers, Fez and Tangier, Morocco, Malaga and the isle of Majorca, Spain, but also from small and out of the way places, such as (Jabal) Nafūsa, Libya, Urbus, Tunisia, and Derʿa, Morocco. In a number of cases, our documents prove that such persons, or even their fathers, had previously emigrated to Egypt. In others, however, we definitely see merchants from Tunisia, Morocco, Spain and Sicily undertaking the long voyage to India and, in some instances, even more than once. To be sure, all this refers to the period before 1147, i.e. before Almohad fanaticism paralyzed the Jewish and Christian communities of the Muslim West for more than two generations.

In a stimulating essay, entitled *The Fatimids and the Route to India,*[2] Professor Bernard Lewis undertook to show that the Fatimid caliphs of Egypt endeavored to take the India trade out of the hands of their Iraqian rivals, the Abbasid caliphs of Bagdad. As is well known, the original base of Fatimid power was Tunisia, where they ruled for sixty years before conquering Egypt and from where they brought with them the Berber contingents of the Kitāma, on which their military might rested. In the light of what has just been said about the predominance of the North African merchants in the India trade, one might ponder whether the Fatimids are not to be regarded as an exponent of North African

[1] Cf. *The Cambridge History of Economics* II, p. 309.

[2] Publ. in the *Revue de la Faculté des Sciences Economiques de l'Université d'Istanbul* II (1953).

expansion. Besides religious and political factors, strong socio-economic forces must have been at work in this development. The economic history of North Africa during the first half millenium of Islam consisted of two contrasting stages: In the early centuries of Islam, North Africa was a colonial area which attracted the enterprising merchants of Persia, Iraq and Syria. Therefore, we find in the Muslim West many persons (including Jews in the Geniza papers) bearing family names derived from Asian cities as remote as Wāsiṭ and Basra, Nīsābūr and Samarqand. By the fourth century, however, North Africa itself had become so rich that inevitably it sought expansion and found an outlet for its surplus in the India and Far Eastern trade. Thus the Fatimids in their effort to push eastwards could make use of the socio-economic upsurge of their North African hinterland. In other words, it was not so much sectarian politics which furthered international trade, as the pressure of an exuberant economy which enabled Fatimid propaganda to spread eastward.[1]

As to the organization of the India trade, no merchant guilds can be discerned in its Middle Eastern branch. The merchants appearing in the Geniza records normally concluded partnerships and travelled in company, but no rigid organization or coercion whatsoever can be discovered in this respect.[2] It is astonishing how many small fry participated in this overseas trade. In order to spread the risk, a Cairene business man would join many partnerships each with comparatively small sums or with limited amounts of goods, and persons possessing little capital would venture on the long and dangerous journey relying mainly on the capital or merchandise confided to them. An important merchant would be accompanied by a slave who served him as a business agent and also as a menial, or he would send a slave out to India instead of going himself.

Yet this great trade did not entirely lack organized leadership. It was provided by the Representative of the Merchants, in Arabic *wakīl al-tujjār*, in Hebrew *peqīd*[3] *ha-sōḥarīm*. This important office,

[1] A similar process is to be assumed for an earlier stage of Ismāʿīlī propaganda in western India, cf. S. M. Stern, "Ismāʿīlī Propaganda and Fatimid Rule in Sind", *Islamic Culture*, October 1949, pp. 1/2 of offprint.

[2] Concerning the so-called Kārim merchants cf. below Ch. XVIII.

[3] This word should not be understood in the sense which it has in modern Hebrew ("official"), but in its medieval Eastern meaning of "attorney", "agent".

which, at least in part, may have formed the prototype for the consuls of the Italian colonies of the Levant, is richly illustrated by the Geniza records, so that its true character and manifold aspects can now be clearly grasped. No substantial difference can be discovered with regard to this office vis-a-vis the Mediterranean and the India trades. For the latter, we are particularly well informed with respect to the wakīls of Aden, about whose activities we have bits of information for a period of about a century and a half, cf. above p. 336.

As the Arabic and Hebrew terms suggest, the origin of the office is probably to be sought in the field of law. A merchant who did business in a foreign country, or even in a city other than his own, needed a legal representative or an attorney to take care of his lawsuits. In case he could not confide the disposal of his goods to a business friend, partner or agent travelling to foreign parts, the legal representative would also supervise the sale of his goods and make the necessary purchases according to his orders. A wakīl who was particularly successful and prosperous, would get many such mandates, until he and his descendants, if they were equally capable and esteemed, would become the generally recognized mandatories and trustees to whom the foreign merchants would regularly confide their affairs. Similarly, the local merchants would take advantage of his ramified connections in order to receive a share in the overseas business. The wakīl would erect a large warehouse (*dār wakāla*), where the goods of his clients would be stored and which served also as a clearing house for business transactions in general or for those commodities in which he specialized. It had become so customary for business to be done in a wakāla, that in an official Geniza document (a deposition in court) it is stated that a promise to let another merchant share in a purchase was binding only when made there or in a store house, but not elsewhere. The merchandise belonging to partners, shipwrecked goods and those of a defunct merchant would be held by the wakīl and he would hand out to each person concerned the share belonging to him. The wakīl served also as a banker, inasmuch as the foreign merchants deposited with him their money and he made payments for them. His wakāla was also a kind of post office to which letters were sent from distant countries to await the arrival of the addressees or to be forwarded to them. In this respect, however, there was no difference between a wakāla and the store of any other prominent merchant.

Most of the Muslim representatives of merchants mentioned in the

Geniza records were cadis, or religious judges, and in a number of instances it is evident that they did not only bear that title, but actually occupied the office of judge. Similarly Maḍmūn, the Jewish Wakīl of Aden, referred to above, was recognized as the local chief justice by the Head of the Diaspora, the secular chief of the Jewish people, who had his seat in Bagdad, as well as by the Head of the Palestinian Academy, who was the highest Jewish religious authority in the Fatimid empire (because of the Crusaders, the latter had his seat in Old Cairo at that time). This recognition was expressed in honorific titles conferred on Maḍmūn from both sides, one of them being Nagīd, or "Prince of the land of Yemen", which, at that time, designated the combined religious and secular leadership of a Jewish community in a country. Moreover, Maḍmūn was characterized as "trusted by all the lords of the seas and the deserts", i.e. he had agreements, in the interest of his clients, with the many petty rulers (or pirates) who controlled the routes of the Arabian and Indian seas, as well as the land route between Aden and Egypt (used at that period in particular for the conveyance of letters).

Thus far, no explicit reference to an official appointment or licensing of a representative of merchants has been encountered. In a Muslim historical source it is said with regard to a person whose son subsequently became Muslim chief judge of Egypt: "after emigrating from Syria to Old Cairo, he opened there a dār wakāla."[1] Of an Egyptian vizier it is stated in the same source: "In this year (516, which began on March 12, 1122 A.D.) he ordered the erection of a dār wakāla in Cairo for the merchants arriving from Iraq and Syria."[2] Since a representative of the merchants occupied a semi-official position, it stands to reason that he had to obtain a license or a confirmation of his office from the head of the market police or the governor of his city. When we read in a Geniza letter: "Mr. So and So sends you his regards, he is today a representative of merchants in partnership with So and So (a Muslim)", one gets the impression that the writer is referring to some sort of official recognition. As may be remarked in passing, such partnerships between a leading Jewish and a prominent Muslim merchant were not infrequent. The same relationship existed between the above mentioned Maḍmūn and Bilāl ben Jarīr, who later became the actual ruler of southern Yemen, cf. p. 338. While licensing a wakīl tujjār—

[1] Ibn Muyassar, *Annales d'Égypte*, ed. H. Massé, Cairo 1919, p. 81, l. 1.
[2] *Ibid.*, p. 62, l. 15. For *al-biḥār*, no doubt *al-tujjār* is to be read.

if such a procedure was practiced at all—the authorities certainly took into consideration his standing among his fellow merchants. Under no circumstances, however, should he be regarded as the head of a merchants' guild, which, as we have seen, was non-existent. He was a self-made, independent agent in a society of independent merchants. Like any other profession, circumstances permitting, the office of a wakīl passed from father to son. There was, however, no hard and fast rule in this matter. The Geniza shows that the father, son and great-grandson of a prominent wakīl tujjār of Old Cairo were physicians and only his grandson followed his own profession.

In a maritime city, the office of a representative of merchants was sometimes combined with that of the superintendent of the port who was in charge of the customs house. This combination is attested to for the Mediterranean with regard to Muslims. In Aden, the above mentioned Maḍmūn ben Ḥasan occupied such a position according to the Geniza records. Moreover, an Arabic literary source tells us about a Jew called David ben Maḍmūn, who fixed the customs tariff of that south-Arabian port.[1] It is very likely that this man was the son, or otherwise a relative, of Maḍmūn II ben David about whom we have read on p. 336.

The letters exchanged between India and Aden contain interesting information with regard to the practice of seafaring and the social and economic conditions prevailing in south-west India. As was usual on the Mediterranean, a ship sailing on the Indian ocean was normally accompanied by another, smaller, ship, belonging to the same proprietor or to his partner. As a rule, ships travelled in convoys. Piracy was rampant. Of one merchant we read that he was robbed both on his way to India and on his return journey. Persons perishing and the loss of goods by shipwreck are frequently referred to. Yet the route between Aden and India must have been comparatively safe. Otherwise, we would not find so many people repeatedly undertaking that journey. The most dangerous part of the passage was the moment when a boat tried to reach the open sea or, vice versa, when it broke through the coastal rollers on its way to a haven. Therefore we encounter several tales of shipwreck shortly after sailing or before arrival, and diving operations undertaken to salvage at least a part of the sunken goods are reported for both the Arabian and the Red Sea coasts. At certain periods of the

[1] O. Löfgren, *Aden im Mittelalter*, Uppsala 1936, p. 49, l. 13.

south-west monsoon the Indian coast is particularly treacherous.[1]

This technical detail may account for an aspect of seafaring which had puzzled the present writer for a long time. Over twenty places on the west coast of India are mentioned in the Geniza records. I had assumed that, after crossing the ocean, a ship would sail along the Indian coast and call at least on all of the major ports. However, as the Geniza indicates, this was not the case. Each ship or convoy had its own port of destination and was labelled accordingly "the one bound for Broach" or Tana, or Kulam etc. Merchants and goods travelling in a ship heading for a port different from their own destination had to change to another ship. An additional reason for this seemingly strange system was perhaps the endeavor to avoid the excessive customs duties levied in each port.

The names of the Indian shipowners, merchants and craftsmen mentioned in the Geniza records will require the attention of the experts.[2] It seems that quite a number of them are not proper names, but designations for officers or members of caste guilds. Thus PTN SWMY[3], whose large ship foundered, after having been driven by winds to Berbera on the African coast (while the accompanying smaller craft arrived safely in Aden), certainly was no other than the *paṭṭaṇa svami*, the head of a large merchants guild, who also served as a kind of mayor.[4] We are reminded of the shipowner Maḍmūn, who was representative of the merchants in Aden and, at the same time, head of the Jewish community of Yemen. Reference is made repeatedly to an Indian shipowner PDYĀR, which word is in some letters preceded by the article, characterizing

[1] Cf. Gus W. Van Beek, *JAOS* 80 (1960), pp. 138/9 and the literature indicated there. The Geniza does not say at which time of the year the shipwrecks on the Indian coast occurred. In the Mediterranean similar conditions prevailed. Ships went down just outside the Pharos, or light tower, of Alexandria, cf. G. R. Monks, "The Church of Alexandria and the City's Economic Life in the Sixth Century," *Speculum* 28 (1953), pp. 359-360.

[2] My thanks are due to Dr. A. L. Basham of the University of London, Sir Harold W. Baily of Queen's College, Cambridge, Professor W. Norman Brown and Dr. Leigh Lisker of the University of Pennsylvania, and to Professor Pierre Meile of Paris for help in these matters.

[3] Hebrew, like Arabic, as a rule does not indicate short vowels. The spelling PTN SWMY indicates that the Jewish merchants heard the word pronounced approximately *patan sōmī*, with which the writing *paṭṭaṇa sāmi* in one Indian inscription (A. Appadorai I, p. 385, Note 217) is to be compared.

[4] See A. Appadorai, *Economic Conditions in Southern India (1000-1500 A.D.)*, Madras 1936, I, pp. 385 and 397. The word literally means "Lord of the mart", as I learned from Dr. A. L. Basham, and thus corresponds to the Arabic *haykh al-sūq*, a term found in the Geniza papers of the Mediterranean area.

it as a title or as a term for an office. The PDYĀR possessed several ships, one of which was commanded by a Muslim,[1] and he was addressed in writing by the above mentioned Maḍmūn. One wonders in which language the two corresponded. Presumably in Arabic. It is, however, not excluded that the Jewish representative of the merchants in Aden kept an Indian clerk for his correspondence with the authorities, shipowners and business friends in the ports of India.

Since the Geniza is essentially a repository of papers written with Hebrew characters, it is natural that it should deal mainly with the commercial activities of Jews and between Jews. It seems also that business was conducted to a large extent along denominational lines, simply because this was the practical thing to do. Members of one religion travelled together in order to be able to fulfill their religious duties, such as prayer, Sabbaths and holidays and the observation of dietary laws. Partnerships were concluded and dissolved and many other civil cases were brought before the courts of the various denominations, and these dealt also with matters of inheritance, so important for families whose fathers and sons were exposed to the hazards of overseas travel.

Moreover, although there were no ghettoes in those days, normally neighborhoods were predominantly occupied by the members of one community or another. This was an additional reason for a certain denominational element in the organization of commerce.

Yet the same Geniza letters reveal an astonishing degree of interdenominational cooperation, matched by almost complete absence of animosity against other communities. Partnerships and other close business relationships between Jews and Muslims, or Hindus, or Christians[2] were commonplace and the members of other religious communities are referred to with the same honoring and amicable epithets as the writers' own brethren. The great dangers shared in common, the feeling that every one's lot was in the hand of the same God, certainly contributed much to that spirit of all-embracing brotherhood which pervades the India papers of the Cairo Geniza.

[1] The term used is *nā-khodā*, a Persian word meaning "lord of the ship" (the same root as in English *nav*y). It designated the shipowner or the "manager" in charge of the passengers and goods, not the captain, who is called in our papers *rayyis*, "head".

[2] As stated above, only one Christian is mentioned by name in the Geniza papers related to the India trade, studied thus far. However, the relationship with him is referred to in a manner which shows that it was by no means anything particular. To be sure, no European Christians were in the Indian waters at that time.

CHAPTER EIGHTEEN

THE BEGINNINGS OF THE KĀRIM MERCHANTS AND THE CHARACTER OF THEIR ORGANIZATION

The Kārim merchants of the late thirteenth, fourteenth and early fifteenth centuries were as prominent in the countries of the Middle East as the German Hanse was in contemporary central and northern Europe. They all but monopolized the trade with India, East Africa and the Far East and constituted the greatest financial power in the Mamluk state besides the government. Unlike their European counterpart, they seem not to have possessed any statutory form of organization and never attained, as a group, political power. The details known about individual merchants and their families show that they formed closely knit groups fortified by intermarriage. However, under the rule of a foreign soldiery no merchant aristocracy could develop or, in any event, persist for long. The power and wealth of a family hardly lasted for more than two or three generations. The rapacious Mamluks, always watchful not to let any one become too prosperous and mighty, destroyed systematically the great merchant houses by imposing on them exorbitant contributions or by wholesale confiscation of the remaining estates. Naturally, there were differences in this respect between the various rulers, but the general trend was unmistakable. The main center of the Kārimīs was Egypt, where at one time reputedly over two hundred of them were found. Others had their seat in Damascus and probably also in other towns of Syria, and, in particular in Yemen, the distributing center for the goods of East Africa, India and the Far East.[1]

What was the nature of this prosperous group of merchants so often referred to by the historians of the Mamluk period? When did it emerge and what is the meaning of its name?[2]

[1] This summary of our knowledge of the Kārimīs, as based on literary sources, is greatly indebted to the studies quoted on page 352, in particular to E. Ashtor's critical evaluation of the material collected by him.

[2] The very pronunciation of the name is not yet definitely established. Arabic script does not indicate the short vowels. The prominent historian of the economic history of Egypt in Islamic times, Carl H. Becker, spelled Kārem in the Encyclopaedia of Islam II, p. 19, and Kāram in his Islam-

A first collection of source material about the Kārimīs was made as early as 1838 and the scholar discussing them characterized them not improperly as *banians*, the Indian term for traders.[1] A comprehensive study, based on Mamluk biographical literature was published in 1937 by W. J. Fischel.[2] It is, however, a telling testimony to the newly aroused interest in the economic development of medieval Islam, that no less than three extensive studies have been devoted to the Kārim group of late, by Dr. Sobhy Labib, Professor Gaston Wiet and Dr. E. Ashtor respectively.[3]

In surveying the results of the studies made so far, Professor Cl. Cahen arrives at the conclusion that the earliest reliable evidence of the existence of the Kārim in Egypt is Maqrīzī's statement about it relating to the year 1181 and the reign of Saladin.[4]

It is the purpose of the following lines to show that we are now in a position to delve even earlier into the history of the Kārim, as it appears already in documents dating undoubtedly from the Fatimid period. These documents—all in Hebrew characters, but mostly in the Arabic language—come from the so-called Cairo Geniza, whose treasures are now dispersed all over the world.[5] That repository of discarded writings contained a great many letters and deeds dealing with trade and travel between the Mediterranean and the Indian Ocean during the eleventh and twelfth centuries.[6] It is most revealing to learn what they have to tell us about the Kārim, both explicitly and by their silence.

studien I, Leipzig 1924, pp. 186 and 214. The studies mentioned in Notes 4 and 5 have unanimously adopted Kārim. If the word is derived from the Indian kāryam (see below), the pronunciation Kāram would perhaps be preferable.

[1] Cf. E. Quatremère, *Notices et Extraits*, Paris 1938, XII, p. 639, XIII, p. 214.

[2] W. J. Fischel, "Über die Gruppe der Kārimī-Kaufleute", *Studia Arabica* I, Rome 1937, pp. 67-82.

[3] Dr. Sobhy Labib, "Al-tijāra al-Kārimiyya wa-tijārat Miṣr fi 'l-'uṣūr al-wusṭā," *Majallat al-jam'iyya al-Miṣriyya lil-dirāsāt al-ta' rīkhiyya*, Cairo 1952. Gaston Wiet, "Les marchands d'épices sous les sultans mamlouks", *Cahiers d'Histoire Égyptienne*, Cairo 1955, pp. 81-147. E. Ashtor, "The Kārimī Merchants", *JRAS*, April 1956, pp. 45-56. It is significant that these three studies have been made independently of each other. Wiet, p. 147, remarks that his manuscript was already in the press, when Labib's article reached him. However, even before Wiet's study was out, Ashtor had sent his to the JRAS. Cf. also O. Spies, *Ibn Fadlallah al-Omari's Bericht über India*, Leipzig, 1943, p. 62.

[4] *Arabica* III 3, p. 339. Maqrīzī relates in his *Sulūk* I, 72-3, that the Kārimīs came to Egypt in 1181, where they had to pay duties for several years.

[5] See Chapter XIV.

[6] Cf. Chapter XVII.

The first two items concern a merchant and shipowner (*nākhodā*) of Aden, Maḥrūz b. Jacob, who is referred to in twelve documents. One of these is dated February-March 1134; however, even without that detail, his time could be fixed, as many other well-known personalities are mentioned in the letters concerned.

Maḥrūz' center of activities was Aden and, as his mother lived there and as he is styled al-ʿAdanī, he was most probably also born in that town. Sometimes he is found travelling in his own ship, which followed the course Aden-Mangalore[1], India, but more often he used others, e.g. one of the ships belonging to Maḍmūn, the Representative of the Merchants of Aden, who was also the Head of the Jewish community of Yemen. Maḥrūz' sister was married to Abū Zikrī Kohen, representative of merchants in Cairo, the scion of a very ancient family with connections in Iraq, Palestine and North Africa. Sometimes we find Maḥrūz also in Cairo, where he conducted the business affairs of the family at the time when his illustrious brother-in-law was away (most probably in India, where he once was captured by pirates), while the latter's brother—perhaps a minor luminary—was sent to Alexandria to supervise the shipment of goods to al-Mahdiyya, Tunisia.

Thus, the scene is set for appreciating the references to the Kārim made in connection with Maḥrūz. One is found in a letter dictated by him in Aden on the very day on which he was embarking for India, after having returned from that country only a short time before. By chance, that letter, which was directed to a son of his brother-in-law in Cairo, has come down to us in two complete copies.[2] Among other items, the writer mentions in it that he had sent various presents, or commodities ordered, with a person travelling from Aden to Cairo, while he had bought for the addressee sixty *mann* of *tabāshīr* (crystals extracted from bamboos[3]), which he had delivered to the representative of the merchants in Aden, Maḍmūn, *yunfidhuha fi'l-Kārim maʿa man yarā* "in order to forward it 'in the Kārim' with whomever he found suitable".

More detailed is the following reference found in a fragment,

[1] Ships used to commute between Aden and one particular port on the coast of India, see above p. 349.

[2] Nos. 134-5 of my India Collection. Ms. University Library Cambridge, TS 16.345 and British Museum Or. 5542, p. 17.

[3] Cf. M. Meyerhof, *Un glossaire de matière médicale composé par Maimonide*, Cairo 1940, p. 84, no. 171, where many details about this material, which served as a constituent in collyriums, tonics, astringents etc. are given.

which was cut out from a letter in order to use its blank reverse side for writing on it a list. Although only a very small part of the letter is preserved, containing neither the name of the sender nor that of the addressee, the name of the former can be ascertained with certainty and that of the latter with great probability. For the handwriting of that letter is none other than that of Abū Zikrī Kohen, the Cairene merchants' representative referred to above, while the mentioning of "my brother-in-law Maḥrūz" confirms the identity, which is, however, beyond doubt, as many letters and deeds have emanated from Abū Zikrī's hand during the years 1132 through 1148. The addressee most probably was his partner in the India trade, Ḥalfōn b. Nethanel, also a member of a very high standing family, who must have been at that time—as he often was—in Aden, because the writer informs him that he was forwarding him his mail through a person, named in the letter, to Maḍmūn, the representative of the merchants in that town.[1]

Owing to its importance, I give the passage referring to the Kārim in full:

Amma 'l-Kārim qad waṣalanī minhu kitāb min ʿind ṣihrī Maḥrūz min Sawākin yaḥkī annahu 3 ālāf ʿidl waqad kharaj fi 'l-Kārim min aṣḥābina 'l-Yahūd 7 Maḥrūz (six other names follow) *lā gayr.*[2]

"As far as the Kārim is concerned—I got a letter from it, from[3] my brother-in-law Maḥrūz from Sawākin, telling that it contained (literally: it was) 3 thousand bales and that there travelled homewards[4] in the Kārim 7 of our Jewish business friends: Maḥrūz etc., not more".

Five out of the six India traders mentioned in addition to Maḥrūz are known from other documents, and as one of these is from 1097, while another is dated 11 September 1149, it is feasible to assume that our letter was written between these two dates, in the twenties

[1] Announcements of this kind are a very common feature in medieval correspondence. They were made in order to enable the receiver of such a message to trace his mail quickly on the arrival of a ship or a caravan. In the case under discussion, the addressee was expected to proceed further to the East. Therefore, his mail was forwarded not to him, but to the representative of the merchants in Aden.

[2] No. 221 of the India Collection. Ms. British Museum Or. 5549, III, fol. 5 recto, l. 6 - margin, l. 5.

[3] Thus, and not "about", which would have to be *ʿanhu* even in the rather vernacular style of the letter.

[4] In the language of the India traders *kharaj* means "coming out from the sea", travelling *homewards*. The same usage prevails in the Arabic spoken in Yemen up to the present day.

or thirties of the twelfth century—which we have already known as the time of Maḥrūz' activities.

The situation reflected in the letter is as follows: the Cairene representative of the Jewish merchants informs his partner, who at that time was in Aden, of the volume of trade carried in that year by the Kārim and of the names of the addressee's business friends who had safely arrived at the Red Sea port Sawākin on their way home (to Egypt and North Africa). From this it follows that the Kārim did not dock in Aden that particular year, but went directly to Sawākin, either from India or from some port in Southern Persia, like Tīz, or in Eastern Arabia, like Mirbāṭ. In the 1097 document, referred to above, we have another instance of ships going directly from Mirbāṭ to the East African coast, without touching Aden—a practice which is in conformity with the conditions of sea travel of those times in general, cf. p. 353, Note 1. We cannot make out, from where the writer dispatched our letter. I suppose, from the Red Sea port ʿAydhāb, which is situated to the north of Sawākin and from where one usually travelled directly to Aden, for the writer mentions that he forwarded the addressee's letters to the latter city; it could be, however, Cairo itself.

As can be ascertained from the names of the persons mentioned, another document referring to the Kārim—very defective, but containing interesting details—is to be attributed to the same period, as those just discussed. In it, a man, who had travelled from Kawlam (Quilon) on the Malabar coast westwards, but was again on his way to India, sends to his wife in Cairo a number of presents, including a six year old slave girl, pearl bracelets, lālis[1] garments, a bronze basin and a ewer. As to the forwarding, he says:

wa-ana, in shāʾ Allāh, unfidhuhum ṣuḥbat man yakh(ruj fi) 'l-Kārim.

"I shall send them, if God will, with somebody who is travelling home[2] in the Kārim".[3]

At the end of the same letter, in a text, which is too badly damaged to be interpreted with any degree of certainty, the writer mentions that a certain Abū Surūr Kohen Ibn al-Dawāniqī carried for him *sufratayn lilmāʾida*, two table cloths, and other commodities *in shāʾ Allāh taṣil ilayka fi l-Kārim mšḥ* (. . .)[4]

[1] For lālis or lānis, cf. above p. 340.

[2] See p. 354, Note 4.

[3] No. 214 of the India book. Ms. University Library Cambridge, TS, New Series J 23.

[4] The word is tentatively complemented as *mashḥūnatan* and translated

"If God will, these commodities will reach you in the Kārim (loaded on the ship?)".

In a letter, sent around 1140 from Alexandria to Aden (or perhaps another port of the Indian ocean), the writer says:

(1) *Wamā kunnā gayr* (2) *qu'ūd nantaẓirak* (3) *fī* (!) *kārim al-sana* (4) *waqad waṣala kitābak*...

"We expected all the time that you would arrive in (!) Kārim this year. Instead, there came your letter..."[1]

This is the first occurrence in these letters of Kārim without the definite article, which indicates that the word is not Arabic.

Another interesting detail in that long letter is the fact that the addressee, whose mother lived in Alexandria, had stayed (*kān yaskun*) in Sarḥa, a little-known anchorage in Yemen.[2] One could hardly conclude from this passage that the Kārim regularly touched that anchorage.

In a long letter written in the thirties or forties of the twelfth century, the well-known Adenese India trader Joseph b. Abraham expresses his regret that the addressee, Abū 'Imrān Ibn Nufay', had been detained a long time and under great hardship in the Red Sea port Dahlak and continues:

fa-arjū anna mawlānā wa-jamī' al-Kārim yakūnū adrakū 'Aydhāb, in shā' Allāh.

"I hope that you and the whole Kārim have reached 'Aydhāb, if God will"[3].

In other Geniza papers of the time, the ruler of Dahlak—which corresponds approximately to modern Massawa'—is mentioned as a dangerous pirate. Our letter seems to indicate that even the Kārim convoys, which were under the protection of the Fatimid navy, see below, were not always safe from the attacks of the pirates.

Concerning the arrival in 'Aydhāb of Jewish merchants travelling in the Kārim we read in a letter sent in December 1140 from Cairo to that Red Sea port:

"loaded on the ship" with the possible explanation, that the shipment referred to formed part of the general cargo and was not forwarded under the supervision of a traveller, as merchandise was usually sent. However, I have not come across, so far, any passage proving such a usage. Cf. p. 357, Note 2.

[1] India book, No. 215, University Library, Cambridge, TS Box 28, fol. 33, p. 1, written upside down on the top of the page.

[2] See Yāqūt, *Geographical Dictionary*, ed. Wüstenfeld III, p. 71.

[3] India book No. 227. Ms. Jewish Theological Seminary of New York, E. N. Adler Collection, Geniza Misc. 4, verso, ll. 11-13.

wa... jamī' man kharaja min aṣḥābinā fi 'l-Kārim bi-atamm al-salām.

"Give best regards to all our coreligionists who are coming home in the K."[1] The sender of the letter was the Cairene representative of the merchants Abū Zikrī Kohen, whom we have already met repeatedly. In an important fragment from Aden, which comes from the beginning of the thirteenth century, a merchant informs his business friend in Egypt about the goods purchased for him and adds:

waṣadara fi 'l-Kārim al-mūbarak. "They have been sent in the blessed K."

Since in such a context the name of the traveller who took care of the transportation would invariably be mentioned, but is not referred to here, it seems that, in this late period, the Kārim company carried goods on its own responsibility.[2]

Finally, in a letter sent from Ma'bar, the Coromandel, or south-eastern coast of India, to Cairo, a man informs his wife that he was sending her several items of Oriental spices and fruits, among them seven and a half *mann* of *jawza* (nutmeg)

mā fi 'l-Kārim mithluhā

"the like of which is not to be had in the Kārim".[3]

Before trying to evaluate the data just collected, a few words must be said about the alleged occurrence of Kārim in the texts published by the late Jacob Mann in his book *The Jews in Egypt and Palestine under the Fatimid Caliphs*, vol. II, Oxford 1922, pp. 246/7. Mann was a very great scholar, but he was not an Arabist and, consequently, his renderings of Arabic texts, even while written in Hebrew letters, have to be used with caution. Thus he read the heading of the list under discussion as "*al-dinār 3*", which is, of course, meaningless, and for which he suggested the reading *al-*

[1] India book No. 244. Univ. Library Cambridge, Or 1080 J. 180. The letter is dated "Month of Teveth", which began on December 13th.

[2] India book No. 229. Univ. Libr. Cambridge, TS NS J 182. The fragment is not dated, but written in the same hand as India book No. 156, whose time is known.

It should be noted that in the fragment No. 299, the writer remarks: "Details in the memorandum" (which, is not said). Thus it is not excluded that the goods were not confided to the Kārim company, but to a traveller mentioned in the memo. Nevertheless, in other Geniza letters, where also reference is made to the memorandum containing details about the shipment, the person in charge of it would be mentioned by name.

[3] India book no. 176. Ms. Jewish Theological Seminary, New York, E. N. Adler Collection 2739, fol. 16.

dhakhīr, "adopted son", a word which never occurs in the Geniza texts. Actually, the original has simply: *alladī kharaj*, which means: Expenditure. For this is not, as Mann believed, a list of donators or taxpayers, but, the reverse; it is a list of persons who were in receipt of emoluments from the community, such as rabbis, judges, scribes, beadles, blind or otherwise disabled people, foreigners, prisoners in need etc. What Mann read as *kārimīn* and *kurrām*, is nothing but *khādimayn* or *khuddām* respectively, meaning the beadles of the two synagogues of Old-Cairo.[1]

Coming back to the authentic Geniza texts mentioning the Kārim in Fatimid times, the following conclusions seem to be obvious:

(1) By the beginning of the twelfth century, al-Kārim had become a household word in Cairo: any woman whose husband was on his way in the countries of the Indian ocean knew that she could expect presents forwarded by him "in the Kārim". Passengers of different creeds and goods of all descriptions (and not only spices and the like) were transported "in" it.

(2) On the other hand, the term *Kārimī*, K. merchant, so common in the Mamluk period, has not yet been found in the Geniza with regard to Fatimid times.

(3) During the twelfth century the K. does not appear as a company handling goods, but rather as a convoy or group of nākhodās, or shipowners, in whose ships merchants travelled and goods were transported under the personal supervision of their owners or the latters' representatives, just as was the case with the ships of nākhodās not belonging to the K. See, however, p. 355, n. 4.

(4) The K. convoy sometimes touched Aden on its way out from India at and other times passed it by. This could have been due to navigational conditions (such as a stormy sea) or political circumstances (such as a siege on Aden),[2] but it is more likely that there operated a certain rotating system, by which the K. one year entered the port of Aden and the other did not.

(5) When an India trader, far out on the Coromandel Coast—cf. above p. 357, writes to his family in Cairo, that he was sending them

[1] Likewise *kārim al-kanīsa* on p. 246 is to be read *khādim*. These beadles were officials with many duties, comparable to, but in many respects also different from, those of the *farrāsh* of a mosque. Four letters of appointment of such beadles have been published by the present writer in the *A. L. Mayer Memorial Volume*, Jerusalem 1964.

[2] Cf. the present writer's paper "Two Eyewitness Reports on an Expedition of the King of Kīsh (Qais) against Aden", *BSOAS* London 1954, XVI/2.

a commodity of a quality "not found even in the K.", this seems to show that the traders cooperating in the K. were renowned for the high standards of their wares.

(6) The quantity of 3000 bales carried by the K. in one year—see above p. 354—is very considerable. The largest single shipment from the East going to Egypt which I have come across in the Geniza papers was one of 60 bales of lacquer, weighing 100 Bahār (totalling 30 000 pounds, one bale (*ʿidl*) normally weighing 500 pounds). However, these were sent by two most prominent persons in partnership, Bilāl b. Jarīr al-Awḥadī, who afterwards became the vizier and actual ruler of southern Yemen,[1] and Maḍmūn, the representative of the merchants of Aden. The total of one million and a half pounds may appear to the modern reader as a relatively small quantity. But one has to keep in mind that the Oriental goods carried were mostly high-priced luxuries, such as spices, drugs, pearls, plants used for dyes etc.

(7) On the other hand, one salient fact is brought out by the Geniza papers on the Indian trade with absolute certainty: up to 1150 approximately, the Kārim by no means monopolized that trade. Rather the reverse: extremely little mention is made of it; against the eight cases discussed here, we could adduce many more of little convoys or single ships owned by rulers, individuals, or merchants forming temporary partnerships which carried goods to and from India.

(8) Nevertheless, the overwhelming importance reached by the K. in Ayyubid and Mamluk times may have had its roots in the Fatimid period. In addition to the very weight of quantity and quality, discussed above under (5) and (6), there might have been the additional factor of special Government protection. It is true that even of Maḍmūn, the representative of the merchants in Aden, it was stated that he had agreements "with the rulers of the seas and the deserts", in order to protect the ships and caravans owned or supervised by him. However, as we learn again from the Geniza papers, piracy was rampant, and there is a far cry from such "Ḥimāya" agreements[2] to the powerful protection by the Fatimid

[1] This outstanding figure in the history of Yemen certainly deserves a special study for the time being cf. Encyclopaedia of Islam s.v. and "(banū al-) Karam" passim, as well as in the article referred to in the previous note, p. 248, and Oscar Löfgren, *Arabische Texte zur Geschichte der Stadt Aden im Mittelalter*, passim (cf. Index). See above, p. 347.

[2] Cf. Cl. Cahen, "Notes pour l'histoire de la Ḥimaya", *Mélanges Louis Massignon*, Institut Français du Damas, 1956, pp. 287-303.

navy stationed at ʿAydhāb, which the Kārim enjoyed according to Qalqashandī's detailed and obviously well informed statement.[1] I am inclined to believe that this special protection had financial, rather than political reasons: the Kārim were able to pay for it, while smaller traders had to put up with the vicissitudes of piracy, which was particularly dangerous in the Red Sea. This additional advantage may explain the final ascendancy of the Kārim.

(9) As to the origins of the Kārim, it is advisable to start again the discussion about the name of this body of merchants. As the word is preceded by the article, it does not represent a proper name, but must be originally a general noun. There is no suitable word in Arabic carrying a meaning connected with the activities of the K. On the other hand, the south Indian language Tamil has a word *kāryam*, which, among other things, means "business, affairs".[2] As business with the Middle East was the main concern of the commercial people on the west coast of India, it is quite feasible that a body of shipowners and traders engaged in it should have been known—or perhaps even called itself—by that designation.

(10) Merchant companies, largely, but not exclusively connected with caste and religious cult, are mentioned in south-Indian inscriptions as early as the eighth century and are particularly well attested to from the twelfth century.[3] The rich epigraphic material proves that commerce in India was conducted largely, if not exclusively, by such guilds; economic cooperation seems to have been less rigid than that of the European merchant guilds of the later Middle Ages. The Geniza papers show how closely the Middle Eastern merchants, irrespective of their religion, were connected with representatives of the Indian companies.[4] Under these circumstances it stands to reason that the formation of the Kārim group was inspired by an Indian model.

[1] Qalqashandī, *Ṣubḥ* III, 524, 2-6. As the many details given show, the writer must have had here an old source at his disposal.

[2] I owe this information to Dr. A. L. Basham of the University of London.

[3] Cf. A. Appadorai, *Economic Conditions in Southern India* (1000-1500 A.D.), Madras 1936, I., pp. 378-402. For the twelfth century cf. the inscriptions quoted on pp. 378, 383, 384, 385, and 391.

[4] See above pp. 349.

CHAPTER NINETEEN

THE PRESENT-DAY ARABIC PROVERB AS A TESTIMONY TO THE SOCIAL HISTORY OF THE MIDDLE EAST

Societies bound by a rigid tradition of fixed moral and religious notions and comprising a large percentage of illiterate persons usually possess a great treasure of proverbs and popular sayings, particularly if they are endowed with a rich and expressive language. The Arabic-speaking countries represent a most conspicuous example of such a society. Many thousands of modern Arabic proverbs have been collected by both European and Arab scholars in the countries of the Middle East and North Africa, and anyone acquainted with the facts will concede that the material is far from being exhausted.

The meritorious "*Critical Bibliography of Spoken Arabic Proverb Literature*" by Charles A. Ferguson and John M. Echols, published in 1952, gives an idea of the rich harvest which already has been gathered.[1] Important additional contributions have been made in this field since the publication of that survey. The following examples may suffice to illustrate the nature and scope of the work done thus far.

For the western end of the Arabic world we have Mohammed Ben Cheneb's three volumes of Algerian and other Maghribi proverbs and sayings, altogether 3127 items arranged in alphabetical order. In addition to the wealth of material collected, this book is especially useful because of its many cross references both to modern Arabic proverbs used in countries other than the Maghrib and in particular to those found in classical Arabic literature.[2] Of an entirely different nature is a collection of 2013 proverbs from Tangier and other places in Morocco, published by the eminent anthropologist E. Westermarck with the aid of a local scholar. They are classified by subject

[1] *Journal of American Folklore*, vol. 65, number 255, quoted here as Ferguson-Echols. This bibliography, which is classified by countries, with a concluding general chapter, contains solely studies which have appeared in the languages of western Europe, not those published in Arabic. For the latter, cf. C. Brockelmann, *EI*[1] s.v. Mathal.

[2] M. Ben Cheneb, *Proverbes arabes de l'Algérie et du Maghreb*, Paris 1905-07.

and introduced by a detailed and highly instructive essay on the Arabic proverb in general.[1] There exist many other collections for the area stretching from Morocco to Libya, some of which are particularly valuable because they are confined to certain localities, social groups or communities.[2]

The numerous publications on the modern Egyptian material were notably inaugurated by the famous Swiss traveller J. L. Burckhardt, who included in his collection of 999 proverbs—a number favorite with the Arabs—a smaller one made about a hundred years before him by a local savant. It is significant that Burckhardt found many items listed by his predecessor no longer in use at his time.[3] Of the books printed in Arabic characters mention should be made of the *Colloquial Proverbs* by the excellent Egyptian scholar Aḥmad Taymūr[4] and of Madame Fā'iqa Rafīq's huge collection, which if continued and completed with the same extensiveness as the volumes published thus far, might well comprise more than ten thousand items.[5] Egypt is especially rich in popular wisdom, a fact due no doubt to the natural inclination of the Egyptians for fun and jesting, as Mme. Rafīq rightly observes.[6] Rural Egypt is represented by proverbs from the Menufeyya district, listed together with other ethnographic and dialect material collected under the supervision of

[1] E. Westermarck, *Wit and Wisdom in Morocco. A Study of Native Proverbs*, London 1930.

[2] E.g. Louis Brunot, "Proverbes et dictons arabes de Rabat", *Hespéris* 8 (1929), pp. 59-121. Of the two hundred items of this collection, according to Ferguson-Echols, not a single one appears in Ben Cheneb.

L. Brunot and Elie Malka, *Textes judéo-arabes de Fès*, Rabat 1939, pp. 184-195 and 379-395. Some items of this collection (e.g. 10, 30, 97) are Arabic adaptions of Hebrew maxims.

Aḥmad ibn Muḥammad Sbiki, *Proverbes inédits des vielles femmes marocaines...*, traduits et commentés par A. Benchedida, Paris 1930.

[3] J. L. Burckhardt, *Arabic Proverbs: or The Manners and Customs of the Modern Egyptians*, London 1830. Between the conclusion of the book in March 1817 (in Cairo) and its publication after the author's death, a part of the manuscript was lost, so that only a total of 782 items remained. Most of those marked as no longer in use were of the more abstract and literary type (e.g. nos. 49, 59, 77, 117-9, 131, 704), but some also were real, popular sayings (e.g. 371 and 506). At least two of those described as obsolete, nos. 55 and 76, are still in use in the twentieth century.

[4] *Al-Amthāl al-ʿAmmiyya*, Cairo 1949, second edition 1956. The author died in 1930, but this, like a number of his other works, was printed posthumously. The collection contains 3188 items.

[5] *Ḥadāʾiq al-Amthāl al-ʿAmmiyya*. The second volume, the last seen by the present writer, appeared in 1943.

[6] *Ibid.*, vol. II, pp. 5-6. The wittiness of the Egyptians is proverbial, cf. Anis Frayha, *Modern Lebanese Proverbs*, no. 3075.

J. Berque and transcribed and partly translated by Nada Tomiche.[1]

The Palestinian Arab proverb has attracted much attention because of its importance for Biblical studies. The Bethlehem pastor Saʿīd Abbūd published "*5000*" *Arabic Proverbs from Palestine* with a commentary in Arabic. M. Thilo provided a German translation with a detailed index of subject matter, which is a useful instrument of research into the modern Arabic proverb at large.[2] Of no lesser scientific value than this and other general collections are the discussions of proverbs included in ethnographic studies made by specialists, among whom Gustaf H. Dalman and H. Granquist are shining examples.[3]

Lebanon, the cradle of modern native research into the Arabic language, has produced important collections of proverbs by local scholars, one made as far back as 1871. Two deserve special mention. Mgr. Michel T. Feghali, who also wrote a grammar of the vernacular of his native village Kfar ʿAbīda and a syntax of the Arabic spoken today in Lebanon in general, published a collection of 3048 proverbs and idioms, with few exceptions all known and used by himself during his younger days. The intrinsic value of this book is enhanced by the detailed explanations provided for many entries, the index of subject matter and a concordance and glossary of the Arabic words.[4] Professor Anis Frayha of the American University of Beirut carried out a similar undertaking in his native village of Rās al-Matn, situated east of Beirut and predominantly Druze. His 4248 proverbs are appropriately elucidated, and parallels from other Arabic dialects are provided. For the English reader, Frayha's book, together with Westermarck's *Wit and Wisdom in Morocco*, is the best introduction to the spoken Arabic proverb.[5]

[1] "Proverbs et Mawwals de la Menufeyya", *Arabica* 6 (1959), pp. 75-90.

[2] Saʿīd Abbūd, *5000 arabische Sprichwörter aus Palästina*, Berlin 1933. Martin Thilo, *Fünftausend Sprichwörter aus Palästina, Aus dem arabischen übersetzt von* M. T., Berlin 1937. Actually the collection comprises 5330 items, but there are many duplicates, as well as classical or semi-classical maxims and translations from the Bible.

[3] Gustaf H. Dalman, *Arbeit und Sitte in Palästina*, 6 vols. in 7, Gütersloh, 1928-39. Hilma Granquist, *Marriage Conditions in a Palestinian Village*. 2 vols. Helsingfors, 1931-5. id., *Child Problems among the Arabs*, Helsingfors 1950. (The proverbs are given here in English translation only.)

Cf. also the studies by Stephan H. Stephan (see *Ferguson-Echols*, nos. 87-90) and Dr. T. Canaan (*ibid.*, 73-75). Cf. also the latter's *The Palestinian Arab House*, Jerusalem 1933.

[4] *Proverbes et dictons syro-libanais*, Paris 1938.

[5] *Modern Lebanese Proverbs*, Beirut 1953.

Many publications of limited scope have been devoted to the modern proverbs of Syria and Iraq both by scholars writing in Western languages and those publishing in Arabic.[1] Some collections are still in manuscript.[2] A gifted young immigrant to Israel from Bagdad has brought together several thousand proverbs used in his native city, carefully discerning between the Muslim, Christian and Jewish usages. As a curiosity, *Proverbia Arabica* by Isaac B. Yahuda should be mentioned. Yahuda was the scion of an old Jewish family of Bagdad and an enormously knowledgeable man. He lived in Cairo and, later on, in Jerusalem as a dealer in Arabic books and had connections all over the Arab world. As for those proverbs gathered by him which were not general Arabic, he indicated their origin and, naturally, those coming from Bagdad are particularly conspicuous. His intimate knowledge of the folkways and folklore of the Middle East render his detailed explanations most illuminating. However, being written in Hebrew, the book is accessible only to a limited number of readers.[3]

The Arabian peninsula is split into many areas of vernacular and social groups differing to a higher degree than even the Fertile Crescent. Next to nothing has been done thus far with regard to the proverbs of bedouins of inner Arabia. The fringes of the peninsula, such as Mecca in the West and Kuwait and Oman in the East, have fared a little better. Yemen with its dense agricultural population has been given considerable attention.[4] The most extensive collection to date of proverbs used in that country is contained in the present writer's *Jemenica*, elicited from immigrants to Palestine coming from the towns of the High Yemen. Each proverb noted was presented to one or more Yemenites and the associations evoked by the latter were included in the commentary, often with the very words used by the informants.[5] In the nineteen-fifties, a

[1] See *Ferguson-Echols*, pp. 75-77 and 80-81, Jalal al-Hanafi, *Proverbs of Baghdad* I, Baghdad 1962 (1562 items, a second volume to follow) and al-Dabbāgh al-Hudhalī, *Mu'jam amthāl al-Mawṣil al-'āmmiyya*, 2 vols. Mosul 1956(Dictionary of Vernacular Proverbs of Mosul).

[2] Cf. A. Frayha (see page 363), p. VIII. A Collection of modern proverbs from Basra is preserved at the Hebrew University Library, Jerusalem.

[3] Isaac Benjamin S. E. Yahuda, *Proverbia Arabica*, Jerusalem 1932 and 1934 (the proverbs, transl. and expl. in Hebrew. Additional title page in Latin. 2502 proverbs. A third volume is still in manuscript).

[4] See *Ferguson-Echols*, pp. 81-82.

[5] *Jemenica. Sprichwörter und Redensarten aus Zentral Jemen*, Leipzig 1934. Comprises 1432 items, which represent however only a selection from a far greater stock of proverbs noted.

wide research program was carried out with immigrants from the rural districts of Lower Yemen, whose vernaculars and social habits differed entirely from those of the townsmen from the central plateau. During those years, a large collection of proverbs from a weavers' village in Lower Yemen was brought together with the aid of a head man. This collection contains many peculiarities not encountered anywhere else.[1]

Where does this immense material come from, and what does it teach us concerning the social history of the peoples using it? It would be futile to attempt to reach an exact answer to these questions. "Never try to find the original of a popular literary composition, for such a thing does not exist," says Professor Marcel Mauss in his classic *Manuel d'Ethnographie*.[2] If this is true of the origin of popular literary creations, it certainly applies to proverbs, which by their very nature express some general human experience, often not confined to any particular place or class, and are therefore prone to migrate from one country to another. However, the modern Arabic proverb possesses certain characteristics, presently to be specified, which render investigation into its origins a promising enterprise, and even a *desideratum* for both philological and historical research.

First, despite the great differences in the stocks of proverbs peculiar to the various Arab countries, localities or sections of population, there remains a considerable *common core* found almost all over the Arab world, from Morocco to Oman or Mosul. It is extremely difficult to appraise the percentage of these common Arabic proverbs to be found in the various local vernaculars, for most of the existing collections try to give the material of a whole country. They are therefore far too comprehensive for exact ethnological research, which prefers to confine itself to locally and socially limited groups—the sole procedure for determining which proverbs are actually alive in any given community. There is of course some difference in this respect between townspeople and the inhabitants of remote villages or bedouins. Still, it would not be far from the truth if one stated that approximately one-third of the

[1] The vernacular of this village has been described by the present writer in "The Language of Al-gades; The Main Characteristics of an Arabic Dialect Spoken in Lower Yemen", *Le Muséon* 73 (1960), pp. 351-394, and its social structure in "Portrait of a Yemenite Weavers' Village", *Jewish Social Studies* 17 (1955), pp. 3-26.

[2] Paris 1947, p. 98.

modern Arabic proverbs recorded thus far is common to the greater part of the Arab world, and that a sizeable portion of these might be found also in Turkish and Persian.

To be sure, it must be borne in mind that the Arabic vernaculars differ from each other almost as greatly as separate languages, so that proverbs sounding very different in wording may in reality be exactly identical. To prove this, there is no need to dwell on commonplaces such as "He who seeks, finds," already current in Hebrew and Latin (*qui quaerit, invenit*), which is represented in classical Arabic literature at least by three variants,[1] while the modern vernaculars express the idea in about ten different ryhmes.[2] The Palestinian version of the commonplace: "When the thieves quarrel the theft comes out" is similar to the one quoted in Maydānī's classical collection, while the Yemenites have a different wording.[3] It is, however, highly significant that proverbs containing unusual notions and being expressed in a particular form are also entirely disparate linguistically in the various vernaculars. Thus both in Bagdad and in Yemen they say: "He who has seen the Sultan's palace destroys his own hut," which means that we are dissatisfied with our own things after having seen what others possess. The Arabic equivalent of the saying is expressed as follows in the two vernaculars. Bagdad: *illī yishūf qaṣr is-silṭān yikharrib kūkhū.* Yemen: *man ubṣar dār al-malik hajam daymatoh.* Even the reader unfamiliar with Arabic realizes that the two versions have not a single word in common. They differ also in grammatical construction, the Yemenite using the preterite, as in classical Arabic, and the Bagdadi the imperfect, as usual in most vernaculars; the former preserves the *h* indicative of the third person, the latter drops it. Yet the English translation of both versions is exactly the same.[4]

A few other examples may illustrate how common these occurrences are. "(It is only) a little pebble (or fruit pit; but it) props a big jar;" which means that everything may be of use, or that even people of modest station may be of help to the great. The present writer heard it from a Yemenite with reference to children who earn some money (e.g. by selling newspapers) and thus contribute to the family income. The large earthen jars used all over the Middle East

[1] Cf. Ḥarīrī, Maqāma No. 9: *man ṭalab jalab; man jāl nāl; man jadd wajad.*
[2] Cf. *Jemenica*, no. 1194. Ḥadā'iq (cf. p. 362), no. 2465.
[3] Maydānī (cf. p. 368), p. 91, Abbūd no. 154, *Jemenica* no. 416.
[4] Yahuda, *Proverbia* 1182, *Jemenica* 1156.

often stand on a base. Where such support is lacking, a pebble or fruit pit helps to keep the balance.

This proverb is attested to for Egypt, Palestine, Lebanon, Syria and Iraq, but in widely differing wording, even inside the same country.[1]

"Strain (hurt) your feet (shoulders, body), but not your head (heart, mind)" seems to be found all over the Arab world, but linguistically in the most diverse forms. Its application, too, varies. It can mean: doing hard physical work is better than worrying how to make ends meet. Or: attend to your business in person, then you will not lose your temper over the slipshod work done for you by others.[2]

"Smear him with his own ointment (or: with [the ointment found on his] own cheek)", i.e. repay him with what you take from him, is common in Bagdad and with a slight variation also in Palestine in the following form: *min dihnū isgīnū*, but in Yemen: *min ṣāburoh ṭulla loh.* Only the little particle *min* is shared by the two versions.[3] All this shows that the divergence in linguistic expression should not conceal the intrinsic identity of content and form.

This fact of the existence of a vast number of proverbs common to most of the Arab countries invites an investigation of their origins, particularly if one bears in mind that this common stock is characteristically different from the proverbs of other areas, including the European, with which Arab civilization shares a heavy indebtedness to the Jewish and Christian as well as to the Graeco-Roman heritage, and with which it has been connected through political and cultural relations for many centuries. The late Professor D. S. Margoliouth stressed this fact in his review of the present writer's *Jemenica*[4] and one has only to compare any one of the above-mentioned collections with the *Oxford Dictionary of English Proverbs* by W. G. Smith and I. E. Heseltine, 1935, to become fully aware of it. Moreover, the degree of difference in this respect of a people geographically and linguistically as near to Arabia as the Abyssinians is very marked as well. In a publication of Gurague proverbs included in a volume on that language by Dr. W. Leslau, not a single item corresponds exactly to those in circulation on the other shore of the Red Sea.[5]

[1] Frayha 3389 and *Jemenica* 891, where parallels are indicated.
[2] Abbūd 54 and 1012. *Jemenica* 257, where there are two versions.
[3] Yahuda, *Proverbia* 1273, Abbūd 4425, *Jemenica* 1196.
[4] *JRAS*, 1935, pp. 405-6.
[5] Viking Foundation 1950.

Finally, the Arabic proverb lends itself easily to an historical approach, because it has been extensively recorded for the last 1,400 years. Pre-Islamic as well as Muslim poets often make allusion to proverbial sayings, and like the early Greek gnomographs, there were poets who specialized in rendering proverbs into verse.[1] I. Goldziher has shown that the Arabs had begun to write down sayings of wisdom, *ḥikam*, in special notebooks even before Islam, and that there existed collections of aphorisms of famous rulers or chieftains, the last instance being one of Manṣūr, the second Abbasid Caliph (died 775), which was still widely circulated at the time of al-Jāḥiẓ (died 869).[2] Side by side with the study of the language, the poetry, the history and the genealogy of the ancient Arabs, the Muslim scholars collected their proverbs, a task almost completed in the fourth century of the Hijra by the works of Ḥamzah al-Iṣfahanī or of al-Ḥasan al-ʻAskarī. The comprehensive collection of al-Maydānī (died 518/1124), now a classic of Arabic literature, is but a later compilation.[3]

The diligent work of the ancient Muslim (mostly Persian) collectors of Arabic proverbs has been discussed in two profound studies made independently of each other and appearing in one and the same year, Rudolf Sellheim's general survey of this type of literature with special reference to the collection of Abū ʻUbayd[4] (died 838) and R. Blachère's essay on the methods and reliability of the ancient scholars.[5]

Of highest importance for an historical investigation of the Arab proverb is the registration of its actual occurrence in the old records of Arabic history and literature. The great Dutch scholar de Goeje has made lists of the proverbs occurring in Ṭabarī's *History of the Prophets and Kings*, the *Kitāb al-Aghānī* and other classical texts.

[1] The chapter on sayings of wisdom (*bāb al-adab wal-ḥikma*) in Abū Tammām's Ḥamāsa may serve as an example.

[2] *Muhammedanische Studien* II, p. 204 ff.

[3] Here the Egyptian edition of 1352 A.H. is used. G. W. Freytag's Latin edition *Arabum Proverbia*, Bonn 1838-43, is referred to only in special cases.

[4] This Abū ʻUbayd should not be confused with his far more famous contemporary Abū ʻUbayda, a son of Persian Jewish parents who was one of the greatest authorities on Arab antiquities. Abū ʻUbayda, too, made a collection of Arabic proverbs, but his was lost and Abū ʻUbayd's was preserved.

[5] Rudolf Sellheim, *Die klassisch-arabischen Sprichwörtersammlungen insbesondere die des Abū ʻUbaid*, 's Gravenhage 1954. R. Blachère, "Contribution à l'étude de la litterature proverbiale des arabes à l'époche archaïque", *Arabica* 1 (1954), pp. 53-83.

His praiseworthy example has been followed by other European scholars, e.g. the editor of al-Mubarrad's *Kāmil*, and by some fine modern Egyptian editions, e.g. that of Ibn Qutayba's *'Uyūn al-Akhbār*. Particularly rich in proverbial sayings—of a different type, to be sure, from those recorded in the early historical works— is religious, especially *Sufic*, literature; these, if I am not mistaken, have, however, not yet been listed in modern editions. We are, on the whole, in an excellent position for tracing an Arabic proverb through the centuries, and the creation of an *historical dictionary of Arabic proverbs*, similar to those in existence for the proverbs of some European languages, is not out of reach at all.

The most striking fact which such an all-embracing study would reveal is the almost complete disappearance of the pre-Islamic proverb. Of about 2,000 proverbs noted by al-Maydānī as classical and occurring in the old texts, hardly a dozen would be found really in current usage over a fairly extended area today. This fact is not easily explained. One may understand why one group of classical proverbs—in fact the most familiar and characteristic of all—*that alluding to a certain personality, occurrence or custom*, has become obsolete: it might be assumed that the majority of such proverbs had originally been confined to certain tribal areas, while their profuse circulation in classical literature was probably due to the fact that most of them constituted a sort of riddle or puzzle, a kind of speech for which Arabs have much predilection, and were quoted in order to show the user's acquaintance with Arabic antiquities and linguistics. It might therefore be concluded that, outside their area of origin, their use was confined to the educated classes, and that they were probably never invoked by the common people even in olden times. In any case, this large group has actually died out. The few proverbs of this type noted in modern collections may be reminiscences from the school bench rather than reflections of real usage. Thus, a proverb of this type, very common in ancient Arabic literature was "Hearing of the Mu'aydī is better than seeing him."[1] Abbūd, no. 254, notes this proverb as modern (Pronouncing *ma'īdī* instead of *mu'aydī*), but its very wording proves that it is not colloquial Arabic and it is not used in Palestine by people other than those who have learned it in school.

[1] Cf. al-Balādhurī, *Ansāb al-Ashrāf*, vol. V, Jerusalem, 1936, p. 42, 10; *Kitāb al-Aghānī*, Cairo, 1345, vol. I, p. 297, 12; Freytag, *Proverbia*, I, p. 223; A. Fischer, *ZDMG*, 63, 394.

The second group of proverbs of which the old Arabs—or perhaps the philologists who collected their sayings—seemed to have been unusually fond, *viz. the elative expression* (e.g., "more grateful than a dog") has left a comparatively little legacy. Here, too, however the majority of the many expressions quoted might not have been in common use over large areas at any time, whilst their diffusion in literature was artificial and declined with active knowledge of classical literature in general.

Furthermore, a great many classical proverbs may have disappeared because they used images taken from *life in the desert*, its physical features, its flora and fauna, which have become unintelligible to the majority of Arabic-speaking people. It seems, however, that classical proverbs of this type have not been preserved in the idioms of the present-day bedouins either, in so far as they are known to us.

Finally, a great many proverbs may have become obsolete, because they included *rare classical words*, with which the educated Arab has ceased to be familiar, or which had never really become common Arabic, except in the dictionaries. For the Arabic language, as the saying has it, is so broad "that only a messenger-prophet is able to master it fully."

However, even if we disregard the four groups just reviewed, there still remains a great mass of classical proverbs, excelling in wisdom, wit and acute observation, couched in comparatively easy language and clad in similes of general human character, of which extremely little has been preserved in contemporary Arabic speech. Express quotations from old Arabic literature are comparatively rare, but even "translations" into the vernacular are less frequent than one might expect.

For instance, one may assume that the Yemenite proverb "If someone dares to say 'Give', dare you to say, 'There is nothing to be had'," is but a modern popular variant of the classical and more abstract original "If the request is strong, so is the refusal".[1] But even cases of this kind are not common.

It would not be correct to account for this fact by the general transitoriness of everything human, for as we shall presently see, a good portion of even the pre-Arabic Near Eastern proverbs has remained alive in the Arabic vernaculars. Some specific agent must

[1] *Jemenica* 1161: *man jazam ugāl iddī ijzim ugūl mābish.* Ibn Qutayba, *ʿUyūn al-Akhbār* I, p. 332, l. 6: *idhā jadd al-suʾāl jadd al-manʿ.*

have been at work here. It seems to me that the fate of the ancient Arabic proverbs has to be studied together with the disintegration and transformation of classical Arabic in general. Despite the great differences between the various Arabic vernaculars, they have much more in common among themselves than they have with classical Arabic. The modern Arab *koine* differs from its classical original—if indeed it was its original—not only in vocabulary, accidence, syntax and style, but in something which might be called the psychology and character of language. The more we know about the development of the Arabic language, the better we shall be able to understand the history of the Arab proverb.[1]

The eclipse of the ancient Arabic proverb is paralleled by the survival of the *pre-Arabic Near Eastern proverb* in Arabic speech. As is well known, the countries of the Fertile Crescent, i.e. Iraq, Northern Mesopotamia, Syria, Lebanon and Palestine, possessed a common language before the Arab conquest—*Aramaic*. Unlike Arabic, however, Aramaic never developed a single literary idiom: every region and every religion cultivated its own dialect, at the same time developing its own separate script. The pre-Arabic proverb of the Near East thus has to be studied through the medium of the literatures of these various groups.

The old pagan Story of Aḥīqār, which contains many sayings and fables, known in an Aramaic version used by the Jews of Elephantine as far back as the fifth century B.C., probably was transmitted to the Arabs through Christian channels, for the first Arab to mention it was ʿAdī b. Zayd, the Christian poet of Ḥīra in lower Iraq.[2] The various branches of Syriac literature themselves yield less than might have been expected from their size, the reason being that most of their products are too formal and scholastic to admit much of the popular proverb, that *enfant terrible* of living speech. The extant Syriac collections of proverbial sayings are translations or

[1] About the common substratum of the Arabic vernaculars see David Cohen, "Koine, langues communes et dialectes arabes", *Arabica* 9 (1962), pp. 119-144, and Charles A. Ferguson, "The arabic Koine", *Language* 35 (1959), pp. 616-30. Cf. also the present writer's *Travels in Yemen*, Jerusalem 1941, p. 72 and Note 1.

[2] Elephantine was a fortress on the southern frontier of Egypt garrisoned by Jewish soldiers. Fragments of the writings used in this military colony have been preserved. ʿAdī b. Zayd lived in the second part of the sixth century A.D., over a thousand years after the date of the oldest extant fragments of the Aḥīqār story. Detailed references about the latter in A. Baumstark, *Geschichte der syrischen Literatur*, Bonn 1922, pp. 11-12.

adaptations of Greek gnomes, while such books as the *Aphorisms of Aphraem* are individual creations.[1] The literature of the Mandaeans—the forefathers of the present-day "Sabaeans"—is too one-sidedly theological and liturgical to provide us with much information as to the proverbs used by them.

There remains the vast post-biblical literature of the Jews of both Palestine and Iraq, of which the Babylonian and Palestinian Talmuds are only conspicuous examples. This literature deals with almost every aspect of life and freely uses the local Aramaic vernacular alongside of Hebrew. No wonder, then, that it teems with proverbs and proverbial expressions, which represent the consummated wisdom of the ancient Near East cast in concise and brilliant Semitic speech at its best. It is comparatively easy to distinguish the proverbs used by the people of Iraq and Palestine in general from those specific to Jews. The former are often introduced as such by the formula "as the folk say" or similar phrases, while the latter often contain allusions to Biblical or other Jewish notions, especially in the field of ethics and religion. Moreover, the Jewish sayings are characterized by a certain pithy, even elliptical way of expression, as is found commonly between scholars or other people who live closely together and understand each other without using many words. In this respect, the specifically Jewish, or "rabbinical", proverb is not unlike the ancient Arabic, and for the same reason: it is perfectly intelligible to the members of the closely knit society in which it is used, and constitutes an enigma only for the outsider. There are however also many rabbinical sayings which are simple and complete in formulation and require no specific commentary when properly translated. A number of such sayings have found their way into the modern Arabic proverb, through the medium of Muslim religious literature. In this study, however, we are not concerned with the history of the Jewish heritage in Islam, but with the living on of pre-Islamic Aramaic popular wisdom in the Arabic vernaculars.

The proverbs, maxims and dictums found in post-biblical Hebrew and Aramaic literature have been listed in various collections, one of which contains as many as thirty thousand items.[2] However, only a fraction of these, say one-tenth, should be regarded as household sayings with which the common people represented in this literature

[1] Cf. Baumstark (see preceding note), pp. 166-170.

[2] Aaron Hyman, *Ōṣār divrē ḥakhāmīm*, Tel Aviv 1947.

were familiar. One comes to a similar conclusion, namely a total of about three thousand sayings, while scrutinizing another and very meritorious collection which lists only 6424 entries, but confines itself to those which have the character of a proverb or quotation.[1] Still, for such an ancient literature this is a very considerable number. Even a superficial comparison of these collections with those of modern Arabic proverbs shows that many of the most current and most characteristic of vernacular Arabic proverbs are but translations or adaptations from the Aramaic. It would be quite erroneous to see in this any specific Jewish influence. Such influence, as said before, existed, and was exercised through the channel of Muslim religious literature. But, in the main, conformity of the Arabic with the Jewish proverb is simply due to the fact that the Jewish literature represents a treasure house of the popular speech prevalent in the Near East prior to the rise of Islam. Even the fact that a proverb appears in Jewish literature only in Hebrew proves nothing, as there exist many post-biblical Hebrew proverbs with variants in Aramaic. Thus the Arabic proverb: "Many a colt's skin served as a cover for its mother"[2] corresponds to an old Hebrew saying[3] which is, however, itself a variant of an Aramaic proverb.[4] The old Arabic proverb: "Do not throw a stone into a well from which you have drunk"[5] repeatedly occurs in pre-Islamic Hebrew literature.[6] Its ultimate source, however, is the Aramaic: "Do not cast a *clod of earth* into a well, etc."[7] which is, of course, more telling, since a clod of earth makes the water muddy, whereas it is hardly affected by a stone cast into it.

It would be far beyond the scope of this paper to attempt to

[1] K. A. Perla, *Ōṣār leshōn ḥakhāmīm*, Warsaw (no date). Together with the sayings quoted in the annotations (some very fine ones) the total of the items amounts to more than 7000. The author provides many parallels from European languages, mostly expressing the same idea as the Talmudic proverb, but differing from it entirely in formulation.

[2] Noted, for instance, for *Oman* by C. Reinhardt in his excellent monograph on that dialect, n. 81.

[3] Perla 2523. The Hebrew version also penetrated into English, cf. *Oxford Dictionary of English Proverbs*, p. 335: "Old camels carry young camels' skins to the market"; the source given: Adag. Hebr.

[4] Perla 4829.

[5] Frayha 1077. A. P. Singer-E. Littmann, *Arabic Proverbs*, Cairo, 1913, no. 84. Ben Cheneb, 1019. *Jemenica* 246.

[6] Perla 1155.

[7] Perla 1210. Here, too, the Hebrew version was accepted by the English, cf. *Oxford Dictionary of E. Proverbs*, p. 311, where again Adag. Hebr. is given as source.

enumerate the correspondences to be found between the vernacular Arabic proverbs on the one hand and those found in post-biblical Hebrew and Aramaic on the other. We quote but a few examples, the specific form of which excludes the possibility that the Arabic proverb originated independently of its Hebrew-Aramaic variant.

"After the ox has fallen, there arise many slaughterers (there come many knives; or: sharpen the knife for it)", meaning: when a powerful man has lost his position, he is attacked by many. This proverb is found in all Arabic vernaculars for which collections exist. For these, as well as the Hebrew and Aramaic antecedents cf. *Jemenica* 85.

"He who adds water must add flour," (or vice versa) i.e. if one adduces new points in a discussion, one must prop them with additional arguments. Noted by Westermarck, *Wit and Wisdom in Morocco*, no. 808, but found already in Hebrew and Aramaic, cf. *Perla* 147.

"He that is unable to master the donkey, bites into the pack-saddle", i.e. a man who is unable to overcome a strong adversary takes advantage of a powerless, but innocent third person. It seems to be found in most Arabic vernaculars from Morocco to Iraq, cf. *Jemenica* 130, and is attested to as a popular saying used in Bagdad during the eleventh century.[1] An ancient Hebrew version in *Jemenica*, ibid.

"It is the fat tail of a sheep (a choice delicacy), but it has a bone in it", i.e. every good thing has its disadvantages, cf. *Jemenica* 269. A tenth century Arabic saying has already an optimistic version of the same saying: "Had it not been for the bone, the meat would not be good."[2]

"Let the drunkard alone. He will fall down by himself." Do not try to correct the sinner, he will ultimately meet the fate he deserves. An Aramaic proverb still used in the Arabic vernacular of Mosul, Iraq, and certainly also in other Arab countries.[3]

"No finger is like another." A euphemism indicating that men differ as to their sexual potency. Common in Arabic as far west as Morocco, but appearing in a Hebrew version in the Talmud.[4]

[1] Ṭālaqānī, *Al-amthāl al-baghdādiyya*, ed. L. Massignon, Cairo 1913, No. 576.

[2] Tawḥīdī, *Kitāb al-Imtāʿ wal-Muʾānasa* III, p. 93.

[3] Perla 5671. A Socin, *Arabische Sprichwörter und Redensarten*, Tübingen 1878, no. 147.

[4] Ben Cheneb 1089. Hyman (see p. 372), p. 439, l. 32.

"If I spit upward, I spit into my own face (If I spit downward, I spit into my beard)." He who behaves insolently against his superiors, does harm to himself. The same fate befalls an irritable person who curses his subordinates or members of his household. Only the first half (for which the Palestinian version has "He who spits against the wind") seems to be common to Arabic and Aramaic.[1]

"He who has been bitten by a snake is afraid of a rope." The Arabic vernacular and the Aramaic versions are literally identical, cf. *Jemenica* 1431. In addition, the contrast "rope-snake" is used in Arabic also in other combinations, e.g. to make a snake out of a rope, i.e. to exaggerate, cf. *ibid.*, 433. A very old woman from the Yemenite countryside took the phrase literally. While speaking in my presence of a great scholar performing miracles she said: he is able to transform a rope into a snake, cf. Exodus 4:2-4.[2]

"The rye grass of your village is better than imported wheat." The rye grass or darnel (*Lolium lentum*) is a poisonous weed sponging upon grainfields. This proverb is found in all Arabic dialects between Egypt and Iraq and uses the same word *zuwān* for rye grass as its Aramaic prototype. The meaning: marry a girl from your native village and not a stranger. The Aramaic version is still more poignant: "Even if the wheat of your village should be rye grass, seed it."[3]

The same idea is expressed without the use of metaphors in countless variations both in Arabic and Hebrew.[4] However only a specific figure of speech is a safe indication of the borrowing of a proverb. For this reason we do not include such proverbs as "oh physician, cure yourself" (meaning: mend your own ways before trying to correct other people), although it is probable that they came into Arabic from the Aramaic.[5]

"The eye gets its fill only by the dust", i.e. human covetousness is

[1] Frayha 447. Abbūd 557. *Jemenica* p. IX. Perla 1821.

[2] That woman was a showpiece. When I was introduced to her, I said: "It is a great privilege for me to meet a person who has reached the age of our Master Moses. I was told that you are 120 years old" (cf. Deuteronomy 34:7). She answered immediately: "This is a lie! I am only 110." I took a picture of her and showed it to a physician, who believed she had not attained the age conceded by her.

[3] Perla 2883. Frayha 1856 and parallels.

[4] Cf. *Jemenica* 1185-6 and Frayha 437, both of which supply copious parallels. See Perla 1052.

[5] *Jemenica* 662. Westermarck, *Wit and Wisdom* 1766. Quoted by the twelfth century Persian poet ʿAttār in his *Tadhkirat al-Awliyā*, vol. I, London-Leiden 1905, p. 28, l. 1.

never completely satisfied until death. This proverb goes back to a well known episode in the legendary story of Alexander the Great and, as in many other respects, Aramaic served here as a transmitter of the Greek heritage to the Arabs.[1]

It may be that some Arabic proverbs taken from earlier sources are mistranslations. Thus, in conformity with the Aesopian fable—which in turn may have been borrowed from the East—a well-known Hebrew-Aramaic proverb says that the camel going to seek horns lost its ears.[2] However, both old Maydānī and the modern Arab vernacular substitute the ass, the typical longeared animal, for the camel,[3] a confusion probably caused by another Arabic proverb concerned with the cropping of the donkey's ears.[4]

Concerning these Arabic-Hebrew-Aramaic correspondences, one interesting fact should be stressed: it seems, though this statement may be qualified by subsequent research, that the percentage of Aramaic proverbs contained in the vernaculars of North Africa, Egypt, North Arabia or Yemen is not considerably smaller than the proportion of those found in the countries of the Fertile Crescent, which had been Aramaic-speaking before Islam. Thus the heritage of the ancient East, of which these Aramaic forms of expression were only a detail, may have been absorbed by the new Arabic civilization at a rather early stage, and diffused all over the present Arabic-speaking countries before the development of local vernaculars had made much progress. It is in conformity with this assumption that the classical collections of Arab proverbs, such as those of al-Maydānī and the *Keshkul* of Bahā' al-Din al-Āmulī (d. 1621) were divided into two sections, one containing the Arab proverbs properly so called, and the other giving those of foreign or mixed origin (*al-muwalladūn*). After all that has been said before, there is no need to add that it is the second section which has contributed most to the present-day Arabic proverb.

Moreover, it appears that the Aramaic proverb had partly found its way into Arabic speech even before the advent of Islam. It is a

[1] Cf. Richard Hartmann, *A Volume of Oriental Studies presented to E. G. Browne*, pp. 182-3. *Jemenica* 1421.

[2] Perla 1536. Also in English, *Oxford Dictionary of English Proverbs*, quoting as source Adag. Hebr.

[3] Abbūd 2119 and parallels.

[4] *Ibid.*, 567. Incidentally, the cropping of a donkey's ear in the way of punishment, e.g. when it damages a garden, is also well attested to among American Indians, cf. J. Smeaton Chase, "Cropping Animal's Ears", *Folk-Lore* 17 (1906), pp. 72-73.

well known fact that many groups of Arabs living in the borderland between the desert and the sown, such as the Nabataeans or the people of Ṣafā, were gradually assimilated into the culture of the sedentary population. Thus it is only natural that those who remained Arabs also adopted, together with many of the other products of the civilizations surrounding the Arabian peninsula, some of their most characteristic similes. Three instances may serve as an illustration.

A common modern Arabic proverb says: "He who hates his hand should cut it off", which means that a man who does not get along with his wife had better divorce her,[1] although a divorce imposed on the husband heavy financial obligations. This phrase is, of course, familiar to everyone from the New Testament[2] but it was very common in old Oriental speech in general.[3] Thus it is not surprising that it is used by a pre-Islamic pagan poet and in the same sense as in modern Arabic (repudiation of the beloved who refuses to yield her favours.)[4]

The phrase, "making a camel (or, as it was said in Babylonia, an elephant) go through the eye of a needle" was widely diffused throughout the Aramaic speaking countries,[5] and became part of Arabic speech long before it was incorporated into the Koran.[6]

The common Arabic proverb "what the goat did to the leaves of the *qaraẓ* tree (*acacia arabica*), the *qaraẓ* did to her"[7] is found in the ancient story of Aḥīqār, chapter 6, no. 2, and may have come to the Arabs before Islam, for, as has been pointed out, ʿAdī b. Zayd, the poet of Ḥīra, already makes mention of that sage of olden times.

Finally, it may be asked whether the borrowing of Arabic speech from that of the ancient East, or the affinities between the two, do not hark back to far older times than the centuries immediately preceding Islam. Arabs are frequently mentioned in Assyrian inscriptions beginning with the ninth century B.C., and in the seventh century the prominence of the desert tribes of North Arabia and

[1] *Jemenica* 1157.

[2] Matthew 5:30. Cf. Asin Palacios, *Logia*, p. 354-5.

[3] Cf. Hermann L. Strack and Paul Billerbeck, *Kommentar zum Neuen Testament aus Talmud und Midrasch*, Munich 1921, I, pp. 302-3.

[4] Al-Muthaqqib al-ʿAbdī, cf. Th. Noeldeke, *Delectus carminum arabicorum*, Berlin 1890, p. 2-3 (from Ibn Qutayba, *Shiʿr*).

[5] Cf. Strack-Billerbeck, I, p. 828, with reference to Matthew 19:24.

[6] 7:40, cf. Goldziher, *Muhammedanische Studien* II, p. 385, n. 1.

[7] Ben Cheneb, 1510; *Jemenica*, 1102. The goat eats the leaves of the *qaraẓ* tree, but these leaves are used also for the tanning of the goat's skin.

the Syrian desert becomes one of the most striking facts of the age. In view of this it seems worth while to inquire how far traces of ancient Eastern ideas and expressions are to be found in Arabic, not only in classical poetry, but even in present-day speech.[1]

The idea of insane obstinacy is expressed in the following proverb which seems to be found all over the Arab world: "I say to him: 'It is an ox'. He replies: 'Milk it'." A Palestinian and Yemenite version replace the ox by the he-goat, which is perhaps secondary, since the latter anyhow is a symbol for stubbornness and stupidity.[2] The paradox of the ox providing milk is found already in a collection of ancient Sumerian proverbs.[3]

"The thief invokes Allah, even while breaking into a house." This Arabic testimony to the power of religion is almost identical in wording with an Aramaic proverb quoted by a Jewish sage living in the fourth century A.D. introducing it with the formula "as the folk say".[4] However both have an antecedent in the famous hymn to the sun-god found in the library of the Assyrian king Ashurbanipal (668-633 B.C.), where it is said: "The burglar, the thief... entreat you."[5]

In the highly interesting "Phoenician" inscriptions of Karatepe in Turkey, King Azita-wadd says of himself several times that he is to his people, the Danunites, "as father and mother".[6] This phrase, which is not found in the Old Testament, is common in classical Arabic literature[7] and often used in modern Arabic. I first heard it many years ago in connection with the British Mandatory administration of Palestine, which then was making great efforts to better the condition of the fellaheen. A fellah describing the benefits received from the government concluded his report by saying, "*al-inglīz mitl al-ab wa-l-umm* (The English are like father and mother)."

This paper tried to drive home four points:

1. Despite their great linguistic diversity, the Arabic vernaculars

[1] For the gnomic literature of the ancient Near East, cf. James B. Pritchard, *Ancient Near Eastern Texts*, Princeton 1955, pp. 412-431, and W. G. Lambert, *Babylonian Wisdom Literature*, Oxford 1961. An excellent survey is contained in Edmund I. Gordon, "A New Look at the Wisdom of Sumer and Akkad", *Bibliotheca Orientalis* 17 (1960), pp. 122-151.

[2] Abbūd 1274 and 2126, *Jemenica* 268 and parallels.

[3] Edmund I. Gordon (see note 1), p. 131.

[4] *Jemenica* 543. Perla 1549.

[5] Literally: "come before you". Pritchard (see note 1), p. 389.

[6] Cf. e.g. Cyrus H. Gordon, *Journal of Near Eastern Studies*, 8 (1949), no. 2, pp. 109ff.

[7] In the formula *bi'abī anta wa'ummī*, used while expressing an entreaty.

spoken today in an area stretching from Morocco to Yemen and Oman have a large stock of proverbs in common.

2. This common stock owes next to nothing to the treasures of pre-Islamic Arabic proverbs so diligently gathered by the ancient Muslim scholars.

3. On the other hand, it contains many proverbs rampant in the lands of the Fertile Crescent prior to the rise of Islam. They are known to us mainly from post-biblical Jewish literature, in which they are preserved partly in Aramaic, partly in Hebrew. This fact does not betray any specific Jewish influence (which existed only in the field of religion), since those proverbs are referred to in Jewish literature as generally used.

4. With regard to the diffusion of the pre-Islamic Near Eastern proverb in modern Arabic vernaculars, there is little or no difference between the region of ancient Aramaic speech: Iraq, Syria and Palestine, and purely Arabic countries such as Yemen and Oman or an area originally remote from both, such as the Muslim West.

Both the negative and positive findings presented here seem to indicate that the racial composition of the populations concerned cannot have had a predominant influence on their beliefs and concepts as expressed in their proverbs. It appears, rather, that it was the great social revolution of the Middle East, which began at the end of the first century of the Hijra, that led the Arabs to adopt the vocations and ways of life prevailing in the conquered countries and to take part in the new economic development, thereby changing their ways of thinking and modes of expression, until that deep gulf between classical and vernacular Arabic was created, to which we have alluded above. The new society of the Middle Eastern civilization differed widely from anything that had preceded it, but still had much more in common with the Hellenized Aramaic speaking Ancient East than with the bedouin civilization of pre-Islamic Arabia. This fact seems to be reflected in the common Arabic proverbs used today all over the Arab world. But, as E. Westermarck rightly observes in the Introductory Essay to his *Wit and Wisdom in Morocco*, p. 52: "Only by an intimate knowledge of the society studied is one able to evaluate its proverbs correctly." Future research into the social development of the Middle East in medieval times will throw more light on the history of the Arabic proverb, just as the former will itself benefit from the lessons to be learned from the study of the latter.

INDEX

The terms Arab(s), Arabia, Christian(s), Christianity, Islam, Muslim(s), Jew(s), Judaism are not included